MIND-BODY MATURITY

MIND-BODY MATURITY
Psychological Approaches to Sports, Exercise, and Fitness

Edited by
Louis Diamant
University of North Carolina
Charlotte, North Carolina

⬤ HEMISPHERE PUBLISHING CORPORATION
A member of the Taylor & Francis Group

New York   Washington   Philadelphia   London

MIND-BODY MATURITY: Psychological Approaches to Sports, Exercise, and Fitness

1 2 3 4 5 6 7 8 9 0   E B E B   9 8 7 6 5 4 3 2 1 0

This book was set in Times Roman by Hemisphere Publishing Corporation. The editors were Nancy Niemann and Mary McCoy; the typesetters were Shirley J. McNett and Linda Andros; the production supervisor was Peggy M. Rote. Cover design by Debra Eubanks Riffe. Edwards Brothers, Inc. was printer and binder.

A CIP catalog record for this book is available from the British Library.

Library of Congress Cataloging-in-Publication Data

Mind-body maturity: psychological approaches to sports, exercise, and
    fitness / editor, Louis Diamant.
        p. cm.
    Includes bibliographical references and index.

    1. Sports—Psychological aspects. 2. Exercise—Psychological
aspects. 3. Physical fitness—Pyschological aspects. I. Diamant,
Louis, date.
    GV706.4.M56 1991
    796'.01—dc20   *90-46147*
                                                                  CIP

ISBN 0-89116-892-3

Contents

III
THEORETICAL CONTRIBUTIONS

Contributors

RICHARD M. BAKER, Community Holistic Health Center, Carrboro, NC, USA

DORCUS SUSAN BUTT, University of British Columbia, Canada

JOHN H. BYRD, University of North Carolina at Charlotte, Charlotte, NC, USA

MICK COLEMAN, University of Georgia College of Agriculture, Athens, GA, USA

DANIEL DERVIN, Mary Washington College, Fredricksburg, VA, USA

LIEF ROBERT DIAMANT, Community Holistic Health Center, Carrboro, NC, USA

LOUIS DIAMANT, University of North Carolina at Charlotte, Charlotte, NC, USA

LISA EISEN, University of Miami School of Medicine, Miami, FL, USA

TIFFANY M. FIELD, University of Miami, School of Medicine, Miami, FL, USA

BETTIE J. GLENN, University of North Carolina at Charlotte, Charlotte, NC, USA

MELISSA HIMELEIN, University of North Carolina at Charlotte, Charlotte, NC, USA

CAROL E. KIRSHNIT, Chicago, IL, USA

DOUGLAS A. KLEIBER, University of Georgia, Athens, GA, USA

P. A. LAMAL, University of North Carolina at Charlotte, Charlotte, NC, USA

SANDRA K. LARSON, University of Miami School of Medicine, Miami, FL, USA

ANN E. MCCABE, University of Windsor, Ontario Canada

ROBERT G. McMURRAY, UNC Chapel Hill, Chapel Hill, NC, USA

THERESA E. MORRIS, University of Windsor, Canada

LOTHAR PICKENHAIN, Holzhauser Strabe 8, Germany

J. THOMAS PUGLISI, Germantown, MD, USA

BRENDA T. ROBERTS, University of Windsor, Canada

ELIZABETH J. ROOT, University of Texas, Austin, TX, USA

IGNATIUS J. TONER, University of North Carolina at Charlotte, Charlotte, NC, USA

Preface

There is at this writing, across socioeconomic, racial, ethnic, and national divisions, a consuming passion with human physical potential. We are called by advertisements and the media—by the enormity of professional and collegiate sports—to diet, to move, to perform, to view and to become involved and immersed. It is a clarion to which incalculable numbers respond. In addition, there is an inexorable current of interest in theoretical and empirical investigation that brings the science of psychology to the understanding of interrelationships between personal development and sports, exercise, and fitness.

In today's world of rapidly widening informational and scientific vistas, innovation is a must in a book with claims to addressing the well-informed and the scientifically oriented reader. While there is some danger that innovation can be a self-serving device, intriguing but not dedicated to productive purpose, the innovative structure of this volume provides a special service: conceptualizing that which has been virtually waiting to be put together. *Mind-Body Maturity: Psychological Approaches to Sports, Exercise, and Fitness* has been structured and organized to depict the gestalt—the irrefutable pattern accepted collectively by those who relate mental processes, physical behaviors and performances to the ongoing process of human development and productivity. Here the reader will find a harmonious and unified orchestration of research, applied experience, theoretical orientation, and scholarly acumen in a readable and innovative book.

Authors from the various fields of psychology (i.e., clinical, developmental, sport, social, industrial) sport medicine, exercise physiology, nursing and education, create an eclectic professional and theoretical resource. The book will be an invaluable source of information and reference for readers whose academic and professional interests include sport psychology, physical education, the social psychology or sociology of sports, exercise and fitness, developmental psychology, health and fitness education, and sport medicine. The material is suitable for advanced undergraduate students, the professional who likes to keep up with things, and the general reader who is serious about this topic.

While the book is divided into three parts, there is no intent to present the notion that they are air-tight compartments—that would be an approach contradictory to the holistic design. The section to which a chapter has been assigned, rather, designates the emphasis given it by the editor and author.

Part I is intended to familiarize the reader with the processes of scientific psychology that are used in relating the discipline to sport exercise and fitness (SEF). (It describes the part theories play in forming frameworks from which to quantify empirical SEF research, and the application of research data to behavioral, emotional, and cognitive changes.) Particular concern has been given to the way psychology views mind, body, and maturity. Part II, Growing and Maturing, has been structured to emphasize the various facets of SEF on the developing individual. Chapters covering a multitude of psychological and psychobiological areas are written toward the understanding of the role of SEF on the developing person from fetus to aging. The topics that have been chosen are representations of those that appear most growth relevant in the psychology of personal development through the life span. Part III is, in the main, concerned with several theories of psychology which are used to explain human behavior, and for this book especially, SEF. Psychodynamic theory, radical behaviorism, motivation, trait, and physiological theories are used to examine SEF concepts.

I wish, at this point, to express gratitude to those who have been helpful, kind, tolerant, understanding, and generous during my labors on this project. I thank the friends and colleagues I have met while putting this project together. Their grasp of the psychological aspects of sports, exercise and fitness has been a source of professional enrichment. I am grateful, also, to many others whom I have never met—both historical and contemporary figures—whose names and works enhance these pages. I extend my appreciation to my colleague and friend Professor Kim Buch for astute observations and to Jeff Mullins, Athletic Director, University of North Carolina at Charlotte for creating an ideal atmosphere for me to approach a variety of sports and performers and for sharing a holistic view of athletic performance. Also, my thanks to Winifred Swinson for contributing her great organizational skills in behalf of this book and to Kathy for her loyalty and personal sacrifice, and to our kids for exercising and behaving decently.

Louis Diamant

I

INTRODUCTION

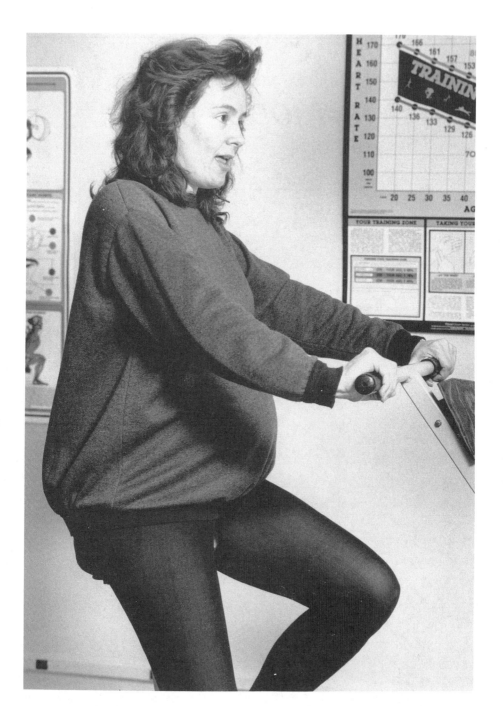

1

How Psychology Relates to Sports, Exercise, and Fitness

Louis Diamant
University of North Carolina at Charlotte

Not a class runner, not a racer, I have an affinity for the solitary run, an affinity for the hills, which, now in steep ascent, are tearing at my fibers, finding flaws in my structure, applying petty pains, and challenging desperate lungs and the self-esteem of a person not young, surviving in the arena of youth. I have made the top, and the tall buildings of campus are below me. Now I can relish the glide down through the still-brown foliage of early spring, consciously holding back against the hill and the downward slope's invitation to maximum speed. Then the kick to the gym where the comraderie of the weight room is waiting for me. Exhilarated, I work around the pain in my left shoulder.

MIND, BODY, AND MATURITY

The notion of a relationship between physical strength and mental strength is not new, but an idea held since antiquity. Some 3,000 years ago, Homer preached a faultless body and a blameless mind. Thomas Jefferson proclaimed a strong body makes the mind strong. Yet certain contemporary psychologists eschew the concept of the metaphysical mind. For example, Skinner (1989) wrote that "extraordinary things have certainly been said about the 'mind.' The finest achievements of the species have been attributed to it; it is said to work at miraculous speeds in miraculous ways. But what it is and what is does are still far from clear" (p. 17). For purposes of this chapter, mental states, attitudes, personality, behavior, cognition, and other psychological constructs are called mind functions (and from all my coauthors and colleagues who find the term mind abhorrent, I'll ask poetic license). The features and functions that can be directly observable and those of neurons, hormones, chemistry, genetics, and actions of the various systems (digestive, respiratory, nervous, cardiovascular, skeletal-muscular) are designated as body functions.

It is the purpose of this chapter to contribute to an understanding of the complex interaction between mind and body and sports, exercise, and physical fitness. To that end psychological theories, research, and experimentation are involved in presenting a thesis (condensed in this chapter title) that a certain admixture of sports exercise and physical fitness will affect maturity. In that regard I accept mind as all that is mental and body as all that is physiological. An abundance of literature supports the validity of these divisions and usages.

Maturity, however, turns out to be a more evasive term, and is neglected in most current and basic texts in the numerous books that I have on my abundancy of shelves. What makes it so surprising is that it is such a common term in psychology, psychiatry, and education. According to common dictionary definition, maturity in plants and in human organisms ordinarily means the attainment of reproductive sexual development. It also means, according to other dictionary usage, the attainment of full development and perfected condition. Psychologists and educators commonly use the term maturity as one that is related to socially acceptable behavior and judgment, and those to whom I spoke were as surprised as I to find that they could not locate the term in the index or glossary in texts they were currently using. Finally, I found the word indexed in a book on someone else's shelf (Gesell et al., 1940). The authors dealt with maturity in terms of the developmental norms of children. They examined four major fields of behavior: (a) motor characteristics; (b) adaptive behavior; (c) language behavior, and (d) personal-social behavior. These divisions are undoubtedly relevant to life's development, and level of personal-social behavior is a variable and commonly assessed in exercise and sports psychology research. However, after citing Gesell et al., the word maturity still defies definition. Norms are only one aspect of measuring growth. The other measure is ongoing and in one sense a defiance of the norm because the norm should be changing constantly in a progressive and evolutionary manner. Ongoing human potential is how I see the spirit of the sports, exercise, and fitness usage. It is this spirit that makes sports records temporary and certain participation with age and gender delimitations meaningless because they address stereotypical notions that are in part atavistic. This view of maturity might be best encapsulated in the current and surprisingly existential slogan of the United States Army recruiting service, "Be all that you can be."

The question of maturity has been, even when not approached in that terminology, still of basic concern to theoreticians. Freudians, egopsychologists, and other psychoanalytically inspired theorists have approached it through different pathways. Narcissism, identity, and self have been concepts that play a part in the structure of maturity and the mature person (Fine, 1986). Narcissism (self-centeredness appropriate to the infants earliest attachment) changes with maturity or as interest and concern involve others. Fine described the pathological narcissism in character disorders and schizophrenia, and allowed for some degree of healthy narcissism. Can there be a healthy narcissism in the satisfied performer? I have considered maturity or maturing a nonlimiting process not too unlike the position taken by Erikson (1950), after the psychoanalytic model, of life stages from infancy to advanced age. In this framework, maturity is appropriate psychosocial and psychosexual functioning at all stages and ages. Call maturity more a movement than a place. Perhaps Maslow (1970) saw maturity at the top of his developmental hierarchy as self-actualization (i.e., maximizing one's potential). Maslow's self-actualized subjects are highly ethical and socially concerned (but not necessarily sociable).

It is apparent that maturity is a mind-body affair from any theoretical view, whether it is a psychodynamic position that sees movement through early narcissism, with its self-centeredness and incompetence to the diminished narcissistic level of existence involving interpersonal relationships and higher levels of mobility, confidence, and sense of self, or in a radical behaviorist perspective, which does not really lend itself to theoretical expansion or maturity but more or less states that one "is what one does."

THE PSYCHOLOGICAL PERSPECTIVE

George Sheehan is a runner, physician, and writer, not a psychologist. Still I mark his *Running and Being* (Sheehan 1978) as the seminal point in my motivation to see the physical aspects of running and exercise in the total mind-body picture. In a thought, it is to see this connection of the mental and the physical in a way that explored potential to improve, not to just the clinically normal but beyond to limitless actualization. True in part, I owed a debt to him just for his inspiring me to remain in the running exercise and fitness mode. After all he was older than I. However, it was somewhat more than cardiovascular improvement, racing, or running competence that connected me to his words. It was rather Sheehan's instant exploration of peoples' potential to move beyond complacency, stagnancy, or deterioration with the aid of body movement, in this case running. For the psychologist in me, this was the application of theory—humanistic existential—toward the improvement of self-concept through the medium of sports and exercise.

Generally the humanistic-existential or holistic view of psychology is eschewed by many psychologists, saying it is weak in its contribution to the empirical position. It also seems true that researchers and exercise specialists have not totally focused on running and choose, a variety of aerobic exercises to study the relationship between emotional and mental disorder, while generally preferring postulates other than the humanistic-existential for study and experimentation; nevertheless, Sheehan prompted me to examine theories and research that link physical fitness to the study of psychology.

Psychology, as a relatively recent science, has struggled to define itself. Essential to the process of its identity is the involvement of special focus and terminology that are essential to scientific inquiry. Psychology has largely satisfied the academic sector that it is a bonafide science in that regard. There was, however, a time when virtually every textbook author whose title bore a psychology designate felt it necessary to elaborate on that proposition. Today fewer authors express such compulsion. This does not mean that psychology is finally free from criticism by those in the natural sciences, but rather that some height, if not Everest, has been reached. Psychologists make serious observations as part of their empirical research leading to the scientific study of behavior. Psychologists studying sports, exercise, and fitness use these methods. Psychology is also theoretical and theoretically diverse. At the risk of tiring those who have heard it before, I will define theory. Weiten (1989) stated that theory is a system of interrelated ideas used to explain a set of observations. Today published research articles in psychology dealing with sports, exercise, and fitness number in the thousands. A large number of these articles are written within a theoretical framework. Many are experimentally or quasiexperimentally designed. This means that there is careful attention given to controlling the variables to be examined, and that hypotheses are accepted or dropped on the basis of statistical tests and inference; however, see Lamal's chapter in this book for an alternative (radical behavioral) viewpoint. "Because no other research method can duplicate this advantage of experiment, psychologists usually prefer to use the experimental method whenever possible" (Weiten, 1989, p. 43). All this means that psychologists and other interested persons can make some predictions and have some effect on a wide range of behaviors related to sports, exercise, and fitness whether it be an attempt to deal with athletes' use of steroids and cocaine, a pregnant woman's use of cocaine, or the effect of imagery in the development of a world-class skier. Such studies might call upon a psycho-dynamic personality theory, psychobiological theory, social reinforcement con-structs, or other theoretical framework. Not all who toil in the area of sports, exercise, and fitness research are satisfied with the current application of theory to experimentation. Iso-Ahola and Hatfield (1986), in their conceptually rich book, cited Kerlinger's (1973) definition of a theory "as a set of related constructs, definitions, and propositions that present a systematic view of phenomena by spec-ifying relations among variables with the purpose of explaining and predicting phenomena" (p. 9). They emphasized that a theory is a set of propositions rather than a single hypothesis, and that theories are put together with many variables that specify relationships. They lamented that sports psychology and social psy-chology generally have operated with an absence of theories using a single hypoth-esis or postulate. I do not necessarily share their dismay, but find that their state-ments do illustrate the importance of theory and experimentation in psychology in general and sports, exercise, and fitness psychology in particular.

HOW SPORTS, EXERCISE, AND FITNESS PSYCHOLOGISTS USE THEORY

In her introduction to *The Psychology of Sport,* Butt (1987) pondered the ques-tion of the athlete's motivation for engaging in sports. She wrote that the motiva-tion of athletes is a fascinating study because it reflects the positive and negative values of the times as well as the psyches of individual athletes. She noted that two people engaged in the same sport may behave overtly in a similar manner, but each may express different feelings about his or her participation, and they react differ-ently to the stress of winning or losing. She felt that the study of the psychological motivations in sport examines an author's theories for these differences.

Of course, the study of motivation in human behavior has much broader appli-cation than sports, on a slightly broad perspective, exercise and physical fitness, and at the broadest level, all aspects of human endeavor. Butt saw the components of the motivational model as life force or energy, aggression, conflict, compe-tence, competition, cooperation, and reinforcement. Cratty (1989) also considered the motivation to engage in sport. He found that children decide to participate in sports because of inherited capacities, parental influence, or perhaps lucky circum-stances that may be as varied as an interested adult or an area in which to partici-pate. Cratty noted that among motivations studied in athletes are: (a) the need for affiliation status and recognition; (b) need for the mastery of achievement; (c) risk taking; (d) character building; and (e) monetary rewards. He saw these motiva-tions as being divided into two major categories; extrinsic and intrinsic. He gave examples of research in motivation in sports with attribution theory, self-efficacy theory, and behavior modification used as theoretical frameworks for various studies.

THE CONCEPT OF MOTIVATION THEORY

I have shown how two outstanding sport psychologists describe the use of motivational concept in discussing the psychology of sports. At this juncture I review the psychological views of motivational theory. I have given the concept of

motivation emphasis because it is a key term for "achievin
motivation has been heard for a long time in the gym and st?
in fitting with the popular interest in athletic participation
household word. How many times have we said or have
after skipping or feeling reluctant about an aerobic wor
with the weights that "I just can't get motivated." Windhoi_
placed the concept of motivation, at least as far as the written recoi_
about 2,500 years to the philosopher Socrates. "He searched for his own m_
and those of his fellow citizens (who unfortunately resented him for it)."

Psychologists have been studying motivation and forming postulates and performing research concerning it for a good part of the history of psychology, which
is often dated from 1879, when Wilhelm Wundt established the first laboratory in
Liepsiz, Germany. If sport and exercise psychologists appear to have trouble or be
ambiguous or at odds with each other in the use of motivational theory, perhaps an
excerpt from Brown's (1961) classic volume on motivation will help the reader
sympathize with their difficulties.

> *The ubiquity of the concept of motivation, in one guise or another, is nevertheless surprising*
> *when we consider that its meaning is often scandalously vague. . . . It will be sufficient to note*
> *that, depending upon the particular writer consulted, motivation can be conscious or uncon-*
> *scious; it can be the same as or different from drive; it may or may not guide behavior; and all*
> *motives can be either learned or instinctive . . . that it is simply the energy that moves the body,*
> *or that it is identical with the neural discharge of specific central nervous system structure. (p.*
> *24)*

Bernstein, Roy, Wickens, and Srull (1988) presented a global view of motivation that can accommodate a number of drive, instinct, and personality theories.
We can examine some of these to see how they might jibe with sports, exercise,
fitness, and maturity concepts. Perhaps after that we can guess what Pat Gillich,
the General Manager of the Toronto Blue Jays baseball team, meant when he told
reporters "we are looking for someone who can work with the modern day player,
someone with the ability to communicate as well as motivate." Alternatively, we
can analyze Greg LeMond's statement made after winning the 1989 Tour de
France cycling classic when experts thought Fignon had an unbeatable lead: "I
wasn't sure if I could take it (the championship) back today. But I am very motivated when it comes to a race like the Tour de France and when it means the
difference between first and second. I had to give it 100%." According to Bernstein et al. (1988), motivation could be explained in terms of instinct theory broad
enough to include Sigmund Freud's psychoanalytic postulates, arousal theory
based on the activity in several physiological systems, incentive theory in which
people think positive rewards (i.e., bonuses, scholarships, longer life through
fitness), and biological motives, which could include hunger, thirst, sex, and perhaps even a primary need for physical activity.

MOTIVATIONAL THEORY IN USE

Drive and activation are often used interchangeably (Cratty, 1989). Attempts to
delineate between the two are often meaningless, and perhaps now is one such
time. An interesting observation concerning drive, motivation, and arousal is that
research in athletic competence appears to support what research in other areas

crates, mainly that motivation (i.e., drive) measured by either physiological
al—activation or anxiety—is facilitates at the middle level and interferes with
.ormance at low or high levels. The inverted U curve effect—low and high
vels being less facilitative of performance—has usually been associated with
Yerkes-Dodson law (1908). Jackson, Buglione, and Glenwick (1988) recently investigated the hypothesis that high drive decreases performance by studying the
playing ability of major league baseball players about to be traded. They presumed
with some substantiation that major league baseball players are in dread of being
traded, possibly to the minors, and are under high levels of stress and are trying
too hard. Using Zajonc's (1965) theory that socially induced drive would account
for social facilitation or impairment effects related to whether a task was simple or
complex, they concluded that the complex task of batting would be impaired by
high levels of drive, and predicted that ball players who were traded and relieved
of the stress concomitant with high drive levels would show an improvement in
their batting performances. That is, when pressure to succeed was reduced to a
medium range, the players would perform more competently. My primary purpose
here is not to report that they hypothesized correctly (although they did) but to
provide a current and vibrant illustration of psychology's application of theory to
practice.

BEHAVIOR MODIFICATION: REINFORCEMENT
AS A MOTIVATIONAL FACTOR

A large number of fitness studies have emphasized behavior modification in the
form of self-control or self-reinforcement. These have been somewhat efficacious
in dealing with weight gain and smoking where reinforcement from cessation of
overeating and smoking are slower to develop. In the area of exercise and especially aerobic exercise, where the reinforcement is in terms of well-being, external
incentives are usually obviated quickly.

Allison and Ayllon (1980) developed a coaching technique that applies principles of behavior modification to football, gymnastics, and tennis. They used positive and negative reinforcement as a means of overcoming bad playing habits and
developing correct procedures. For example, if a coach thought that a performance
was correct, he or she would give strong social reinforcement to the athlete. When
movement was incorrect, the coach might instantly shout at the player to freeze.
The coach gives verbal feedback about the error and corrects and models the
appropriate movement. The researchers reported that the results of their studies
indicated that a behavioral approach to coaching brings about significantly improved performance. A definitive article on behavioral coaching was developed by
Martin and Hyrcaiko (1983), in which they described six major characteristics that
could make behavior modification a valuable instrument in the coach's armamen-
tarium.

Of the role of radical behaviorism in sports psychology, Butt (1987) mused that
it tended to neglect what she considered the first aspect of human function, mainly
the individuality or personality of the client. She stated that few practice radical
behaviorism today in sports because of this. She did advocate cognitive psychology, along with the skillful use of reinforcement, which she indicated has provided
an array of clinical techniques that sometimes have innovative or direct application

in sport. For most radical behaviorists, the terms *mind* and *mental* present the problem of being inconcise; therefore, they have avoided dealing with a concept such as cognition, which might mean also belief, thought, idea, or perception. Since the past decade or thereabouts, there has been a meeting or mating between the two (cognitive and behavioral psychology), which has resulted in the designate cognitive behaviorist or cognitive behavior modification (Martin & Pear, 1983).

PSYCHODYNAMIC THEORY

Psychodynamic theory, and here I think mainly of psychoanalytic theory, has not played a primary role in the psychology of sports, exercise, and fitness. Still psychoanalytic theory is given some words of mention in a number of volumes that deal with motivation and touched upon in some sport psychology books. On the basis of the Freudian (1923) premise that two main drives—sex and aggression— propel us through our stages of development and the commensurate activities, it seems reasonable to include it in systems of motivation.

The following is an interpretation of a soccer game with the use of psychoanalytic concepts. This writer sees the soccer match as a therapeutic outlet for the unconscious fears of homosexuality. The design of the game according to Suarez-Orozco (1982) reflects homosexual taboos and the unconscious and thus unknown fantasies associated with it. Fears of castration and anal attack are, unconsciously of course, handled through mastery of the ball and protection of the goal. Intrapsychic conflict dealing with the foregoing fantasies may be relieved by participating or even being a spectator at a soccer game. As you might suspect, no experimental and empirical evidence supported Suarez-Orozco's postulate given from a unique perspective.

A HOLISTIC POINT OF VIEW

Some years ago, nearer the genesis of the fitness world, a 59-year-old physician postulated ties between physical activity and mental state. Because I have been a running advocate and, from early on, a fan of George Sheehan, I chose him as one of the most eloquent spokespersons of our time on the relationship between the physical and mental aspects of sports and exercise and, of course, in the ultimate sense, fitness. All of this comes together in his book *Running and Being: The Total Experience*. The theoretically initiated, would recognize the psychological theory as an humanistic existential and holistic expression of that relationship (mind, body, the self, and the world). Humanistic-existential examinations strive to understand human behavior in terms of wholeness, feelings, the now, and involvement in a deep sense intended by my choice of words. Valerie Andrews in her book *The Psychic Powers of Running* also makes one of the strongest claims to the nature of running both as an enhancer of personality and as a treatment for mental disorder. She described running from a holistic frame of reference. Psychiatrist Thaddeus Kostrubala (1976) is also an example of the runner with existential verve who uses running to restructure personality and to treat even major mental disorder. Kostrubala involved both the holistic framework and Jungian view of the personality structure. He saw running as a means of accessing the layers conscious-unconscious and collective-unconscious to the behavior pattern of our animal and prehuman ancestry into the archtypal inhabitant as postulated by Jung (1953).

A DISCURSIVE OVERVIEW

Looking through a pile of papers and books that were being used to help create this one, I came upon an opening sentence that said something like this: Today everyone appears obsessed with physical fitness. Search as I did I could not find the source of this statement once I put it back on the pile. Did I really need a citation for an idea that sounds so common and so like something we commonly mutter aloud, feeling that its all right to be careless with a clinical term like obsessed? Karen Rubenstein highlighted the intensity with which fitness is being pursued "like so many Gatsbys in jogging suits, Americans are chasing an ideal of perfect health" (1982). Being involved with sports, exercise, and fitness is not so much at this time in history a matter of getting in but rather more of a being swept along. When opening my front door on any reasonably decent day and, to a surprising degree, even in bad weather, I will not have to wait long (I can really hold that proverbial breath) until a runner comes by, and try Manhattan's Central Park on any Sunday no matter what the weather. My emphasis on running is not meant to establish its superiority over other forms of athletics, recreation, or exercise, but rather because it is a phenomenon that symbolizes the new wave. Can 50 million runners be wrong? If I run through my old, rather tough neighborhood today, I will go unnoticed. In the early 1960s, adolescents shouted "bird legs"! Were adult Americans always so involved in strenuous sports, exercise, and fitness? Hardly. Once out of school, past tendencies were to drop to the lowest level of inertia, except for a certain few who were often labeled as eccentric. Even physicians who commonly admonished patients to remember their ages when soreness, pain, or fatigue was reported now advocate some athletic endeavor for that same type of complaint.

Spectator sports and college athletic events have always had a prominent part in our lives and have fired our imaginations and provided our heroes, but psychology was rarely involved with them before the 1970s. To support these contentions, I reviewed the *Psychological Abstracts* index from July to December 1969, just 20 years before this writing. There were no separate listings or headings for sports but rather "See recreation education/physical." Physical fitness was not indexed, and for exercise one was referred to "work" (I think no joke intended). The change of awareness and concern in sports, exercise, and fitness may be reflected by the items in Dialog Files, Psycinfo, last load, May, 1989. The headings in the germane topics have appeared as follows: Exercise, 1973; Physical Fitness, 1973; Sports Psychology, 1982; Sports, 1982. It listed 522 published works on physical fitness, 131 on sports psychology, 1395 on physical fitness, and 993 on sports. The degree of psychology's interest and involvement in these areas and the rise of interest in 2 decades is impressive.

Earlier research on the use of behavioral modification as an instrument of coaching was discussed. Other articles have investigated the relationship of sports to a variety of psychological phenomena including personality traits. Psychologists have studied the relationships between sport participation and social, moral, and character development.

Nutrition, which is covered under the umbrella of fitness, has had too little attention by clinical, sport, and developmental psychology, escaping mention in my most recently acquired texts. The mental response to legal drug use, as well as diet and food supplement fadding by athletes and nonathletes, warrants consideration by physical fitness, coaching, and clinical personnel. The threads between psychology and sports, exercise, and fitness appear complexly and inextricably woven.

The preceding pages have defined psychology as a science and, more pointedly, how that science has been used to understand the role that exercise, sports, and fitness play in our behavior and our mental states. We note here, although it is probably obvious, that the three—sports, exercise, and physical fitness—have a related but not identical meaning. Brief descriptions are here culled from the literature to ensure that they are the popular if (perhaps) not the only definition of these terms.

SPORTS

There are a number of authorities defining sport, and they do so wearing a variety of scholarly cloaks: sport psychology, sport historian, history, sport sociology, sport philosophy, and sport anthropology are among them. For a neat, brief, readable, yet highly erudite summary, there is Allen Guttmann's (1988) *A Whole New Ballgame*. Guttmann's definition of sports calls for competition. It also calls for some kind of morality in the sense that fair play and rules and reasonable challenge are essential, which makes inclusion in this volume of psychological investigation of social, moral, and developmental issues so appropriate. Sports also, according to Guttmann, are physical, obviously in some sports more than others, which makes exercise and fitness so related to sports. Sports appear also to have a division relating to the importance or level of the competition, which means that sports may be called "recreational" when the competition lacks prominence, (i.e., all the marathoners behind the front runners in the Boston Marathon may be thought of as recreational runners). The distinction may be frivolous or useless except that serious (not recreational) competitors at the college and professional level, especially in popular sports, produced the social psychology of the sport spectator, and as celebrities, the athletes invoke the role-model phenomenon.

EXERCISE

Robert Maynard Hutchins might be best remembered for his comment that when he got the urge to exercise, he laid down until it went away. The time when that statement tickled the sophisticated is long gone, but it still tells us at least one thing: that exercise is movement and, as used in common parlance, body movement or exertion for improvement for training. In the context in which we use it now (operationally), it is sustained and deliberate physical activity performed to increase physical strength, flexibility, and cardiovascular and mental health. Loading trucks can be exercise, but we refer to that activity as work. Most psychological research dealing with the mental concomitants of exercise do so within a more traditional physical education construct.

Isometrics

These exercises are done by pushing or pulling against immovable objects for several seconds. They were once popularized through body builder Charles Atlas' magazine ads depicting the muscular bully kicking sand on the little guy, who then took Atlas' course and was no longer referred to as "skinny" on the beach. This form of exercise, however efficacious for the former "skinny," is not considered adequate by most trainers. However, Robert W. Boyce (personal communication, July 1989) reported success with isometrics equal to that with isotonic exercise, in particular strength development for the United States Air Force.

Isotonic Exercises

These are the most frequently used exercises to develop muscle tone, strength, and definition. Calisthenics, push-ups, pull-ups, free weights, and Nautilus machines may be used for this type of exercise. Isotonics are used in body building at many levels, and both male and female models for fitness center advertisements and fitness equipment usually display that defined kind of body gained from equipment, weights, and other isotonics. Intrigued by the toned physique phenomenon, Gary Long, Michael Masterson, and I have become involved with muscles and personal attraction research.

Isokinetic Exercise

These exercises get brief mention because they refer to muscle development using complex and expensive equipment not found in most gyms (not mine anyway). Isokinetics involve the movement of weights with a consistency of speed.

Anaerobic Exercise

These exercises involve short distance and short periods of time. Many games in sports are anaerobic (i.e., tennis doubles, baseball, softball, and sprinting) because the movement is not sustained for any long period of time without stopping. Calisthenics with frequent breaks in activities are anaerobic. Although anaerobic exercise develops speed and endurance, it does not demand the cardiovascular and respiratory involvement of aerobic exercises.

Aerobic Exercise

Most of the research relating to mood, depression, anxiety, and tension to physical exertion appear to involve aerobic exercise. Morgan (1987), in investigating the effect of acute physical activity on state anxiety, used vigorous walking and running with his subjects. Ryan (1983) indicated that physicians surveyed concerning the use of exercise for the treatment of depression and anxiety mainly favored walking, swimming, cycling, strength training, and running. Folkins and Sime (1981), in their investigation of physical fitness and mental health, emphasized studies that used those cardiovascular models of physical fitness. Experts divide exercise into discreet categories. The main characteristics of aerobics are duration and intensity. Running or jogging is the major form of aerobic activity today, and represents a social and psychological phenomenon. Among other activities that have similar effect upon the cardiovascular and respiratory systems are swimming, cycling, cross-country skiing, aerobic dancing, vigorous walking, and possibly racquet sports played vigorously enough. Some aerobic exercises are recreational and competitive sports as well as exercise. Finally, there is that exercise that is itself called "aerobics". Ordinarily done in groups with a leader, it may combine a variety of vigorous heart-pumping movements with catchy musical beats. A contemporary product, it has become, at its highest levels, "sport" with national and international championships.

PHYSICAL FITNESS

Physical educators, health educators, and health psychologists usually consider physical fitness to mean an ability to meet the routine physical requirements of life and to have enough left in reserve to meet unaccustomed demands. Whereas sports and exercise are ordinarily activities for behavior, fitness is more a statement of the condition of the individual. Fitness is generally seen in terms of adequacy of flexibility, cardiovascular function, and muscular strength and endurance. On the basis of the importance given to obesity by most health and physical educators as well as the medical profession, some have included freedom from obesity as another dimension (Johnson & Nelson, 1979). However, the term total weight control might be more appropriate than just obesity control because there is an additional feature involved when considering weight: the problem of eating disorders. Anorexia, quite polar to obesity, has recently been observed in many exercise-addicted individuals as well as in runners. In that regard Leon (1984) proposed that athletes involved in rigorous training and who also keep a low weight level through food intake reduction are much like those clinically diagnosed with anorexia nervosa, and may be in some respects undistinguishable from patients bearing the diagnosis of anorexia nervosa. The elusive path to fitness, although certainly involving sports and exercise, also calls for nutritional wisdom, drug wisdom, and mental and emotional adjustment. From the psychologist's point of view, all these relationships demand investigation.

ATHLETES

This may be bold on my part. Most sport psychology books do not define athletes, but it seems they rather take it for granted that the author and reader understand. I, too, took this position until an article by Sheehan alerted me to the amorphous nature of the term. "Athlete" on its own bears some mystique, some loftiness. George Sheehan commented in *Runners World* (March 1989) that fitness became a personal matter to him long before Ken Cooper's reports on aerobics and before the other experts came on the scene. He believed as the Greeks did that his body was tuned to the self. It was for Sheehan the rediscovery of an ancient law: knowing your body. For him, all questions he had about running were answered by his body; the main one for him and for every successful life-long fitness program was: "Am I having fun?" Sheehan concluded that his body answered that question soon after he started running. Running was play. He had fun because his body had fun. In the midst of all that, he became better and better at running, and he declared "I became fit. Even better, I became an athlete."

When the wife of our all-American, all-Pro basketball coach introduced me to a sportswriter saying, "he is quite an athlete himself," I did not know where to put my feet, hands, or gaze. To me it was kind, complimentary, far-fetched, and embarrassing.

At the time of this writing, I solicited a definition from those who work with competing athletes, including a sports information director. Answers were as illuminating as "good question" and "athletes perform athletics." I retreated to the American Heritage Dictionary, Second College Edition (1982). According to this source, an athlete is: (a) one who takes part in competitive sports; (b) a person containing the natural aptitudes for physical exercises and sports, as strength, agility and endurance. According to my very worn *The American College Dictionary* (1956), an athlete is any one trained to exercise physical agility and strength.

REFERENCES

Allison, K. E., & Ayllon, T. (1980). Behavioral coaching in the development of skills in football, gymnastics and tennis. *Journal of Applied Behavioral Analysis, 13,* 297–314.

Andrews, V. (1978). *The psychic powers of running.* New York: Rawson Wade.

Bernstein, D. A., Roy, E. J., Wickens, C. D., & Srull, T. K. (1988). *Psychology.* Boston: Houghton Mifflin.

Brown, J. S. (1961). *The motivation of behavior.* New York: McGraw-Hill.

Butt, D. S. (1987). *The psychology of sport: The behavior, motivation, personality, and performance of athletes.* New York: Van Nostrand Reinhold.

Cratty, B. J. (1989). *Psychology in contemporary sport.* Englewood Cliffs, NJ: Prentice Hall.

Erikson, E. H. (1950). *Childhood and society.* New York: W. W. Norton.

Fine, R. (1986). *Narcissism: The self and society.* New York: Columbia University Press.

Folkins, C. H., & Sime, W. E. (1981). Physical fitness training and mental health. *American Psychologist, 36,* 373–389.

Freud, S. (1923). The ego and the id. In J. Strackey (Ed.), *The standard edition of the complete psychological work of Sigmund Freud.* London: Gordon Hogarth Press.

Gesell, A., Halverson, H. M., Thompson, H., Ilg, F. L., Costner, B. M., Ames, L. B., & Amatruda, C. S. (1940). *The first five years of life.* New York: Harper & Brothers.

Guttmann, A. (1988). *A whole new ballgame.* Chapel Hill: The University of North Carolina Press.

Iso-Ahola, S., & Hatfield, B. (1986). *Psychology of sports.* Dubuque, IA: William C. Brown.

Jackson, J. M., Buglione, S. A., & Glenwick, D. S. (1988). Major league baseball performance as a function of being traded. *Personality and Social Psychology Bulletin, 4*(1), 46–56.

Johnson, B. L., & Nelson, J. K. (1979). *Practical measurement for evaluation in physical education.* Minneapolis, MN: Burgess.

Jung, C. G. (1953). *Two essays on analytical psychology.* New York: Pantheon.

Kerlinger, F. N. (1973). *Foundation of behavior research.* New York: Holt, Rinehart & Winston.

Kostrubala, T. (1976). *The joy of running.* Philadelphia: Lippincott.

Leon, G. (1984). Anorexia nervosa and sports activities. *Behavior Therapist, 7*(1), 9–10.

Martin, G., & Hrycaiko, D. (1983). Effective behavioral coaching: What's it all about? *Journal of Sports Psychology, 5*(1), 8–20.

Martin, G., & Pear, J. (1983). *Behavior modification.* Englewood Cliffs, NJ: Prentice-Hall.

Maslow, A. H. (1970). *Motivation and personality.* New York: Harper & Row.

Morgan, W. P. (1987). Reduction of state anxiety following acute physical activity. In W. P. Morgan & S. E. Goldston (Ed.), *Exercise and mental health.* Washington, DC: Hemisphere.

Peterson, C. (1988). *Personality.* New York: Harcourt Brace Jovanovich.

Rubenstein, C. (1982, Month). Wellness is all. *Psychology Today,* pp. 28–37.

Ryan, A. J. (1983). Exercise is medicine. *The Physician and Sports Medicine, 11*(10).

Sheehan, G. (1978). *Running and being: The total experience.* New York: Simon & Schuster.

Skinner, B. F. (1989). The origins of cognitive thought. *American Psychologist, 44*(1), 13–18.

Suarez-Orozco, M. M. (1982). A study of Argentine soccer: The dynamics of its fans and their folklore. *Journal of Psychoanalytic Anthropology, 5*(1), 7–28.

Weiten, W. (1989). *Psychology themes and variations.* Pacific Grove, CA: Cole.

Windholz, G., & Sternlicht, M. (1985). *The psychology of human adjustment.* Lexington, MA: Ginn Press.

Yerkes, R. M., & Dodson, J. D. (1908). The relation of strength of stimulus to rapidity of habit formation. *Journal of Comparative Neurology, 18,* 459–482.

Zajonc, R. B. (1965). Social facilitation. *Science, 149,* 269–274.

II

DEVELOPMENT: GROWING AND MATURING

2

Environmental Effects on the Fetus: The Examples of Alcohol, Cocaine, and Exercise

Lisa Eisen, Tiffany M. Field
University of Miami School of Medicine

Sandra K. Larson
University of Denver

During pregnancy, a mother-to-be often continues living her life as if nothing has changed, engaging in activities that might directly or indirectly affect the fetus. The nine months of gestation are a period of rapid and extensive growth and development as well as one of enhanced susceptibility and sensitivity. Many factors may influence the course of prenatal development. Whatever a pregnant woman eats or drinks and whatever drugs she takes may be transmitted to the fetus. Whether she is healthy or ill, whether her diet is nutritious or not, and whether she is exposed to environmental toxins or not may affect the development of the fetus. These agents that may produce malformations in the fetus are called *teratogens*. They include maternal diet, disease, drugs, hormones, and irradiation. In addition, maternal characteristics such as age, emotional state, number of previous pregnancies, and exercise influence prenatal development.

Until the 1940s, it was generally accepted that the human embryo was protected from environmental agents by the fetal membranes and the mother's abdominal walls and uterus. In 1941 Gregg documented that maternal rubella infection could cause malformations in human fetuses, leading to the first generally accepted realization that human embryos were susceptible to environmental influences. However, it was the thalidomide tragedy of the late 1950s and early 1960s (McBride, 1977) that first focused attention on the role of drugs during pregnancy in the cause of fetal malformations. Still, the potential harmful effects of more commonly used drugs and alcohol were generally ignored. It was not until 1973 that the issue of prenatal effects of alcohol consumption was raised and the fetal alcohol syndrome (FAS) (Jones & Smith, 1973) was defined. Today there is an increased interest and awareness in both the lay and scientific communities of the impact of environmental influences on prenatal development. Not only is there an awareness of teratogens resulting in gross physical abnormalities and mental retardation, but there is also an awareness of more subtle behavioral and cognitive teratogenic effects.

One of the best ways to understand environmental risks to the embryo or fetus is by the use of examples. This chapter discusses three different environmental influences on prenatal development: alcohol, cocaine, and exercise. Alcohol is one of the most extensively researched teratogens, and is a commonly used substance. Cocaine-exposed infants are the new epidemic in hospital neonatal units. The problem has spurred research, but it is still in the preliminary stages. Maternal exercise during pregnancy is a presumed healthy activity made popular by increased health consciousness; but in reality very little is known about the effect of maternal exercise on the developing fetus.

ALCOHOL

Drinking is often considered less lethal for the fetus than heroin or cocaine. However, alcohol, like other legal drugs such as nicotine and caffeine, has its undesirable effects on the fetus.

In 1968, Lemoine and his colleagues in Paris reported in a French medical journal on abnormalities observed in 127 children of alcoholic parents (Lemoine, Harousseau, Borteyru, & Menuet, 1968). They found these children to have common characteristics including: highly distinctive facial features; considerable growth retardation; high frequency of malformations, including cleft palate, limb malformations, and heart defects; and psychomotor disturbances. Lemoine and colleagues findings went virtually unnoticed until 5 years later when Jones and his associates, working independently in Seattle, discovered the same set of characteristics in children of alcoholic mothers (Jones & Smith, 1973; Jones, Smith, Streissguth, & Myrianthopoulos, 1974a; 1974b; Jones, Smith, Ulleland, & Streissguth, 1973), and termed this pattern of altered growth and morphogenesis FAS (Jones & Smith, 1973). The striking similarities in the independent findings of Jones and Lemoine in two different populations lent much credibility to these observations of the prenatal effects of alcohol.

Over the next several years, studies of the offspring of alcoholic mothers confirmed initial findings of altered growth and morphogenesis (Clarren & Smith, 1978; Jones, Smith, & Hanson, 1976; Smith, Jones, & Hanson, 1976; Ulleland, 1972). Several studies reported mental deficiency of varying degrees in children with FAS (Jones et al., 1976; Shaywitz, Cohen, & Shaywitz, 1980; Streissguth, 1976; Streissguth, Herman, & Smith, 1978a, 1978b). They also found a significant relationship between severity of morphogenesis and mental dysfunction, suggesting that the intellectual handicap, like the morphogenesis and growth deficiency, is of prenatal origin.

Behavioral problems, as well as growth deficiency, morphogenesis, and mental retardation, were reported in children with FAS (Iosub, Fuchs, Bingol, & Gromisch, 1981). These behavioral problems included irritability, hyperactivity, and feeding problems during infancy and the preschool years. A high incidence of speech and language problems ranging from mild to severe dysfunctions was also found. Impaired development of speech and language is a common early indicator of cerebral dysfunction, and behavior problems such as hyperactivity are indicators of minimal brain dysfunction. These problems are believed to be a result of the teratogenic effects of alcohol on the brain.

Effects of the Central Nervous System (CNS)

Alcohol readily crosses the placenta and enters the fetus' bloodstream. Alcohol is metabolized and eliminated much more slowly in the fetus and in the newborn than in the mother (Idanpaan-Heikkila et al., 1972). Thus, blood alcohol levels of the fetus may reach or surpass those of the mother. Even a small oral dose of alcohol exerts a depressant effect on the Fetal CNS. As little as one ounce of 40% alcohol consumed by the mother was found to significantly decrease infants' breathing movements within half an hour (Fox et al., 1978). After birth, the nursing newborn may continue to receive alcohol from the mother because alcohol is present in breast milk at the same concentration as in maternal blood (Borges & Lewis, 1981).

The potential effects of alcohol on the developing CNS are devastating. Studies reporting on autopsies of infants who died during the neonatal period whose mothers had a history of alcohol use have described extensive developmental anomalies of the brain, which resulted primarily from aberrations of neuronal migration (Clarren, Alvord, Sumi, Streissguth, & Smith, 1978; Jones, 1975). It is believed that interference with normal cerebellar and brainstem development occurred before 45 days gestation, and that cerebral abnormalities were initiated before 85 days gestation (Clarren et al., 1978). The level of maternal alcoholism in these cases ranged from chronic alcoholics to a binge drinker, who reported drinking at least five drinks at one time at approximately weekly intervals. Thus, intermittent high doses of alcohol can also cause severe damage. It is interesting that only a few of the infants from these studies were considered to have FAS from external criteria, indicating that abnormalities of CNS development can occur without external anomalies.

The effects of maternal alcohol use on fetal development have been investigated by controlled animal models as well (Streissguth, Landesman-Dwyer, Martin, & Smith, 1980). Despite differing methodologies, studies using animal models have the common findings of increased fetal mortality and decreased birth weight being related to maternal alcohol intake. For example, Reyes, Rivera, Saland, and Murray (1983) found alcohol-treated rat offspring to exhibit growth retardation, microcephaly, low birth weight, and decreased survival rates. Offspring from the alcohol group had brain weights that were 10% to 15% smaller than the control group. Further examination showed a decrease in dendritic spines and vacuolated area in layer V of the parietal cortex in the alcohol-treated pups. These findings parallel human findings of autopsies of FAS infants revealing incomplete brain development and lack of normal neuronal migration (Clarren et al., 1978; Jones, 1975).

Animal models have allowed a more controlled means of studying the mechanism of CNS damage related to maternal alcohol consumption. In monkeys, an impairment of the fetal-placental circulation system was found following administration of ethanol to the mother (Mukherjee & Hodgen, 1982). This impairment of umbilical function produced hypoxia and acidosis in the fetus. Although this condition was transient, brain cells are extremely sensitive to low oxygen levels, and significant brain damage may occur despite a short duration of severe hypoxia.

It seems clear that maternal alcohol consumption can have a dramatic effect on the developing CNS. Abnormalities of the CNS can occur in the absence of external anomalies. In addition, binge alcohol drinking may produce damage similar to chronic alcohol drinking.

Dosage and Critical Period

The questions of how much alcohol a mother can drink before damaging her baby and when during pregnancy is the fetus vulnerable to alcohol still remain unanswered. The susceptibility to teratogens varies with developmental stage (Wilson, 1973). There is a degree of vulnerability to teratogenesis throughout the total span of development, but research has demonstrated that the greatest danger is associated with a relatively short period between germ-layer differentiation and completion of major organ formation. This period of tissue and organ differentiation occurs between Gestation Days 18 or 20 to 55 or 60 (Wilson, 1973).

Two vulnerable or "critical" periods have been identified in the development of the human brain (Abel, 1980). The first occurs between 12 and 18 weeks of gestation during a period of neuronal multiplication. The second occurs during the third trimester and continues through the first 18 months after birth. This period is characterized by dendritic branching and formation of synaptic connections. Thus, a teratogenic agent may have maximal effects on the developing brain in the first and third trimesters.

These "critical periods" have some implications with regard to alcohol consumption during pregnancy. External anomalies characteristic of the full-blown FAS are likely to occur in children of chronic alcohol drinkers and those who drink heavily during the first trimester. CNS damage such as mental retardation and more subtle brain damage may occur without external anomalies when maternal alcohol intake occurs before or after the period of organogenesis. Before organogenesis, heavy alcohol intake may produce death, which is one explanation for the higher rate of miscarriages in alcoholic mothers. In the third trimester, after organogenesis is complete, the fetus is still susceptible to alcohol intake. Even a single binge during this period may lead to irreversible brain damage (Mukherjee & Hodgen, 1982). In addition, there may be little structural alteration to be found in the fully formed brain, yet the functional effects may be significant, and obvious behavioral deficits may result (Rodier & Reynolds, 1977).

Whether a particular developmental deviation is produced depends not only on the period of development but also on dosage. The susceptible early embryo is readily malformed or killed by a relatively small dose of suitable agents, but much larger doses may be needed to harm the fetus (Wilson, 1973). Higher levels of alcohol intake may be required at some periods during prenatal development than at others to produce deviant development. What may be a "safe" level of alcohol intake during one period of prenatal development may not be at another period.

Manifestations of deviant development increase in frequency and degree as dosage increases, from the no-effects level to the totally lethal level (Wilson, 1973). Whether there is a threshold below which no manifestation of abnormality is seen is still unresolved. This threshold is bound to change with the period of prenatal development, as well as with the genotype of the individual fetus and mother. Although there may be a theoretical safe level for any agent, finding it is a very difficult task. For alcohol it is even more so because of the many confounding variables associated with chronic maternal drinking: maternal health, maternal nutrition, poverty, physical stress, and other drug use. Further, as yet there has been no teratogen studied that clearly shows a threshold above which the substance is teratogenic and below which the substance is safe (Smith, 1979).

What is a "safe" level of maternal alcohol consumption remains unanswered. It is known that chronically alcoholic mothers and mothers who binge drink often produce offspring with FAS. Researchers have now begun investigating the effects of moderate alcohol consumption or social drinking on the developing fetus. They are not only looking for death and external anomalies in these infants of social drinkers, but for differences in growth and behavior as well.

Social Drinking During Pregnancy

Since 1974, several prospective studies have focused on the question of whether social drinking during pregnancy is harmful. Among the largest and most prolific were the Boston and the Seattle studies. In addition, there have been several epidemiological studies that have dealt with the prenatal effects of alcohol.

Boston Studies

A pilot prospective study at Boston City Hospital, which serves a poor inner-city area, began in 1974 interviewing 633 women and examining 322 babies (Ouellette & Rosett, 1976; Ouellette, Rosett, Rosman, & Weiner, 1977; Rosett, Ouellette, & Weiner, 1976). They found that the frequency of abnormalities was twice as great in offspring of heavy drinkers as that in offspring of abstinent or moderate drinkers. Congenital anomalies were found in 32% of the infants of heavy drinkers compared with 14% in moderate drinkers and 9% in abstinent drinkers (Ouellette et al., 1977). Infants of heavy drinkers had smaller birth lengths, birth weights, and head circumferences, and were more likely to be born prematurely, than infants of abstinent or moderate drinkers. Infants of mothers who drank heavily were significantly more likely to be jittery, have poor muscle tone (hypotonia, and have poor sucking ability compared with infants whose mothers were classified as moderate drinkers or abstainers (Ouellette & Rosett, 1976; Ouellette et al., 1977).

Maternal drinking was also related to neonatal sleep state regulation (Rosett et al., 1979; Sander et al., 1977). Sleep state organization is generally considered an indicator of infant CNS organization and maturity. Heavy alcohol consumption throughout pregnancy was associated with a decrease in the total time spent sleeping, more quiet sleep periods interrupted by indeterminate sleep, and greater restlessness with more frequent body movements. However, heavy-drinking mothers who were able to modify consumption and abstain or significantly reduce drinking for the third trimester had babies who slept longer (Rosett et al., 1979).

Following this report, Rosett, Weiner, Zuckerman, McKinlay, and Edelin (1980) further investigated the impact of reduced alcohol consumption during the third trimester. They found significantly less growth retardation among infants born to women who reduced their alcohol consumption during pregnancy. This finding further indicates that alcohol consumption late in pregnancy, as well as earlier in pregnancy, has a detrimental impact on the unborn baby.

A later Boston study was conducted to control for numerous confounding factors such as cigarette smoking, other drug use, maternal weight change during pregnancy, nutrition, history of maternal illness, race, maternal age, and socioeconomic status that may contribute to adverse fetal development (Alpert et al., 1981; Hingson et al., 1982). Heavy-drinking women were compared with other women in the sample on a variety of life-style factors. It was found that women who drink heavily are different in a number of ways from those who do not (Alpert et al.,

1981). Women who drank heavily were less likely to attend school or work, even though no difference in income level was noted. Those women who drank heavily were more likely to be smokers, and they smoked more heavily than other women. Drug use before pregnancy was reported more frequently among heavy drinkers. Although there was no reported difference in prenatal care, heavy drinkers had twice as many previous miscarriages, had higher parity, and were less likely to take prenatal vitamins and iron than other women. These findings emphasize the importance of evaluating other life-style variables that may also impact prenatal development when investigating the prenatal effects of alcohol.

Seattle Studies

The first Seattle study involved 801 middle-class women from a health maintenance organization, analyzing birth weight for a selected sample of 263 infants and assessing the behavioral development of 130 children at 4 and 5 years of age (Landesman-Dwyer, Ragozin, & Little, 1981; Little, 1977; Little, Schultz, & Mandell, 1976, 1977).

This study found that maternal alcohol use before pregnancy and late in pregnancy is significantly related to infant birth weight. Daily consumption of 1 oz of absolute alcohol per day before pregnancy was associated with a decrease in birth weight of 91 grams, whereas 1 oz per day consumed in late pregnancy was associated with a decrease in birth weight of 160 grams (Little, 1977). A follow-up of study subjects was conducted to examine behavioral differences when the children were 4 years old (Landesman-Dwyer et al., 1981). Children of moderate drinkers generally were less attentive, less compliant with parental commands, and more fidgety during mealtimes than were children of light drinkers or abstainers.

The second Seattle study is the most comprehensive to date in its assessment of pregnancy outcomes in 1,529 women and in detailed, repeated evaluation of 500 children from birth on (Hanson, Streissguth, & Smith, 1978; Landesman-Dwyer, Keller, & Streissguth, 1978; Martin, Martin, Lund, & Streissguth, 1977; Martin, Martin, Streissguth, & Lund, 1979; Ragozin, Landesman-Dwyer, & Streissguth, 1978; Streissguth, Barr, & Martin, 1983; Streissguth, Barr, Martin, & Herman, 1980; Streissguth, Barr, Sampson, Darby, & Martin, 1989; Streissguth, Martin, Martin, & Barr, 1981).

Women receiving prenatal care at two Seattle area hospitals were interviewed during the fifth month of pregnancy. A follow-up sample of 500 infants was selected at birth according to criteria including maternal smoking and alcohol use patterns. The mothers participating in this study were primarily Caucasian, married, middle-class, and well educated. This larger project gave rise to numerous smaller studies examining the various aspects of prenatal alcohol consumption on neonatal outcome (Streissguth et al., 1981).

Streissguth et al. (1983) administered the Brazelton Neonatal Behavioral Assessment Scale (NBAS) to 417 infants when they were between 9 and 35 hours old. The NBAS evaluates infants on many different items including state control, reflexes, responsiveness to auditory and visual stimuli, social interaction, motor development, and habituation to repeated stimuli. Infants exposed to relatively greater amounts of alcohol prenatally performed poorer on the habituation part of the NBAS. That is, they were not as capable of shutting out redundant stimuli when in a state of light sleep. Martin et al. (1979) evaluated the sucking patterns of 151 study infants by using electronic recordings of amplitude, frequency, and duration. Infants whose mothers smoked or were moderate to heavy drinkers had significantly weaker sucking ability, drawing a parallel between infants of moderate drinkers and FAS babies who are known to have poor sucking skills and feeding difficulties. Landesman-Dwyer et al. (1978) found that infants of social drinkers showed to a lesser degree some to the behavioral characteristics of infants with FAS. Increased maternal alcohol use was associated with more time spent with eyes open, more body tremors, increased head orientation to the left (atypical for newborns), decreased amount of time spent in high levels of body activity, and increased hand-to-mouth behavior. These behaviors are characteristic of other populations at-risk for CNS dysfunction (such as narcotic withdrawal); however, excessive irritability and hyperactivity, two salient behavioral signs reportedly present in newborns with FAS or neonatal narcotic withdrawal, were not observed in the infants of social drinkers.

In addition to studies of infant assessment, medical records of 1,439 subjects were reviewed (Streissguth et al., 1978). Increased amounts of maternal drinking were related to lower Apgar scores at one minute, more fetal heart rate abnormalities (bradycardia and variable decelerations), and an increased need for ventilatory resuscitation during the first few days of life.

The evidence from the second Seattle project suggests that the effects of social drinking may be seen in the newborn. How long-lasting these effects are was the next question the Seattle project set out to answer. Streissguth, Barr, Martin, & Herman, (1980) followed up 462 of the study infants at 8 months of age and found that maternal drinking during early pregnancy was significantly related to lower mental and motor scores on the Bayley Scales of Infant Development. These effects could not be attributed to other agents (such as smoking, caffeine, or street drugs), other risk factors (such as parity, gestational age, or maternal education), or other obvious intervening variables occurring after birth (such as head injuries, fevers, maternal illness, or level of environmental stimulation). A follow-up of these same children at 4 years of age revealed a significant relationship between maternal alcohol use and IQ scores, even when a large number of other potentially confounding variables were adjusted for in the statistical analyses (Streissguth et al., 1989). Maternal use of more than 1.5 oz (approximately three drinks) of alcohol per day during pregnancy was significantly related to an average IQ decrement of almost 5 points (one-third of a standard deviation).

The behavioral effects of these follow-up studies are relatively small in magnitude and by themselves probably do not constitute impairment of the children's general functioning. However, the effects of prenatal exposure to moderate levels of alcohol are enough to impact development at 4 years and possibly longer. Still unanswered are the questions of how long term the influences may be, and how much alcohol is safe to drink during pregnancy.

Epidemiological Studies

Several epidemiological studies have analyzed the physical development and survival of offspring in relation to alcohol use. These studies include a French investigation of more than 9,000 pregnancies (Kaminski, Rumeau-Rouquette, & Schwartz, 1978), a California study of more than 32,000 pregnancies (Harlap, Schiono, & Ramcharan, 1979), and a Cleveland study of more than 12,000 pregnancies (Sokol, Miller, & Reed, 1980).

One finding of these studies was that increased maternal alcohol use is related to decreased infant birth weight (Kaminski et al., 1978; Sokol et al., 1980). In the Cleveland study, the risk of intrauterine growth retardation was estimated to be increased 2.4-fold in association with alcohol alone, 1.8-fold with smoking alone, and 3.9-fold with these risks together (Sokol et al., 1980).

In the French study, the risk of stillbirths was increased two and one-half times for women reported drinking an average equivalent of three or more glasses of wine per day. This risk was even greater for mothers who also smoked, came from lower socioeconomic classes, had more prior pregnancies, or were older (Kaminski et al., 1978). The California study also detected a significant increase in spontaneous abortions, which increased with the amount of maternal drinking, even after adjusting for important variables correlated with drinking (Harlap et al., 1979).

The Cleveland study found a significant increase in congenital anomalies (38%) related to maternal alcohol use. Cigarette smoking did not appear to account for the observed anomalies. In addition, women who used alcohol had a higher risk of infection and premature placental separation during labor. Evidence of fetal distress during labor and neonatal depression were also more common in their infants (Sokol et al., 1980).

An epidemiological study at Loma Linda University in California, collected data on more than 12,000 pregnancies (Kuzma & Kissinger, 1981; Kuzma & Phillips, 1977). In this project, different groups of women ranked according to absolute alcohol intake were compared with regard to their smoking practices, drug use, nutritional history, socioeconomic status, education, income, number of abortions, number of miscarriages, and prenatal care. They found that drinking habits appear to be associated with age, ethnicity, marital status, income, education, church attendance, and prenatal care, but not with gestational age, breast-feeding, or self-reported health (Kuzma & Kissinger, 1981). Women from higher education and income brackets had a higher frequency of moderate drinking during pregnancy. Being widowed, separated, or divorced was also associated with higher alcohol use. Greater church attendance was associated with lower alcohol use or abstinence. Heavy drinkers tended to have fewer prenatal checkups than lighter drinkers. In addition, drinking and smoking were closely interrelated. This study emphasized that subgroups of women with different prenatal drinking habits may not be comparable on other characteristics that are also likely to influence either maternal complications of pregnancy or the health of the newborn (Kuzma & Kissinger, 1981).

The findings of these various epidemiological studies suggest a few points. First, although FAS is relatively rare, a range of adverse outcomes including spontaneous abortions, intrauterine growth retardation, and increased congenital anomalies is much more common. Second, alcohol use is associated with other pregnancy risks such as smoking that may contribute to, but do not appear to explain, the observed adverse outcomes associated with alcohol use.

COCAINE

Recreational drugs such as heroin, methadone, cocaine, crack, and marijuana have been noted to have deleterious effects on the fetus and newborn when used by the mother during pregnancy. In recent years there has been a marked increase in cocaine use in the United States. According to national surveys, the greatest increase in use of cocaine has occurred in the population group of child-bearing age. It can be inferred from these statistics that the number of pregnant women using cocaine has also increased.

In 1982, 70 of 2,500 new mothers at Bronx-Lebanon Hospital reported drug use, with 25% using cocaine. In 1985, the number of self-reported drug users increased to 120, with 75% using cocaine (Newald, 1986). Of 18 hospitals recently surveyed by the Select Committee on Children, Youth, and Families, 15 reported an increase in the incidence of substance abuse during pregnancy and the number of drug-exposed births since 1985 (Miller, 1989). One New York City hospital reported that the number of newborns with a positive urine screen for cocaine increased from 12% to 13% of 2,900 to 3,000 total births in 1985 to 15% of 2,900 to 3,000 births in 1988 (Miller, 1989). At the University of Miami's Jackson Memorial Hospital, the prevalence of perinatal cocaine exposure was 12% (26 of 215) when all infants born were monitored for a one-week period during the summer of 1988 (Bandstra, Steele, Burkett, Palow, and Levandoski, 1988). As a result of the increased use of cocaine in pregnant women, researchers have begun to focus on the impact of cocaine on the infant.

The fetal risks of maternal drug use may take different forms. Some drugs are addictive, some are toxic, and some are teratogenic. Both addictive and toxic drugs can cause the newborn to be sick, small for gestational age, of low birth weight, premature, or a combination of these (Jones & Lopez, 1988). Addictive drugs may also cause the neonate to experience withdrawal, after which the infant will grow and develop normally. Toxic drugs may cause direct injury to the infant. Teratogenic drugs are more complex in that they effect the developing embryo or fetus. As seen in the alcohol literature, teratogenic effects are influenced by time and dosage of exposure, the systems that are under development at the time of exposure, and the genetic susceptibility of the individuals. Teratogens may result in easily identifiable physical anomalies or in less easily observed behavioral differences. Researchers have explored prenatal cocaine exposure from both a teratogenic and addictive point of view.

Teratogenicity of Cocaine

Cocaine's mechanism of action can partially explain some of its teratogenic effects. Cocaine is a CNS stimulant of short duration with acute effects similar to those produced by the naturally occurring hormone adrenaline and almost identical to the effects of amphetamine (Nichols & Clone, 1987). Crack, a more concentrated form of cocaine, has a "high" that lasts for an even shorter time (approximately 30 minutes) than that of cocaine. Cocaine's short duration generally leads to frequent repeated use. Crack's extremely short duration leads to even more repeated use to regain the euphoric state, thereby resulting in a higher level of fetal exposure (Leblanc, Parekh, Naso, & Glass, 1987).

Cocaine acts peripherally to inhibit nerve conduction and prevent norepinephrine (NE) uptake at the nerve terminals, producing increased NE levels with subsequent vasoconstriction and tachycardia and a concomitment abrupt increase in blood pressure. Placental vasoconstriction can occur, which decreases blood flow to the fetus and increases uterine contractions (Woods, Plessinger, & Clark, 1987). This may account for the high incidence of spontaneous abortions and abruption placenta found in cocaine-addicted women (Chasnoff, Burns, Schnoll, & Burns, 1985).

Like other drugs that act upon the CNS, cocaine has high-water and lipid solubility features, has a low molecular weight, and is capable of rapidly penetrating mucosal membranes (Bingol, Fuchs, Diaz, Stone, & Gromisch, 1987; Smith, 1988). These characteristics make it easy for cocaine to cross the placenta and the fetal blood-brain barrier. The intrapartum effects that can occur are fetal tachycardia, excessive fetal activity, and a sudden onset of strong uterine contractions at the beginning of labor (Smith, 1988). Bingol et al. (1987) speculated that in pregnant cocaine-abusing women, vasoconstriction, sudden hypertension, or cardiac arrhythmias may interrupt the blood supply to the various fetal tissues causing deformation or disruption of morphogenesis. Because maternal cocaine use places the fetus at risk for tachycardia and hypertension, it also places the fetus at risk for a cerebrovascular accident. One such incident was reported of an infant who developed a cerebral infarction after delivery at term to a woman who had used a large amount of cocaine before delivery (Chasnoff, Bussey, Savich, & Stack, 1986).

Prenatal cocaine exposure has also been related to a higher incidence of infants born small for gestational age, of shortened gestational periods, of lower Apgar scores, and of lower birth weights and smaller head circumferences (Bingol et al., 1987; MacGregor et al., 1987; Ryan, Ehrlich, & Finnegan, 1987; Smith, 1988). The shortened gestational period and low birth weight reported in cocaine babies, if accurate, may be due to the vasoconstrictive and catecholamine effects of cocaine (Leblanc et al., 1987). The reduction of blood flow to the placenta and fetus caused by cocaine also limits the nutrients to the fetus, which in turn may retard growth (Bingol et al., 1987).

Cocaine Withdrawal Symptoms in Neonates

Between 50% to 90% of newborns of narcotic-addicted mothers show some withdrawal symptoms (Chavez, Ostrea, Stryker, & Smialek, 1979; Lipsitz, 1975; National Clearinghouse for Drug Abuse Information [NCDAI], 1974). Maternal narcotic and ethanol addiction produces a variety of physical symptoms in the newborn, which usually appear within the first 4 days after birth (NCDAI, 1974). These symptoms include: tremors and seizures; irritability with excessive or high-pitched crying and wakefulness or restlessness; tachypnea and other respiratory problems; abnormal reflexes; increased flexor tone and hypertonia; gastrointestinal problems such as vomiting, regurgitation, diarrhea, poorly formed stools, weight loss, and poor feeding; autonomic instability manifested as sweating, cyanosis, inability to maintain temperature, and fever; excessive mouthing such as fist sucking; and repetitive sneezing or yawning (Coles, Smith, Fernhoff, & Falden, 1984; Doberczak et al., 1986; Lipsitz, 1975; Madden et al., 1977; NCDAI, 1974; Ostrea, Chavez, & Strauss, 1976).

Cocaine-exposed infants do not seem to experience the classic neonatal abstinence syndrome, the dramatic withdrawal symptoms associated with alcohol and opiates (Rosecan & Gross, 1986; Ryan et al., 1987; Smith, 1988). The symptoms may simply be more subtle or manifested at a later time than thus far examined. Also it is difficult to identify cocaine's unique withdrawal symptoms given that infants are rarely exposed to cocaine alone without alcohol or other drugs (Rosecan & Gross, 1986). A recent study conducted by the present authors found that although cocaine-exposed neonates tended to show more withdrawal symptoms than nonexposed neonates, a multiple regression revealed that maternal alcohol use and obstetric complications accounted for a significant amount of the variance in withdrawal symptoms, whereas cocaine use did not (Eisen et al., 1989).

Only a limited number of studies have been published on the withdrawal symptoms of infants exposed to cocaine alone (without opiates) (Chasnoff et al., 1985; Leblanc et al., 1987; Madden, Payne, & Miller, 1986), and these studies are inconsistent in both their methodology and their findings. The physical symptoms paralleling narcotic withdrawal that have been reported include: tremulousness, irritability, wakefulness or restlessness, muscular rigidity (hypertonia), and abnormal elicited reflexes.

One hypothesis for the apparently more severe withdrawal symptoms of narcotic versus cocaine addiction could be related to the relatively greater effects of narcotic addiction on the developing fetus. Narcotics, with their longer lasting effects, may prevent the development of an endogenous endorphin system in the fetus. In contrast, cocaine and especially crack, with their very brief high, may not completely alter the naturally developing endorphin system. Following birth, the infant who has been exposed to narcotics such as methadone and heroine may experience withdrawal not only from the mother's supply, but also from his or her own endorphin system. This may explain the continuum of increasing severity of withdrawal symptoms reported for the infants of crack-, cocaine-, heroine-, and methadone-addicted mothers.

Another possibility is that researchers have looked for withdrawal symptoms too soon in cocaine-exposed infants. In the adult, cocaine withdrawal first results in a "crash" occurring after the high and lasting anywhere from nine hours to four days. This crash, consisting primarily of depression and exhaustion, is followed by a period of anxiety, intense cocaine craving, and other overt symptoms of withdrawal (Nunes & Rosecan, 1987). If the infant's withdrawal parallels the adult's, then withdrawal symptoms such as those that have been described for narcotics withdrawal may not appear until four days after birth (possibly after hospital discharge) or perhaps even longer because of the neonate's slow metabolism. Depression and exhaustion, which may be experienced before other symptoms, may go undetected because the agitation-like withdrawal symptoms are expected instead.

Behavioral Effects of Prenatal Cocaine Exposure

Several researchers have used the Brazelton NBAS (Brazelton, 1984) to assess differences in behavior of newborns exposed prenatally to cocaine. Cocaine-exposed newborns have been found to show increased startle responses, poor state organization, rapid state changes, decreased reactivity to environmental stimuli, depressed interactive behavior, and less consolability than nonexposed newborns (Chasnoff, 1988; Chasnoff et al., 1985; Leblanc et al., 1987; MacGregor et al., 1987; Madden et al., 1986). Additionally, Eisen et al (1989) found that cocaine-exposed neonates differed from controls on the habituation portion of the NBAS, indicating that they were not as capable of shutting out redundant stimuli when in a state of light sleep.

Few findings have been published on the long-term effects of prenatal cocaine exposure, partly because of the relative recency of the problem and the cost and difficulties of longitudinal research. One short-term longitudinal study found motor development delays at 4 months of age in the infants of mothers who consumed cocaine or crack during pregnancy (Schneider, 1988). Certainly, much more work needs to be performed to determine the potential long-term effects of prenatal cocaine exposure.

EXERCISE

In the past several years, a fitness craze has hit the United States. People are more aware of health issues, and many people are eating healthier diets and engaging in proper exercise programs. Health and fitness clubs and aerobic classes are as popular as ever. With this increased interest in fitness has come the question of whether exercise during pregnancy is beneficial or harmful. This is not an easy question to answer. Many factors including the intensity and duration of the exercise, the time during pregnancy, maternal weight gain during pregnancy, and the level of maternal fitness before pregnancy influence the answer.

Evidence From Animal Studies

Research on the effects of maternal exercise is sparse and has typically involved the forced exercise of pregnant animals. In a recent review of that literature, Goodlin and Buckley (1984) concluded that reduced birth weight is the only typical finding when pregnant animals are exposed to forced exercise. Additionally, these animal studies have failed to find beneficial pregnancy outcomes to forced prenatal exercise.

Several potentially harmful pregnancy outcomes have been noted from these animal studies. Increased mortality and delayed ossification have been reported in research using rodents, guinea pigs, and sheep (Fisher, 1984), although these animals did not differ from controls in fetal body, brain, or heart weights. Various explanations have been offered for the negative delivery outcomes observed in these studies. They include a reduced oxygen supply reaching the fetus, the decreased capacity of the placenta to diffuse carbon monoxide in the blood, and reduced blood circulation following strenuous exercise.

Although there is relatively little research on the effects of maternal exercise on the developing fetus, there are several studies in the animal literature on the effects of maternal stress on pregnancy outcome. Stress is typically defined as any manipulation that activates the pituitary-adrenal axis. Given this definition, exercise may be considered a stressor. Thus, examining the effects of general maternal stressors on the developing fetus may lend some insight to the potential effects of maternal exercise.

Studies of the effects of prenatal stressors have generally involved stressing pregnant animals with electric shock, body restraint, hormone injections, or intense light. Such prenatal stressors have led to poor delivery outcomes including late deliveries, premature deliveries, prolonged labor, and fetal resorption (for review see Fisher, 1984; Istvan, 1986). The effects of these stressors on offspring behavior are less conclusive. Some studies have reported that offspring of mothers stressed during pregnancy exhibit heightened arousal as indicated by decreased activity and increased defecation in unfamiliar environments, whereas other studies have failed to find such behavioral differences (for review see Archer & Blackman, 1971; Daly, 1973; Thompson & Giusek, 1970). These contradictory findings may be due to the different types of stressors, the timing of the stress during gestation, and the variable duration and intensity levels of the stressors used in the different studies. Although these behavioral findings appear to be controversial, prenatal manipulations clearly alter the physiology of the offspring. For example, prenatally stressed female rats have shown disorganized estrus cycles, reduced fertility, and disruptive maternal behavior (Herrenkohl, 1979; Herrenkohl & Whitney, 1976).

Although primate models may be more analogous to the human, very few studies have investigated the effects of exercise or stressors on fetal primates. When primates have been stressed prenatally, increased rates of miscarriages and lower birth weights have been noted (Myers, 1975). Explanations for these findings have included altered chemical, hormonal, cardiovascular, and respiratory functioning in the pregnant animal. Myers (1975), for example, suggested that stress increases levels of norepinephrine and epinephrine, which in turn leads to reduced uterine blood flow. A reduced uterine blood flow would mean a reduced amount of oxygen and nutrients reaching the fetus.

Although animal models allow for carefully controlled experimentation on the prenatal effects of exercise, care must always be taken when attempting to generalize results to humans. Contradictions between animal and human studies may be due to the voluntary nature of exercise in humans, which may be less stressful than forced exercise or other stressors used in animal studies. In addition, the level of stress and exercise these pregnant animals have been exposed to is probably excessive in comparison to that of most human mothers. The intensity and duration of the exercise or stressor are undoubtedly important factors.

Evidence From Research With Humans

The exercise of pregnant women must be closely monitored because of the dramatic physiological changes induced by pregnancy (Goodland & Buckley, 1984). Softening of the joints and connective tissue make the pregnant woman vulnerable to injury. Increased blood volume and cardiac output can lead to a rapid increase in blood pressure and heart rate during exercise. In previously trained pregnant women, exercise further increases blood volume, which is beneficial to the fetus because the amount of maternal expansion of blood volume during pregnancy determines the size of the newborn. However, exercise without prior training is associated with a relative failure to expand maternal blood volume (Goodlin & Buckley, 1984). Most studies have involved women who were already exercising before pregnancy because of the general recognition that it is unhealthy for both the mother and fetus to initiate a vigorous exercise regime during pregnancy.

The immediate effect of exercise is that blood is diverted from the uterus to the legs. Changes in norepinephrine and epinephrine levels, irregular uterine activity, and increased maternal and fetal heart rate also occur during exercise (Artal et al., 1986, Collings, Curet, & Mullin, 1983; Morton, Paul, Campos, Hart, & Metcalfe, 1985; Rauramo, Anderson, Laatikainen, & Patterson, 1982). Typically, the increase in fetal heart rate continues for 30 minutes following moderate to strenuous exercise (Artal et al., 1986; Clapp, 1985; Collings & Curet, 1985; Hauth, Gilstrap, & Widemer, 1982). In contrast to the increase in fetal heart rate noted by others, Jovanovic, Kessler, and Peterson (1985) reported fetal bradycardia during and immediately after vigorous maternal exercise by using ultrasound monitoring. Their findings suggest that maximal exertion could result in fetal hypoxia, although this hypoxia is assumed to be mild and transient in nature because all fetuses in this study had normal nonstress test results within 30 minutes of exercise cessation.

Mixed findings are also seen regarding the effects of typical exercise levels and delivery outcome. Clapp and Dickstein (1984) reported that women who engaged in regular strenuous exercise such as running and cross-country skiing throughout pregnancy gained less weight, delivered earlier, and had lighter infants than women who quit exercising in mid-pregnancy. In a similar study, Collings et al. (1983) found no differences between infants whose mothers regularly exercised during pregnancy and those whose mothers did not. Other researchers failed to find a relationship between level of maternal physical fitness and length of gestation, length of labor, infant's size, Apgar scores, or the number of obstetric complications (Dibblee & Graham, 1983; Pomerance, Gluck, & Lynch, 1974).

Two recent studies have reported more favorable outcomes for pregnant women who were encouraged to increase their usual amount of exercise. Hall and Kaufman (1987) had pregnant women visit a gym where fitness levels and exercise programs were monitored. These women were less likely to undergo caesarean delivery, had shorter hospital stays, and had heavier babies with higher Apgar scores than women in a control group. Kulpa, White, and Visscher (1987) assigned pregnant women to low- and high-exercise groups, varying on the amount of aerobic exercise per week. They found no differences between low- and high-exercise groups for type of delivery, length of gestation, birth weight, or Apgar scores.

None of the studies to date have included forms of exercise associated with leisure and household activities when monitoring maternal exercise during pregnancy (Caspersen, Powell, & Christenson, 1985). This may be an important consideration because one survey of 7,700 pregnancies found that women who continued to work in their third trimester bore infants who weighed from 5 to 14 oz less than infants born to women who remained at home (Naeye & Peters, 1982). However, this weight deficit was greatest when the mother herself was underweight or had high blood pressure; and the women whose jobs required them to stand for long periods of time had fetuses who were more likely to weigh less, probably because the blood supply to these mothers' uteri and placentas was poor.

In summary, the published findings on the effects of maternal exercise on fetal development have not noted any consistent negative effects. Thus, physicians have tended to suggest exercise within guidelines during pregnancy. The American College of Obstetricians and Gynecologists (ACOG) introduced guidelines for exercise during pregnancy in 1985. Since then there has been considerable controversy over the guidelines; among criticisms were that the guidelines were too general or too specific and had a questionable hard data basis (Gauthier, 1986). Despite the debate, ACOG stands behind their guidelines. According to these guidelines, although unexplained fetal bradycardia during maternal exertion of any intensity is rare, it would be prudent to recommend pregnant women to limit their vigorous exercise to activities requiring a heart rate of 150 beats per minute or less (Carpenter et al., 1988).

METHODOLOGICAL ISSUES

Studies of environmental risks to the embryo or fetus are inherently wrought with problems. Regardless of the prenatal risk being investigated, researchers must deal with measurement problems and associated risk factors.

Measurement Problems

Measures of alcohol consumption have relied on self-reports. Measures of cocaine consumption have relied on self-reports and toxicology screens. The accuracy of self-report appears to be questionable. In the case of alcohol, accuracy varies with the level of drinking reported (Little, 1981) and with who is doing the interviewing (Little, 19760. Alcohol use reported to an independent interviewer may be at least somewhat accurate, whereas use reported to a physician appears far less accurate (Little, 1976). In the case of cocaine, self-report is an even larger problem. Given that cocaine is an illegal substance, women are less likely to report its use. In a Miami prevalence study, only 27% of the pregnant women testing positive for drug use at labor and delivery had admitted drug use (Bandstra et al., 1988). Toxicology screening is also problematic in that it has a high rate of false-negative results and detects substance use only within the previous few days (Miller, 1989).

Then there is another problem in measuring consumption. People drink different kinds of alcoholic beverages, and they combine and dilute these beverages in many ways. Street drugs such as cocaine are diluted to differing degrees with different substances such as lactose, mannitol, lidocaine, and procaine (Bingol et al., 1987). In addition, people vary their consumption from day to day and week to week. In addition, people metabolize these substances at different rates.

Another problem is standardizing self-report measures used to detect prenatal use of these substances. Although there are standardized self-report methods to assess alcohol consumption based on interview questions, different studies have used different methods. The Boston studies used a method by Cahalan, Cisin, and Crossley (1969), which categorizes drinkers according to a combination of their daily intake and the average and maximum volumes consumed per drinking episode. The Seattle studies used a method by Jessor, Graves, Hanson, and Jessor (1968), which estimates the average daily number of ounces of absolute alcohol intake. An individual classified as a "heavy drinker" by one method frequently is not classified as such by another method (Abel, 1982); this is an important point to consider when comparing studies using different methods of assessing alcohol consumption.

It is known that teratogenic effects are influenced by time and dosage of exposure. Clearly, if researchers are to be able to answer questions regarding dosage and critical periods during prenatal development, measures are needed that include the pattern of consumption as well as the average amount consumed.

These issues also apply to the risks of maternal exercise. Some women exercise more intensely than other women, and women change their exercise habits from day to day and week to week. Research in this area has yet to deal with the issue of how to measure amount of exercise. Increased attention needs to be paid to assessing the intensity and duration of maternal exercise and to the timing of the exercise during pregnancy.

Associated Risk Factors

Drinking alcohol, using cocaine, and engaging in exercise programs are not isolated events randomly distributed across the population. Different kinds of women engage in these various activities.

Different kinds of women drink than abstain, and different kinds of women drink heavily than moderately (Abel, 1982; Rosett & Sander, 1979). Alcohol consumption is correlated with a variety of other risk factors including smoking, drinking caffeine, other drug use, age, number of previous miscarriages, number of prior pregnancies, socioeconomic status, amount of prenatal care, and marital status (Alpert et al., 1981; Kuzma & Kissinger, 1981; Sokol et al., 1981; Streissguth et al., 1981). In addition, there is evidence that women with a history of heavy drinking or alcoholism who totally abstain during pregnancy still have infants with decreased birth weight (Little, Streissguth, Barr, & Herman, 1980). Whether this is due to a history of maternal alcohol use directly or to maternal characteristics associated with past alcohol use is not known.

Similarly, cocaine use is highly related to other risk factors. Women who use cocaine are more likely to use other drugs, to smoke, and to drink alcohol (Baucher, Zuckerman, Amaro, Frank, & Parker, 1987; Eisen et al., 1989). MacGregor et al. (1987) reported that only 24% of 70 pregnant cocaine users used cocaine alone. Thus, studies of cocaine-exposed neonates are likely to actually be studies of polydrug exposure. Drug-abusing women have other associated risks as well. Substance-abusing pregnant women are up to four times less likely to receive prenatal care than other women (Miller, 1989). They are also at increased risk for venereal disease (Miller, 1989).

To date there are no studies providing such statistics for women who exercise during pregnancy, but it is not hard to imagine that women who engage in exercise programs during pregnancy differ in a variety of ways from those who do not..

Even in studies discussing associated risk factors and attempting to deal with them, the problem of covarying risks remains an integral part of this research. Experimental control over these confounding variables is not possible, so other methods of adjustment must be used. Multivariate statistical techniques, such as multiple regression, canonical correlation, and discriminant analysis, may be used to statistically partial out the contribution of covarying risk factors to pregnancy outcome; but they, too, have problems.

The purpose of this type of research is to distinguish between the outcomes of infants whose mothers engage in a particular activity and those whose mothers do not. Associated risks along with this activity may be considered part of a package being studied. Although there is still the need to try to tease out which part of the package is most related to infant outcome, we must realize that these various factors are most likely interacting in complex ways, and our statistical tools are limited.

Indeed, research on the effects of the prenatal environment on the fetus is difficult. Animal studies provide the only controlled experiments possible, eliminating many of the problems of accurately measuring dosage and associated risks. Studies with humans have difficulty isolating and identifying single agents as the cause of abnormal fetal development and neonatal outcome. Although the problems inherent in this area of research are many, this does not negate the value of conducting human studies, but it should set realistic expectations of what can be learned from such work. The impact of an individual maternal behavior is relatively minor compared with the impact of a life-style that combines many factors.

REFERENCES

Abel, E. L. (1982). Characteristics of mothers of fetal alcohol syndrome in children. *Neurobehavioral Toxicology and Teratology, 4*(1), 3–4.

Abel, E. L. (1980). Fetal alcohol syndrome: Behavioral teratology. *Psychological Bulletin, 87*(1), 29–50.

Alpert, J. L., Day, N., Dooling, E., Hingson, R., Oppenheimer, E., Rosett, H. L., Weiner, L., & Zuckerman, B. (1981). Maternal alcohol consumption and newborn assessment: Methodology of the Boston City Hospital prospective study. *Neurobehavioral Toxicology and Teratology, 3*(2), 195–201.

Archer, J. E., & Blackman, D. E. (1971). Prenatal psychological stress and offspring behavior in rats and mice. *Developmental Psychobiology, 4,* 193–248.

Artal, R., Rutherford, S., Romem, Y., Kammula, R. K., Dorey, F. J., & Wiswell, R. A. (1986). Fetal heart rate response to maternal exercise. *American Journal of Obstetrics and Gynecology, 155,* 729–733.

Bandstra, E. S., Steele, B. W., Burkett, G. T., Palow, D. C., & Levandoski, N. (1989). Prevalence of perinatal cocaine exposure in an urban multi-ethnic urban population. *Pediatric Research, 25,* 247A.

Baucher, H., Zuckerman, B., Amaro, H., Frank, D. A., & Parker, S. (1987). Teratogenicity of cocaine. *Journal of Pediatrics, 111*(1), 160–161.

Bingol, N., Fuchs, M., Diaz, V., Stone, R. K., & Gromisch, D. S. (1987). Teratongenicity of cocaine in humans. *Journal of Pediatrics, 110*(1), 93–96.

Borges, S., & Lewis, P. D. (1981). Effects of alcohol on the developing nervous system. *Trends in Neurosciences, 4*(1), 13–15.

Brazelton, T. B. (1984). *Neonatal behavioral assessment scale (2nd ed.).* London: Spastics International Medical Publications.

Cahalan, D., Cisin, I. H., & Crossley, H. M. (1968). *American drinking practices: A national study of drinking behavior and attitudes.* New Brunswick, NJ: Rutgers Center of Alcohol Studies.

Carpenter, M. W., Sady, S. P., Hoegsberg, B., Sady, M. A., Haydon, B., Cullinane, E. M., Coustan, D. R., & Thompson, P. D. (1988). Fetal heart rate response to maternal exertion. *Journal of the American Medical Association, 259,* 3006–3009.

Caspersen, C. J., Powell, K. E., & Christenson, G. M. (1985). Physical activity, exercise and physical fitness: Definitions and distinctions for health-related research. *Public Health Reports, 100,* 126–131.

Chasnoff, I. J. (1988). Cocaine: Effects on pregnancy and the neonate. In I. J. Chasnoff (Ed.), *Drugs, alcohol, pregnancy and parenting.* Boston: Kluwer.

Chasnoff, I. J., Burns, W. J., Schnoll, S. H., Burns, K. A. (1985). Cocaine use in pregnancy. *New England Journal of Medicine, 3*(13), 666–669.

Chasnoff, I. J., Bussey, M. E., Savich, R., Stack, C. M. (1986). Perinatal cerebral infarction and maternal cocaine use. *Journal of Pediatrics, 70*(2), 210–213.

Chavez, C. J., Ostrea, E. M., Stryker, J. C., Smialek, Z. (1979). Sudden infant death syndrome among infants of drug dependent mothers. *Journal of Pediatrics, 95*(3), 407–409.

Clapp, J. F. (1985). Fetal heart rate response to running in midpregnancy and late pregnancy. *American Journal of Obstetrics and Gynecology, 153,* 251–252.

Clapp, J. F., & Dickstein, S. (1984). Endurance exercise and pregnancy outcome. *Medicine and Science in Sports and Exercise, 16,* 556–562.

Clarren, S. K., Alvord, E. C., Jr., Sumi, M., Streissguth, A. P., & Smith, D. W. (1978). Brain malformations related to prenatal exposure to ethanol. *Journal of Pediatrics, 92*(1), 64–67.

Clarren, S. K., & Smith, D. W. (1978). The fetal alcohol syndrome. *New England Journal of Medicine, 298*(19), 1063–1067.

Coles, C. D., Smith, I. E., Fernhoff, P. M., & Falden, A. (1984). Neonatal ethanol withdrawal: Characteristics in clinically normal nondysmorphic neonates. *Journal of Pediatrics, 105,* 445.

Collings, C., & Curet, L. B. (1985). Fetal heart rate response to maternal exercise. *American Journal of Obstetrics and Gynecology, 151,* 498–501.

Collings, C. A., Curet, L. B., & Mullin, J. P. (1983). Maternal and fetal responses to a maternal aerobic exercise program. *American Journal of Obstetrics and Gynecology, 145,* 702–707.

Daly, M. (1973). Early stimulation of rodents: A critical review of present interpretations. *British Journal of Psychology, 64,* 435–460.

Dibblee, L., & Graham, T. E. (1983). A longitudinal study of changes in aerobic fitness, body composition, and energy intake in primigravid patients. *American Journal of Obstetrics and Gynecology, 147,* 908–914.

Doberczak, T. M., Kandall, S. R., Rongkapan, O., Davis, L., Weinberger, S. M., & Lowenstein, W. (1986). Peripheral nerve conduction studies in passively addicted neonates. *Archives of Physical Medicine and Rehabilitation, 67,* 4–6.

Eisen, L., Field, T. M., Bandstra, E. S., Roberts, J. P., Morrow, C., & Larson, S. K. (1989). *Effects of perinatal cocaine exposure on neonatal behavior with withdrawal symptoms.* Manuscript submitted for publication.

Fisher, D. M. (1984). *The effects of vestibular stimulation on growth and motor behavior in the rat* (Doctoral dissertation, University of Missouri-Columbia, 1985). *Dissertation Abstracts International, 46* 1371–B.

Fox, H. E., Steinbrecher, M., Pessel, D., Inglis, J., Medvid, L., & Angel, E. (1978). Maternal ethanol ingestion and the occurrence of human fetal breathing movement. *American Journal of Obstetrics and Gynecology, 132*(4), 354–358.

Gauthier, M. (1986). Guidelines for exercise during pregnancy: Too little or too much? *Physician and Sports Medicine, 14*(4), 162–169.

Goodlin, R. C., & Buckley, K. K. (1984). Maternal exercise. *Clinics in Sports Medicine, 3,* 881–894.

Gregg, N. M. (1941). Congenital cataract following german measles in the mother. *Transactions of the Ophthalmol Society of Australia, 3,* 35.

Hall, D. C., & Kaufman, D. A. (1987). Effects of aerobic and strength conditioning on pregnancy outcome. *American Journal of Obstetrics & Gynecology, 157,* 1199–1203.

Hansen, J. W., Streissguth, A. P., & Smith, D. W. (1978). The effects of moderate alcohol consumption during pregnancy on fetal growth and morphogenesis. *Journal of Pediatrics, 92*(3), 457–460.

Harlap, S., Shiono, P. H., & Ramcharan, S. (1979). Alcohol and spontaneous abortions. *American Journal of Epidemiology, 110,* 372–373.

Hauth, J. C., Gilstrap, L. C., & Widemer, K. (1982). Fetal heart rate reactivity before and after maternal jogging during the third trimester. *American Journal of Obstetrics and Gynecology, 142,* 545–547.

Herrenkohl, L. (1979). Prenatal stress reduces fertility and fecundity in female offspring. *Science, 206,* 1097.

Herrenkohl, L., & Whitney, J. (1976). Effects of prepartal stress on postpartal nursing behavior, litter development, and adult sexual behavior. *Physiology and Behavior, 17,* 1019–1021.

Hingson, R., Alpert, J. J., Day, N., Dooling, E., Kayne, H., Morelock, S., Oppenheimer, E., & Zuckerman, B. (1982). Effects of maternal drinking and marijuana use on fetal growth and development. *Pediatrics, 70*(4), 539–546.

Idanpaan-Heikkila, J., Jouppila, P., Akerblam, H. K., Isoaho, R., Kauppile, E., & Koivisto, M. (1972). Elimination and metabolic effects of ethanol in mother, fetus and newborn infant. *American Journal of Obstetrics and Gynecology, 112*(3), 387–393.

Iosub, S., Fuchs, M., Bingol, N., & Gromisch, D. S. (1981). Fetal alcohol syndrome revisited. *Pediatrics, 68*(4), 475–579.

Istvan, J. (1986). Stress, anxiety, and birth outcomes: A critical review of the evidence. *Psychological Bulletin, 100,* 331–348.

Jessor, R., Graves, T. D., Hanson, R. C., & Jessor, S. L. (1968). *Society, personality, and deviant behavior: A study of a tri-ethnic community.* New York: Holt, Rinehart and Winston, Inc.

Jones, C. L., & Lopez, R. (1988). *Direct and indirect effects on the infant of maternal drug abuse.* Washington, DC: U. S. Department of Health and Human Services/National Institute of Health.

Jones, K. L. (1975). Aberrant neuronal migration in the fetal alcohol syndrome. *Birth Defects, 11*(7), 131–132.

Jones, K. L., & Smith, D. W. (1973). Recognition of the fetal alcohol syndrome in early infancy. *Lancet, 2,* 999–1001.

Jones, K. L., Smith, D. W., & Hanson, J. W. (1976). The fetal alcohol syndrome: Clinical delineation. *Annals of the New York Academy of Sciences, 273,* 130–137.

Jones, K. L., Smith, D. W., Streissguth, A. P., & Myrianthopoulos, N. C. (1974b). Outcome in offspring of chronic alcoholic women. *Lancet, 1,* 1076–1078.

Jones, K. L., Smith, D. W., Ulleland, C. N., & Streissguth, A. P. (1973). Pattern of malformation in offspring of chronic alcoholic mothers. *Lancet, 1*, 1267–1271.

Jovanovic, L., Kessler, A., & Petterson, C. M. (1985). Human maternal and fetal response to graded exercise. *Journal of Applied Physiology, 58*, 1719–1722.

Kaminski, M., Rumeau-Rouquette, C., & Schwartz, D. (1978). Alcohol consumption in pregnant women and the outcome of pregnancy. *Alcoholism: Clinical and Experimental Research, 2*(2), 155–163.

Kulpa, P. J., White, B. M., & Visscher, R. (1987). Aerobic exercise and pregnancy. *American Journal of Obstetrics and Gynecology, 156*, 1395–1403.

Kuzma, J. W., & Kissinger, D. G. (1981). Patterns of alcohol and cigarette use in pregnancy. *Neurobehavioral Toxicology and Teratology, 3*(2), 211–221.

Landesman-Dwyer, A., Keller, L. S., & Streissguth, A. P. (1978). Naturalistic observations of newborns: Effects of maternal alcohol intake. *Alcoholism: Clinical and Experimental Research, 2*(2), 171–177.

Landesman-Dwyer, S., Ragozin, A. S., & Little, R. E. (1981). Behavioral correlates of prenatal alcohol exposure: A four year follow-up study. *Neurobehavioral Toxicology and Teratology, 3*(2), 187–193.

Leblanc, P. E., Parekh, A. J., Naso, B., Glass, L. (1987). Effects of interuterine exposure to alkaloidal cocaine ('crack'). *American Journal of Diseases of Children, 141*(9), 937–938.

Lemoine, P., Harousseau, H., Borteyru, J. P., & Menuet, J. C. (1968). Les enfants de parents alcooliques. Anomalies observess: Apropos de 127 cas. *Quest Medical, 21*, 476–482. (English translation available from National Clearinghouse for Alcohol Information, Dept. STIAR, P. O. Box 2345, Rockville, MD 20852).

Lipsitz, P. J. (1975). Proposed narcotic withdrawal score for use with newborn infants. *Clinical Pediatrics, 14*, 592–594.

Little, R. E. (1976). Alcohol consumption during pregnancy as reported to the obstetrician and to an independent interviewer. *Annals of the New York Academy of Science, 273*, 588–592.

Little, R. E. (1977). Moderate alcohol use during pregnancy and decreased infant birth weight. *American Journal of Public Health, 67*(12), 1154–1156.

Little, R. E. (1981). Epidemiologic and experimental studies in drinking and pregnancy: The state of the art. *Neurobehavioral Toxicology and Teratology, 3*(2), 163–167.

Little, R. E., Schultz, F. A., & Mandell, W. (1976). Drinking during pregnancy. *Journal of Studies on Alcohol, 37*(3), 375–379.

Little, R. E., Schultz, F. A., & Mandell, W. (1977). Describing alcohol consumption. *Journal of Studies on Alcohol, 38*, 554–562.

Little, R. E., Streissguth, A. P., Barr, H. M., & Herman, C. S. (1980). Decreased birth weight in infants of alcoholic women who abstained during pregnancy. *Journal of Pediatrics, 96*(6), 974–977.

MacGregor, S. N., Keith, C. G., Chasnoff, I. J., Rosner, M. A., Chism, N. M., Shaw, P., & Minogue, J. P. (1987). Cocaine use during pregnancy: Adverse perinatal outcome. *American Journal of Obstetrical Gynecology, 157*(3), 686–690.

Madden, J. D., Chappel, J. N., Zispan, F., Gumpel, J., Mejia, A., Davis, R. (1977). Observation and treatment of neonatal narcotic withdrawal. *American Journal of Obstetrics and Gynecology, 127*(2), 199–201.

Madden, J. D., Payne, T. F., & Miller, S. (1986). Maternal cocaine abuse and effects on the newborn. *Pediatrics, 77*, 209–211.

Martin, J. C., Martin, D. C., Lund, C. A., & Streissguth, A. P. (1977). Maternal alcohol ingestion and cigarette smoking and their effects on newborn conditioning. *Alcoholism: Clinical and Experimental Research, 1*(3), 243–247.

Martin, D. C., Martin, J. C., Streissguth, A. P., & Lund, C. A. (1979). Sucking frequency and amplitude in newborns as a function of maternal drinking and smoking. In M. Galanter (Ed.), *Currents in alcoholism* (Vol. V, pp. 359–366). New York: Grune & Stratton.

McBride, W. G. (1977). Thalidomide embryopathy. *Teratology, 16*, 79–82.

Miller, G. (1989). Addicted infants and their mothers. *Zero to three: Bulletin of National Center for Clinical Infant Programs, 9*(5), 20–23.

Morton, M. J., Paul, M. S., Campos, G. R., Hart, M. V., & Metcalfe, J. (1985). Exercise dynamics in late gestation: Effects of physical training. *American Journal of Obstetrics and Gynecology, 152*, 91–97.

Mukherjee, A. B., & Hodgen, G. D. (1982). Maternal ethanol exposure induces transient impairment of umbilical circulation and fetal hypoxia in monkeys. *Science, 218*, 700–702.

Myers, R. E. (1975). Maternal psychological stress and fetal asphyxia: A study in the monkey. *American Journal of Obstetrics and Gynecology, 122*, 47–59.

Naeye, R. L., & Peters, E. C. (1982). Working during pregnancy: Effects on the fetus. *Pediatrics, 69*, 724–727.

National Clearinghouse for Drug Abuse Information. (1974). *Neonatal Narcotic Dependence.* (Report Series #29). Rockville, Maryland.

Newald, J. (1986). Cocaine infants: A new arrival at hospitals steps? *Hospitals, 60*, 96.

Nichols, C. E., & Clone, E. R. (1987). Neonatal nightmare: Devastating effects of cocaine. *Florida Nurse, 35*(2), 5.

Nunes, E. V., & Rosecan, J. S. (1987). Human neurobiology of cocaine. In H. I. Spitz, & J. S. Rosecan (Eds.), *Cocaine abuse: New directions in treatment and research.* New York: Brunner/ Mazel.

Ostrea, E. M., Chavez, C. J., & Strauss, M. E. (1976). A study of factors that influence the severity of narcotic withdrawal. *Journal of Pediatrics, 88*(4), 642–645.

Ouellette, E. M., & Rosett, H. L. (1976). A pilot prospective study of the fetal alcohol syndrome at the Boston City Hospital. Part II: The infants. *Annals of the New York Academy of Sciences, 273*, 123–129.

Ouellette, E. M., Rosett, H. L., Rosman, P., & Weiner, L. (1977). Adverse effects on offspring of maternal alcohol abuse during pregnancy. *New England Journal of Medicine, 297*(10), 528–530.

Pomerance, J. J., Gluck, L., & Lynch, V. A. (1974). Physical fitness in pregnancy: Its effect on pregnancy outcome. *American Journal of Obstetrics and Gynecology, 119*, 867–872.

Ragozin, A. S., Landesman-Dwyer, S., & Streissguth, A. P. (1978). The relationship between mother's drinking habits and children's home environment. In F. A. Seixas (Ed.), *Currents in alcoholism, volume IV: Psychiatric, psychological, social and epidemiological studies* (pp. 39–50). New York: Grune & Stratton.

Rauramo, I., Anderson, B., Laatikainen, T., & Patterson, J. (1982). Stress hormones and placental steroids in physical exercise during pregnancy. *British Journal of Obstetrics and Gynecology, 89*, 921–925.

Reyes, E., Rivera, J. M., Saland, L. C., & Murray, H. M. (1983). Effects of maternal administration of alcohol on fetal brain development. *Neurobehavioral Toxicology and Teratology, 5*(2), 263–267.

Rodier, P. M., & Reynolds, S. S. (1977). Morphological correlates of behavioral abnormalities in experimental congenital birth damage. *Experimental Neurology, 57*, 81–93.

Rosecan, J. S., & Gross, B. F. (1986). Newborn victims of cocaine abuse. *Medical Aspects of Human Sexuality, 20*(11), 30–35.

Rosett, H. L., Ouellette, E. M., & Weiner, L. (1976). A pilot prospective study of the fetal alcohol syndrome at the Boston City Hospital. Part I: Maternal drinking. *Annals of the New York Academy of Sciences, 273*, 118–122.

Rosett, H. L., & Sander, L. W. (1979). Effects of maternal drinking on neonatal morphology and state regulation. In J. D. Osofsky (Ed.) *Handbook of Infant Development*, New York: Wiley, 809–836.

Rosett, H. L., Snyder, P., Sander, L. W., Lee, A., Cook, P., Weiner, L., & Gould, J. (1979). Effects of maternal drinking on neonate state regulation. *Developmental Medicine and Child Neurology, 2*(4), 464–473.

Rosett, H. L., Weiner, L., Zuckerman, B., McKinlay, S., & Edelin, K. C. (1980). Reduction of alcohol consumption during pregnancy with benefits to the newborn. *Alcoholism: Clinical and Experimental Research, 4*(2), 178–184.

Ryan, L., Erlich, S., & Finnegan, L. (1987). Cocaine abuse in pregnancy: Effects on the fetus and newborn. *Neurotoxicology and Teratology, 9*, 295–299.

Sander, L. W., Snyder, P. A., Rosett, A. L., Lee, A., Gould, J. P., & Ouellette, E. (1977). Effects of alcohol intake during pregnancy on newborn state regulation. *Alcoholism: Clinical and Experimental Research, 1*(3), 233–241.

Schneider, J. W. (1988). Motor assessment and parent education beyond the newborn period. In I. J. Chasnoff (Ed.), *Drugs, alcohol, pregnancy and parenting.* Boston: Kluwer.

Shaywitz, S. F., Cohen, D. J., & Shaywitz, B. A. (1980). Behavior and learning difficulties in children of normal intelligence born to alcoholic mothers. *Journal of Pediatrics, 96*(6), 978–982.

Smith, D. W. (1979). Fetal drug syndromes: Effects of ethanol and hydantoins. *Pediatrics in Review, 1*(6), 165–172.

Smith, J. E. (1988). The dangers of prenatal cocaine use. *American Journal of Maternal Child Nursing, 13*, 174–179.

Sokol, R. J., Miller, S. I., Debanne, S., Golden, N., Colings, G., Kaplan, J., & Martier, S. (1981).

The Cleveland NIAAA prospective alcohol-in-pregnancy study: The first year. *Neurobehavioral Toxicology and Teratology, 3*(2), 203–209.

Sokol, R. J., Miller, S. I., & Reed, G. (1980). Alcohol abuse during pregnancy: An epidemiologic study. *Alcoholism: Clinical and Experimental Research, 4*(2), 135–145.

Streissguth, A. P. (1976). Psychologic handicaps in children with fetal alcohol syndrome. *Annals of the New York Academy of Sciences, 273,* 140–145.

Streissguth, A. P., Barr, H. M., & Martin, D. C. (1983). Maternal alcohol use and neonatal habituation assessed with the Brazelton Scale. *Child Development, 54,* 1109–1118.

Streissguth, A. P., Barr, H. M., Martin, D. C., & Herman, C. S. (1980). Effects of maternal alcohol, nicotine, and caffeine use during pregnancy on infant mental and motor development at eight months. *Alcoholism: Clinical and Experimental Research, 4*(2), 152–164.

Streissguth, A. P., Barr, H. M., Sampson, P. P., Darby, B. L., & Martin, D. C. (1989). IQ at age 4 in relation to maternal alcohol use and smoking during pregnancy. *Developmental Psychology, 25,* 3–11.

Streissguth, A. P., Herman, C. S., & Smith, D. W. (1978a). Intelligence, behavior, and dysmorphogenesis in the fetal alcohol syndrome: A report on 20 patients. *Journal of Pediatrics, 92*(3), 363–367.

Streissguth, A. P., Herman, C. S., & Smith, D. W. (1978). Stability of intelligence in the fetal alcohol syndrome: A preliminary report. *Alcoholism: Clinical and Experimental Research, 2*(2), 165–170.

Streissguth, A. P., Landesman-Dwyer, S., Martin, J. C., & Smith, D. W. (1980). Teratogenic effects of alcohol in humans and laboratory animals. *Science, 209,* 353–361.

Streissguth, A. P., Martin, D. C., Martin, J. C., & Barr, H. M. (1981). The Seattle longitudinal prospective study on alcohol and pregnancy. *Neurobehavioral Toxicology and Teratology, 3*(2), 223–233.

Thompson, W. R., & Giusec, J. E. (1970). Studies of early experience. In P. H. Mussen (Ed.), *Carmichael's manual of child psychology* (3rd ed., pp. 565–654). New York: Wiley.

Ulleland, C. N. (1972). The offspring of alcoholic mothers. *Annals of the New York Academy of Sciences, 197,* 167–169.

Wilson, J. G. (1973). *Environmental and birth defects.* New York: Academic Press.

Woods, J. R., Plessinger, M. A., & Clark, K. E. (1987). Effect of cocaine on uterine blood flow and fetal oxygenation. *Journal of American Medical Association, 257*(7), 957–961.

3

Nutrition and Psychological Response

Elizabeth J. Root
University of Texas, Austin

GENERAL NUTRITIONAL CONSIDERATIONS

If one is to appreciate the importance of nutrition to a sound mind and to good athletic performance, one needs to consider several aspects of nutrients and their use by cells.

Loss and Replacement of Nutrients

Cells of all tissues, as well as products released from cells such as those that form connective tissue and body fluids, are made of nutrients. These nutrients are in a state of more or less continual turnover. This is obvious in the case of cells with a short life span, which die and must be completely replaced. Examples of such cells include those lining the stomach and digestive tract, which live about 3 days, and red blood cells, which live about 3 months. It is less obvious in very long-lived cells, such as neurons of the brain, but even in these cells components of the cell are in constant turnover. This turnover involves recycling and reuse of some nutrient molecules and also destruction or loss from the body of others. Lost nutrients must be replaced by the nutrients found in one's food.

Energy

Quantitatively, of course, the greatest turnover involves the nutrients metabolized to provide energy. We are all aware of the need to eat to have energy. Energy is most efficiently released from carbohydrates, obtained from sugars and starches, and from lipids, obtained from fats and oils. (A well-known exception is the lipid cholesterol, which is not significantly metabolized to provide energy.) Protein can also be metabolized for energy, and will be used for energy rather than muscle building or other structural purposes if intake of other energy sources is too low, or if the quality of the protein is poor. Protein quality depends upon the balance of the amino acid subunits, which comprise the protein.

The energy provided by carbohydrates, lipids, and proteins is usually measured in calories, or more properly, kilocalories. A kilocalorie is the amount of energy expressed as heat required to raise 1 liter of water 1 °C. As most of us are aware, if one eats enough food to provide more kilocalories than are used, the excess energy-producing nutrients will be converted to fat and stored in adipose tissue. Conversely, fat is mobilized from adipose tissue to provide energy when fewer kilocalories are furnished by food than are needed. Most people engaged in sports have little trouble with excess fat storage because the energy demands of the sport use up large numbers of kilocalories.

It should be noted that the supply of energy is critical to life at the cellular level. Energy is needed for biochemical reactions within cells. Energy is needed for transport of such nutrients as calcium, sodium, and potassium in and out of cells to help maintain the normal intracellular and extracellular environments. Severe disruption of these environments can rapidly cause cell death. To appreciate this, one has only to think of the consequences of the block in energy production caused by lack of oxygen or by cyanide poisoning. Both of these cause death by a rapid and complete block in energy production and consequent deterioration of the cellular environment.

Energy production is also affected by decreased activity of enzymes, which catalyze the biochemical reactions of the pathways of energy production. Dietary deficiencies can hamper energy production in several ways. Energy-producing enzymes are protein in nature, synthesized under genetic control from the amino acids obtained from dietary protein. Many enzymes, in addition, require for their activity nonprotein "cofactors," such as vitamins or minerals. In real-life situations, such vitamin and mineral cofactors are depleted only slowly so that their lack does not completely block energy production, but impaired energy production can easily occur. The point here is that one needs not only the macronutrients (carbohydrates, lipids, proteins), which are metabolized to yield energy, but also the micronutrients (vitamins, minerals), which make such metabolism possible. Extra amounts of one or two of these micronutrients will not do much good, and may sometimes do harm. One needs adequate, but not excessive, amounts of all.

In similar manner, essential nutrients must also be supplied from the diet for synthesis and maintenance of structural elements of the body: muscles, nerves, brain, bone, tendons, connective tissue, and the like.

What are these nutrients? How much is enough?

A list of essential nutrients, those that cannot be synthesized but must be obtained directly from food, is given in Table 1, together with a recommended intake, or range of intakes, where known. Unless indicated otherwise, figures presented are the recommended daily allowances (RDA), as set in 1989 by the National Academy of Sciences (Food and Nutrition Board, National Research Council, 1989), and are given as a range of the lowest to highest recommendations for adults 19 to 50 years of age. Except for iron, the lower recommendations are for women and the higher ones for men. Figures labeled with the [a] are tentative recommendations (for vitamins) or estimations of minimum and maximum desirable intakes (for minerals). Nutrients with no adjacent figures are believed to be essential, but too little information in available to make any recommendation for intake. For the amino acids, recommendations are given in relation to body weight. Eating patterns likely to provide these nutrients are suggested later.

Like the rest of the body, the brain is dependent upon an adequate supply of essential nutrients for both energy and maintenance of its normal structure. A sound mind, capable of coping with intellectual and environmental challenges and of urging the rest of the body to its utmost in athletic performances, depends upon normal structure and normal biochemistry. Neither of these will be maintained without a sufficient supply of the nutrients upon which they depend.

Table 1 Recommended intakes of essential nutrients

Vitamin	Amount	Mineral	Amount	Essential fatty acids	Amount (of kcal)	Essential amino acids	Amount (mg/kg body wt)[b]
Thiamin	1.1–1.5 mg	Calcium	800–1,200 mg	Linoleic acid	2–3%	Valine	14
Pantothenic acid	4–7 mg[a]	Phosphorus	800–1,200 mg	Alpha-linolenic acid	0.5%	Leucine	16
Riboflavin	1.3–1.7 mg	Magnesium	280–350 mg			Isoleucine	12
Niacin	15–19 mg	Sodium	500–3300 mg[a]			Lysine	12
Biotin	30–100 μg[a]	Potassium	2000–5625 mg[a]			Phenylalanine plus tyrosine	16
Vitamin B6	1.6–2.0 mg	Chloride	750–5100 mg[a]			Methionine plus cysteine	10
Vitamin B12	2.0 μg	Sulfur	Obtained from protein			Tryptophan	3
Folacin	180–200 μg	Iron	10–15 mg			Threonine	8
Vitamin C	60 mg	Iodine	150 μg				
Vitamin A	800–1000 RE or 4000–5000 IU	Zinc	12–15 mg				
Vitamin D	5–10 μg or 200–400 IU	Copper	1.5–3 mg[a]				
Vitamin E	8–10 mg of alpha-tocopherol equivalent	Manganese	2–5 mg[a]				
Vitamin K	65–80 μg	Selenium	55–70 μg				
		Chromium III	0.05–0.2 mg[a] (50–200 μg)				
		Fluoride	1.5–4.0 mg[a]				
		Molybdenum	75–250 μg[a]				
		Silicon	NR				
		Nickel	NR				
		Vanadium	NR				
		Tin	NR				
		Boron	NR				
		Bromine	NR				

Note. NR, probably or certainly essential, but no recommendation exists. Unless otherwise indicated, quantities are value or range of values for men and women aged 19 to 50.

[a]Tentative recommendations (for vitamins) or estimations of minimum and maximum desirable intakes (for minerals).
[b]To compute weight in kilograms, divide weight in pounds by 2.2.

45

Effect of Deficiencies Upon the Nervous System

Nutritional insufficiencies or excesses may cause psychic disturbances as well as problems with the peripheral nervous system affecting sensory or motor function. Symptoms can vary because of individual differences in metabolism or because of differences in diet. Although it is possible for single nutrient deficiencies to occur, causing classic deficiency symptoms, multiple deficiencies are much more likely to occur, since a less-than-optimum eating pattern will probably fail to provide a number of nutrients. Thus, the pattern or balance of deficiencies may influence which symptoms occur.

Neurological symptoms can stem from biochemical defects without important changes in cell structure, from edema, or from degenerative changes in cell structure. The latter may involve demyelination, degeneration of axons with myelin left intact, or changes in neuronal structure leading eventually to cell death. A brief description of cellular structure of the brain is given here to provide a basis for information about effects of specific nutrients.

The brain and spinal cord comprise the central nervous system (CNS) and the nerves innervating the muscles, organs, and other tissues comprise the peripheral nervous system (PNS). Both CNS and PNS contain two basic types of cells: neurons and glial cells. Neurons receive and transmit nerve impulses, whereas glia of various types may assist neurons in metabolism or may form the myelin "coating" of nerves. A typical multipolar neuron, such as the one shown in Figure 1, includes a cell body, or perikaryon, which contains the cell nucleus and performs much of the metabolic activity of the cell, together with numerous short to long extensions of neuronal cytoplasm termed dendrites, and a long, slim extension of cytoplasm termed an axon. The neuron receives nerve impulses upon its dendrites or perikaryon at synapses, which are specialized sites in the plasma membrane surrounding the cell. Many, but not all, synapses are formed upon tiny protuberances called spines. These features of a typical neuron are shown in Figures 1 and 2. The neuron continually receives many nerve impulses from other neurons. These impulses are communicated by means of molecules called neurotransmitters, which are released from the end, or terminal, of each incoming axon at the synapse. Some neurotransmitters are excitatory, and some are inhibitory. In response to the sum of these positive and negative impulses, the neuron either generates, or fails to generate, a nerve impulse of its own, which travels rapidly along its axon to the synapse or synapses formed by that axon upon other cells. The speed at which the nerve impulse travels depends partly upon the diameter of the axon and partly upon myelination. Myelin, composed of plasma membranes of glial cells, serves to insulate the axon and greatly increase the speed of impulse transmission. The message depends upon the frequency of such impulses, the amplitude of all impulses being the same (Carpenter & Suting, 1983).

An example of the simplest sort of message transmission is furnished by a spinal cord reflex, such as the one that controls quick withdrawal of one's finger upon touching a hot stove. Nerve endings in the finger sensitive to heat and noxious stimuli generate nerve impulses that travel up the nerve fiber and into the spinal cord to synapse directly upon motor neurons causing muscles to contract. The finger is already withdrawn by the time the sensation of pain has traveled along other axons to the brain and is perceived consciously. This is an automatic reaction, not under conscious control.

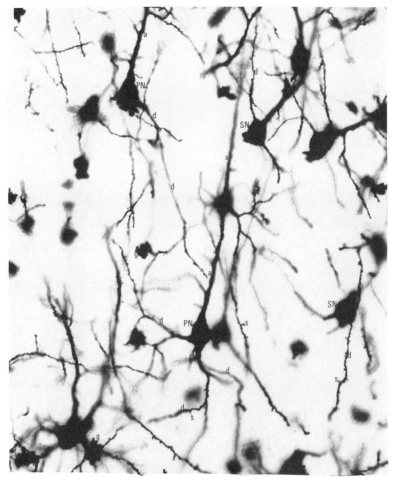

Figure 1 Brain cells from the cerebral cortex of a rat as seen in a light microscope. This tissue is prepared by a method called Golgi impregnation, which turns 5% to 10% of the cells black, leaving others invisible. In this preparation, cell bodies and dendrites have impregnated, but axons are not seen. (*PN* = perikaryon of pyramidal neuron; a = apical dendrite; d = basal dendrites; s = spines; sn = perikaryon of stellate neuron; g = glial cells.

A much more complex sort of message transmission on the other hand is required for sports. Consider an example from baseball. The batter sees the ball leave the pitcher's hand and begins to judge its path and speed as it approaches. This involves visual input from the retina of the eye traveling along the optic nerve to an area of the brain called the thalamus and from there to the primary visual cortex at the back of the brain. Neurons there react to separate aspects of the visual image, synapse with each other to integrate the information, and send impulses to the secondary visual cortex and from there to association areas of the cortex. At the same time information about the position of the batter's own limbs travels up

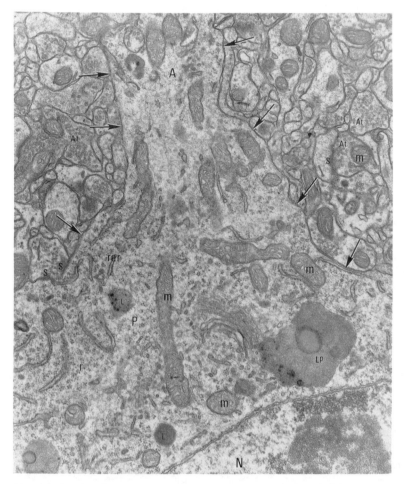

Figure 2   Interior of a pyramidal neuron similar to those labeled PN in Figure 1, as
seen in an electron microscope. Arrows point to the plasma membrane
enclosing the cell. A = apical dendrite close to the perikaryon; P =
cytoplasm in the perikaryon; N = the nucleus of the cell, surrounded by a
double membrane, the nuclear envelope; the dark area within the nucleus is
the nucleolus; m = mitochondria, which house the Krebs cycle and are the
site of most energy production. Sites of protein synthesis are the rough
endoplasmic reticulum (rer) and the ribosomes (r). L = lyosomes,
representing the cell's internal digestive apparatus; Lp = lipofuscin; GA =
Golgi apparatus. Outside the plasma membrane of the neuron, one sees
cross-sections of axons and dendrites, which collectively are called
neuropil. AT = axon terminals filled with vesicles of neurotransmitter.
Synapses(s) are indicated by dark-staining synaptic densities.

the spinal cord to the cerebellum and, after processing there, reaches other areas of the brain called the basal ganglia and somatosensory area of the cerebral cortex. Association areas of the cortex in turn receive all of this incoming information and further integrate it, not only forming, an assessment of the probable location of the ball as it approaches, but also planning a response to be mediated by the motor cortex. It is necessary to control motor impulses to stimulate contraction of the muscles appropriate to bring not only the arms and bat but also the rest of the body into the proper position for making contact with the ball.

One's mental set may affect considerably the efficiency with which all this is performed. Memory of prior experiences, as well as strategy based on knowledge of the pitcher's repertoire, will also have an influence. Many areas of the brain must cooperate. Hundreds if not millions of synaptic transmissions must occur in the fraction of a second it takes the ball to leave the pitcher's hand and reach an accessible area over the plate. This requires amazing speed of neural transmission. Neural transmission, in turn, depends upon normal myelination and normal metabolic activity of the neurons involved.

It is evident as well that normal cell structure is necessary for accuracy of neural function. If synaptic contacts or portions of the dendritic tree have been lost, neural function cannot be optimal. In addition, impairment of neurotransmitter synthesis can decrease synaptic transfer of nerve impulses so that neural function cannot be optimal. Both maintenance of cellular structure and neurotransmitter synthesis depend upon an adequate supply of nutrients. These nutrients are continually lost during turnover of molecules comprising the tissue and therefore must be replaced by adequate diet.

Effects of Specific Nutrient Deficiency and Excess, with Emphasis on Neural Effects

Although depletion of several nutrients at once is likely, and effects of multiple deficiencies may differ from the effects of single deficiencies, certain mental or neural symptoms have been observed to stem from lack of individual nutrients. A partial list of such symptoms follows, together with some typical nonneural signs and symptoms that may help to identify the deficiency.

Thiamin

Deficiency of thiamin most frequently causes peripheral neuropathy. Initially there are minor changes in cellular structure, but in severe deficiency leading to the disease beri beri there can be complete degeneration of the myelin sheath and axon itself, with eventual death of the parent neuron. The portion of the axon farthest from the neuronal perikaryon suffers first, as do the longest axons. Because the longest axons extend from neurons in the spinal cord to the feet, symptoms appear first in the lower legs, feet, and ankles. Muscle cramps are early symptoms, followed by weakness or aching, stiffness, tightness, or tenderness of the muscles. Abnormal sensations, termed paresthesias, may occur as numbness, tingling or "pins and needles" sensations. There can be diminished sense of touch or loss of sensation, beginning in the feet, or ankles, or hands. An unsteady gait may develop. There may be apathy, irritability or depression. Edema in the feet and lower legs may develop (Cruickshank, 1976). There is usually constipation.

As mild deficiency progresses to the classic deficiency disease, symptoms spread upward to involve the trunk and become more severe. Beri beri is no longer a common deficiency disease, but mild lack of thiamin, leading to occasional muscle cramps and perhaps constipation, is probably not uncommon.

A severe, rapidly developing deficiency of thiamin, such as sometimes develops in alcoholics, can instead lead to degeneration of neurons in certain areas of the brain; unless this is promptly treated a permanent memory deficit will follow (de Wardener, 1947).

Pantothenic Acid

The gastrointestinal distress, bloating and gas pains that sometimes appear in early pantothenic acid deficiency (Nutrition Foundation, Inc., 1984) may actually stem from involuntary nervous system malfunction associated with decreased synthesis of the neurotransmitter acetylcholine (Novelli, 1953). More severe deficiency brings on a group of symptoms affecting particularly the feet. The typical manifestation of this is called the "burning foot syndrome." There is aching, burning, or sharp stabbing pain centered at the balls of the feet. The pain may radiate to the heels and sometimes up the shins. The discomfort is worse at night and after a long day of activity. It can become bad enough to prevent sleep for weeks. A more general insomnia, depression, or forgetfulness may also be present. There can be dimness of vision and loss of hearing (Cruickshank, 1976).

Structural changes found postmortem include diffuse loss of myelin in posterior and lateral areas of the spinal cord. The optic nerve may also show demyelination (Cruickshank, 1976).

Niacin

Niacin deficiency may produce different symptoms in different individuals. Nervous system symptoms may predominate with no sign of the skin changes or gastrointestinal effects, although the latter are probably more common. Earliest mental symptoms include depression, insomnia, headaches, irritability, memory defects, and sometimes dizziness. Later there is a general dulling of intellect and mental confusion. Severe dementia may follow. Mental symptoms, even the most severe, improve rapidly in response to large amounts of niacin (Cruickshank, 1976).

Paresthesias, which are abnormal sensations such as numbness, tingling, or the sensation of bugs crawling on the skin, may be present and severe in niacin deficiency. Often these involve a burning sensation similar to that of pantothenic acid deficiency but affecting the body generally rather than centering on the feet. There are accounts of people jumping into water in an effort to relieve the burning sensation.

Structural changes similar to those of pantothenic acid deficiency have been reported to follow deficiency of niacin. These include diffuse demyelination of the posterior and lateral tracts of the spinal cord. Atrophy of the optic nerve may also occur, with symptoms of visual fatigue, a slight hypersensitivity to light, a decrease in visual acuity and sometimes blurring of vision, headache behind the eyes, or loss of vision in small areas of the visual field (Cruickshank, 1976).

Typical extraneural symptoms of early niacin deficiency include dermatitis with roughened, thickened, pigmented skin in areas exposed to sunlight or pressure and irritation of the gastrointestinal tract with a tendency to diarrhea (Nutrition Foundation, Inc., 1984).

Riboflavin

Riboflavin deficiency may also be associated with degeneration in the optic nerve and related symptoms similar to those listed for niacin (Cruickshank, 1976). Subtle effects upon personality and actual neuropathy have been reported in riboflavin deficiency, but mental effects are uncommon because transport of vitamin B2 into the brain is such that activity of riboflavin-dependent coenzymes in the brain is maintained even in fairly severe deficiency. Thus, mental effects of riboflavin deficiency are rare.

Mild deficiency may cause the eyes to become watery and very sensitive to light, with increased prominence of the blood vessels in the white of the eye, resulting in a bloodshot appearance. Deficiency may also affect the skin, causing fissures at the corners of the mouth or an acne-like dermatitis (usually described as seborrheic dermatitis) (Nutrition Foundation, Inc., 1984).

Folacin (Folate, Folic Acid)

Neurological symptoms of mild folate deficiency include insomnia, irritability, and forgetfulness. Worsening of symptoms to produce dementia, or "organic brain syndrome," is possible (Food and Nutrition Board, National Research Council, 1989). Sometimes a peripheral neuropathy similar to that of thiamin deficiency responds to folate administration. The restless leg syndrome (which describes the symptoms well) may be a mild manifestation of peripheral nervous system effects.

Nonneural symptoms of mild deficiency of folacin include soreness of the tongue, especially the periphery of the tongue, where lesions may develop. Fatigue is common, and anemia may occur. The fatigue may precede the anemia as well as result from it (Holvey & Talbott, 1972). Scores on IQ tests have improved in some individuals following treatment for folate deficiency (Botez, Peyronnard, Bérubé, & Labrecque, 1979). Deficiency of vitamin C can induce a secondary folate deficiency (Holvey & Talbott, 1972).

Vitamin B6 (Pyridoxine)

Mental symptoms of deficiency of vitamin B6 can occur before any other symptoms. Depression and confusion are common mental symptoms. Weakness, lassitude, and loss of appetite as well as difficulty walking are reported as also typical. Folkers, Wolaniuk, and Vadhanavikit (1984) linked B6 deficiency to carpel tunnel syndrome, which includes inability to flex fingers completely, weakness of grasp so that the individual is prone to drop objects and pain in the hands and shoulders. This syndrome may be exacerbated by combined deficiencies of vitamin B6 and riboflavin. Folkers, Willis, Takemure, Escudier, and Shorey (1981) also identified, as a symptom of mild vitamin B6 deficiency, "transitory nocturnal paralysis of the arm and hand" in which the blood supply to the affected limb is readily decreased by lying upon it, so that the arm "goes to sleep" and cannot be moved until circulation is restored.

Vitamin B12 (Cobalamin)

In advanced deficiency, breakdown of myelin sheaths occurs in the dorsal and lateral columns of the spinal cord, beginning in the midthoracic (chest) region.

Degeneration of the axons follows. Ultimately this results in difficulty walking and finally in paralysis of the lower extremities. Foci of demyelination occur in the brain as well as in the spinal cord. Once this happens, one never recovers. Peripheral nerves are also affected but, in contrast to the brain and spinal cord, are capable of good recovery with repletion of the vitamin (Cruickshank, 1976).

Earliest symptoms of deficiency usually include abnormal sensation (paresthesias) and muscle weakness beginning equally in both legs. Alternatively, poor memory, poor concentration, irritability, depression, or variations in mood may be initial symptoms. Judgment is usually impaired, as is coordination (Cruickshank, 1976). There can be apathy, somnolence, euphoria, seizures, deterioration of vision, or visual or auditory hallucinations (Rosenthal & Goodwin, 1985). The anemia, which is well known as the initial symptom of vitamin B12 deficiency, may never occur if the individual's diet provides large amounts of folacin.

Fortunately, vitamin B12 deficiency is unlikely to occur in most people. The vitamin is plentiful in foods of animal origin, so that diets containing meat, poultry, fish, cheese, eggs, or milk provide generous amounts. Problems arise for persons with a family history of pernicious anemia or for persons who have had part of the stomach removed as treatment for ulcers. In such cases, the stomach cannot synthesize a glycoprotein necessary for absorption of vitamin B12, called the "intrinsic factor." The vitamin then cannot be absorbed, and deficiency develops. Persons who eat no animal protein are the only ones likely to develop neurological symptoms because of dietary deficiency of vitamin B12.

Biotin

Deficiency of vitamin B12 can be induced by excessively high levels of bacteria in the intestinal tract, (*Escherichia coli,* for example) because of the high need of the bacteria for the vitamin. Vitamin B6 appears needed for synthesis of the intrinsic factor; therefore, vitamin B6 deficiency may affect vitamin B12 status.

Deficiency of biotin most commonly leads to hyperesthesia, an increased sensitivity to sensation such that ordinary stimuli, such as the touch of clothing upon the skin, become uncomfortable or even painful. Other possible symptoms stemming from an effect on the nervous system include mild depression, anxiety, lassitude, somnolence, hallucinations, and muscle pain. A dermatitis resembling eczema may also occur.

Biotin is synthesized by intestinal flora of the human digestive tract, so that dietary intake is usually not a matter of concern. Persons undergoing antibiotic therapy for long periods of time can develop symptoms if their food does not provide enough biotin; however, historically, biotin deficiency is associated with drinking egg nog or other beverages containing raw eggs. This is because raw egg white contains a protein, avidin, which binds biotin, making it unavailable for absorption. Cooking the egg denatures the protein so that it no longer affects biotin absorption.

Vitamin C (Ascorbic Acid)

Deficiency of vitamin C can induce a secondary deficiency of folacin, with some of the milder of the neurological manifestations of folate deficiency. Nonneural effect of vitamin C deficiency concerns mainly synthesis and repair of the connective tissue proteins, collagen and elastin, leading to capillary fragility, gums that bleed easily and recede from the teeth, poor healing of cuts, and pain in bones and joints in more severe deficiency. Excess vitamin C increases the requirement for copper, and under some circumstances can induce symptoms of copper deficiency.

Vitamin A (Retinol)

Vitamin A deficiency is known to affect the inner ear and sense of balance and the translation of visual images into nerve impulses by its role as a component of visual pigments. Vitamin A is required by the brain, and is held within brain cells by cellular retinol-binding protein (Nutrition Foundation, Inc., 1984). However, its role in the brain is not well defined, and vitamin A deficiency affects primarily nonneural tissues.

Mild Vitamin A deficiency causes poor vision in dim light, or night blindness, causes decreased resistance to colds and other respiratory infections, and promotes roughening of the skin on the upper arms and legs. Severe deficiency can lead to blindness by causing opacity of the cornea. Excess vitamin A is toxic, and may cause headaches that can be mistaken for symptoms of brain tumor.

Vitamin D (Calciferol)

Vitamin D is present in a few foods such as sardines and fortified milk, but is synthesized in the skin under the influence of ultraviolet light. By this process, the body produces only as much as it needs. For persons living in cloudy or cold areas, calciferol becomes a dietary essential. Any effect of vitamin D upon the nervous system is felt through its effect upon blood levels of the mineral calcium. Vitamin D deficiency results in low blood levels of calcium, or hypocalcemia. Conversely, excess vitamin D causes high blood calcium, or hypercalcemia. Both hypocalcemia and hypercalcemia affect the nervous system. Hypocalcemia can cause seizures or convulsions, which can be mistaken for epilepsy. More typically, a collection of symptoms arises that is known as tetany (Katzman & Pappius, 1973). Tetany is described in detail by Katzman and Pappius (1973). It begins with paresthesias felt as a tingling sensation around the mouth and in the hands and feet. This sensation becomes stronger and spreads over the face and up the extremities. Later a sensation of tension or spasm is felt in the mouth, hands, and lower legs, and spreads in the same way as the paresthesias. Subsequently, spasms set in, affecting the same areas. These spasms are involuntary contractions of muscles of the lower and upper extremities, causing flexion of the fingers and toes at the joints that are closest to the trunk and extension at the further ones. The wrist and elbow are generally flexed as well. Spasms may last only a few minutes, or may persist for hours or days. There is considerable pain with prolonged spasms. Sometimes epileptic fits accompany the tetany. In individuals prone to tetany, tapping the face in front of the ear, over the site of the facial nerve, will induce twitching of the eyelid on the same side. This response is called a positive Chvostek sign (Katzman & Pappius, 1973).

Hypercalcemia can be induced in some individuals by rather modest excesses of vitamin D. Supplements of this vitamin should not exceed 400 IU per day. In adults, symptoms of hypercalcemia vary from one individual to another. Most typically there are headaches, paresthesias, dizziness, depression, or, at very high levels of vitamin D, mild psychosis or stupor. Alternatively, there may be weakness, nausea, vomiting, unsteady gait, speech difficulties, and blurring of vision, or confusion, disorientation, loss of ability to calculate, unsteadiness, and weakness, or personality changes, a disinclination to move, depression, and sometimes memory impairment along with severe constipation, loss of appetite, and nausea. In hypercalcemia there is muscle weakness, and deterioration and death of muscle fibers are found upon biopsy (Katzman & Pappius, 1973).

There is great variation in individual susceptibility to vitamin D toxicity. Some individuals can tolerate the vitamin in amounts far above the RDA, whereas in others smaller excesses induce hypercalcemia. In nonneural tissues, vitamin D excess induces inappropriate calcium deposit. The kidneys usually suffer the most damage. Death from toxicity is usually from kidney failure.

Vitamin E (Tocopherol)

Vitamin E deficiency has been shown to cause degeneration in the brain in rats. Axons from sensory neurons carrying information to the brain show a dying-back type of degeneration. The peripheral nervous system is similarly affected (Towfighi, 1981). In people, effects of deficiency upon the nervous system are rare, but have occurred in association with impaired intestinal absorption. Poor coordination, impaired sense of touch, abnormal eye movements, and difficulty walking have been reported, all of which showed improvement upon treatment with vitamin E (Weder, 1984).

The usual nonneurological symptom of vitamin E deficiency in people is hemolytic anemia, a type of anemia with accelerated destruction of red blood cells.

Vitamin K (Menaquinone, Menadione)

Vitamin K is required for synthesis of several blood-clotting factors. No effect of vitamin K deficiency upon the brain or peripheral nervous system has been identified, nor is a role for the vitamin known in the brain. Some role in the brain may eventually be found, however; the role of vitamin K is thought to be much broader than currently understood.

Calcium

Most of the calcium in the body resides in bone and in tooth enamel. Bone serves as a storage site for the mineral, which is released from bone as necessary to maintain blood calcium levels. Therefore, under conditions of low dietary intake, blood levels of calcium are maintained at the expense of bone, and hypocalcemia, with its attendant neurological symptoms, does not occur. The dietary cause of hypocalcemia or hypercalcemia is usually deficient or excessive intake or production of vitamin D. Therefore, neurological effect of hypocalcemia and hypercalcemia are discussed in relation to vitamin D. An additional possible dietary cause of hypercalcemia is the ingestion of large amounts of alkali, from antacids together with large amounts of milk. In the past this sort of intake characterized conventional treatment for gastric ulcers, and led in some individuals to elevated blood calcium, with nausea, vomiting, and deposit of calcium in soft tissues.

Without the conditions just mentioned, and with normal levels of parathyroid hormone, blood calcium is maintained at normal levels. If calcium withdrawn from the bones exceeds that replaced from the diet, the bones gradually become demineralized, leading eventually to softening and deformity of the bones (osteomalacia) or to increased susceptibility to osteoporosis (weak, brittle bones subject to spontaneous fracture) in later life. In dietary deficiency of calcium, deposit of calcium into bones is impaired still further if magnesium is deficient (Nutrition Foundation, Inc., 1984).

Magnesium

Deficiency of magnesium is said to show "clinical polymorphism"; that is, it produces a wide variety of symptoms in different individuals. Most symptoms affect the nervous system. there may be anxiety, insomnia, headaches, tremors, the sensation of "a lump in the throat," a feeling of blocked breathing similar to asthma, dizziness, and vocal or visual fatigue. More common, perhaps, are involuntary muscle twitchings, heart palpitations, and inappropriately rapid heartbeat known as tachycardia. there can be paresthesias, cramps affecting muscle or gastrointestinal tract, and chest pain (Durlach, 1985). Severe deficiency of magnesium can produce tetany, which is indistinguishable from the tetany of hypocalcemia (see *Vitamin D*).

Nonneural signs of chronic deficiency include brittle fingernails, hair, and teeth. Animals show a reddening of paws and ears, which may be transient or persistent. There may be a counterpart to this in red ears or palms of human hands, but this is not established.

Certain environmental conditions are known to increase the need for magnesium or to precipitate symptoms of deficiency. Insufficient water intake or excessive water loss, because it increases secretion of antidiuretic hormone, increases urinary magnesium excretion. Ingestion of alcohol can increase excretion of magnesium to three times the normal level. Adaptation to heat or cold appears to require extra magnesium. Adaptation to increased exercise also appears to increase the need for magnesium, probably because the mineral is generally needed wherever energy, as adenosine triphosphate, is used or produced.

Approximately 6 mg magnesium per kilogram of body weight (weight in pounds divided by 2.2) is required in the diet so that uptake of magnesium will exceed loss.

Sodium and Potassium

These two minerals are considered together to emphasize the effect of sodium depletion upon potassium status and the relationship of both to the body's supply of water. When water losses exceed the capacity of antidiuretic hormone secretion to prevent dehydration, reuptake of water by the kidneys is augmented by secretion of aldosterone. The latter hormone is secreted in response to depletion of water, depletion of sodium, or excessive blood levels of potassium. It promotes reuptake of sodium by the kidneys, which augments reuptake of water because water follows sodium. When sodium is reabsorbed, potassium is generally excreted to maintain balance of the electrical charges these minerals acquire when they dissolve in body fluids (Whitney & Hamilton, 1987).

Vigorous exercise, especially in hot environments, promotes sweating and loss of body water. If such water is not promptly replaced, loss of both sodium and potassium is likely to ensue. In hot climates this sequence of events can be of considerable importance. Sodium depletion may cause weakness, irritability, lethargy, confusion, nausea, and vomiting. Coma and death can follow if depletion continues. Potassium depletion, which, as indicated previously, can occur in response to sodium loss, may produce muscular weakness and even paralysis owing to changes in neuromuscular sensitivity. Effects upon smooth muscle of the gastrointestinal tract may produce paralytic ileus, a purely functional block passage of intestinal contents, which may be accompanied by abdominal pain (Holvey & Talbott, 1972). Weakness of vascular musculature may lead to low blood pressure. The most serious effect of potassium deficiency is on heart rhythm. Cardiac arrest and death can occur.

Sodium excess persisting over long periods of time is associated with high blood pressure. In some individuals sodium excess is associated with accumulation of fluid in the body. Acute sodium toxicity is unlikely under normal conditions because sodium is readily excreted, but it has occurred when salt has been accidentally ingested in large amounts. Multiple small hemorrhages in the cerebral cortex arise in sodium toxicity.

Increased potassium increases excretion of sodium (Nutrition Foundation, Inc., 1984) and, as one would expect, counteracts the effect of sodium upon blood pressure. Potassium excess, although virtually impossible from dietary intake, induces symptoms quite similar to those of potassium deficiency, with abnormal heart rhythm, and a possibility of skeletal muscle paralysis and cessation of heartbeat. (Holvey & Talbott, 1972). Potassium depletion can sometimes be induced by a magnesium deficiency (National Foundation, Inc., 1984).

Iron

Although deficiency of iron mainly impairs delivery of oxygen to tissues and affects energy production, several of the symptoms of deficiency indicate a more direct effect upon the nervous system. There may be irritability, loss of appetite or capricious appetite, and numbness, tingling, or pain in the extremities (Holvey & Talbott, 1972). Levels of the catecholamine category of neurotransmitters, particularly norepinephrine, increase in iron deficiency and return to normal with correction of the deficiency (Nutrition Foundation, Inc., 1984). Nonneural symptoms of iron deficiency include fatigue, weakness, and pallor stemming from anemia. Gastrointestinal symptoms sometimes also occur, including heartburn, flatulence, and abdominal pain (Holvey & Talbott, 1972).

Absorption of iron from the diet is impaired by concomitant ingestion of tannins (in tea) and phytates (in coffee and unleavened breads and cereals). The effect can be substantial, amounting to a decrease of almost two thirds in the case of tannins. In contrast, iron absorption is facilitated by foods and beverages containing vitamin C.

Iodine

Lack of iodine has a devastating effect upon the developing nervous system, causing mental retardation in many cases. Once the nervous system is mature, iodine deficiency produces exclusively nonneural symptoms; decreased levels of thyroid hormone and enlargement of the thyroid gland, or goiter.

Zinc

Human deficiency of zinc is reported to produce neurological symptoms including apathy, lethargy, irritability, headaches, insomnia, "bad dreams," depression, paranoia, and amnesia (Baer et al., 1985; Pfeiffer & Bravermen, 1982), with considerable individual variation as to what group of changes appear.

Taste acuity is quite sensitive to zinc deficiency (Nutrition Foundation, Inc., 1984) and is a favorite measurement of zinc status used by scientists in studies of mild deficiency in human volunteers.

In animals, deficiency of zinc during the prenatal period has been shown to lead to impaired behavioral development and a permanent deficit in learning and memory, even after repletion (Nutrition Foundation, Inc., 1984). Comparable deficits may exist for people, but have not been identified as such.

In animals, dietary zinc deficiency is reported to decrease neural transmission in mossy fibers of the hippocampus. The hippocampus is a part of the brain essential to memory, presumably mediating the storage of information in long-term memory and its retrieval from storage. The hippocampus contains a great deal of zinc, much of it in nerve terminals of the mossy fiber tract.

Excess zinc increases the need for copper, and appears to interfere with metabolism of cholesterol, resulting in decrease in high-density lipoprotein cholesterol. Such a change can be expected to increase susceptibility to heart disease.

Copper

Effects of copper deficiency upon the nervous system during development are quite different from effects upon the mature brain. Perinatal copper deficiency is strongly associated with defective myelination and degeneration of white matter, whereas myelin undergoes little damage from copper deficiency in adults.

In adults, synthesis of the neurotransmitters dopamine and norepinephrine is decreased in copper deficiency (Nutrition Foundation, Inc., 1984). Copper repletion restores norepinephrine levels to normal, but not dopamine levels, suggesting damage to dopamine-releasing neurons. In rats electron microscope evidence of neuronal degeneration has been reported (Root & Longenecker, 1983). In humans, a case of severe depression with hallucinations that improved in response to supplementation with copper, but not with other nutrients, has been reported (Hansen, Malecha, Mackenzie, & Kroll, 1983).

Manganese

Both manganese deficiency and toxicity are capable of affecting the brain. Deficiency in rats increases susceptibility of the animals to convulsions (Hurley, Wooley, Rosenthal, & Teineras, 1963). A similar action in humans is suggested by increased seizure frequency in epileptics who have low blood levels of manganese (Papavasiliou et al., 1979).

A possible mechanism for this overexcitability of the brain lies in altered metabolism of the excitatory neurotransmitter, glutamate. Glutamic acid, or glutamate, is a nonessential amino acid both obtained from the diet and synthesized in the body. It is not only used for protein synthesis but is also released by certain neurons as a neurotransmitter. Excessive glutamate at the synapse can produce too much excitation and be toxic to postsynaptic neurons. To prevent this, the glutamate is removed by uptake into glial cells, which convert it to nontoxic glutamine and release it for reuptake by the neurons, which can in turn reconvert it to gutamate as needed. The glial enzyme, which converts glutamate to glutamine, requires manganese for its activity (Tholey et al., 1988). Lacking manganese, the enzyme will be inactive, glutamate can be expected to accumulate in the glial cell and in the synaptic cleft, and overexcitement of neurons with glutamate receptors can be expected to occur, with convulsions a likely result.

Toxicity of manganese has occurred in miners who were exposed to dust from manganese-containing ore; it is unlikely from excessive dietary intake. It causes symptoms similar to those of Parkinson's disease (Nutrition Foundation, Inc., 1984).

Nonneural effects of manganese deficiency, observed in people who volunteered for short-term studies, include a skin rash with tiny fluid-filled pustules, which give way to small reddish spots, and impaired ability of the blood to clot. Animals show bone abnormalities.

Selenium

Deficiency of selenium occurs only in areas were selenium content of the soil is low, such as the Keshan province in northeast China. Deficiency has not been associated with neural disease, but it could theoretically make the brain more susceptible to damage from free radicals, reactive molecules with unpaired electrons arising from some normal biochemical reactions in the body. There is a normal mechanism for detoxifying free radicals, which produces hydrogen peroxide, which is in turn detoxified by being converted to water using the tripeptide glutathione and the enzyme glutathione peroxidase. The predominant form of glutathione peroxidase is selenium-dependent (Nutrition Foundation, Inc. 1984). Breakdown of neurotransmitters such as dopamine or norepinephrine by the enzyme monamine oxidase produces hydrogen peroxide, which if not detoxified can itself give rise to free radicals, so nerve terminals of neurons releasing these catecholamine neurotransmitters are areas that could theoretically be affected in selenium deficiency. Lack of activity of glutathione peroxidase would lead to elevated levels of hydrogen peroxide, which could start a new cycle of free radical generation, resulting in damage to membranes of the neurons. This is a hypothetical situation that is not known to actually occur.

Nonneural effects of selenium deficiency include damage to heart muscle, causing a degeneration of heart muscle, or cardiomyopathy, known as Keshan disease. Until selenium was supplemented, this was an important cause of death in northeast China (Xia, Hill, & Burk, 1989).

Excessive selenium is highly toxic. Cattle pastured in high-selenium areas develop a disease called "blind staggers" and ultimately die of hemorrhages into the lungs. Early signs of selenium excess in people include loss of hair, deterioration of fingernails, and a smell of garlic on one's breath. (A smell of garlic also occurs in excess intake of arsenic.)

Chromium

The mineral chromium exists in two valence states: one with a positive charge of three, the other six. The plus-six form is toxic, whereas the plus-three form (chromium III) is essential. Water faucets are plated with the plus-six form.

Insufficient chromium intake in free-living individuals has not been related to any neurological changes; however, deficiency of chromium III has occurred in 2 patients maintained on total parenteral nutrition, and in these persons has caused either peripheral (Jeejeebhoy, Chu, Marliss, Greenburg, & Bruce, 1977) or central (Freund, Atamian, & Fischer, 1979) neuropathy. Symptoms improved rapidly with chromium supplementation. The peripheral neuropathy is described as being similar to diabetic neurpathy, with incoordination, paresthesias including numbness, tingling of the hands and feet, and sometimes pain, which worsens at night. Chromium is needed for effective use of insulin. Nonneuronal symptoms include high blood sugar and a diabetes-like condition.

Silicon

Silicon, one of the minerals more recently identified as an essential nutrient, has been reported to have a protective effect against accumulation of aluminum in the brain (Carlisle, 1988; 1989). Elevated aluminum is found in brains of persons dying of Alzheimer's disease. Silicon is also reported to aid in homeostasis of other minerals as well. In contrast to this probable neuroprotective effect, excessive silicon is postulated to have a neurotoxic effect in persons with inadequately kidney function (Hershey et al., 1988). It is not unusual for minerals to perform beneficial or essential functions at low levels and yet be toxic at high levels.

The nonneural role of silicon as a structural component of at least some glycosaminoglycans is well established. It is thus important for strong connective tissue and normal bone structure.

Other Trace or Ultratrace Element

Cobalt is important as a part of the vitamin B12 molecule, but is not known to have other essential roles. Vanadium, nickel, tin, boron, and bromine are believed to be essential, but there is little or no information about any role in the nervous system.

Eating to Obtain the Needed Nutrients

This information concerning effects of deficiency should have convinced the reader that nutrition is important to the nervous system as well as to the rest of the body. The rather severe effects of nutrient deficiency described will occur only as the result of severe or long-standing deficiency. However, with mild deficiency, some tendency in the same direction can be expected so that function of the nervous system cannot be optimal. Slightly impaired function may go unnoticed by some, but not by the athlete. Performance will be limited, perhaps severely, by any part of the body that is not at its best, the brain and nervous system included. Indeed, activity of most, if not all, of the body is absolutely dependent upon nervous system function.

Fortunately, the best diet for all parts of the body is the same. Foods should provide adequate amounts of the 12 or more vitamins, the 15 or more minerals, and the 8 amino acids known to be essential, but no great excess. Foods should also provide enough energy to balance energy use. Choosing foods that provide these things is neither difficult nor excessively expensive in our Western culture, but it is still not a trivial matter. It is probably safe to say that most people, including many athletes, are less than optimally nourished.

We do have some guidelines to help us choose foods. "Dietary Goals," the product of a United States Senate committee hearing that sought a consensus from eminent nutritionists concerning ways to improve public health, gives some specific recommendations: protein in one's diet should provide 12% of the kilocalories; fat, 30%; and carbohydrate (starches and sugars), 58%. Cholesterol should be restricted to 300 mg per day. Most nutritionists would agree that we can amend the calorie recommendations slightly under some circumstances, letting the protein rise to 20% and the carbohydrate decrease in compensation to 50%. Fat should stay close to 30%. The altered percentages would be better for people with diabetes, people on diets for weight reduction, and perhaps athletes trying to increase muscle mass. More protein than enough to furnish 20% of kilocalories would be counterproductive even for athletes. This is discussed later.

The use of protein, fat, and carbohydrate requires vitamins and minerals. These are all needed for both protein synthesis and energy production. They are needed for proper function of the nervous system. Because these together form the basis for health and optimum performance, it is impossible to stress enough that one needs all the essential nutrients.

How then, does one ensure obtaining all of these nutrients without spending all one's time perusing food composition tables? Fortunately, we have guidelines for this too. Foods can be classified into groups with similar composition, so that eating a specific number of servings from each group each day is likely to provide the needed nutrients. The "basic four" food group is the best known of these classifications. Similar food groupings, known as the exchange lists (Guthrie, 1989; Whitney & Hamilton, 1987), enable one to control intake of carbohydrate, protein, and fat, and therefore kilocalories. These exchange list groupings were established jointly by the American Dietetic Association and the American Diabetic Association for use by diabetics, who must follow a lifelong diet, but the exchanges proved so useful that they have been used for many other purposes. The exchanges include only foods of relatively high nutrient density.

Nutrient density refers to amounts of vitamins, minerals, and protein in a food relative to the kilocalories it provides. Foods that contain substantial amounts of sugar or fat are generally of low nutrient density because sugar and fat are concentrated sources of kilocalories. Candy, soft drinks, alcoholic beverages, doughnuts, cakes, pies, cookies, and most other desserts can be assumed to be of low nutrient density. High nutrient density foods include vegetables, legumes (navy beans, pinto beans and so on), lean meats, whole-grain breads, and most fruits, so long as all of these are prepared without much added fat or sugar. Athletes involved in prolonged exercise will need some foods of low nutrient density to provide enough kilocalories without requiring excessive bulk. However, the basis of the diet should come from high nutrient density foods.

With this information, then, let us consider some specific advice about what to eat. The following suggestion is a "core" of foods providing approximately 1,600 kcal from high nutrient density foods to which additional foods of either high or low nutrient density can be added to provide additional kilocalories. The core consists of:

1. Two 3-oz. servings of lean meat, poultry, or fish.
2. Two 8-oz. glasses of lowfat milk (approximately 2% butterfat).
3. Two cups (8-oz.) of cooked vegetables (or larger amounts of salad).
4. Three large pieces of fruit.
5. Three slices of bread.
6. One and one-half cups of cereal, rice, pasta, potato or starchy beans, or some combination thereof.
7. Five tsps (25 gm) of butter, margarine, salad oil, mayonnaise, or other fat.

For readers familiar with the exchange lists (Guthrie, 1989; Whitney & Hamilton, 1987) this core is equivalent to six low-fat meat exchanges, two medium-fat milk exchanges, four vegetable exchanges, six fruit exchanges, five bread exchanges, and five fat exchanges. It is an attempt to simplify use of the diet. If followed carefully with an effort to avoid adding extra fat or sugar, the diet provides 20% of kilocalories from protein (at 4 kcal/gm), 29% from fat (at 9 kcal/gm), and 51% from carbohydrate (at 4 kcal/gm). If other foods are added, these percentages will change, but at least this provides a starting point. If one chooses foods to obtain some variety and to provide good sources of nutrients that are unevenly distributed in foods, this eating pattern should easily provide the RDAs for both men and women.

What nutrients are unevenly distributed? Vitamins A and C are very concentrated in some foods and entirely absent from others. A single orange can provide the entire day's requirement for vitamin C, and a single large carrot or serving of spinach can do the same for vitamin A. However, there is no vitamin A or C in muscle meats or breads. Folacin is similarly associated mainly with fruits and vegetables, although it has a somewhat wider distribution.

The calcium in two glasses of milk amounts to about three quarters of the RDA of 800 mg, and the remaining amount is accumulated in small amounts from other foods. A similar situation exists for riboflavin.

Zinc in four to five oz of red meat amounts to a substantial part of the day's requirement, so that the remaining need can be met from small amounts in other foods. Oysters are richer sources than red meat, but poultry and fish are less rich sources, providing only about one fourth as much as beef. The amount of zinc needed is affected strongly by amounts of phytate in the diet. Phytate is found mainly in cereal grains, and is partially degraded by the leavening action of yeast so that it no longer binds zinc, preventing its absorption. So using at least part yeast-leavened bread rather than hot breads leavened with baking powder will keep one's requirements for zinc within usual bounds.

Other nutrients, for example thiamin, pantothenic acid, vitamin B6, iron, copper, and magnesium, are more widely distributed in foods in smaller amounts so that the daily requirements must be met from many foods. Although the entire RDA for these nutrients will not be obtained from any one food, some of the relatively richer food sources of these nutrients need to be included frequently. Good sources of various nutrients are listed in Table 2. Choosing the core foods to include good sources of the nutrients listed in Table 2 should ensure a good nutrient intake.

For most people, more food than the core amounts will be needed to provide enough energy, or kilocalories. The total amount of food one eats is controlled mainly by the need for kilocalories. Hunger and satiety mechanisms may be imperfectly understood, but they nevertheless function quite well, so that for most of us energy intake and energy use are well balanced, and body weight remains quite stable. This is why it is important to be aware of nutrient density. One should be sure one can eat all of the core foods in the amounts indicated as foods of high nutrient density before adding low nutrient density foods to supply extra kilocalories. If one eats the low nutrient density foods first, one may be too full to eat the others, and consequently fail to obtain the needed vitamins and minerals. Continuing to eat after one feels satisfied is likely to cause deposit of unwanted fat.

Sometimes people wonder why they cannot obtain the vitamins and minerals they need from supplements, and eat anything they like. Someday this may be possible, but at the present state of nutritional knowledge, supplements do not provide everything one needs. We have probably identified all of the vitamins, but may not have identified all of the essential minerals. Certainly we do not yet know

Table 2 Foods that are sources of selected nutrients

Nutrient	Source
Thiamin	Pork, ham, oranges or orange juice, bran cereal, dry cooked beans,[a] whole wheat or "enriched" bread, watermelon, sunflower seeds
Pantothenic acid	Liver,[b] eggs,[b] avocado, celery mushrooms, milk, cauliflower, broccoli, nuts
Riboflavin	Liver,[b] milk, cheese, yogurt, meats, bran, spinach, broccoli
Niacin	Chicken, tuna fish, peanuts, peanut butter, beef, other meats, poultry and fish, dry cooked beans[a]
Biotin	Liver,[b] oatmeal, cooked eggs,[b] milk, salmon, clams, brown rice
Vitamin B6	Liver,[b] meats, bananas, avocados, dry cooked beans,[a] corn, potatoes, watermelon, salmon
Vitamin B12	Liver,[b] meat, cheese, milk, eggs,[b] fish, shellfish, sauerkraut
Folacin	Liver,[b] oranges, spinach, romaine lettuce, cantaloupe, broccoli, green peas, strawberries, asparagus, dry cooked beans[a]
Vitamin C	Oranges, orange juice, grapefruit, tangerines, strawberries, broccoli, tomatoes, cantaloupe, green pepper
Vitamin A	Liver,[b] egg yolk,[b] spinach, carrots, winter squash, broccoli, cantaloupe, romaine lettuce, watermelon
Vitamin K	Turnip greens, lettuce, cabbage, broccoli, liver[b]
Calcium	Milk, hard cheese, yogurt, sardines (with softened bones)
Magnesium	Dry cooked beans,[a] peanuts, spinach and other green leafy vegetables, bananas, avocados, tuna fish, nuts, chocolate
Potassium	Bananas, potatoes, milk, avocado, chicken
Iron	Liver,[b] bran flakes, dry cooked beans,[a] beef, egg,[b] tomato sauce
Zinc	Oysters, beef, other red meats, chicken, lima beans and dry cooked beans,[a] soup made with beef or chicken broth, milk, cheese
Copper	Liver,[b] meats, dry cooked beans,[a] bran, oysters, shrimp, nuts
Manganese	Spinach, carrots, other vegetables, whole grain breads and cereals, nuts, dry cooked beans, tea, rice
Selenium	Meats, poultry, eggs,[b] milk, whole grain breads and cereals
Chromium III	Liver,[b] cheese, whole wheat bread, black pepper
Silicon	Apples, oranges, beef broth
Nickel	Oysters, green leafy vegetables, tea

[a]Dry cooked beans refers to mature beans or peas that must be softened by cooking, such as navy beans, pinto beans, kidney beans, lentils, and so on.

[b]High in cholesterol (shellfish, including oysters, clams, and shrimp, are moderately high in cholesterol).

what amounts to supply for some of the recently recognized minerals. In addition to essential minerals, amino acids, and vitamins, foods provide many other substances useful to the body. The body could synthesize these substances, but is benefited by not having to do so. For this reason it is unlikely that supplements will ever have any advantage over foods in promoting good athletic performance. Some nutritionists feel strongly that supplements should never be used. Others feel that a broad-spectrum vitamin-mineral supplement providing amounts at or near the RDAs (Table 1) does no harm and may provide a sort of insurance against increased need for certain nutrients such as may be induced by environmental factors such as illness, stress, or injury. Certainly there is no benefit from supplements added to an already adequate diet. Nor is there any benefit from amino acid supplements, or even from adding extra protein (more than 20% of kcal) from foods, as is sometimes suggested to promote muscle building.

The reason that extra protein exerts no magic with respect to muscle building lies with control of synthesis of muscle proteins (mostly actin and myosin) within the cell. Skeletal muscle cells are large cells with many nuclei, formed from fusion of the many small muscle cells, which form by cell division early in development. The large cells can increase or decrease the actin/myosin fibrils they contain, and thus become larger or smaller. Increase occurs in response to demand (exercise), whereas decrease may occur in response to lack of demand (no exercise) or to a need for amino acids elsewhere in the body. Muscle proteins will be broken down to release amino acids not only when protein intake is too low but also when carbohydrate is insufficient to support energy production. To metabolize fat for energy, a certain biochemical pathway, the Krebs cycle, must be operating. Carbohydrate or protein can keep it operating, but fat cannot. Amino acids, then, can be used in place of carbohydrate in producing energy and will be used if carbohydrate is insufficient. Excess protein, above the amount needed for protein synthesis, will be metabolized for energy or stored as fat, but energy is released more efficiently from carbohydrate or from fat. Exercise is believed to stimulate protein synthesis largely because the binding of the neurotransmitter acetylcholine to its receptors simultaneously leads to muscle contraction and to activation of mechanisms for metabolic control within the cell. Thus, metabolic activity, including muscle building, and physical activity are coupled. This presumably explains the atrophy of denervated muscle. Although the need for protein thus rises with activity, the need for energy increases more. If the amino acids must be used to produce this energy, they cannot be used to form muscle. The best advise for muscle building, then, is to consume a little extra protein (13%-20% of kilocalories) and enough carbohydrate and fat to cover the energy needs of increased exercise. Use of protein, fat, and carbohydrate both for protein synthesis and energy production requires vitamins and minerals. One cannot stress enough that one needs all of the essential nutrients to promote both health and optimum performance. The core foods can be amended slightly for use by children and younger athletes who are still growing. They will need more milk than specified for the core foods: a minimum of three glasses for younger children and four glasses for teenagers. Smaller but proportional mounts of the other core foods can be used if energy requirements are less than 1,600 kcal.

For all ages, as indicated previously, foods should be chosen to provide variety. Use different vegetables, different fruits, different meats, different breads, and cereals. Variety not only promotes a better balanced intake of minerals and vitamins, but also prevents too great an intake of any of the many slightly toxic substances found in foods. Most foods contain some deleterious substances; the body can detoxify and excrete modest amounts of these substances with ease, but may sustain some damage from large amounts before they can be entirely processed. Even minor damage could theoretically take the edge off athletic performance.

There yet remains something to say about several topics of current interest. One of these topics is cholesterol. The relation between cholesterol and heart disease is well known. The dietary goals recommendation of 300 mg cholesterol per day represents an attempt to help decrease incidence of heart disease; however, individuals whose blood cholesterol is low (200 mg per deciliter or less) and who have no family history of heart disease can probably tolerate larger amounts. A single egg provides 213 to 250 mg of cholesterol, and meat and milk products provide smaller amounts, so it is easy to exceed 300 mg. The core diet will provide about 250 mg cholesterol if eggs and other foods high in cholesterol such as liver and shrimp are avoided.

Fiber is related to cholesterol because some forms of fiber promote excretion of cholesterol from the body. These forms are the soluble fibers found in fruits, vegetables, and oat bran. Insoluble fibers, found in wheat bran, promote rapid passage of material through the gut, and help to prevent colon cancer but have little or no effect upon cholesterol. Both types of fiber are desirable. In following the core diet, choice of whole wheat breads, whole grain cereals, dry cooked beans, apples, oranges, and a variety of vegetables will provide adequate fiber.

SUMMARY

There is continual need for replacement of nutrients to replace those lost during the continual turnover of molecules in the body as well as those used up for energy production. Failure to replace vitamins and minerals can affect the nervous system and the mind as well as the rest of the body. Excess intake also is likely to have adverse effects. Any adverse effects can be expected to impair athletic performance. Optimal nutrition, in contrast, promotes the best possible performance. An eating pattern is suggested that will normally supply good nutrition.

REFERENCES

Baer, M. T., King, J. C., Tamura, T., Morgan, S., Bradfield, R. B., Weston, W. L., & Dougherty, N. A. (1985). Nitrogen utilization, enzyme activity, glucose intolerance and leukocyte chemotaxis in human experimental zinc depletion. *American Journal of Clinical Nutrition, 41,* 1220–1235.

Botez, M. I., Peyronnard, J. M., Bérubé, L., & Labrecque, R. (1979). Relapsing neuropathy, cerebral atrophy and folate deficiency. *Applied Neurophysiology, 42,* 171–183.

Carlisle, E. M., Curran, M. J., & Duong, T. (1988). The effect of dietary calcium and silicon. *FASEB Journal, 2,* A841.

Carlisle, E. M., Curran, M. J., & Duong, T. (1989). The effect of the thyroid and dietary silicon and aluminum on zinc content in brain. *FASEB Journal, 3,* A761.

Carpenter, M. B., & Sutin, J. (1983). *Human neuroanatomy* (8th ed.). Baltimore: Williams & Wilkins.

Cruickshank, E. K. (1976). Effects of malnutrition on the central nervous system and the nerves. In P. J. Vinken & G. W. Bruyn (Eds.), *Handbook of clinical neurology: Volume 28. Metabolic and deficiency diseases of the nervous system. Part II.* Amsterdam: North-Holland.

deWardener, H. E., & Lennox, B. (1947). Cerebral beri-beri (Wernicke's encephalopathy). Review of 52 cases in a Singapore prisoner-of-war hospital. *Lancet, 252;* 11–17.

Durlach, J. (1985). Neurological disturbances due to magnesium imbalance, In S. Gabay, J. Harris, & B. T. Ho (Eds.), *Metal ions in neurology and psychiatry* (pp. 121–128). New York: Alan R. Liss.

Folkers, K., Willis, R., Takemure, K., Escudier, S., & Shorey, R. (1981). Biochemical correlations of a deficiency of vitamin B6, the carpal tunnel syndrome and the Chinese restaurant syndrome. *IRCS Medical Science, 9,* 444.

Folkers, K., Wolaniuk, A., & Vadhanavikit, S. (1984). Enzymology of the response of the carpal tunnel syndrome to riboflavin and to combined riboflavin and pyridoxine. *Proceedings of the National Academy of Sciences USA, 81;* 7076–7078.

Food and Nutrition Board, National Research Council. (1989). *Recommended dietary allowances* (10th ed.). Washington, DC: National Academy of Sciences.

Freund, H. A., Atamian, S., & Fischer, J. E. (1979). Chromium deficiency during total parenteral nutrition. *Journal of the American Medical Association, 241;* 496–498.

Gershell, W. J. (1981). Psychiatric manifestations and nutritional deficiencies in the elderly. In A. J. Levenson & R. C. W. Hall (Eds.), *Neuropsychiatric manifestations of physical disease in the elderly,* New York: Raven Press.

Guthrie, H. A. (1989). *Introductory nutrition* (7th ed.) St. Louis: Times Mirror/Mosby.

Hansen, C. R., Jr., Malecha, M., Mackenzie, T. B., & Kroll, J. (1983). Copper and zinc deficiencies in association with depression and neurological findings. *Biological Psychiatry, 18;* 395–401.

Hershey, C. O., Ricanati, E. S., Hershey, L. A., Varnes, A. W., Lavin, P. M. J., & Strain, W. H. (1988). Silicon as a potential uremic neurotoxin. *Neurology, 33;* 786–789.

Holvey, D. N., & Talbott, J. H. (Eds.). (1972). *The Merck manual of diagnosis and therapy.* Rathway, NJ: Merck, Sharp and Dohme Research Laboratories.

Hurley, L. L., Wooley, D. E., Rosenthal, F., & Teineras, P. S. (1963). Influence of manganese on susceptibility of rats to convulsions. *American Journal of Physiology, 204;* 493–496.

Jeejeebhoy, K. N., Chu, R. C., Marliss, E. B., Greenburg, G. R., & Bruce, R. A. (1977). Chromium deficiency, glucose intolerance and neuropathy reversed by chromium supplementation, in a patient receiving long-term total parenteral nutrition. *American Journal of Clinical Nutrition, 30;* 531–538.

Katzman, R., & Pappius, H. M. (1973). *Brain electrolytes and fluid metabolism.* Baltimore: Williams & Wilkins.

Novelli, G. D. (1953). Metabolic functions of pantothenic acid. *Physiological Reviews, 33;* 525.

Nutrition Foundation, Inc. (1984). *Nutrition review's present knowledge in nutrition* (5th ed.). Washington, DC: The Nutrition Foundation, Inc.

Papavasiliou, P. S., Kutt, H., Miller, S. T., Rosal, V., Wang, Y. Y., & Aronson, R. B. (1979). Seizure disorders and trace metals. Manganese tissue levels in treated epileptics. *Neurology, 29;* 1466–1473.

Pfeiffer, C. C., & Braverman, E. R. (1982). Zinc, the brain and behavior. *Biological Psychiatry, 17;* 513–532.

Root, E. J., & Longenecker, J. B. (1983). Brain cell alterations suggesting premature aging induced by dietary deficiency of vitamin B6 and/or copper. *American Journal of Clinical Nutrition, 37;* 540–552.

Rosenthal, M. J., & Goodwin, J. S. (1985). Cognitive effects of nutritional deficiency. *Advances in Nutrition Research, 7;* 71–100.

Tholey, G., Ledig, M., Mandel, P., Sargentini, L., Frivold, A. H., Leroy, M., Grippo, A. A., & Wedler, F. C. (1988). Concentrations of physiologically important metal ions in glial cells cultured from chick. *Neurochemical Research, 13;* 45–50.

Towfighi, J. (1981). Effects of chronic vitamin E deficiency on the nervous system of the rat. *Acta Neuropathologica, 54;* 261–267.

Weder, B., Meienberg, O., Wildi, E., & Meier, C. (1984). Neurologic disorder of vitamin E deficiency in acquired intestinal malabsorption. *Neurology, 34;* 1561–1565.

Whitney, E. N., & Hamilton, E. M. N. (1987). *Understanding nutrition* (4th ed.). St. Paul, MN: West Publishing.

Xia, Y., Hill, C., & Burk, R. F. (1989). Biochemical studies of a selenium-deficient population in China. Measurement of selenium glutathione peroxidase and other oxidant defense indices in blood. *Journal of Nutrition, 119;* 1318–1326.

4

Psychophysiology of Sports, Exercise, and Fitness: Developmental Aspects

Lothar Pickenhain

Active movement is one of the most characteristic features of each self-organizing living system, including humans. It exists as an internal drive, organizes the adaptive realization of the genetic potential under the condition of different epigenetic influences, and secures the existence of the organism within its changing surroundings. Within the social network, this drive is consciously organized as sports and exercise with the declared aim to acquire and retain fitness.

For better understanding of the laws governing the development and the character of this special feature of the human personality, the following four scientific topics are examined.

1. The relationship between genetic and epigenetic factors providing the predisposition for human movement activity.
2. The ascending maturation of the central steering and controlling levels of movement.
3. The unity of perception and action.
4. The increasing internalization of movement initiation and movement control.
5. The neurophysiological mechanisms of ideomotor training.
6. Psychophysiology of movement.

I wish to stress that the holistic approach is the single way to understand the psychophysiology of sports, exercise, and fitness. This does not deny the necessity of the analytic research on different biotic or psychic elements and complex parts of the whole system. However, it must be acknowledged that neurophysiological (biotic) and psychic events cannot be dissected one from another and understood separately. They are developing—and I try to show this—as an integrated entire feature of the behaving human organism, and only the special situation (internal motivation, external situation and influences, the state of the organism, or the lack of any morphological or functional essentials) decides whether the psychic or the biotic factors are more influential and more visible.

This holistic concept of human behavior as a self-organizing system in a changing environment includes the assumption that it is based on and uses many subordinated self-organizing subsystems of different complexity. However, as long as we look to the behavior of the entire human organism—as in sports and exercise—the deciding link is the highest psychic level that is part of self-organizing systems of higher order of complex subject-environmental (physical, biotic, societal) systems.

THE RELATIONSHIP BETWEEN GENETIC
AND EPIGENETIC FACTORS

We only can understand the development of the living organism if we consider the interrelationship between the genetic and epigenetic factors involved. The genetic factors are inherited and coded in the genetic rules, which are localized within the genome of each cell of the organism. During evolution, these genetic rules have been developed by selection and determine the principle directions and possibilities of the development of the new organism. However, the way in which these rules are realized under the respective conditions is decided by the epigenetic factors and influences. In humans, these epigenetic factors are biotic as well as social.

Let us demonstrate this by a well-studied example. It concerns the development of the motor innervation during the embryonic phase of the chicken (Figure 1). During the first embryonic days about 23,000 motoneurons are growing from the lumbar cord to reach the muscle cells in the periphery. Not all motoneurons find their target, and if more than one motoneuron comes in contact with one muscle cell, only one motoneuron survives and forms a synaptic junction; the others disappear. Those motoneurons that survive are the ones that are actually used. In

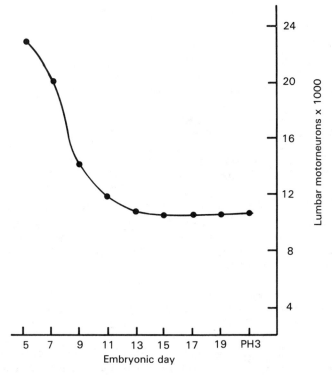

Figure 1   The number of motorneurons in the lumbar spinal cord during the development of the chicken embryo. Ordinate = number of lumbar motorneurons; abscissa = embryonic days, PH = after hatching.

many similar experiments, it was confirmed that about 50% of the genetically preprogrammed neurons are canceled during the time when the connections between the different cells are arranged. The same holds true for the development of the neuronal networks in the different levels of the central nervous system.

Therefore, we can formulate the following rules for the interrelationship between the genetic and epigenetic factors during early development. First, the genetic code determines the principles of the time scale and the spatial direction of the developing cellular elements, but not their final number and all details of their future connections. It begins the surplus production of cellular elements capable of performing the prospective function. Second, the selection of which of these elements survive and which disappear is accomplished by the influence of complex epigenetic factors, the most important of which is the use of the presumptive function. The only genetically possible programs that are realized are those that are used by the self-organizing organism to accomplish its vital aims within its respective environment.

In our special case (Figure 1), this means that the early movements of the embryo within the uterus are necessary to form the vital connections between the outgrowing motoneurons and their muscle targets. This process begins at a very early time and comprises elementary motor actions anticipatory before their final inclusion into vital goal-directed movements: flexion and extension of the extremities, movements of the head and of the body, sucking, and swallowing among others. This first use of the developing functional arcs is an instinctive training and the precondition for the realization of the possibilities given by the genetic code.

At birth, the division of nerve cells in the central nervous system is completed (i.e., their number can no longer increase). However, the forming of new connections between neurons and the development of intricate neuronal networks at the ascending levels in the central nervous system continues. The dynamics of this development, which is realized by the outgrowth of new axonal and dendritic branches and the formation of additional synapses, are also guided by the functional use—now we can call it a real training—of the respective pathways. It is overlapped by increasing learning processes. However, the priming of the inborn, inherited possibilities in the central nervous system by epigenetic influences continues at least up to 8 years of age. This is demonstrated by the fact that children with only one hemisphere (this damage may be inherited, or one hemisphere might have been removed for therapeutic reasons) later on can display completely normal behavior.

Therefore, the inborn drive to perform different movements must not be suppressed during this early age. Their continuously repeated performance is one of the most important—biotic as well as social—factors ensuring good preconditions for further physical and psychophysical education.

THE MATURATION OF THE ASCENDING LEVELS OF MOTOR PROGRAMMING AND MOTOR CONTROL

The behavioral acts of the living organism are organized, initiated, and controlled by neuronal ensembles or neural networks in the different levels of the central nervous system from the spinal cord up to the cortex. During the time in which the embryo develops to the adult organism, we have an ascending maturation of their morphofunctional biotic basis. Already in the uterus the embryo performs locomotory-like leg movements by which it can change position in the womb. Because they consist of coordinated agonistic and antagonistic movements of the extremities on both sides, already at this time a coordination program must exist in the spinal cord.

If shortly after birth we move a neonate in a vertical position slowly over a floor with the feet slightly touching the surface, the newborn performs regular locomotory movements. These rhythmic movements are elicited by the excitation of the sensory receptors in the skin of the sole and of the kinesthetic receptors of the passively moved legs, and are guided by a specific program in the neural network within the respective segment of the spinal cord. This shows that in the central nervous system there are self-organizing neural networks with inborn preprogrammed specialized functions.

At this age, the locomotory function is not needed, because the postural innervation of the body is not yet matured. Only at the end of the first year—after the stages of crawling, scrambling, and other movements on the ground—is the coordinated innervation of the body muscles matured so far that the child can try to perform the first spontaneous steps. Also, this much more complex program (dynamic maintenance of the vertical posture of the body, coordination of arm, head, and leg movements to maintain the balance, rhythmic locomotory movements, and so on) is initiated and controlled by the interconnected cooperation of neural networks hierarchically organized at different levels of the central nervous system. This can be shown by experiments in cats. If we stimulate a special small area in the midbrain of the cat, it performs rhythmic locmotory movements, and we can derive feedback signals from the dorsal spinal pathways going to the cerebellum (Arshavsky, Berkenblit, Gelfand, Orlovsley, & Fukson, 1972b).

During the following years, the child learns more and more skillfully to move in his or her changing environment; however, it lasts about 10 years, until a skillful, aesthetically looking locomotion is acquired. This type of locomotion is worked out and controlled by the highest level of brain functions, which are primed by social influences and goals and are guided by the conscious or unconscious intention to perform special goal-directed acts. These highest levels formulate the goals and initiate and control the more automatized motor programs in the deeper coordination levels of the brain and the spinal cord. The programs of these deeper levels must be relatively stable and self-regulating, whereas the flow of functions on the higher levels is more versatile and more adaptable to the changing situations.

In principle, all that was said regarding the development of locomotion also is valid for the development of all other types of motor actions including that associated with the development of speech and language. Therefore, an extensive performance of diverse motor activities by young children provides a good basis for their later physical and psychic development.

THE UNITY OF PERCEPTION AND ACTION

If we discuss the psychophysiology of sports, exercise, and fitness, we must always have in mind the unity of perception and action. Regarding the behavior of the entire organism, it is clear that any perceptions does not occur without action and no action occurs without perception. This is one of the basic principles of all organisms as self-organizing living systems (Figure 2). We can demonstrate this at all sensory modalities and at all behavioral output channels.

One of the best known examples is the sense of touch. If we try to recognize anything by touching with eyes closed, we handle the object with our fingers moving along the surface, around all its corners and so on. This is one of the most effective ways in which newborn children explore the objects they can grasp; in addition, they actively make use of their lips and their tongue, which are equipped with a great number of tactile receptors (sensory end organs for touching). Differently the motor output influences the events occurring in the auditory system. During normal hearing, the sound waves must be transmitted through the middle ear from the tympanic membrane to the oval window, the entrance to the cochlea. With the highest energy, this transmission is performed by three interconnected ossicles: the malleus, the incus, and the stapes. At the malleus and the stapes, two small muscles are attached, which, by the strength of their contraction, can change the transmission capability of the ossicles' chain.

The most important distant sense—the visual sense—has the most intricate motor control. This is already valid at the level of the retina. If the image of an object

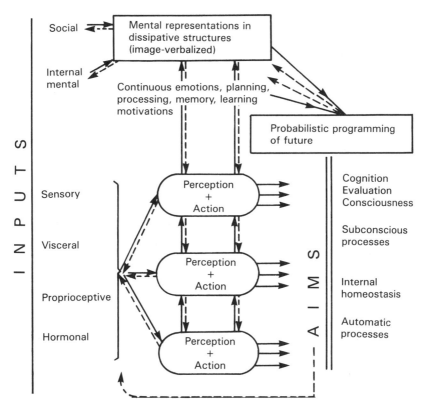

Figure 2 Unity of perception and action. The interrupted bottom line indicates the continuous feedback mechanism. See text for discussion.

is continuously projected to the same retinal cells, it fades after some seconds and finally disappears, because the rhodopsin within the retinal cells cannot be regenerated. Therefore, our eyes continuously perform tiny saccades of which we are not aware. In addition, the muscles of the eye and of the head and the movements of the whole body actively change the direction of the gaze and, in this way, the projection of the external objects on the retina. Ivo Kohler (1951) performed a very interesting experiment that demonstrated the importance of the motor activity for the correct adaptive functioning of the visual system. Instead of the usual eyeglasses, normal subjects had to wear glasses with prismatic lenses, which gave an inverted image of the surrounding world. The subjects had to wear these inverting glasses all day under their usual living conditions. On the first day, they performed all manipulations and locomotions wrong, because there was a lack of concordance between the real situation in the environment and the visual information. However, during the following days they adapted more and more to the new situation, and about 2 weeks later they could—wearing the inverting prisms—nearly behave in the correct way. The visual image of the surrounding world seemed to be inverted again, giving the correct visual information. If now the subjects took away their inverting prisms, the same disturbance occurred as at the beginning of the experiment, but the new adaptation took place in a much shorter time.

Kohler asked himself what could be the neurophysiological mechanism of this surprising adaptation to the reversed image of the surrounding environment. In response, he made a crucial experiment. The subject with the inverting prism was seated on a wheelchair, and his head and his hands were fixed so that he could not move them, and he was passively driven around in the same environment in which the other subjects could actively move and manipulate. After 2 weeks there was no sign of adaptation to the inverted world! This is a clear proof of the fact that the correct visual sensory function depends on the active motor behavior of the subject in the surrounding world. The visual system provides the morphofunctional preconditions for the representation of the environmental situation in our internal world, but this occurs only in the active coping with the real biotic and social influences of this world. There exists a complex self-organizing system between the integrated sensory-motor internal representations with all its additional subjective factors, such as emotion, motivation, memory, and so on, and the environmental opposing situation. This unity of perception and action also exists at the highest integrating levels of the human brain (Figure 2). Only thinking of a special situation includes subthreshold motor components, as may be seen by recording the electromyographic (EMG) activity of the muscles of the larynx, lips, or tongue.

Concerning the movements of our body and our extremities during daily life as well as during sports and exercise, the unity of motor and sensory functions is realized in a very well-studied specialized form. Each active, goal-directed movement may be regarded as being a self-organizing, self-controlling system consisting of efferent command signals and a complex sensory afferent input, which confirms whether the intended goal has been reached or not. This feedback control has been studied by many authors and at many different self-organizing levels. The first one who gave a principle scientific description of this system was N. A. Bernstein in 1929. He later published a scheme that includes all essential elements of this neurophysiological mechanism (Figure 3), which were also analyzed by

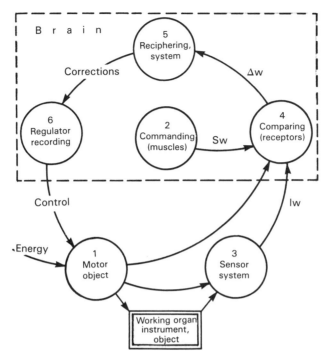

Figure 3 The feedback control system according to Bernstein (1967). It is the simplest possible block diagram of an apparatus for the control of movements. Sw = Sollwert (set-point value); Iw = Istwert (value of the performed action).

other authors (Anokhin, 1935; Sperry, 1950; Miller, Galanter, & Pribram, 1960; von Holst & Mittelstaedt, 1950). The crucial fact is that the efferent (motor) signal is stored for a short time as an efference copy (Soll-Wert), which after the performance of the motor act will be compared with the (reafferent) information (Ist-Wert) on the performed task. Anokhin (1967) called this the "receptor of the action results," and Sperry (1950) talked about the "corollary discharge." In the meantime many neurophysiological experiments have confirmed the existence of such a short-time storage of efferent commands.

The result of the comparison between the real result and the stored efference copy either confirms the adequacy of the executed program or, in the case of incongruity, it triggers a new behavior by looking for new external information ("orienting reaction") and using additional internal information, especially from higher coordination levels. This feedback confirmation is the neurophysiological basis of one type of learning. It is a way to better adapt the actual behavior to the conditions of the surrounding world.

The greatest part of this continuous control and of the small corrections of the performance of the motor actions occurs automatically at a subconscious level. The organism uses old automatized pathways with relatively fixed programs as long as they are sufficient. Therefore, the lower levels of the central motor organization are relatively stable and rigid. However, as soon as a disturbance occurs, higher levels with more complex and more adaptable programs are included to regulate the insufficiently coordinated movements and to develop a new, better fitting motor program. This process also may occur subconsciously, or conscious elements that are connected with the intended goal are included. If we are quickly going down a well-known staircase and unexpectedly the height of one stair has been changed, we stumble and are in danger of losing our balance. In this case, some more complex automatic reflex mechanisms are elicited immediately (reflectory changes of posture, grasping any support, and so on) to avoid a fall (i.e., to find a new equilibrium of the self-organizing system at the deeper levels). However, in addition the highest conscious (and unconscious) levels of the brain are set into action, evaluate the existing new situation, and initiate further measures to avoid an accident.

Therefore, one can conclude that the self-organizing, self-regulating systems at deeper levels are enlarged by including higher levels comprising more complex functions adaptable to the actual situation. As we see, the fitness of the organism depends on the interdependence of automatic genetic-epigenetic mechanisms, which are trained during the ontogenesis, and higher steering and controlling functions, which ensure the subtle regulation of the complex interrelationship between humans and their environment. In humans, this highest level is primarily dominated by subjective, psychic processes.

How may we understand the origin, development, and plastic efficacy of this qualitatively new, highest steering, controlling level?

THE INCREASING INTERNALIZATION OF MOVEMENT INITIATION AND MOVEMENT CONTROL

During evolution, the internal representation of signs of the surrounding environment in the central nervous system has grown more and more. At first, in the invertebrates and the lower vertebrates, this internal representation of external signs was mostly included in the genetic code and part of the self-organizing systemic interrelationship between the individual and the environment. By selection, only those individuals could survive who had inborn reactive programs—in correspondence with the internal situation—correctly reacting to the different external ecological cue stimuli. This phenomenon is called innate releasing mechanism.

With the increase of the central neural networks forming a more and more intricate biotic basis for information storage and information processing, an immense plastic field developed the processing, which was broadly extended by genetic-epigenetic mechanisms as shown previously here. Now, by the combined realization of the sensory-motor processing and the active behavior of the organism, the traits of the environmental situation that could elicit active behavioral acts ᵍrew. This means the internal storage of an increasing amount of of the environment, which, by learning, could trigger the correct ivity.

s of internalization, already in higher vertebrates and especially in ght on the storage of such a large number of environmental cues that the animal gets an optimal complex representation of all life-important ecological characteristics. This can be used not only to execute relatively rigid motor programs, but also to formulate new ones, to improve them for better adaptation, and to perform new strategies within the frame of the possibilities of their respective species.

In humans, however, these mental representations in dissipative brain structures acquire a new quality: subjective psychic experience, primarily determined by the social environment (Figure 2). This is a very important fact, if we talk about training and exercise. The biotic basis for this new quality at the highest steering level of the human brain is given by an immense increase in the number of neuronal cells that are organized in cortical columns and connected in dissipative neural networks. The number of neurons in each cortical column is estimated to be in the order of 10^3 and the number of columns amounts to about 10^7. If, in addition, we consider that each neuron has about 10^3 to 10^4 synapses, which undergo plastic changes if necessary, then the possibilities of forming and changing connections within the dissipative neural network of the brain are unimaginable. At this highest level of brain function, we no more have relatively rigid preprogrammed behavioral patterns, but continuously the connections within and between the neural networks at a large amount are changing and adapted to fit to the actual situation. According to the special individual (social or biotic) behavioral goals, which are formulated at this highest steering and controlling level of the human brain, the phenomena of which appear as (unconscious and conscious) psychic subjective experience, different types of network programs are continuously proved. In principle, the whole brain is participating in this highly intricate process (Edelman, 1987). The formulation of the goal and of the strategy to reach it is a probabilistic (stochastic) process. Bernstein (1967) indicated that the past is determined, and the present time is only the transition from the past to the future. However, our future behavioral activity is probabilistic, and its final execution may be decided in completely different ways. This process is going on at the highest psychic level of the brain with its immense plastic imaging and verbal representations.

The record of the electrical activity of the brain during a simple motor act can give us an obvious example for understanding this phenomenon. In Figure 4, a subject was instructed to press a key at a self-determined time. From the subject's scalp, the bioelectrical activity of the brain is recorded continuously. At time 0, the subject executes the task. However, already 800 msec in advance, an increasing negativity is indicating that neuronal circuits are beginning to be activated. This "readiness potential" (Bereitschaftspotential = BP) is recorded with its highest amplitude on both sides of the front and middle parts of the scalp (i.e., extensive neural networks of the brain are probabilistically participating in this central activation, as can also be seen by brain-mapping methods). In psychological terms, this is the period in which the subject "intends" to perform the voluntary movement (the period of probabilistic programming). In this process, widely distributed cortical areas, including areas in the frontal, association, and sensorimotor cortex, are participating. This BP is followed by a premotor positivity (PMP), which is expressed differently at the derivation points of both hemispheres. Only shortly before the execution of the movement (i.e., after the individual has decided what voluntarily to do) do we see a negative motor potential (MP) which is clearly restricted to the representation area in the motor cortex contralateral to the finger that will be moved. At the same time, we can record tonic preinnervation impulses

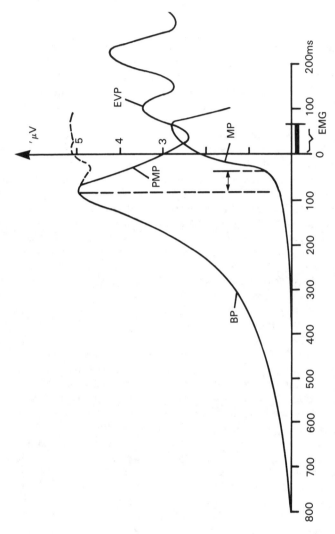

Figure 4 Derivation of the slow-wave electrical activity from the human brain immediately before and during the performance of a finger movement (pressing a button). BP = "Bereitschaftspotential" (readiness potential); PMP = premotor positivity; MP = motor potential; EVP = evoked potential. See text for discussion. (Adapted from "Distribution of Readiness Potential, Pre-Motion Positivity and Major Potential of the Human Cerebral Cortex, Preceding Voluntary Finger Movements" by L. Deecke, P. Scheid, and H. H. Kornhuber, 1969, *Experimental Brain Research, 7,* p. 758. Copyright 1969 by *Experimental Brain Research.* Adapted by permission.

in the periphery, preparing the optimal performance of the intended movement by the respective motor units. After all these internal preparations, which are mentally elicited (the subject has the intention to press) and are organized (according to the existing motor program) in the biotic central neural networks and by efferent impulses to the prospectively participating motor units, the subject presses the key.

In this example, the subject has only to perform a well-trained simple movement. Usually, during the continuously ongoing behavior, this probabilistic programming within the complex neural network of the brain is proceeded permanently. In children, the biotic basis of the higher psychic functions is slowly developing. It may and must be improved by supporting the optimal organization and fixation of the central representation of movement. This can be realized by imaging and verbal methods. The imaging method produces an image-like internal representation of the movement performed by the subject. At the beginning (in young children or during the learning of new motor coordinations in older people), this method gives a relatively feeble image with a large variability, if it is based only on its spontaneous appearance. This image may become more exact and more stable if the coach makes correcting remarks and explains what details of the entire movement must be improved. In addition, this method may be supported by the observation training. This means that the teacher, coach, or any experienced sportsperson demonstrates the correct execution of the respective exercise. This also can be realized by a demonstration on a monitor screen on which the correct performance is shown.

Another additional method is the application of biofeedback. Using this method, the performance of the motor program executed by the subject is recorded by videocamera and then displayed by a videorecorder shortly after the end of the exercise. In this case, as in the other ones, the teacher or coach gives a verbal explanation of the mistakes and how to perform the program in a better way. This additional verbal explanation is especially important in older children and in adult subjects. However, the verbal explanation may not be too abstract and must produce a vivid internal image of the exercise. For example, the description may be "performing a wheel along the vertical axis" instead of the usual nonillustrative professional term. The aim must be to create an easily understandable vivid image of the exercise intended.

All these methods are aimed at the fact that the subject receives a clearer and more vivid internal representation of his or her own movement. They confirm the subjective experience of the training athlete that arises by the afferent signals from the muscle, joint, and skin receptors. This helps to assimilate the imagined execution to the aspired prototype. However, one must consider that it is impossible consciously to imagine all details of the special exercise. The conscious representation is restricted to the exercise as a whole, to its fluent execution, and to single subtle details that are especially difficult to perform or that may be disturbed by any unexpected influence. We must bear in mind that, for the performance of the entire training program, all the deeper automatized programs are used, and only during the development of the automatization, or if the performance is not yet enough automatized or their automatized execution is disturbed, the highest unconscious and conscious psychic levels are included.

THE NEUROPHYSIOLOGICAL MECHANISM
OF THE IDEOMOTOR TRAINING

If, at the highest level of our central neural networks, we have a representation of our well-trained, learned motor programs that is well tuned to the motor programs stored at deeper levels, which are used for their performance, one can imagine that it must be possible mentally to train at this representation level, to make the already existing programs more precise, and to develop new connections between existing program details. Such a possibility actually exists, but regarding the considerations in our preceding chapters we must attend to some special rules.

Already in the middle of the last century, Carpenter (1877) stated that if a subject is asked to exert a motor action of his or her arm in the mind without actually doing any movement, the observer can feel—palpating the muscles of this arm—a real muscle tension. This means that the mere idea of the muscle contraction is accompanied by a flow of impulses going from the brain to the respective muscles. Carpenter interpreted this observation correctly and called it "ideomotor phenomenon."

About 15 years ago, we decided systematically to study this phenomenon, which already was empirically and sometimes intentionally applied in the training process of physical culture. Most people called it "mental training." In this article I demonstrate this phenomenon in the special case of swimming and try to give a neurophysiological explanation.

One male subject, well trained in swimming, is sitting on a comfortable chair. The subject is completely relaxed and not disturbed by external influences. He is asked to concentrate on a special imaginative process: In his mind, he should imagine that he is in a competitive situation standing on the starting place at the swimming pool. Then, at a moment decided by himself he should spring into the water and pass over the distance of 50 m and back with his highest possible velocity. He is ordered to press a button, when he is mentally starting (Figure 5). He is ordered to press the button once more, if he stroked the goal, and then ended his imagined swimming.

In Figure 5 we give the record of the respiration rate of one subject during this ideomotor swimming. The record was accomplished by a heat-sensitive transistor fastened before his nose. We measured the intervals between the single breathings, as can be seen on the ordinate. Therefore, the decline on the curve means an increase in respiration rate. Figure 5 shows that immediately after the imagined start (first arrow) the respiration rate increases very much; at the imagined turn (after the first 50 m) it diminishes a little; and on the second half of the distance it increases again. At the end of the imagined swimming (second arrow), the respiration rate decreases beyond its initial value, because the hyperventilation without any physical work has produced a hyperoxemia (surplus of oxygen in the blood).

If we look to Figure 5, we can follow what is going on in the mind of the subject. We have numerous records of this type, and many of which demonstrate that the subjects did not really perform an intensive mental training. Sometimes one can clearly see that they are doing nothing in their mind. The background of this complete congruence between the respiration rate and the imagined velocity of the ideomotor swimming is given by the fact that during real swimming the athlete has the possibility to breathe only if his nose is outside of the water. This means in well-trained subjects we have a complete synchronization between the arm strokes

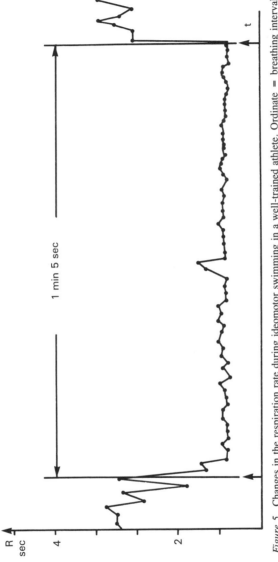

Figure 5 Changes in the respiration rate during ideomotor swimming in a well-trained athlete. Ordinate = breathing intervals; abscissa; first arrow = mentally springing into the water; second arrow = arriving at the goal (Pickenhain, 1979).

and the breathing rate (the relation between them must be a constant integer value like 1:1, 2:1, or so). This synchronization must be a part of the complex central program for swimming. As we see, these central programs for the performance of special types of exercise include not only motor but also vegetative components.

It is very informative to compare the changes of the vegetative functions and of the electroencephalogram (EEG) parameters. For this purpose, during ideomotor training one of my collaborators (Weisz, 1988) simultaneously recorded the heart rate and one parameter of the alpha-frequency of the EEG at the precentral and occipital derivation points. These experiments were done in well-trained bobsled athletes. The ideomotor task was to train a competitive run three times with interruptions of 3 minutes. In Figure 6 the heart rate changes are demonstrated. One can see that during each ideomotor training period the heart rate increases to high values. However, during the intervals without ideomotor activity the heart rate rapidly decreases to its initial values. The EEG data display a completely different picture (Figure 7). The alpha-frequency also increases during the first ideomotor training, but during the following 3 minutes of rest the value does not decrease again. It remains at the heightened level and shows an additional, but smaller increase with the next ideomotor training period, and it also does not return to the initial value after the three times that ideomotor training has been finished.

What can we conclude from this different behavior of vegetative and central nervous functions during the ideomotor training? Obviously, the EEG changes reflect the motivation of the subjects, which was produced by the given instruction. This instruction elevated the attention and activated widely distributed neural

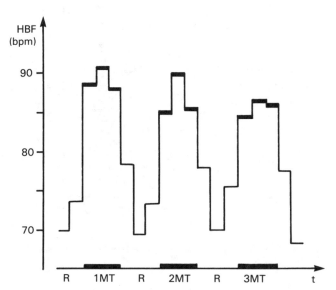

Figure 6 Heart rate (HBF) during three consecutive ideomotor training (MT) with intervals (R) of 3 min. (Adapted from "Einflusz Bunterschiedlicher Belastungen auf Kenziffern zentralnervaler Aktivievungsprozesse" by T. Weisz, 1980, unpublished doctoral dissertation, University of Leipzig. Adapted by permission).

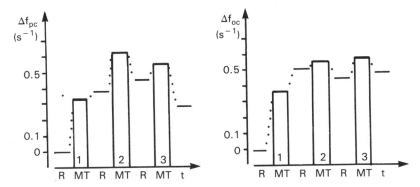

Figure 7 Differences of the alpha = frequency (Δf) related to the initial frequency in the precentral (pc) (left) and occipital (oc) (right) derivation during three repetitions (R) of ideomotor training (MT) with intervals of 3 minutes. (Adapted from "Ernflusz Bunterschiedlicher Belastungen and Kennizeffern zentrvalnervaler Aktivierungsprozesse" by T. Weisz, 1980, unpublished doctoral dissertation, University of Leipzip. Adapted by permission).

networks in the brain in which the goal-directed behavior—in this case the ideomotor behavior—was probabilistically programmed, maintained, initiated, and corrected. This central processing can be followed at the permanently increased EEG values in the occipital as well as in the precentral areas. On the other hand, the vegetative functions (heart rate and respiration rate) are included only during the (mental) realization of the efferent function. This clearly shows that the guiding mechanism of the whole process is organized at the highest (i.e., psychic) level with its probabilistically organized neural networks from which the deeper functional levels of the central nervous system and of the periphery are triggered. They include the different participating vegetative—and as may be supposed also some metabolic—changes. Therefore, one can conclude that the vegetative parameters are not necessarily parts of the guiding central (psychic) program. The subject does not imagine faster breathing or a higher heart frequency. The subject only imagines that the goal given by the instruction and the accompanying vegetative changes are the consequence of the fact that the imagined program triggers lower levels of the central nervous function for the execution.

There arises one principal question. As we have seen, the learning process is realized by the intermodal feedback and the feedback of the result. However, in our examples, both are lacking because there does not occur any movement at all. Some people have questioned whether, during the ideomotor training, any training could occur at all. However, the practical application of these methods shows that actually the fixation of already learned processes as well as real new learning are possible. The compelling conclusion must be that in these cases an additional internal feedback at the different levels of the central nervous system occurs (Figure 8).

In each active behavior, the subject, on the basis of needs, experience, memory, and other internal arguments—in our case on the basis of the instruction—formulates a goal that may be vital or only given by the actual situation (or instruction). By probabilistic programming, the subject is proving with internal models in

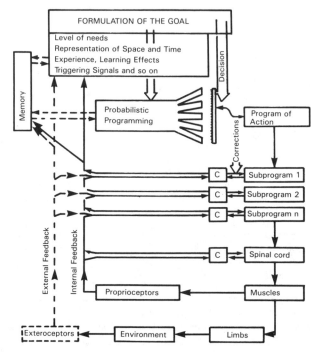

Figure 8   Scheme of planning and performance of a voluntary
movement with its different biofeedback information
channels. Uninterrupted lines = obligatory information
channels; interrupted lines = facultative information
channels; C = comparator elements (corollary
discharge). (Adapted from "Das Verhalten" in
Neurobiologie, edited by D. Biesold and H. Matthies,
1977, Jena, East Germany: Fischer. Copyright 1977 by
Fischer. Adapted with permission.)

which way this goal may be reached. Finally, a decision is made—also coming
from the highest steering level of the brain—and a special program is initiated. To
perform it, many subprograms at deeper levels must be activated, including vegetative functions. At each deeper level, efferent copies (corollary discharges = C)
are stored and compared with the feedback signals of the subprograms of the next
deeper level (or levels). Already at this stage corrections may be possible, if the
internal loop of the respective levels makes this necessary.

The existence of such internal feedback loops between different levels was
shown by Arshavsky et al. (1972a, 1972b). During acute experiments in decere-
brated cats, the authors stimulated the midbrain locomotion center and, in this
manner, elicited rhythmic locomotory movements. They then interrupted the ventral and dorsal roots of the spinal cord through which the motor and sensory
impulses to and from the muscles are transmitted. This operation abolished the
motor innervation of the leg muscles as well as the sensory feedback. They next
introduced microelectrodes into the ventral (efferent, motor) and the dorsal (afferent, sensory) spinocerebellar pathways within the spinal cord. In this preparation

they observed that the impulse trains in the ventral pathway, elicited by the stimulation of the midbrain "locomotory center" and only signaling a "fictive" locomotion, after a short delay were followed by similar impulse trains in the dorsal afferent pathway. This demonstrates that the efferent impulse trains were transmitted at the spinal level through interneurons to the dorsal afferent pathways (i.e., to higher levels of the central nervous system). Therefore, we can assume that indeed at different intermediate levels internal feedback and comparison mechanisms exist (Pickenhain, 1977). Other authors have confirmed these experiments.

In conclusion, it can be stated that because of these internal feedback loops during ideomotor training learning processes are possible. However, from these results one can also conclude some principal assumptions concerning the necessary type of this ideomotor training, if it should be effective:

1. The subject who wishes to perform ideomotor training must have previous training experience with the respective exercise or parts of it. Up to some degree, the subject must already master and have performed the respective program or parts of it with the adequate subprograms included.

2. The subject must very vividly imagine the respective training program as being actively exerted by him- or herself. This imagination must be so vivid that the subject feels a real exertion of the participating muscles without any real movement. This means that the deeper levels of the motor system are included. Therefore, we prefer to use the term ideomotor instead of mental (at the highest level only) training (Figure 8). According to our concept, ideomotor training includes more than only mental training, more than mere concentration and elevation of attention, which are only an obligatory part of it.

3. After several (perhaps 6 to 10) performances, the ideomotor training program must alternate with one or some real performances of the respective exercise. This feedback confirmation by the real performance effect is necessary, because the self-sustaining internal feedback mechanisms underlie the fundamental working principle of the central neural networks, which follow probabilistic rules. Small changes (errors) in the stored programs at the different central levels included can summarize and cause small deviations from the intended optimal program. This can be prevented by the interpolation of some real exercises with the whole intermodal feedback and the feedback of result.

Considering all these internal mechanisms during ideomotor training, one question remains. If the neuronal motor impulses actually reach the respective muscles, and in many cases may be recorded by means of the EMG, why do the (perhaps slightly) innervated muscles not move? The answer is simple. The coach or the experimenter simultaneously gives two instructions: At first, in mind to perform the ideomotor training; and second, not to perform any movement. Of course, the second instruction triggers the innervation of the respective antagonists (the effect of which also can be recorded by EMG), and therefore no movement occurs. This additionally makes a difference between the ideomotor and the real training, but obviously the inhibition of the real movement by the innervation of the antagonistic muscles does not disturb the ideomotor training effect.

PSYCHOPHYSIOLOGY OF MOVEMENT

The formation, development, and performance of human motor acts can be understood only as an intrinsic part of human behavior, as a step-wise development of a self-organizing system consisting of the human organism and the biotic and social environment in which the human organism plays the primary active role to maintain its integrity and to accomplish by training and exercise a better physical and psychic fitness. Obviously, the highest level of the brain with subtly organized and adaptively working intricate neural circuits plays the leading role in this system. By the new quality of the brain's function, the psychic function, the human organism has a much better possibility not only of storing the past events in nonverbal and verbal terms, but also of constructing varying probabilistic models of the future events (Bernstein, 1967). Considering the high complexity of these central sensory motor programs, we never may forget their composition of self-organizing systems, their plasticity, and their existence as a unified adaptive whole.

The internal representation of the internalized motor programs is mostly unconscious. Only the crucial points of it (the general goal or deciding parts of it, the basic strategy to reach the goal, special learning sets, real or supposed disturbances of the performance, and so on) are experienced consciously. This shall be demonstrated by two experiments.

One part of our internal representation is the so-called body scheme. It is of fundamental importance because it is necessary for the organization of spatially oriented motor behavior, for the mutual relationship among the different parts of the body, and for their plastic adaptation to the environmental situation. Gurfinkel, Debreva, and Levik (1986) showed that this internal body scheme disposes a high degree of autonomy. In subjects with eyes closed, the authors partially ligated the right arm for 30 to 40 minutes by this ligature to produce a permanent ischemia. The effect was a model of an artificial "phantom limb," as if a limb must have been amputated. With the eyes closed, the subject has the impression that the removed limb yet exists. However, it seems to be shortened and to perform uncontrollable movements. Also in Gurfinkel et al.'s model experiment, the artificial phantom limb was seemingly shortening more and more, and the subject exerted spatially shifted fictive flexor and extensor movements. If the subject (with eyes closed) performed aiming movements with the unimpaired left arm, these movements were correct. However, if these movements were directed to circumscribed points on the right (phantom) arm, they failed their aim. Rather, these movements were directed to the respective points on the phantom extremity. This means the movement was performed according to the spatial representation field in the mentally imagined "body scheme," which had been changed by the experimental conditions. This experiment shows the immense importance of the internal representation for the planning and execution of movements. However, in the same experiment it could be shown that the situation immediately changed if the subject opened his or her eyes. This confirms the great importance of the visual afferences for spatial orientation and movement control.

Very important results concerning the organization and control of posture and movement were reported by Berthoz (1987). He instructed his subjects to maintain special postures, as if they were prepared and intended to perform different visuomotor tasks: throwing the javelin, putting the shot, expecting the start in the starting hole, simulating boxing, and so on. Berthoz, took photographs of the different postures and diligently analyzed the positions of the entire body, the extremities, the head, and the eye movements. Interestingly, Berthoz found that the mere observation of the gaze and the eye movements gave the possibility of predicting the intended type of movement. He proposed that the eye movement-related afferent signals adjust postural mechanisms according to the intended direction of gaze. They are measurable expressions of the shifts that occur at the level of the internal representation of the body in space depending on the sensory-motor goal.

In conclusion, Berthoz (1987) assumed that "posture and movements are controlled at two levels: (a) by servo-assisted, vectorial, continuous, nonpredictive, local mechanisms (akin to local self-sustaining reflex-like systems and subserved by hard-wired synergies), and (b) by topological, discontinuous, predictive, global mechanisms based upon internal representation, which allows posture and movement to be planned and simulated without motor execution" (p. 575). This second level elaborates motor strategies (i.e., combinations of strategies), and specifies sensory cues to be sampled according to the postural task and context. Again, analyzing the dynamic changes of posture in combination with movements, it is found that the distinction between the top level of neural networks and circuits at which the probabilistic planning of future behavior is organized in plastic continuously changing self-organizing systems and the deeper levels with relatively fixed self-sustaining and self-correcting programs, which are used for the execution of the entire complex behavioral program. One aim of training must be to organize and stabilize the mostly automatic operation of the functions on these deeper levels, which, however, must be changeable enough to serve different purposes in a stable way. The second aim is directed to train the variability and disposability of the highest (psychic) steering and controlling level to build up and initiate many different programs to reach the intended goals.

In summary the following principal scheme is presented (Figure 9). The interrelationship between the human organism and the environment may be interpreted as a self-organizing, adaptive system that consists of a great number of self-organizing subsystems. The human organism and human behavior are determined by closely interwoven biotic and social structures and functions and according to the individual's special living conditions, the social factors and influences play the leading role. This is realized in the individual by the fact that the highest steering and controlling level has the specific new quality of the human psychic phenomena and processes. They have their biotic basis at the highest level of the human brain, which is characterized by an immense amount of intricate neural circuits and neural networks. Their capacity for information storage and processing is so gigantic that their representational possibilities with their great variabilities are capable of storing and processing symbolic and semantic contents that give humans the possibility for social communication and social life in a respective social environment. This is no reductionist view, but only the acknowledgment of the fact that without the individual human brain there are no psychic phenomena at all, and there is no social life.

To understand these highly integrated complex processes as a whole, we must apply the results and ideas of modern scientific theories like system theory, synergetic, and so on. These theories give the possibility of comprising the dynamics and the development in very complex systems, which consist of parts possessing completely different qualities (in our case inorganic matter, organic matter, psy-

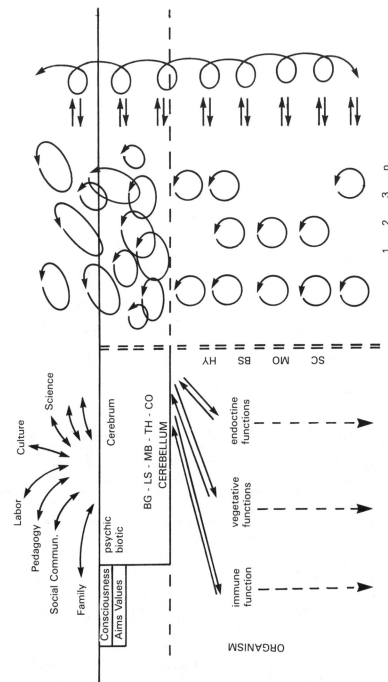

Figure 9 Scheme demonstrating the self-organizing system of subject and society, the self-organizing subsystems within the organism, and between the organism and its environment, and the downward and upward influences between the different levels of organization. SC = spinal cord; MO = medulla oblongata; BS = brainstem; HY = hypothalamus; BG = basal ganglia; LS = limbic system; TH = thalamus; CO = cerebral cortex.

chic functions, social relations). Regarding our scheme in Figure 9 the following points should be stressed. First, the highest steering and controlling level of the organism is the level of the higher brain functions (or as Pavlov called it, the higher nervous activity). Its semantic content is primed by multiple external social influences coming from the past (tradition, education, culture) and actual societal influences, the information of which is processed and evaluated in the internal semantic representational field. The evaluation is accompanied by emotional and affective effects (in which the limbic structures play the deciding role) and followed by the motivation to execute more or less adapted motor behavior. Second, this highest psychic steering level of the human brain uses all endocrine and vegetative functions for the realization of its aims. As we now know, psychic influences are also very important for the optimal activity of the immune functions of the human body. Third, the bionic basis of this psychic level is organized within the highly integrated neural networks of the cerebrum—the cerebral cortex, thalamus, basal ganglia, limbic system, midbrain, and cerebellar structures. They are inborn and by learning later on changed, and developed connection patterns in dissipated brain structures are the plastic, adaptable representation field in which different self-organizing systems may be activated according to the actual needs of the organism and the given environmental conditions. During the dynamic information processing, the probabilistic search for solutions at this dissipated representational level can include different parts of various neural networks within the mentioned higher brain structures into the necessary self-organizing functional systems. This dynamic process also uses environmental bionic and social factors as essential components of the actual self-organizing systems. I only wish to remind readers that the human being continuously uses self-produced external symbols and signs as part of an internalized probabilistic information processing (Pickenhain, in press).

Fourth, contrary to this higher level self-organizing system, which is organized with many degrees of freedom, the deeper levels up to some parts of the hypothalamus have relatively stable self-organizing functional systems used by the higher dynamic levels to perform the intended behavioral acts (goal-directed movements, posture stabilization, the inclusion of metabolic and vegetative functions, and so on). They are, as Berthoz (1987) indicated, servo-assisted and secured by nonpredictive, local, self-controlling mechanisms. With the numbers 1, 2, 3, and n (in Figure 9), we have marked some functions that dispose on self-organizing systems at several hierarchically built-up levels (No. 1 for locomotion, No. 2 for grasping, No. 3 for any other specialized movements of the foot and so on).

Fifth all these functional systems with their self-organizing working principles are continuously connected together by upward and downward signal (indicated at the right side of Figure 9). The upward signals are the biofeedback information working at all levels and including feedback information from outside the organism, as shown. The downward signals are the trigger impulses from the higher levels, including the highest (psychic) steering and controlling level, which can change all functions at the deeper levels (changing the set point for the body temperature during long-distance running, lowering the pH values of the blood during long-lasting heavy exercise to such deep values that are normally incompatible with the life functions).

CONCLUSIONS

To understand the importance of psychophysiology for sports, exercise, and fitness, one must elucidate how psychophysiological mechanisms develop and how they work. Sports and exercise are societal phenomena organized by individuals within their social environment. However, at the same time these people must train their body functions to become competitive. Therefore, it seems necessary to understand the relationship between the biotic and social factors for the development of the highest steering and controlling level of the human being.

Most people working in sports education and training are only looking for the fitness of the body functions and do not acknowledge that the athlete also has a brain. However, now we must note that the highest brain functions are more important for an effective training, because the usual body-oriented training programs are well known and their possibilities for further development are nearly exhausted. In this situation, the most important and deciding factor in modern sports—on the background of a well-organized and effective body training—is the psychic influence. The fundamentals, the frame, and the deciding factors for this influence on the better development of training efficacy and fitness development were, I hope, demonstrated in this article.

Again, in humans the deciding level for the solution of all behavioral problems including the questions of training exercise and fitness is the psychic level, which has its biotic fundamentals in the highest neural network systems of the human brain.

REFERENCES

Anokhin, P. K. (Ed.). (1935). *The problem of the center and the periphery in the physiology of nervous activity.* Gorki, University Press.

Anokhin, P. K. (1967). *Das funktionelle System als Grundlage der physiologischen Architektur des Verhaltensaktes.* Jena, East Germany: Fischer.

Arshavsky, J. I., Berkenblit, M. B., Gelfand, I. M., Orlovsky, G. N., Fukson, O. I. (1972a). Activity of the neurons in the dorsal spinocerebellar pathway during locomotion. *Biofizika, 17,* 487–494.

Arshavsky, J. I., Berkenblit, M. B., Gelfand, I. M., Orlovsky, G. N., Fukson, O. I. (1972b). Activity of the neurons in the ventral spinocerebellar pathway during locomotion. *Biofizika, 17,* 883–890.

Bernstein, N. A. (1967). *The coordination and regulation of movements.* Oxford: University Press.

Berthoz, A. (1987). Influence of gaze on postural mechanisms. *Neuroscience, 22,* (Suppl.), S575.

Carpenter, W. B. (1877). *Mesmerism and spiritualism.* London.

Deecke, L., Scheid, P., & Kornhuber, H. H. (1969). Distribution of readiness potential, pre-motion positivity and motor potential of the human cerebral cortex, preceding voluntary finger movements. *Experimental Brain Research, 7,* 158–168.

Drowatzky, J. N. (1975). *Motor learning: Principles and practices.* Minneapolis, MN: Burgess.

Edelman, G. (1987). *Neural Darwinism: The theory of neuronal group selection.* New York: Basic Books.

Ford, D. H. (1987). Humans as self-constructing living systems. Hillsdale, NJ: Erlbaum.

Gurfinkel, V. S., Debreva, E. E., & Levik, J. S. (1986). The significance of the internal model for the position perception and movement control of the hand. *Fiziologicheskii Cheloveka.* (Moscow), *12,* 769–776.

Kohler, I. (1951). Über Aufbau und Wandlungen der Wahrnehmungswelt, insbesondere über 'bedingte Empfindungen.' Sitzungsber. österr. Akad. Wiss. Wien, Phil.-histor. Klasse, *227,* 1–118.

Miller, G. A., Galanter, E., & Pribram, K. H. (1960). *Plans and the structure of behavior.* New York: Holt, Rinehart and Winston.

Oppenheim, R. W. (1985). Naturally occurring cell death during neural development. *Trends in Neuroscience, 8,* 487–493.

Pickenhain, L. (1976). Die Bedeutung innerer Rückkopplungskreise für den Lernvorgang (gezeigt am Beispiel des motorischen Lernens). *Zeitchrift fur Psychologie, 184,* 551–561.

Pickenhain, L. (1977). Das Verhalten. In L. Biesold, H. Matthies, (Eds.), *Neurobiologie* (pp. 693–733). Jena, East Germany: Fischer.

Pickenhain, L. (1984). Towards a holistic conception of movement control. In H. T. A. Whiting (Ed.), *Human motor actions—Bernstein reassessed* (pp. 505–528). Amsterdam: North-Holland.

Pickenhain, L. (in press). *Evolutionsgeschichtliche Voraussetzungen tierieschen und menschlichen Verhaltens.*

Pickenhain, L. (in press). *Das ideomotorische Training und seine neurophysiologischen Grundlagen.*

Sperry, R. W. (1950). Neural basis of the spontaneous optokinetic response produced by visual inversion. *Journal of Comparative and Physiological Psychology, 43,* 482–489.

Stelmach, G. E. (Ed.). (1976). Motor control. Issues and trends. New York: Academic.

von Holst, E., & Mittelstaedt, H. (1950). Das Reafferenzprinzip. *Naturwissenschaften, 37,* 464–476.

Weib, T. (1980). *Einflub unterschiedlicher Belastungen auf Kennziffern zentralnervaler Aktivierungsprozesse (EEG-Studie).* Unpublished doctoral dissertation, University of Leipzig.

5

Athletic Activity, Body Image, and Adolescent Identity

Ann E. McCabe, Brenda T. Roberts, and Theresa E. Morris
University of Windsor

This chapter is concerned with adolescents' participation in athletics, the impact of this participation on body image, and how this relationship affects the development of a sense of identity. A review of the literature on the relationships among these variables reveals a preponderance of data indicating that boys and girls differ with respect to how athletic ability and participation affect body image and identity. Thus, it is often necessary to consider these issues separately for boys and girls.

In our discussion, we review some of the issues surrounding identity, body image, and athletic ability. We then consider the complex interrelationships that exist among these phenomena in adolescence, focusing on the aspects of these issues that are involved in their interaction.

IDENTITY

Few readers will be unfamiliar with the term "identity crisis." Since Erik Erikson (1950) introduced the argument that the development of a sense of identity is the major task confronting the adolescent, the term "identity crisis" has been borrowed and used to refer to virtually any life event that involves an individual questioning his or her sense of self. The term has become so popular that the majority of people who currently use it probably know nothing of Erikson's work or the original intent of the term.

Erikson viewed the period of adolescence as one during which the combination of internal and external forces acting upon the individual brought about the need to form a definition of self that would provide a sense of continuity between past, present, and future. If successful in resolving this crisis, the adolescent would go forward into adult life with a strong and stable sense of self, ready to tackle subsequent life crises. If unsuccessful, the adolescent would be left with a sense of "role confusion" and stumble forward into adulthood without a core sense of self. The lack of a sense of identity would leave the individual adrift in adulthood, unable to deal adequately with future crises or to experience a satisfying life.

Why should adolescence be the time of the identity crisis? As the individual embarks on the transition from childhood to adulthood, a wide variety of changes, both internal and external, provide the impetus for a fundamental self reevaluation. As described by Remschmidt (1975), sudden physical changes occur in adolescence before the individual is socially or economically mature. The adolescent must attempt to establish a sex role, confirm a value system, and prepare for a role in society at the same time he or she is attempting to deal with biological maturity and the reactions of others to that new maturity. The combination of these changes and demands brings the need for a reevaluation of self. It is the process of this reevaluation that is the adolescent identity crisis.

For much of the first 10 years of life, the child operates with a degree of certainty concerning what is expected of her or him by others and a confidence in who she or he is. Although it is obviously untrue that childhood is free of worry or conflict, it is clear that when compared with the uncertainty facing the adolescent, childhood can be seen as a relatively quiescent period. Once having entered the transition period of adolescence, internal and external changes of such a fundamental nature occur that it is necessary to redefine oneself.

James Marcia (1966) subsequently refined and extended Erikson's notions by obtaining empirical evidence of the process of identity formation among adolescents. Marcia defined four statuses in identity formation. From Erikson's writings, one can expect to see a sequence in the formation of identity whereby the individual moves from a child's sense of self through a period of questioning and searching to the eventual establishment in adolescence of a mature sense of identity, or if the process is not successful, to a state where the individual has given up the search for an identity. The achievement of a mature sense of identity is Marcia's "identity achieved" status. Those who consider themselves to have failed in the process and are no longer seeking an identity are referred to as, in Erikson's term, "identity diffused." Individuals who are in the active search process are in a "moratorium status." Marcia also defined an additional group—"identity foreclosed"—which includes individuals who have not experienced the crisis of searching for an identity, but have instead accepted a preformed identity. These adolescents may have adopted a definition of themselves that corresponds with one that their parents prescribed for them or that was provided by some other external agency.

Erikson's early writings and those of Marcia tended to focus on occupational choice. That is, the selection of one's life's work and the initial preparation for it were considered by these writers to constitute a major part of identity formation. Subsequent writers have discussed identity in a broader context. In addition to the beginning of career preparation in adolescence and its accompanying changes, other changes also occur: physical changes, changes in the adolescent's cognitive abilities, changes in the social milieu in which the adolescent operates, and changes in the way familial and extrafamilial others behave toward the adolescent.

The most obvious changes in adolescence are the extensive and rapidly occurring physical changes associated with the onset of puberty. How the adolescent experiences these changes and comes to terms with his or her new physical status has a major impact on the sense of identity.

The physical changes of adolescence begin with a rapid increase in the length of the long bones in arms and legs. Increases of 6 inches in a year are common. Rapid changes in facial features, particularly the growth to adult size of the lower jaw and the nose, also occur at this time. Sex organs begin to mature and secondary sex characteristics, such as pubic and axillary hair and breasts, emerge. The majority of these changes take place within a relatively short period of time, typically between the ages of approximately 11 and 13 for girls and about 12 and 14 for boys (Santrock, 1987).

Thus, the adolescent sees a physically different person upon looking in the mirror (which most adolescents do quite often!). How does one reconcile this new physical appearance with the sense of who one is?

The reaching of sexual maturity brings about not only changes in appearance, but also changes in feelings and interests. Sexual urges and interests, which have been relatively quiet during childhood, now become much more intense. Adolescents do not become all consumed by sexual motives as some have charged; nevertheless, interests in sex and in the opposite sex in general begin to occupy much more of the adolescent's consciousness. The role as a being who may be attractive to as well as attracted by the opposite sex becomes part of the new self-definition. As is discussed later, the extent to which one's physical appearance matches an ideal is a factor in the process of self-evaluation and in the extent to which the adolescent is comfortable with the new identity of semiadult.

Along with these physical changes are concomitant changes in the individual's cognitive capacities. Theorists of cognitive development (Inhelder & Piaget, 1958; Werner, 1948) have described the thought processes of adolescence as qualitatively different from those of younger children. In childhood, thinking is on a concrete level and nonreflective. Although children can often reason logically, the range of this logic is limited, confined to things with which they are familiar. With adolescence comes the capacity to think abstractly, to consider what is possible, to reflect on one's own thinking, and to recognize these same capacities in others. Thus, unlike the child who understands what is, the adolescent begins to consider what is possible. The ability to consider what is possible fundamentally changes how the world is viewed. People are no longer seen as simply playing defined roles in society, but as making choices of the roles they play. The adolescent begins to question the choices made by others, for example, with respect to occupation, religious affiliation, and political persuasion, and more important, begins to see how his or her own choices will affect her or his own life and the functioning of society as a whole. The choice of how to be, then, becomes crucial. The ramifications of the change in thinking ability are pervasive, but despite these advances in cognitive capacities, the adolescent's thought processes remain immature relative to those of the adult.

This lack of maturity in the adolescent's thinking is expressed well by Elkind (1967). The new capacities for abstract thinking and reflection along with an inability to take a detached view produce a peculiar kind of egocentric thinking in the adolescent. Insight into the features of this adolescent egocentrism as described by Elkind provide, in the view of the present authors, some of the most useful clues to the understanding of adolescent thought and behavior.

According to Elkind, there are two related facets of adolescent egocentrism; the imaginary audience and the personal fable. The former is dependent on the adolescent's new-found capacity for reflection. This reflectivity of thinking allows an assessment and evaluation of self in broad terms, but also in terms of details of appearance and behavior. Furthermore, the adolescent recognizes this capacity of thinking in others. The egocentric aspect of this thinking is the adolescent's failure to recognize that the object of her or his own thought—him or herself—is not necessarily the object of the thought of others. As is easily imaginable, the assumption that oneself is the object of the thought and evaluation of everyone with whom one comes in contact creates some considerable stress for the individual. The adolescent knows him or herself excruciatingly well, including knowing all the failings in behavior and the imperfections in appearance. The assumption that others are as immediately and acutely aware of these shortcomings contributes to the depressed feelings not uncommon among adolescents. The imaginary audience has its positive aspects as well. The adolescent equally assumes that others are aware of her or his strengths and achievements, which contributes to the euphoric feelings also not uncommon among adolescents. The effect of the imaginary audience on the adolescent is that he or she feels constantly "on stage" to a highly critical audience.

The second facet of adolescent egocentric thinking, according to Elkind, is the "personal fable." The capacity to consider possibilities leads the adolescent to dream and plan for the future. These dreams and plans generally are elaborate constructions of the great things that will be achieved by the dreamer. There is no limit, and there are no obstacles to what can be achieved in the imagination. Usually these constructions take the form of the adolescent achieving something of great value of humankind such as discovering the cure for a disease or finding the secret to universal and lasting peace. The idealism implicit in these mental constructions is both useful and healthy because the pursuit of such goals serves as a strong motivating force. However, they can create difficulties for the individual in several ways. Because the achievements dreamed of have never been attained by anyone, it is unlikely, to the adolescent's way of thinking, that they could be understood by anyone. Thus, they are private plans. From this comes the adolescent cry that "nobody understands me." Moreover, if one is destined for greatness, it is inconceivable that the "powers that be" (i.e., God or whatever force in which the adolescent believes) would allow anything negative to happen to one. This latter way of thinking often leads adolescents to take foolish risks in the belief that they are immune from harm.

In addition to and partially as the result of the physical and cognitive changes occurring in adolescence, there are pressures from others to assume more adult roles. Parents, peers, and community agencies such as schools begin to demand more mature behavior from the adolescent. The adolescent, in concert with these pressures, begins to expect more autonomy.

The striving for independence from the family is the result of both internal and external forces acting on the adolescent. It has been argued (Havighurst, 1972) that the major task of adolescence is to achieve some measure of independence from the family. Indeed, it can be argued that the entire period of childhood and adolescence is directed toward attaining independence from the family. During the period of adolescence, however, the process reaches a peak. Achieving independence and attaining a sense of identity interact in a complex manner during the adolescent period. With the adolescent's increasingly adult physical appearance, both the adolescent and others begin to expect more adult privileges and responsibilities. Typically, the adolescent presses for more privileges, while family members and others press for more responsibilities. Contrary to popular opinion, there are usually not high levels of conflict between parents and adolescents. Commonly, the adolescent and the family work out ways to meet these new mutual expectations without major conflict (King, 1972). The change in roles does cause adolescents to think of themselves in more adult terms, which requires some self-redefinition.

The adolescent's peers are experiencing the same pressures and, thus, the peer group provides a haven in which individuals can share their experiences. The peer group, then, becomes a vehicle to which the adolescent can transfer some of the loyalty that previously had been invested almost exclusively in the family. The process is interactive in that as the peer group provides increasing support, the adolescent spends more time with peers and less time with family and, consequently, presses for more independence from the family. The peer group serves as a source of at least temporary identification in that the adolescent can see similarities between him or herself and the individuals in the peer group and can use the group as a kind of mirror of self.

This transfer of loyalty to the peer group provides additional opportunities for the formation of identity. In the adolescent peer group, one's status is dependent on one's own characteristics rather than being derived from one's membership in a family that has a certain community status. Generally, the extent to which the individual possesses characteristics most valued by the peer group is a determinant of status within the group. For example, a peer group that values athletic achievement will hold in highest regard those members of the group who are most athletically accomplished. In a peer group that values attractiveness to the opposite sex, individuals who are most sought after by members of the opposite sex will have the highest status. In striving for status and acceptance within the group, the adolescent evaluates his or her own characteristics and may attempt to modify them to achieve a certain status. Particularly in early adolescence, the individual may "try on" different roles within the peer group. The young adolescent may play one role within the group for a period of time and then later shift and play another role for a time. For example, the adolescent may for a time play the role of the group clown and then at a later time take on a leadership role within the group. This process of shifting roles requires that the adolescent emphasize different qualities at different times, allowing the individual to assess those roles and characteristics with which she or he is most comfortable. The importance of the peer group in providing support for this experimentation tends to be greatest in early adolescence and then declines as the individual becomes increasingly confident and independent (Brown, Fischer, & Petrie, 1986).

In addition to the increased role of the peer group in early adolescence, other social changes also impact on the adolescent. The first of these changes for most adolescents is the shift from elementary school to secondary school. School systems differ with respect to both the number and the timing of school-to-school transitions, but in most a shift to senior high school comes at Grade 9 or 10. This is an important transition because, for the first time, the adolescent is placed in an environment in which the peer group sees itself as being much closer to adult status. One's place in the peer group, then, is determined by how one is able to handle the task of becoming more adult. Responsibilities for performing in school and for performing social roles fall more directly on the shoulders of the adolescent. As some degree of independence from the family is achieved, parents become less directly involved in the adolescent's curricular and extracurricular activities. Teachers, who often see well over 100 different students in the course of a day, have less direct involvement in the performance of the individual student than was the case in elementary school. Thus, the adolescent must assume greater responsibility for his or her own performance.

In summary, the process of identity formation in adolescence is multifaceted. Physical, cognitive, and social changes converge, creating a need for reevaluation of self and a new conceptualization of self as a fledgling adult. We have noted the extent of physical changes that occur during adolescence. We have not yet addressed how the individual copes with this new physical appearance. It is to that issue which we turn next.

BODY IMAGE

With the physical changes confronting the adolescent, the sense of his or her body undergoes a radical shift (Koff, Rierden, & Silverstone, 1978). There is considerable evidence to suggest that the development of a new body image following pubertal change is a difficult and somewhat negative experience for the adolescent (Blyth, Simmons, & Zakin, 1985; Davies & Furnham, 1986a; D'Hondt & Vandewiele, 1982; Levinson, Powell, & Stellman, 1986; Rosenbaum, 1974).

Girls appear to experience greater difficulty in adjusting to a new body image than do boys. Societal notions of the ideal body shape have changed over time. Over the past several decades we have seen an increasingly thin ideal, particularly, although not exclusively, for girls. Through a variety of mechanisms, especially the media, adolescents are influenced by these ideals and think more or less positively about themselves on the basis of how closely they perceive themselves to match these ideals. Again, girls seem to be more influenced by societal values on the ideal body than are males. A consideration of some potential reasons for this sex difference is warranted. Pubertal development for females results in increased proportions of fat tissue especially associated with breast and hip development. Even in childhood, the proportion of body fat is always greater on average for girls than for boys. Pubertal development increases the differential. Considering that fat is perceived negatively, it is not surprising that girls tend to devalue their maturing bodies.

Many readers will be familiar with the body image distortions, which are reported by eating-disordered, particularly anorectic, individuals. Distorted body image is one of the diagnostic signs of an eating disorder. Such distortions usually involve the individuals seeing themselves as fat even though their actual body weight is dangerously low. Evidence (Davies & Furnham, 1986b; Levinson et al., 1986; Wardle & Beales, 1986) suggests that eating-disordered individuals represent only the extreme of body image distortion. Many adolescents hold images of their bodies that are a distortion of their actual size and shape. Female adolescents tend to see themselves as much larger and fatter than they actually are and often engage in dieting in an attempt to make their bodies conform to an idealized image (Davies & Furnham, 1986a, 1986b; Wardle & Beales, 1986). This is occasionally the case with boys, but they are more likely to see themselves as weighing less than their idealized image (Levinson et al., 1986).

One might expect that negative body images are the result of the initial change at puberty and would lessen as the adolescent becomes more familiar with his or her new shape and size. This does not appear to be the case, however. Conversely, concern about body image and negative evaluations of one's body both increase throughout adolescence (Adams & Jones, 1981; Davies & Furnham, 1986b). There is little evidence to indicate the age at which this trend discontinues. It is unlikely, however, that there is continual increase in negative evaluation of body images through adulthood.

Not only do adolescents distort their view of themselves, but they also tend to hold distorted beliefs about what is considered attractive by the opposite sex (Cohn et al., 1987). Adolescent females tend to believe that boys prefer thinner figures than they actually prefer and thinner figures than the girls actually have. Boys also have a tendency to estimate the preferences of girls inaccurately, but assume that they prefer larger, more muscular figures than are actually preferred.

The consequences of distorted body image are unfortunately not neutral. Relationships between negative body images and depression have been shown by several investigators (Kaplan, Busner & Pollack, 1988; Noles, Cash, & Winstead, 1985; Rierdan, Koff, & Stubbs, 1987; Teri, 1982). This is not to say that negative body images cause depression; the converse may be true, or both variables could be related via a third, unmeasured variable. However, anyone acquainted with an adolescent is no doubt aware of the strong association between body image and emotional reaction to it.

Negative body images also appear to be related to lower levels of self-esteem among adolescents, again particularly among girls (Lerner, Iwawaki, Chihara, & Sorell, 1981; Mendelson & White, 1985; Rosen, Gross, & Vara, 1987). Not surprisingly, girls who see themselves as fatter than their ideal, or their perception of society's ideal, think less well of themselves generally. Among girls, lower self-esteem is also related to a tendency toward eating disorders (Grant & Fodor, 1986). It is difficult to determine the direction of these relationships, and it can be argued that individuals who present as eating disordered have difficulties other than simply seeing themselves as failing to meet the societal ideal in terms of body type. There is, however, a disturbing convergence of evidence relating wishes to be thinner, negative feelings about oneself and more serious disorders among adolescent girls. Among boys, relationships have also been found between negative body images, lower levels of self-esteem, and tendencies toward antisocial behavior (Jurich & Andres, 1984; Maitra, 1981). However, as with most other relationships between body image and other variables for boys, the relationships tend to be weaker and not present in the literature as consistently as those for girls.

Not only the fact of maturing but also the age at which one matures appear to exert an effect on body image. The age of attaining pubertal status varies from individual to individual. Because the reaching of puberty is considered a major life event, the effects of being an early maturer versus a later maturer have long been of interest to developmental psychologists. As usual, sex differences are found. Although there may be mitigating factors, in general, early maturation appears more advantageous for boys. Early maturers tend to have positive self-images, are popular among peers, and are successful in athletics. Although findings have been less consistent for girls, early maturing girls are generally reported to be less advantaged than age mates who mature at an average age or later than the majority of their peers. Duncan, Ritter, Dornbusch, Gross, and Carlsmith (1985) studied more than 5,000 adolescents aged 12 to 17. They found that, among the groups, early maturing boys were the most satisfied with their bodies, whereas the early maturing girls were the least satisfied, at least with respect to weight. In fact, all groups of girls became dissatisfied with their weight as they matured. In the authors' words, "a normal developmental process is being viewed negatively by females and positively by males" (p. 227). Blyth et al. (1985) studied only adolescent girls at the time of school transition and found consistent negative relationships between early maturation and satisfaction with weight and figure. These authors concluded that the cultural ideal of thinness was a more powerful predictor of body satisfaction than were any of the other variables under investigation.

In summary, the overwhelming body of evidence on body image satisfaction substantiates the adage that "thin is in" for girls at this time in history. During a period of life when body image is of particular salience, girls who do not perceive themselves as thin, regardless of actual body weight, are less than happy with themselves. Boys also evaluate themselves relative to a cultural ideal, that of the large muscular figure. However, they tend to perceive much less mismatch, regardless of actual body shape and size, and any perceived mismatch with their ideal is of much less consequence to them.

ATHLETIC ACTIVITY

Rates of participation in physical activity have changed over time. Societal pressure toward fitness peaked in the late 1980s and appears to be continuing at a high level. Although this societal pressure probably has its greatest impact on adults, adolescents are also very much influenced by the social desirability of fitness. Again, sex differences are apparent. For boys, participation and quality of performance in athletic activity are important, but for girls fitness appears equated with thinness.

Apart from the obvious health and physical fitness benefits of athletic participation, adolescents may perceive athletic participation and excellence as providing other extrinsic rewards. Within the adolescent community, one may derive status from being an athlete. Among this age group, the opportunity for interaction with peers may also hold appeal as may the opportunity just to have fun. A survey of 1,138 adolescent athletes by Gill, Gross, and Huddleston (1983) indicated that these were important reasons for participation but that only boys perceived sports as an avenue of gaining status and a sense of achievement.

Participation and excellence in athletic activity have traditionally been viewed as falling within the male domain (Nixon, Maresca, & Silverman, 1979). Women have engaged in athletics and exhibited high levels of performance, but with the exception of a few notable athletes, in particular, those in "gender-neutral" sports (e.g., tennis, golf), female athletic activity has not been high visible. For adolescents, then, it is perhaps not unexpected that the visibility of athletic activity, the meaning of participation, and the rewards for participation and excellence differ for boys and girls (Borman & Kurdek, 1987; Eder & Parker, 1987).

The conclusion indicated by the literature on adolescent athletic activity is that gender differences exist with regard to what is important in sports activity. For boys, success appears to be the primary aim, whereas girls focus instead on appearance. Athletic events for boys tend to be primary social events in high schools, and female roles with respect to these events are primarily supportive. Athletic events in which girls are the participants are generally less well attended than those involving male participants and tend not to impart the same prestige to participants within the school culture. In other words, even in the late 1980s, it is still the male athlete and the female cheerleader who are viewed as ideals by the student population (Eder & Parker, 1987).

Rates of participation in athletic activities tend to be higher for boys than for girls. These differential participation rates may be the result of a number of factors, including general societal attitudes toward the appropriateness of athletic activities for girls. Public attitudes toward women's athletic participation have become more positive over time, but there remains a belief that women should participate only in certain sports such as tennis or gymnastics (Snyder & Spreitzer, 1983). Adolescents themselves, particularly boys, are likely to perceive certain sports as being inappropriate for girls (Colley, Nash, O'Donnel, & Restorick, 1987). Because girls are more influenced by the opinions of others than are boys (Striegel-Moore, Silberstein, & Rodin, 1986), attitudes concerning the appropriateness of certain activities are likely to have a substantial impact, particularly in the vulnerable adolescent period. So although girls tend not to sex stereotype sports as much as do boys (Nixon et al., 1979), they are more likely to be influenced by stereotypes in their choice of participation.

Participation in athletics appears to have a variety of benefits. Improvements in self-image have been reported for both boys and girls as a function of participation in sports, with boys reporting greater benefits than girls (Douctre, Narris, & Watson, 1983). A study comparing late-adolescent athletes with nonathletes found significant positive relationships between self-concept and athletic participation (Schumaker, Small, & Wood, 1986). Both male and female athletes scored higher than nonathletes on a global measure of self concept as well as on a variety of subscales. The authors reported that differences were greater for boys than girls; nevertheless, female as well as male athletes showed differences.

For male athletes, positive benefits of participation are long lasting. Varca, Shaffer, and Saunders (1984) reported that boys who have high levels of sport participation in high school continue to have higher levels of life satisfaction through their university years and as long as 5 years after they have graduated from university. These high school athletes also continued athletic participation into adulthood. Similar relationships were not found for females.

Although boys tend to benefit more from athletic participation, girls who do participate in sports tend to be those who are independent, self-confident, and assertive (Butcher, 1983). They also show benefits from this participation and achievement with respect to their self-images. Comparisons of female athletes and nonathletes of high school age (Jackson & Marsh, 1986; Marsh & Jackson, 1986) indicated higher self-concepts of physical abilities among the athletes but not necessarily higher self-concepts in other areas. The athlete groups did attach, however, a greater importance to physical self-concept than the nonathletes. The athlete group also viewed themselves as having more masculine characteristics but no fewer feminine characteristics than did nonathletes, indicating a more androgynous sex role orientation for the athletes.

The availability of athletically oriented role models may influence girls to participate in and attempt to excel in sports as well as to adopt a more androgynous sex role orientation. For instance, female adolescents whose parents, particularly mothers, were achievers in sports were more likely to be participants in athletic activity than girls whose parents were not involved (Gregson & Colley, 1986).

In summary, athletic participation appears to have positive influences on self-concept for those who do participate. These benefits are much greater for boys than for girls, with the result that boys participate at higher rates and more publicly than do girls. The developmental trend for participation also differs for boys and girls. Male participation rates appear to remain relatively constant throughout adolescence and early adulthood. Female participation rates fluctuate; higher rates of participation are found in early adolescence, a sharp decrease in rates of participation in midadolescence, and a partial recovery of participation rates in later adolescence and early adulthood.

INTERRELATIONSHIPS

We have attempted to examine the issues of athletic ability, body image, and identity during the period of adolescence. There are few data that speak directly to the question of the relationships among these variables. Thus, our discussion of relationships is necessarily speculative. It is our sincere hope that this discussion will stimulate the research needed to provide a clearer picture of them. Because the patterns with respect to the individual variables differ for boys and girls, we must assume that these different patterns are also reflected in the interrelationships.

For boys, the pattern of relationships between athletic ability, body image, and identity appears to be relatively straightforward. Male athletic participants perceive themselves as more physically effective and generally feel more positive about themselves than do nonathletes. Physical effectiveness is an important dimension of body image satisfaction for boys, so perceptions of increased physical effectiveness contribute to higher levels of self-esteem (Lerner, Orlos, & Knapp, 1976). Thus, the evaluative dimension of identity is positively influenced by athletic participation and success.

High status is generally accorded to the male athlete within the school culture at both high school and university levels (Murray, 1976). The athlete's positive self-perception coincides with the positive regard communicated by his peers. Consistency of information from internal and external sources contributes to the individual's developing sense of identity.

The high status accorded the athlete affords other benefits as well. The importance of the peer group to adolescents and its role in identity formation has already been documented. The availability of peers with whom to interact is enhanced for male adolescent athletes. Team members, for athletes engaged in team sports, provide a ready-made group of individuals having similar interests. Because of status considerations, other adolescents within the school usually consider athletes desirable individuals with whom to associate. Thus, for the adolescent, the process of transferring loyalty from the family to the peer group, and the consequent increase in emotional independence from the family, is facilitated.

The diminishing of adolescent egocentrism is generally seen to come about as a result of interaction with others and the growing realization of the true views of others that it provides. Here again the adolescent male athlete has an advantage because of his position with the peer group.

The pattern that emerges for girls is less consistent than that for boys. In early adolescence, athletic participation is valued, although it does not appear to afford particular status to the individual; instead, girls appear to participate because they enjoy the activity. However, some extrinsic rewards for participation may exist. Because athletic participation is an activity that is generally sanctioned by parents, it may provide an opportunity for periods of freedom from parental supervision. This freedom may provide the young adolescent girl with some sense of independence.

Participation also provides opportunities for increased interaction with peers, and this interaction provides similar benefits for girls as it does for boys. Peer support for athletic participation and excellence is temporally limited, however.

As pubertal changes advance, however, there is a change in the value of athletic activity for girls. Young adolescents have strongly stereotyped notions of appropriate male and female activities. Athletic participation, and particularly athletic excellence, are not viewed as feminine. Female athletes tend not to have high status within the peer culture during middle adolescence. Not only do they not enjoy the peer support associated with male athletic excellence, they may also be negatively evaluated by peers because of their participation in what are perceived to be masculine activities. Female athletes, then, may have a more restricted peer group than their nonathletic counterparts, a peer group composed primarily of other adolescent female athletes. This group itself is not particularly prestigious and, although it may provide some of the important opportunities for interaction discussed previously, membership does not confer the positive evaluation enjoyed by male athletes.

Given the lack of reward for athletic participation among adolescent females, there is decreased motivation for girls to participate, at least in highly visible sports activities. Moreover, because girls tend not to value physical effectiveness as much as physical attractiveness, both the types of activities in which they participate and their reasons for participating tend to be different from those of boys. When girls do participate, they tend to participate in less competitive and less visible activities. This may be partially attributable to a reluctance to be seen in a state that might be considered not well groomed or in a stance that might be perceived as aggressive. The reasons for girls participating in athletic activity are also often quite different from those of boys. Adolescent girls are likely to participate in athletic activity as a means of weight control, that is, in service of appearance.

Unlike boys, girls' athletic participation does not appear to enhance body image, except to the extent that it leads to thinness. It is weight that is the overwhelming predictor of body image satisfaction among girls. Thus, in middle adolescence, neither athletic participation nor athletic excellence appear to contribute substantially to positive self-image and that aspect of identity formation.

By late adolescence, athletic activity for girls begins to regain some of its appeal and to begin to become a factor in the process of identity formation. By this age, the extreme sex stereotyping of activities has diminished, and there is greater permissiveness among the peer group for individuals to pursue their own interests. Although appearance continues to be a significant concern for girls well into (perhaps even throughout) adulthood, its role as the major dimension of self-evaluation begins to lessen.

CONCLUSIONS

On the basis of currently available evidence, we are led to conclude that the relationships among athletic participation and excellence, body image and identity follow different paths for boys and for girls. For boys, participation and success in athletics leads to a sense of physical effectiveness and, in turn, a positive body image. Although body image is only one component of identity, it is an important one. For the athletically accomplished boys, the establishment of a positive sense of identity is facilitated. Among girls, a similar pattern might prevail were it not for both personal and societal attitudes concerning the appropriateness of athletic activity and excellence for girls. In early adolescence, patterns for boys and girls are not markedly different. It is in midadolescence, when the influence of societal attitudes becomes acute, that girls lose the sense of a value in athletic excellence. Body image is a significant contributor to a sense of identity, but body image is influenced by factors other than athletic ability. Not until several years later does the pattern of athletic activity and achievement contributing to positive body image return. Because identity formation is well advanced by this time, the contribution of athletic participation and excellence to identity formation is diminished.

REFERENCES

Adams, G. R., & Jones, R. M. (1981). Imaginary audience behavior: A validation study. *Journal of Early Adolescence, 1*, 1–10.

Blyth, D. A., Simmons, R. G., & Zakin, D. F. (1985). Satisfaction with body image for early adolescent females: The impact of pubertal timing within different school environments. *Journal of Youth and Adolescence, 14*(3), 207–225.

Borman, K. M., & Kurdek, L. A. (1987). Gender differences associated with playing high school varsity soccer. *Journal of Youth and Adolescence, 16*(4), 379–400.

Brown, R. B., Fischer, S. A., & Petrie, S. (1986). The importance of peer group ("crowd") affiliation in adolescence. *Journal of Adolescence, 9*(1), 73–96.

Butcher, J. (1983). Socialization of adolescent girls into physical activity. *Adolescence, 18*(72), 753–766.

Cohn, L. D., Adler, N. E., Irwin, C. E., Millstein, S. G., Kegeles, S. M. & Stone, G. (1987). Body-figure preferences in male and female adolescents. *Journal of Abnormal Psychology, 96*(3), 276–279.

Colley, A., Nash, J., O'Donnell, L., & Restorick, L. (1987). Attitudes to the female sex role and sex typing of physical activities. *International Journal of Sport Psychology, 18*,(1), 19–29.

Davies, E., & Furnham, A. (1986a). Body satisfaction in adolescent girls. *British Journal of Medical Psychology, 59*(3), 279–287.

Davies, E., & Furnham, A. (1986b). The dieting and body shape concerns of adolescent females. *Journal of Child Psychology and Psychiatry and Allied Disciplines, 27*(3), 417–428.

D'Hondt, W., & Vandewiele, M. (1982). Attitudes and behavior at adolescence perceived by secondary school students in Senegal. *Journal of Genetic Psychology, 140*(2), 319–320.

Douctre, G. P., Narris, G. A., & Watson, K. E. (1983). An analysis of self-image differences of male and female athletes. *Journal of Sport Behavior, 6*(2), 77–83.

Duncan, P. D., Ritter, P. L., Dornbusch, S. M., Gross, R. T., & Carlsmith, J. M. (1985). The effects of pubertal timing on body image, school behavior, and deviance. *Journal of Youth and Adolescence, 14*(3), 227–235.

Eder, D., & Parker, S. (1987). The cultural production and reproduction of gender: The effect of extracurricular activities on peer group culture. *Sociology of Education, 60*(3), 200–213.

Elkind, D. (1967). Egocentrism in adolescence. *Child Development, 38*, 1025–1033.

Erikson, E. (1950). *Childhood and society.* New York: Norton.

Gill, D. L., Gross, J. R., & Huddleston, S. (1983). Participation motivation in youth sports. *International Journal of Sport Psychology, 14*(1), 1–14.

Grant, C. L., & Fodor, I. G. (1986). Adolescent attitudes toward body image and anorexic behavior. *Adolescence, 21*(82), 269–281.

Gregson, J. F., & Colley, A. (1986). Concomitants of sport participation in male and female adolescents. *International Journal of Sport Psychology, 17*(1), 10–22.

Havighurst, R. J. (1972). *Developmental tasks and education.* New York: McKay.

Inhelder, B., & Piaget, J. (1958). *The growth of logical thinking from childhood to adolescence.* New York: Basic Books.

Jackson, S. A., & Marsh, H. W. (1986). Athletic or antisocial? The female sport experience. *Journal of Sport Psychology, 8*(3), 198–211.

Jurich, A. P., & Andrews, D. (1984). Self-concepts of rural early adolescent juvenile delinquents. *Journal of Early Adolescence, 4*(1), 41–46.

Kaplan, S. L., Busner, J., & Pollack, S. (1988). Perceived weight, actual weight, and depressive symptoms in a general adolescent sample. *International Journal of Eating Disorders, 7*(1), 107–113.

King, S. H. (1972). Coping and growth in adolescence. *Seminars in Psychiatry, 4*(4), 355–366.

Koff, E., Rierden, J., & Silverstone, E. (1978). Changes in representation of body image as a function of menarcheal status. *Developmental Psychology, 14*(6), 635–642.

Lerner, R. M., Iwawaki, S., Chihara, T., & Sorell, G. T. (1981). Self-concept, self-esteem and body attitudes among Japanese male and female adolescents in S. Chess and A. Thomas (Eds.). *Annual Progress in Child Psychiatry and Child Development,* 494–507.

Lerner, R. M., Orlos, J. B., & Knapp, J. R. (1976). Physical attractiveness, physical effectiveness, and self-concept in late adolescents. *Adolescence, 11*(43), 313–326.

Levinson, R., Powell, B., & Stellman, L. C. (1986). Social location, significant others and body image among adolescents. *Social Psychology Quarterly, 49*(4), 330–337.

Maitra, A. K. (1981). The DAP differentials of the delinquents. *Psychological Research Journal, 5*(1–2), 59–66.

Marcia, J. E. (1966). Development and validation of ego-identity status. *Journal of Personality and Social Psychology, 3,* 551–558.

Marsh, H. W., & Jackson, S. A. (1986). Multidimensional self-concept, masculinity, and femininity as a function of women's involvement in athletics. *Sex Roles, 15*(7–8), 391–415.

Mendelson, B. K., & White, D. R. (1985). Development of self-body-esteem in overweight youngsters. *Developmental Psychology, 21*(1), 90–96.

Murray, C. (1976). Valuation of athletic performance in male adolescent peer groups. *Perceptual and Motor Skills, 43*(3), 1003–1011.

Nixon, H. L., Maresca, P. J., & Silverman, M. A. (1979). Sex differences in college students' acceptance of females in sport. *Adolescence, 14*(56), 755–764.

Noles, S. W., Cash, T. F., & Winstead, B. A. (1985). Body image, physical attractiveness, and depression. *Journal of Consulting and Clinical Psychology, 53*(1), 88–94.

Remschmidt, H. (1975). New results in psychology and psychiatry of adolescence. *Zeitschrift fur Kinder und Jugenpsychiatrie, 3*(1), 67–101.

Rierdan, J., Koff, E., & Stubbs, M. L. (1987). Depressive symptomatology and body image in adolescent girls. *Journal of Early Adolescence, 7*(2), 205–216.

Rosen, J. C., Gross, J., & Vara, L. (1987). Psychological adjustment of adolescents attempting to lose or gain weight. *Journal of Consulting and Clinical Psychology, 55*(5), 742–747.

Rosenbaum, N. T. (1974). Gender-specific problems in the treatment of young women. *The American Journal of Psychoanalysis, 37*(3), 215–221.

Santrock, J. W. (1987). *Adolescence: An introduction* (3rd ed.). Dubuque, IA: W. C. Brown.

Schumaker, J. F., Small, L., & Wood, J. (1986). Self-concept, academic achievement and athletic participation. *Perceptual and Motor Skills, 62*(2), 387–390.

Snyder, E. F., & Spreitzer, E. (1983). Change and variation in the social acceptance of female participation in sports. *Journal of Sport Behavior, 6*(1), 3–8.

Striegel-Moore, R. H., Silberstein, L. R., & Rodin, J. (1986). Toward an understanding of risk factors for bulimia. *American Psychologist, 41*(3), 246–263.

Teri, L. (1982). Depression in adolescence: Its relationship to assertion and various aspects of self-image. *Journal of Clinical Child Psychology, 11*(2), 101–106.

Varca, P. F., Shaffer, G. S., & Saunders, V. (1984). A longitudinal investigation of sport participation and life satisfaction. *Journal of Sport Psychology, 6*(4), 440–447.

Wardle, J., & Beales, S. (1986). Restraint, body image and food attitudes in children from 12 to 18 years. *Appetite, 7*(3), 209–217.

Werner, H. (1948). *Comparative psychology of mental development.* New York: International Universities Press.

6

Sports Participation and Social Development

Mick Coleman
University of Georgia

Perhaps nowhere do sports have as great an impact than on the lives of the 20 million young people between the ages of 6 and 18 who participate in nonschool youth sport programs (Martens, 1988). Following a line of thought began earlier in this century, some argue that youth sports promote social skills that young people need in adult life (e.g., self-confidence, leadership, cooperation). Others contend just the opposite, noting the aggressive and demanding behavior of parents and coaches at Little League games to argue that youth sports have become part of the "hurried child" (Elkind, 1981) American ethos in which young people are being pushed to grow up too soon too fast.

Regardless of one's feelings about the current operation of youth sports, most would agree that the institution of sport has itself become an important socialization agent (Leonard, 1988) in which life values and skills—good or bad—are learned. In this chapter, attention is focused on the social development of youth sport participants from three perspectives. From a historical perspective, a brief account of the youth sports movement in America is given to provide a context within which to consider sport as a socialization agent. From a research perspective, the limited studies conducted on the social development of youth sport participants are reviewed. Finally, from a theoretical perspective, the social readiness of young people to enter into youth sports is examined.

YOUTH SPORTS IN THE 20TH CENTURY

Much of the controversy over the developmental impact of youth sports today can be traced back to the early part of this century. First introduced into American society in the last decade of the 19th century (Wiggins, 1987), organized youth sport programs were viewed as a means of building character through achievement and motivation and learning assertiveness and fair play (Berryman, 1988; Coakley, 1986). Unfortunately, professional recreation leaders and physical educators dropped their support of nonschool youth sport programs in the 1930s, criticizing their elitism and competitiveness (Figler, 1981; Wiggins, 1987). Volunteer youth groups subsequently assumed sponsorship, although the adult volunteers responsible for conducting the sport programs often had no training in child development (Berryman, 1988).

Today control of nonschool youth sport programs continues to be held by untrained volunteer coaches (Gould, 1987a). Furthermore, sponsorship of these programs is diverse, lacking a national coordinating body (Martens, 1988). There is also no nationally accepted system of certification for coaches (Kimiecik, 1988).

Fortunately, there is evidence of a shift in the public's appraisal of youth sports. A recent national survey found that although 59% of the respondents strongly agreed that competition was good for young people, an even larger majority believed that youth sport coaches took the game too seriously (82%), placing too much emphasis on winning and not enough on physical and psychological development (86%) (Miller Brewing Company, 1983). A majority (80%) of the respondents believed that sport programs for young people 12 years of age or younger should allow all participants to play an equal amount of time.

It is because of concerns such as those expressed in the Miller Brewing Company survey that physical educators are taking a more active role in making youth sport programs more developmentally appropriate (Gould, 1981). One of the most important challenges now facing physical educators is to understand themselves the impact of youth sports on the social development of young people.

THE SOCIAL DEVELOPMENT OF YOUTH SPORT PARTICIPANTS

Does participation in youth sports contribute to or detract from the social development of young people? There is wide consensus among sport scholars (Coakley, 1986; Figler, 1981; Gill, 1986; Gould, 1982; Heyman, 1987; Kerr & Fowler, 1988; Leonard, 1988; Lucas, 1986; Silva, 1984; Stevenson, 1975) that this question, studied for the past two decades, remains unanswered. In short, one can find within the literature support for a number of different opinions regarding the developmental impact of sports (Gavin, 1988).

The reasons for the contradictions found within youth sports research have been examined in detail elsewhere (Fishwick & Greendorfer, 1987; Gavin, 1988; Gill, 1986; Gould, 1982; Weiss & Bredemeier, 1983). The include: (a) poor methodological designs, including a lack of attention to confounding variables like race, gender, and family background; (b) the lack of an applied justification for conducting youth sports research; (c) an overgeneralization of results across situations; (d) an inappropriate focus on global personality traits that are poor predictors of specific behaviors; and (e) insufficient use of developmental theories in planning and interpreting youth sport research studies.

It is because of problems like these that we are as yet unable to make cause and effect linkages between the participation of young people in sports and their social development. For example, it is routinely noted that we do not yet know whether the differences found between young athletes and nonathletes are an effect of their sports participation or whether something in their personal makeup or background attracted them to sports in the first place.

Of all the social developmental issues addressed in youth sports, most can be categorized under one of its three social functions (Leonard, 1988); (a) catharsis, through which life tensions are released; (b) belonging, through which one develops a sense of social acceptance and self-worth; and (c) ritual, through which one develops a sense of stability and security in a changing world.

The Cathartic Function of Sports

The cathartic function of sports is to help young people learn to reduce tension and conflict in a socially acceptable manner. Juvenile delinquency and stress management are two social developmental issues that are often associated with the cathartic function of youth sports.

Juvenile Delinquency

Youth sports have long been viewed as a cathartic mechanism through which young people might void delinquent behavior (Purdy & Richard, 1983; Segrave, 1983). For example, the basic tenet of the surplus energy theory is that it is through sports participation that young people are able to channel their tensions. Without sports, some young people may "blow off" their tensions through such destructive behavior as vandalism or gang assaults. The basic tenet of strain theory is that young people from disadvantaged backgrounds can, through their success in sports, overcome what would otherwise be a life filled with frustration at attempting to achieve social prestige. Success in sports supplies these young people with a valued identity, thereby reducing the possibility that they will seek prestige through gang membership. Finally, the basic tenet of control theory is that the structure imposed by youth sports serves as a social control mechanism, teaching young people to respect and abide by social norms. Segrave's (1983) review of the limited research on the relationship between youth sports and delinquency reveals some trends that support the cathartic function of sports.

1. There is a negative association between participation in sports and juvenile delinquency. Young athletes tend to engage in less delinquent behavior than their nonathletic peers.
2. The overall relationship between youth sports and delinquency is primarily an association among lower socioeconomic groups. Athletes from lower socioeconomic families are particularly less likely to engage in delinquent behavior than their nonathletic peers from similar socioeconomic families.
3. The overall relationship better youth sports and delinquency is a function of the seriousness of the offense. Young athletes are less involved in more serious offenses like vandalism and physical assault than are their nonathletic peers.
4. The personality profiles of young athletes and nonathletes are different. Young athletes have a higher self-image and peers status and participate more in school and nonschool activities. They also assume more leadership roles than their nonathletic peers.

It should be noted that these trends must be tempered with the many caveats offered in the literature, including the following.

1. Most of the data available on youth sports and delinquency are descriptive and correlational. There is no evidence of a cause and effect relationship between participation in youth sports and social conformity (Segrave, 1983).
2. Some studies have found a positive relationship between delinquent behavior and young athletes who participate in certain sports like football, basketball, and ice hockey. These studies suggest that highly publicized and aggressive sports may

actually contribute to the delinquent behavior of young athletes (Segrave & Hastad, 1982).

3. Mediating variables like age, gender, race, and family background have received limited attention in studies on youth sports and delinquency (Segrave & Hastad, 1982). It is not known how these variables may interact with sports participation to affect the social behavior of young athletes.

4. Dependent measures of delinquency have often been limited to official court records documenting only more serious offenses. We do not know the relationship between minor "middle-class" offenses and sports participation (Purdy & Richard, 1983; Segrave, 1983).

5. As is true with most youth sports research, a self-selection process may be operating in studies on delinquency. Social conformers may remain in youth sport programs, whereas nonconformers withdraw or are cut from sport teams (Hastad, Segrave, Pangrazi, & Peterson, 1986; Purdy & Richard, 1983; Segrave, 1983).

Stress

Sport psychologists and practitioners have identified the competitive stress placed on young people as a major issue in youth sports (Gould, 1982). The findings of Passer (1982) and Scanlan's (1984) review of the limited research conducted on this issue follow.

1. Young athletes who display high competitive trait anxiety (i.e., a stable trait disposition) experience greater precompetitive stress than do low competitive trait anxiety athletes.

2. Young athletes who display a low self-esteem experience greater precompetitive stress than do their high self-esteem peer athletes.

3. Young athletes participating in individual sports experience more precompetitive stress than do their peers participating in team sports.

4. In team sports, team expectancies are more important predictors of stress than personal performance. Young athletes with low expectancies that their team will win experience greater precompetitive stress than do their peers with high team expectancies.

5. Young athletes who worry about failure and evaluations by parents and coaches and who feel under pressure from parents to participate in sports experience greater precompetitive stress than do their peers who worry less about failure, evaluation by others, or parental pressure.

6. Game outcomes influence postcompetitive stress. Winning decreases stress, and losing or tying increases stress. Losing a very close game is the most stressful.

7. Young athletes who report to have had less fun during a game experience greater postcompetitive stress than do their peers who report more fun. This relationship is independent of victory; winners do not necessarily have more fun than losers.

8. Some young athletes experience ongoing stress symptoms such as sleeping and eating disorders (see Gould, 1987a).

Finally, it should be noted that there is no evidence at this time that youth sports are more stressful than other activities involving comparisons and evaluations (Passer, 1982). Further research is needed to address the various social contexts within which youth sports are conducted before more conclusive statements can be made about their cathartic function in relation to stress.

The Belonging Function of Sports

The belonging function of sports is to help young people develop a sense of personal worth and social acceptance. Some researchers have addressed this function by studying the reasons young people give for entering into and withdrawing from youth sports. Other researchers have studied the perceived competence of young athletes. Still other researchers have studied the social identity of young athletes.

Entering Into and Withdrawing From Sports

Some of the reasons cited by young people for participating in youth sports include skill development, affiliation, achievement, and fun (Coakley, 1986; Gill, Gross, & Huddleston, 1983; Gould, Feltz, & Weiss, 1985; Passer, 1982). Fun, in fact, has consistently been cited as a primary reason for young people entering into youth sports, leading Wankel and Kreisel (1985) to study the importance of intrinsic versus extrinsic rewards to young people's sports participation. Their results indicated a consistent patterning of enjoyment factors across age groups (7–8 years; 9–10 years; 11–12 years; and 13–14 years) and sport groups (soccer, hockey, baseball). Intrinsic factors, such as skill improvement and excitement, took precedence over social factors, such as being part of a team and friendship, which in turn took precedence over extrinsic factors, such as playing for others, obtaining rewards, and winning.

These findings seem to support the idea that young people pursue youth sports as a means of achieving an intrinsic sense of accomplishment and belonging. With this in mind, special note should be made of the emphasis currently placed on extrinsic rewards in many, if not most, youth sport programs.

Although even very young people have in some cases been found to emphasize the extrinsic rewards associated with winning, we do not yet know the reasons why (Passer, 1982). It could be based on their need to compare themselves with others or on an overemphasis placed on winning by significant adults. Smoll and Smith (1984) noted that although winning seems to make little difference to youth sport participants, they nevertheless know that it is important to adults. Whatever the reasons, an overemphasis on extrinsic rewards and winning in youth sports can have both short- and long-term negative consequences for the social development of young people.

In the short term, an emphasis on extrinsic rewards can drive away those young people who lack the interest or abilities to perform at a level that meets the expectations of adults. Likewise, youth participants can view performance pressure as a form of control that undermines their intrinsic motivation to continue in youth sports (Vallerand, Deci, & Ryan, 1987). In either of these situations, the belonging function of youth sports is ill-served.

In the long term, an emphasis on extrinsic rewards may contribute to the establishment of a life pattern in which young people become dependent upon extrinsic information and rewards to measure their life successes. As noted by Singer and Gerson (1980), "if the purpose of athletic competition is to aid the youthful athlete in developing feelings of competence, and rewards are to be used effectively, they must be contingent upon the personal achievement (not necessarily winning) of the participants" (p. 256). Otherwise, young people may continue to strive for a sense of belonging and acceptance through extrinsic rewards, never accepting responsibility for their own behavior or abilities. Other participants may simply give up trying to meet the expectations of adults and withdraw from youth sports.

In fact, some of the reasons young people give for withdrawing from youth sports include lack of playing time, lack of success or skill improvement, dislike for the coach, too much competitive stress, boredom, lack of fun, conflict with other activities, and injury (Gould, 1987a, 1987b; Martens, 1980). Activities that conflict with youth sports and injury deserve special attention, because they provide insight into the process by which young people may withdraw from youth sports when their sense of social belonging and self-worth are threatened.

The decision to withdraw from youth sports is not made in a vacuum but, according to Gould and Petlichkoff (1988), involves a cost-benefit analysis. That is, the decision to withdraw from sports participation is mediated by a comparison of the costs of continuing in sports versus: (a) the availability of other positive activities; and (b) the benefits of pursuing these activities. Only if valued alternative activities are available that offer benefits exceeding those of sport participation do young people decide to withdraw from sports.

Gould and Petlichkoff (1988) further contended that it is inappropriate to assume that young people who discontinue their participation in a given sport will never again participate in sports. Rather, they suggested a continuum of withdrawal. At one end of the continuum, sport-specific withdrawal involves withdrawal from only one sport. Young people continue in another sport or pick up a new one. This type of withdrawal specificity was recently found among young athletes who, although withdrawing from competitive swimming (Gould, Feltz, Horn, & Weiss, 1982) and gymnastics (Klint & Weiss, 1986), continued their sport participation in other programs.

At the other end of the continuum, domain-general withdrawal involves a withdrawal from all sport activities on a permanent basis. Given the importance of sports to American youth, permanent withdrawal from sports would seemingly be a difficult decision for young people to make. One possibility is that sport injuries may provide young people with a means for rationalizing a permanent withdrawal from sports.

Kerr and Fowler (1988) estimated that stressful life events may explain 10% to 20% of the injuries that occur in sports. For youth sport participants, the pressures of living up to adult performance expectations may themselves lead to sport injuries. For example, Kerr and Fowler (1988) suggested that a high incidence of stress among youth sport participants can result in mental disruptions that lead to inattention, a resulting decrease in performance, and injury. One potential form of mental disruption is the intrusion of inappropriate thoughts (anxiety over adult evaluations) that interfere with the ability of youth participants to concentrate on their performance. Likewise, excessive concern over the need to win can detract youth participants from "letting go" of skilled actions that would otherwise be automatically performed. Still other youth participants may take unnecessary risks that result in injury, thereby providing an excuse for their withdrawal from the stressful demands of sports (Hellstedt, 1988; Klint & Weiss, 1986. It is also possible that overuse injury caused by repeated trauma during sport competition can, if ignored or hidden by youth participants, lead to physical damage that forces sport withdrawal (Kozar & Lord, 1988).

Perceived Competence

Within recent years, researchers have addressed the belonging function of youth sports by studying the perceived athletic competence of participants. Harter's (1978, 1981) theory of competence motivation in particular has been used to understand the basis by which young people evaluate their self-worth as athletes.

In general, Harter's theory holds that a young person's assessment of his or her degree of competence influences performance in three developmental domains: physical, cognitive, and social. Those young people whose early performance in one or more of these achievement domains results in success and reinforcement from significant adults develop a positive perception of competence. With maturity and continued reinforcement, the positive perceptions of young people increasingly become internalized so that there is less dependence upon external information and reinforcements. In contrast, young people who develop a low sense of competence continue to rely upon external sources of information about their performance.

When considered within the context of youth sports, Harter's theory holds that young people who perceive themselves to be competent in the achievement domain of physical sports will be more motivated to continue their involvement than those who have a low sense of perceived physical competence. A number of studies have been conducted within the past decade using Harter's theory and competence scale (1978, 1981) or another related scale (see Horn & Hasbrook, 1984) to address the relationship between youth sport participation and perceived competence.

One study conducted by Roberts, Kleiber, and Duda (1981) measured the perceived competence of fourth and fifth-grade youth sport participants and nonparticipants. The results supported Harter's theory in that participants scored significantly higher on perceived physical competence than did their nonparticipant peers. However, subsequent analysis of the correlation between years of participation and perceived physical competence among the participants failed to reach significance. This finding thus failed to support the idea that participation in sport itself instills a sense of competence in young people. Rather, the researchers argued that the youth participants who perceived themselves as having a high level of physical skill competence may have selected out youth sports as a social environment in which to display their competence.

A second study by Feltz and Petlichkoff (1983) focused on the relationship between perceived physical competence and length of involvement in sports among junior and high school athletes. Contrary to the findings of Roberts and his colleagues (1981), these researchers found a significant, although low, relationship between years of sport involvement and perceived physical competence. In comparing their results to those of Roberts and his colleagues (1981), the researchers concluded that the impact of youth sports on perceived physical competence may not be apparent until the adolescent years. Measures of physical competence taken before this time may be masked by the limited years of experience young people have in sports. It also follows that younger participants will have had less exposure to the benefits of sports, as touted by parents and coaches, than their older peers.

A third study conducted by Horn and Hasbrook (1984) found that the types of information young people used to evaluate their physical competencies differed across the childhood years. Older soccer players aged 12 to 14 rated social comparison information (e.g., comparisons with peers) as more important in evaluating their athletic competence than did their younger peers. In contrast, younger children aged 8 to 11 rated evaluation feedback from parents and spectators as more important in evaluating their athletic competence than did their older peers. The youngest children (those aged 8 to 9) placed the greatest reliance upon external information (winning or losing) in evaluating their athletic competence, suggesting a concrete mind-set not yet able to rely upon internalized standards of performance or reinforcement. These findings support the idea of a developmental progression over the childhood years away from a reliance upon external standards of performance evaluation toward a greater reliance upon internal standards.

In a related study, Horn and Hasbrook (1987) investigated the influence of age and locus of performance control on perceived athletic competence. As hypothesized, soccer players, aged 10 to 14, with a greater sense of internal performance control made greater use of internal standards (e.g., amount of effort exerted, degree of skill improvement over time) in judging their athletic competence. In contrast, soccer players with a greater sense of external performance control displayed greater dependence on external standards (e.g., game outcome, parental feedback) in judging their athletic competence. Interestingly, there was no relationship between perceived competence, performance control, and reliance upon a particular informational source of 8- and 9-year-olds. This finding was in obvious contrast to the researchers' (Horn & Hasbrook, 1984) earlier study in which 8- and 9-year-olds reported a preference for external information about their athletic performance.

Most recently, Klint and Weiss (1987) used Harter's theory to investigate whether the type of perceived competence was related to the different motives young people have for participating in youth sports. Their study of young gymnasts aged 8 to 16 indicated that those young athletes scoring high in perceived physical competence rated skill development as a more important reason for participating in gymnastics than did their peers scoring lower in this domain. In contrast, and as hypothesized, those young athletes scoring high in perceived social competence were more motivated by the affiliation aspects of gymnastics than their peers scoring lower in the social competence domain. These findings suggest that even within the same sport young people's sense of physical versus social competence is an important factor in determining their continued involvement.

Although these studies differed in many methodological aspects (e.g., age range, type of sport, years of sport participation), their results generally supported Harter's (1978) developmentally based theory of social competence in which young people progress from a dependence upon external standards of performance evaluation and reinforcement to greater reliance upon internal standards and reinforcement. This small body of work also suggests that youth sport programs should not only be operated differently from adult sports, but that they should be operated differently across age groups and with the individual child's competencies (i.e., social, cognitive, and physical) in mind. Some strategies for physical educators to use in promoting a healthy sense of athletic competence in young people are given in Table 1 (also see Coakley, 1984; Gould & Horn, 1984).

Identity

As already suggested, a young athlete's sense of social belonging is in part based on his or her perceived competence in the physical skills domain. Put another way, it is through the demonstration of one's physical skills that an athletic

Table 1 Strategies for building young people's sense of physical competence through youth sports

Keep in mind the reasons that young people give for participating in youth sports as well as their need for early successes that are free from adult pressures.

1. Structure activities so that everyone gets to play and scores are kept close. Rotating positions on a regular basis is one way to achieve both tasks. Youth participants will be allowed to build skills across different positions, and scores will be kept close because no one will specialize in one particular position.
2. Encourage youth participants to explore a number of different play, game, and sport activities rather than specialize in one sporting event.
3. Keep practice sessions active and fun, not repetitive and boring. Asking young people what they like and dislike about their participation in games and sports is one way to modify practice sessions and game rules so that they remain fun and challenging.
4. Provide opportunities and time during and outside the game for young people to socialize. Social events need not always center around athletics.
5. Help young people identify and feel good about their strengths, while also motivating them to work on areas in need of improvement. Try using the "sandwich approach" (Smith, Smoll, & Curtis, 1979). Begin by responding to a skill error with reinforcement for a positive behavior (e.g., "your concentration was terrific"). Then follow with instruction on how to improve performance (e.g., "be sure to follow through on your swing"). End with encouragement (e.g., "Keep up the good work. You're beginning to bring it all together").
6. Control the impact of competitive outcomes for people younger than age 12 by using techniques like "do-overs" and handicap systems, as well as by focusing on individual physical skill development as opposed to individual or team points and rewards (Coakley, 1984).
7. Follow-up all games and sports with an active discussion of the events that occurred and the player's feelings about those events. Encourage participants to reinforce one another for their efforts, regardless of the game outcome. Avoid making comparisons between participants, instead reinforcing each participant for their unique effort or continued improvement.
8. Establish rules of "sportsmanship" for parents to follow while observing games. If necessary, ban parents whose behavior becomes disruptive.
9. Conduct educational programs for volunteer youth coaches to help them plan and facilitate developmentally appropriate game and sport activities for young people (see Coleman, 1985; Kimiecik, 1988; Seedfeldt, 1987; Smith et al., 1979; Smoll & Smith, 1981).

identity if formed, giving one a sense of belonging to a special social group and the privileges that it provides.

It is generally agreed that the development of an athletic identity begins with the family (Lewko & Ewing, 1980; Snyder & Spreitzer, 1983) and peer group (Lewko & Greendorfer, 1988). Parents are responsible for the early sport socialization of young people (Lewko & Ewing, 1980; McElroy & Kirkendall, 1981; Snyder & Spreitzer, 1983), providing them with the support and opportunities to practice, learn, and display physical skills through the use of sport equipment, camps, lessons, and teams (Cratty, 1981). Peers provide an affective climate, serving as sources of athletic comparison, feedback, and recognition. In fact, the athletic identity carries a high status within most youth peer groups. In the 1960s (Coleman, 1961) and again in the 1970s (Eitzen, 1975), male high school students reported that they would rather be remembered as a star athlete than as a brilliant or popular student. Given the continued popularity of sports, there is reason to believe that athletic prowess would continue to lead as a preferred identity among young men (and women) today.

Unfortunately, an athletic identity can also have negative consequence, especially in relation to the stereotyped and contradictory social expectations that young athletes must face (see Table 2). For example, young athletes who accept the label of "tough jock" may adopt a life script in which aggression is viewed as normal and academics are viewed to be of limited value. Pursuing athletics at the expense of academics, these young athletes may subsequently confirm the "dumb jock" expectations of peers, parents, and teachers. Obviously, none of these labels are fair. Nevertheless, it is such stereotyped and contradictory expectations that can prevent some young athletes from developing an understanding and acceptance of their true selves, setting the stage for personal problems during adulthood. Heyman (1986, 1987) documented through case studies the personal and interpersonal problems encountered by adult athletes who have become caught up in the stereotyped and contradictory nature of the athletic identity. Some suggested strategies for high school and college administrators to follow in helping young athletes avoid this situation by integrating their athletic and social identities are given in Table 3.

The Ritualistic Function of Sport

The ritualistic function of youth sports is to provide young people with a sense of stability and security in an otherwise changing world. Youth sports and school are two of the most important social institutions whose rituals introduce young people to the values and beliefs of American society. Sport researchers have long been interested in the relationship between these two social institutions, especially in regard to the potential conflict that can arise between young people's academic and athletic achievement.

Academic Achievement

Because of the methodological limitations of youth sports discussed previously here, conclusions about the relationship between youth sports and academic achievement are also at best tentative. Eitzen (1987) and Sack (1987) reviewed the existing trends.

Table 2 The contradictory expectations of athletes

An athlete must:	Versus:
Be a team player to gain the respect of others	Be competitive to maintain his or her team position
Display courteous behavior	Win at all costs
Have self-control to compete effectively	Be aggressive to compete effectively
Be self-motivated in taking the competitive initiative	Demonstrate "trainability" by following the directions of coaches and officials
Be empathic to put him or herself in a competitor's role and thereby plan a competitive strategy	Be impersonal to avoid feeling sorry for a competitor and thereby losing the competitive edge
Be self-confident in one's own expectations and abilities	Be responsive to the feedback of coaches, parents, and spectators to remain in their favor
Be willing to accept and learn from defeat	Never be satisfied with defeat
Be dedicated to sport to remain on the team and win a college scholarship	Be dedicated to academics to graduate and go on to college
Place team needs above personal needs	Be ambitious to succeed as an athlete

Table 3 Strategies for integrating athletic and student identities

School administrators should:

Provide counseling services or educational classes that allow young athletes to explore their strengths and weaknesses outside the athletic domain.

Do away with athletic dormitories that isolate athletes from the greater student body.

Develop eligibility policies making it mandatory for student athletes to become involved in social or civic groups that are unrelated to athletics.

Form student athletic advisory committees made up of both student athletes and nonathletes.

Encourage coaches to communicate with student athletes about their interests and activities outside of sport as a means of demonstrating their interest in the athletes beyond that of their performance on the playing field.

Provide reinforcements for athletes' academic and civic successes that are equal to those provided for on-field playing success.

1. High school athletes display better academic skills only when their sport involvement is paired with academic support and encouragement from parents and friends (Coakley, 1986). Only if significant others treat young athletes seriously as students does their success on the playing field generalize to success in the classroom.

2. College athletes involved in sport programs resembling the "corporate model" (e.g., football and basketball at National Collegiate Athletic Association Division I schools that are highly commercialized and generate revenue) are less likely to fair well in academia than athletes in sport programs that contain less commercialization and that generate little or no revenue. College athletes in corporate model sport programs tend to have lower grade point averages and are less likely to earn degrees.

3. College athletes in corporate model sports programs are under greater pressure by coaches to give preference to their athletic responsibilities over their student responsibilities to win games.

4. Black student athletes are least prepared for the demands of college academics and display poor academic performance.

5. College athletes, especially men, are more likely to take academic shortcuts by "clustering" in the same easy major (e.g., general studies).

6. Female student athletes are better prepared for college and perform better academically than male athletes.

Although controversial, strategies have been suggested for improving the negative association that currently seems to exist between youth sports and academic achievement. Some of these strategies are listed in Table 4 (see Coakley, 1986; Eitzen, 1987).

Summary

Given the limited and contradictory research on the cathartic, belonging, and ritualistic functions of sport, many people nevertheless continue to believe in youth sports as a character-building institution. Coakley (1987) identifies three factors that promote this belief. First, organized youth sport programs attract young people with certain characteristics (e.g., advanced physical skills) that ensure their success. In contrast, young people with undesirable skills or traits either voluntar-

Table 4 Strategies for improving the academic performance of student athletes

---

Eliminate play-offs as a means of keeping the importance placed on sports in balance with other school-sponsored activities.

Establish fixed budgets for athletic programs that do not depend upon gate receipts and fund-raising. This should reduce pressure on coaches, and thereby students, to emphasize athletic performance over academic performance.

Hire and reward coaches on the basis of educational criteria rather than on their win-loss records. Tie coaches' tenure to something other than their win-loss records (e.g., grades and graduate rates of athletes).

Shift resources away from highly selective athletic teams toward intramural activities that emphasize individual skill development and social affiliation for the entire student body.

Place athletic programs directly under the leadership of school principles and university presidents as opposed to coaches, athletic directors, or athletic boards.

Publish an annual report documenting the academic progress of athletes.

Enforce college policies regarding the admission of only those students, including athletes, who have a reasonable chance of academic success.

Provide career counseling for athletes, noting especially those barriers (e.g., injury, the aging process) that can limit one's career as a professional athlete.

Limit the time devoted to off-season practice sessions.

Limit athletes to playing in a certain number of games per season.

These suggestions were adapted from *Sport in Society: Issues and Controversies* by J. J. Coakley, 1986, St. Louis: Mosby; and "The Educational Experiences of Intercollegiate Student-Athletes" by D. S. Eitzen, 1987, *Journal of Sport and Social Issues, 11,* pp. 15–30.

ily withdraw or are cut from teams. As already discussed, this selective process is not adequately accounted for in existing research or by the general public. Second, a selective generalization occurs in youth sports by which people focus on the development of an outstanding young athlete, assume that the positive behaviors they observe have resulted directly from sports, and generalize those behaviors to all youth sport participants. However, and also as just discussed, there is no evidence of a cause and effect relationship between participation in youth sports and advanced social development. Finally, because young athletes display their best skills (i.e., their physical domain skills) in a public arena, spectators see only their successes. Not seen are the competencies of young athletes when faced with the challenges of everyday life. However, and again as just discussed, there is no consistent evidence that success on the playing field necessarily transfers to the classroom or contributes to a positive social adjustment.

Because of the limited and contradictory nature of youth sport research, an additional approach is needed to address the social development of young people who participate in youth sports. Developmental theories provide a means of assessing the social readiness of young people to enter into various types of physical activities, an issue of concern to both sport psychologists and practitioners (Gould, 1982).

THE SOCIAL READINESS OF YOUNG PEOPLE
TO ENTER INTO YOUTH SPORTS

Although most young people are selected to participate in youth sport teams based upon their physical development, it is obvious that motor skills are not easily separated from cognitive or social skills. No amount of physical strength or motor proficiency can compensate for mental confusion or social immaturity on the playing field. Given the interdependence of the physical, cognitive, and social development of young people, it is nevertheless sometimes necessary to consider each factor separately to gain a better understanding of its relative contribution to the whole child's involvement in sports. This section thus deals only with the social readiness of young people to enter into play, games, and sports.

Although the term *sports* is often used interchangeably with *play* and *games*, each activity has distinguishing characteristics (Callois, 1961; Coakley, 1980; Figler, 1981; Huizinga, 1970; Piaget, 1951, pp. 147–150) that must be addressed to understand the social readiness of young people to enter into youth sport programs.

Play, Games, and Sport

Key characteristics of play are its freedom from time, space, and rule limitations. Play is self-directed and spontaneous, lacking externally imposed rules. Play also is nonproductive in the sense that there are no extrinsic rewards. Instead, the reward of play is intrinsic: fun. Indeed, fun is essential to play, because play ceases when fun ceases (Figler, 1981).

Unlike play, games operate within a loosely organized social system that is defined and controlled by the participants themselves. Although some time, space, and rule limitations are usually built into games, they are not fixed and can be readily modified by the participants. Games are moderately productive in the sense that someone usually "wins." According to Figler (1981), fun is usually but not always present in a game. Young people may continue in a game out of a sense of obligation to their peers or to a self- or peer-imposed rule, even after fun ceases.

Sports involve highly structured activities with governing officials who specify and strictly enforce rule, location, space, and time limitations. Sports also are highly productive, the outcome of competition being ritualized through the awarding of trophies or money as well as through social recognition (e.g., banquets, media releases). According to Figler (1981), although fun may be hoped for in sport, it is not necessary. Sports, unlike the individual freedom afforded through play or the negotiated group norms of games, are externally controlled by representative officials who are not themselves active participants.

As noted in Figure 1, play and games are a primary influence in the early lives of young people. In contrast, sport is primarily an adolescent and adult activity, reflecting the social reality of externally imposed rules and norms. Movement between these physical activity categories is transitional rather than absolute. That is, as we mature we gradually come to enjoy and follow more structured physical activities. However, even as adults we have a continued need for child-like games and play. This progression from play to games and finally to sports is best appreciated from a developmental perspective.

Social Development Theory

A number of developmental theories can be used to address the readiness of young people to enter into play, games, and sports. Two are reviewed in this section: (a) Erikson's (1963) theory of social-emotional development; and (b) Selman's (1971, 1976) theory of role taking. Unlike Harter's (1978) theory, these two theories have not been directly tested within youth sports research settings. Yet

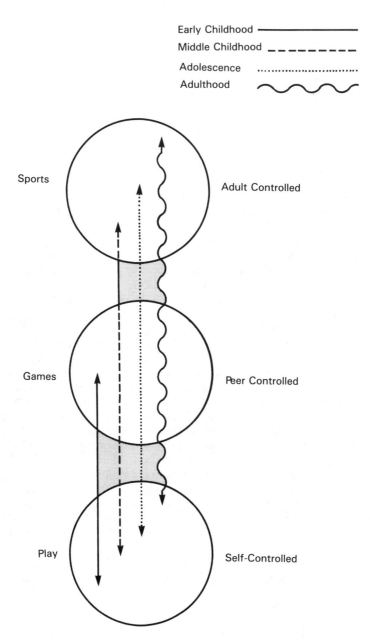

Early Childhood ——————
Middle Childhood — — — — — — —
Adolescence   ....
Adulthood   ∿∿∿∿∿

Sports   Adult Controlled

Games   Peer Controlled

Play   Self-Controlled

Figure 1 The developmental sequencing and control of play, games, and sports.

they remain valuable as heuristic models in addressing the social readiness of young people to enter into various phases of the youth sports' experience.

Erikson

According to Erikson (1963), the social-emotional development of an individual proceeds through a series of eight stages, each of which contains certain life dilemmas or crises that must be resolved if the individual is to successfully progress to the next stage. For most young people, youth sports first become a factor in their social development between the ages of 6 and 12. It is during this time that young people begin to deal with the life dilemma of "industry versus inferiority." They seek praise for their achievements, and they seek out social comparisons with others. As noted by Erikson (1963), it is through "doing things beside and with others" that young people develop their "first sense of division of labor and of differential opportunity" (p. 260). That is, it is through social comparisons that young people begin to develop a sense of their personal strengths and self-worth. Those young people who compare themselves favorably with others and who receive positive feedback from significant adults develop a sense of industry and trust in themselves. In contrast, young people who compare themselves unfavorably with their peers or who receive negative feedback from significant adults run the risk of developing a sense of inferiority over their abilities and self-worth.

For those few young people who possess advanced physical skills, youth sports can become a source of pride, self-reinforcement, and self-worth (Heyman, 1987) that will carry them forward into their next stage of social development during the adolescent years. However, there is also a potential downside for successful young athletes. If their early success is reinforced by parents, teachers, and coaches at the expense of other aspects of childhood, then a danger exists that they will develop a constricted sense of self that can lead to identity problems during adolescence. This is especially true in those situations where athletic abilities diminish or are lost during adolescence as a result of injury or the sudden motor skill advances of peers who during early and middle childhood, exhibited normal or delayed motor development.

Young people—most young people in fact—who possess normal or delayed motor skills during the early and middle childhood years face a different set of circumstances when competing in youth sports. These individuals may develop feelings of inadequacy and inferiority as they are cut from teams, provided with limited playing time, or ridiculed by parents or spectators for performances that fail to match up to those of their more advanced peers. As noted previously here, in extreme cases, these experiences may lead some young people to avoid physical activities altogether, setting the stage for a sedentary life-style and health problems.

Young people aged 12 to 18 enter into a new stage of social development in which the life dilemma revolves around "role identity versus role confusion." The goal during this stage is for adolescents to develop role identities for a range of social contexts, including family, work, and society in general. This process typically involves experimentation with values and behaviors that may at times seem ideological. However, as noted by Erikson (1963), although adolescence is characterized by an "ideological mind . . . it is the ideological outlook of a society that speaks most clearly to the adolescent who is eager to be affirmed by his (or her) peers, and is ready to be confirmed by rituals, creeds, and programs which at the same time define what is evil, uncanny and inimical" (p. 263).

Sports can serve an important function in helping adolescents to feel "affirmed." The rituals associated with sport nicknames, uniforms, and activities can contribute to adolescents' perception of themselves as an important part of the social order. When conducted in a developmentally appropriate manner, sport programs also can help instill lifelong values relating to health practices, social cooperation, and fair play.

However, when the athletic identity is reinforced at the expense of other aspects of the adolescent's life, role confusion may result as new demands are made that fall outside the playing field. For example, some high school or college athletes may try unsuccessfully to translate their athletic identity and skills to the classroom, work site, or dating relationship (Heyman, 1987). That is, they may narrowly define self based upon a life dominated by an athletic peer group. Time commitments to practicing, participating in, and observing sports may prevent adolescent athletes from taking part in school, occupational, and general interpersonal experiences (Heyman, 1987; Snyder, 1983) that are necessary prerequisites for successfully carrying out adult life roles.

From a developmental perspective, it is a mistake to assume that sport involvement can build total character. At a time when the unethical behavior of successful college and professional athletes is under scrutiny by the media, a danger also exists that the ideological mind-set of adolescent athletes may lead them to confuse what is socially appropriate and socially inappropriate behavior on and off the playing field.

Selman

As suggested by Erikson (1963), to fully appreciate and participate in competitive sports, young people must be able to put themselves in the roles of their teammates and opponents. Such role taking is necessary to coordinate one's own performance with that of fellow teammates and plan counterstrategies against one's opponents. Even young people involved in individual sports like track or swimming must pace themselves in relation to their expectations about the performance of other participants. Without such role taking, it becomes difficult to effectively compete, and, as a result, the competitive quality of sport is lost.

Selman (1971, 1976) identified a number of stages through which young people move in their role-taking ability. Young people between the ages of 6 and 8 are in the "social-informational" stage. They are aware that others hold social perceptions that may or may not be similar to their own, but nevertheless they tend to focus only on their own perceptions in carrying out activities. Young people in this stage of role taking have a limited ability to coordinate their roles when involved in a group activity, making it difficult for them to comprehend or carry out the logistics of team sports.

Young people aged 8 to 10 are in a self-reflective stage, having a more sophisticated level of self- and "other" awareness. That is, young people are now able to reflect on the self's behavior and motivation as it might be viewed from another person's perspective. However, their role-taking ability is often limited to a two-person interaction. They are unable to coordinate the different self-perceptions of a group of individuals, making it difficult for youth coaches to successfully coordinate team positions and activities containing more than two individuals.

During the next stage, the mutual role-taking ability of young people aged 10 to 12 begins to encompass group self-perceptions. That is, young people are now able to move beyond a two-person interaction and consider the perspectives of three or more people simultaneously. Young people are now able to recognize the relativity of an issue or task across a number of individual perceptions, allowing them to better understand and appreciate differences of opinions. This might be viewed as a period of transition during which the loosely organized structure of games can become more organized.

For adolescents 12 years of age and older, the mutuality of group perceptions is expanded to "social and conventional system role taking." It is during this stage that adolescents realize that mutual perspective taking does not necessarily result in mutual agreements. Instead, adolescents begin to consider the perceptions of the "generalized other" as represented by greater society. Their behavior is now guided by a decision-making process that takes into account the values and rules of society and its institutions, including the institution of sport.

Summary

The social development of young people suggests that it is not until age 12 that they are able to fully understand and respect the need for the external sanctions and reward systems imposed by sports as a social institution (Coakley, 1984). Before age 12, young people should move from an initial involvement in spontaneous and unorganized play during the early school years to the challenges of loosely organized games in the later elementary school years.

Unfortunately, as discussed previously here, this developmental sequencing is not occurring. It is thus not surprising that a sizable number of young people are in turn withdrawing from organized physical activities. One large-scale study found that youth sport involvement increased up to ages 11, 12, and 13, but declined dramatically thereafter (Sapp & Haubensticker, 1978). Similar findings have been reported by others (Eifermann, 1971). Overall, it is estimated that approximately 35% of all young people eventually withdraw from youth sports (Gould, 1987b). The withdrawal of young people from physical activities around the ages of 11 to 13 supports the argument against imposing the demands and stress of adult-governed sports onto young people before the adolescent years (Eifermann, 1971; Iso-Ahola, 1980, p. 113–114). Some specific guides for assessing the social readiness of young people to enter into play, games, and sports are given in Table 5.

CONCLUSION

Although it is too soon to draw firm conclusions about the impact of youth sports on the social development of young people, three outcomes are possible when youth sport programs are conducted with an adult-centered philosophy: (a) washout; (b) burnout; and (c) super athlete (Figler, 1981). These outcomes, depicted in Figure 2, relate well to the research and theoretical work reviewed in this chapter.

As youth sports move away from a child-centered philosophy to an adult-centered philosophy (Figler, 1981; McPherson, 1986), increasing pressure is placed on young people to function under adult-imposed rules and expectations. Those young people who lack the physical skills or cognitive or social maturity to

Table 5 Guides for assessing the readiness of young people to enter into play, games, and sports

---

1. Based on the research and theory reviewed in this chapter, the following guides apply to considering a young person's social readiness to enter into different types of physical activities.
   - Young people in preschool and the early elementary grades need the freedom and flexibility to learn about themselves and others through play and loosely constructed, simple games. The focus should not be on social comparison or competition but on individual strengths and skill development (Coakley, 1984).
   - Young people in the middle-school grades who are better able to make social comparisons can be introduced to group games that are peer governed. Adults should serve as facilitators in reinforcing participation rather than as coaches. Orlick's (1982) cooperative games provide a good reference source of learning how to facilitate peer-dominated games.
   - Beginning around age 10, young people can gradually be introduced to the competitive aspects of sports. However, rules and operational standards should be based not on adult expectations but on the expectations and developmental abilities of children involved. Practical suggestions for this transitional period from games to sport can be found in a number of resources (Coakley, 1986; Morris, 1984; Orlick, 1984; Pooley, 1984).
   - Only upon entering adolescence will most young people be fully able to understand, appreciate, and accept the adult world of organized competitive sports in which rules and operational standards are external to the players involved.
2. Assess the developmental readiness of young people to enter into play, games, and sports by observing their play and asking questions of significant adults (e.g., parents and teachers). Some possible questions to ask include:
   - How well does this child cooperate with peers?
   - How well does this child follow instructions?
   - Is this child self-motivated?
   - Does this child have good impulse control?
   - How does this child respond to frustration?
   - How does this child respond to limits?
3. Use the following guides to assess the play, game, and sport characteristics of physical activities. If necessary, redesign an activity so that it is more developmentally appropriate for the young people involved.
   - Structure refers to the degree of outside involvement in an activity, as defined by time, space, and rule limitations. Play has low structure, wheres games have moderate structure, and sports have high structure.
   - Productivity refers to the emphasis placed on the extrinsic rewards (trophies and social recognition) associated with an activity. Play has low productivity, whereas games have moderate productivity, and sports have high productivity.
   - Skill refers to the degree to which one must possess certain physical abilities to successfully participate in an activity. Play ranks low in skill proficiency, whereas games have moderate skill requirements, and sports have high skill requirements.
   - Separation refers to the ease by which one's identity and self-worth can be separated from one's involvement in a physical activity. Play has a high degree of separateness, whereas games have a moderate degree of separateness. Because of the personal sacrifices associated with "making a team" and the status of being an athlete, sports usually have a low degree of separateness.

---

cope with this pressure washout while transitioning into sports or soon thereafter. Other young people who have the physical skills to successfully compete in sports nevertheless burnout as the demands of maintaining their team position and competitive edge detracts them from other social aspects of their childhood lives. Finally, those young people who posses the skills, support, and personal interests to succeed in sports stand a chance of becoming one of the relatively few "super athletes." However, as discussed previously here, there is no conclusive evidence that even the success of these young super athletes on the playing field extends to all other aspects of their lives.

As also noted in Figure 2, it is the transitional periods between play, games, and sports that are critical to the continued involvement of young people in physical activities. Care should be taken to slowly transition young people between these physical activity categories, focusing on their readiness to engage in increasingly structured and competitive activities. Throughout all transitions, focus should be on the individual's skill development and enjoyment of physical activities as opposed to comparisons and outcomes.

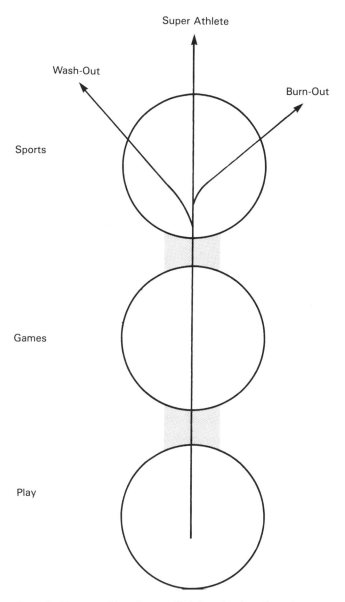

Figure 2 Three possible outcomes of adult-centered youth sport programs.

Given the problems found in the institution of sport for young people, there nevertheless remains a potential for it to fulfill its social function of instilling life values and skills. Researchers will no doubt continue to document the ways in which changes in youth sports contribute to or detract from the social development of youth participants.

REFERENCES

Berryman, J. W. (1988). The rise of highly organized sports for pre-adolescent boys. In R. A. Magill, M. J. Ash, & F. L. Smoll (Eds.), *Children in sport: A contemporary anthology*. Champaign, IL: Human Kinetics.

Callois, R. (1961). *Man, play and games*. New York: Free Press.

Coakley, J. (1980). Play, game, and sport: Developmental implications for young people. *Journal of Sport Behavior, 3*(2), 99–118.

Coakley, J. (1984). When should children begin competing? A sociological perspective. In M. R. Weiss & D. Gould (Eds.), *Sport for children and youths*. Champaign, IL: Human Kinetics.

Coakley, J. J. (1986). *Sport in society: Issues and controversies*. St. Louis, MO: Times Mirror/Mosby.

Coakley, J. J. (1987). Children and the sport socialization process. In D. Gould & M. R. Weiss (Eds.), *Advances in pediatric sport sciences*. Champaign, IL: Human Kinetics.

Coleman, J. S. (1961). Athletics in high school. *Annals of the American Academy of Political and Social Science, 338*, 33–43.

Coleman, M. (1985). Promoting children's well-being through developmentally appropriate sport programming. *Wellness Perspectives, 2*(2), 9–12.

Cratty, B. J. (1981). *Social psychology in athletes*. Englewood Cliffs, NJ: Prentice-Hall.

Eifermann, R. R. (1971). Social play in childhood. In R. E. Herron & B. Sutton-Smith (Eds.), *Child's play*. New York: Wiley.

Eitzen, D. S. (1975). Athletes in the status system of male adolescents: A replication of Coleman's *the adolescent society*. *Adolescence, 10*(38), 267–276.

Eitzen, D S. (1987). The educational experiences of intercollegiate student-athletes. *Journal of Sport and Social Issues, 11*(1,2), 15–30.

Elkind, D. (1981). *The hurried child*. Reading, MA: Addison-Wesley.

Erikson, E. H. (1963). *Childhood and society*. New York: Norton.

Feltz, D. L., & Petlichkoff, L. (1983). Perceived competence among interscholastic sport participants and dropouts. *Canadian Journal of Applied Sport Sciences, 8*(4), 231–235.

Figler, S. K. (1981). *Sport and play in American life: A textbook in the sociology of sport*. Philadelphia: Saunders.

Fishwick, L., & Greendorfer, S. (1987). Socialization revisited: A critique of the sport-related research, *Quest, 39*(1), 1–8.

Gavin, J. (1988). Psychological issues in exercise prescription. *Sports Medicine, 6*(1), 1–10.

Gill, D. L. (1986). *Psychological dynamics of sport*. Champaign, IL: Human Kinetics.

Gill, D. L., Gross, J. B., & Huddleston, S. (1983). Participation motivation in youth sport. *International Journal of Sport Psychology, 14*(1), 1–14.

Gould, D. (1981). The role of the physical educator in nonschool youth sports. *Physical educator, 38*(2), 99–104.

Gould, D. (1982). Sport psychology in the 1980s: Status, direction and challenge in youth sport research. *Journal of Sport Psychology, 4*(3), 203–218.

Gould, D. (1987a). Promoting positive sport experiences for children. In J. R. May & M. J. Asken (Eds.), *Sport psychology: The psychological health of the athlete*. New York: PMA.

Gould, D. (1987b). Understanding attrition in children's sport. In D. Gould & M. R. Weiss (Eds.), *Advances in pediatric sport sciences*. Champaign, IL: Human Kinetics.

Gould, D., Feltz, D., Horn, T., & Weiss, M. (1982). Reasons for discontinuing involvement in competitive youth swimming. *Journal of Sport Behavior, 5*(3), 155–165.

Gould, D., Feltz, D., & Weiss, M. (1985). Motives for participating in competitive youth swimming. *International Journal of Sport Psychology, 16*(2), 126–140.

Gould, D., & Horn, T. (1984). Participation motivation in young athletes. In J. M. Silva & R. S. Weinberg (Eds.), *Psychological foundations of sport*. Champaign, IL: Human Kinetics.

Gould, D., & Petlichkoff, L. (1988). Participation motivation and attrition in young athletes. In F. L.

Smoll, R. A. Magill, & M. J. Ash (Eds.), *Children in sport* (3rd ed.). Champaign, IL: Human Kinetics.

Harter, S. (1978). Effective motivation reconsidered: Toward a developmental model. *Human Development, 21*(1), 34–64.

Harter, S. (1981). A new self-report scale of intrinsic versus extrinsic orientation in the classroom: Motivational and informational components. *Development Psychology, 17*(3), 300–312.

Hastad, D., Segrave, J. O., Pangrazi, R., & Peterson, G. (1986). Causal factors of deviant behavior among youth sport participants and nonparticipants. In L. V. Veldden & J. Humphrey (Eds.), *Psychology and sociology of sport: Current selected research* (Vol. 1). New York: AMS.

Hellstedt, J. C. (1988). Kids, parents, and sports: Some questions and answers. *The Physician and Sports Medicine, 16*(4), 59–71.

Heyman, S. R. (1986). Psychological problem patterns found with athletes. *The Clinical Psychologist, 39*(3), 68–71.

Heyman, S. R. (1987). Counseling and psychotherapy with athletes: Special considerations. In J. R. May & M. J. Asken (Eds.), *Sport psychology: The psychological health of the athlete.* New York: PMA.

Horn, T. S., & Hasbrook, C. (1984). Informational components influencing children's perceptions of their physical competence. In M. R. Weiss & D. Gould (Eds.), *Sport for children and youth.* Champaign, IL: Human Kinetics.

Horn, T. S, & Hasbrook, C. A. (1987). Psychological characteristics and the criteria children use for self-evaluation. *Journal of Sport Psychology, 9*(3), 208–221.

Huizinga, J. (1970). *Homo ludens: A study of the play element in culture.* New York: Harper & Row.

Iso-Ahola, S. E. (1980). *The social psychology of leisure and recreation.* Dubuque, IA: William C. Brown.

Kerr, G., & Fowler, B. (1988). The relationship between psychological factors and sports injuries. *Sports Medicine, 6*(3), 127–134.

Kimiecik, J. C. (1988). Who needs coaches' education? U. S. coaches do. *The Physician and Sports Medicine, 16*(11), 124–136.

Klint, K. A., & Weiss, W. R. (1986). Dropping in and dropping out: Participation motives of current and former youth gymnasts. *Canadian Journal of Applied Sport Sciences, 11*(2), 106–114.

Klint, K. A., & Weiss, M. R. (1987). Perceived competence and motives for participating in youth sports: A test of Harter's competence motivation theory. *Journal of Sport Psychology, 9*(1), 55–65.

Kozar, B., & Lord, R. H. (1988). Overuse injuries in young athletes: A "growing" problem. In F. L. Smoll, R. A. Magill, & M. J. Ash (Eds.), *Children in sport.* Champaign, IL: Human Kinetics.

Leonard, W. M. (1988). *A sociological perspective of sport* (3rd ed.). New York: Macmillan.

Lewko, J. H., & Ewing, M. E. (1980). Sex differences and parental influence in sport involvement of children. *Journal of Sport Psychology, 2*(1), 62–68.

Lewko, J. H., & Greendorfer, S. L. (1988). Family influences in sport socialization of children and adolescents. In F. L. Smoll, R. A. Magill, & M. J. Ash (Eds.), *Children in sport.* Champaign, IL: Human Kinetics.

Lucas, J. (1986). Predictions for the year 2000. *Journal of Physical Education, Recreation and Dance, 57*(8), 7.

Martens, R. (1980). The uniqueness of the young athlete: Psychologic considerations. *American Journal of Sports Medicine, 8*(5), 382–385.

Martens, R. (1988). Youth sport in the USA. In F. L. Smoll, R. A. Magill, & M. J. Ash (Eds.), *Children in sport.* Champaign, IL: Human Kinetics.

McElroy, M. A., & Kirdendall, D. R. (1981). Conflict in perceived parent/child sport ability judgments. *Journal of Sport Psychology, 3*(3), 244–247.

McPherson, B D. (1986). Policy-oriented research in youth sport: An analysis of the process and product. In C. R. Rees & A. W. Miracle (Eds.), *Sports and social theory.* Champaign, IL: Human Kinetics.

Miller Brewing Company. (1983). *The Miller Lite report on American attitudes toward sports: 1983.* Milwaukee, WI: Author.

Morris, G. S. D. (1984). Developing a sense of competence in children through game modifications. In M. R. Weiss & D. Gould (Eds.), *Sport for children and youth.* Champaign, IL: Human Kinetics.

Orlick, T. D. (1982). *The second cooperative sports and games book.* New York: Pantheon.

Orlick, T. D. (1984). Evolution in children's sport. In M. R. Weiss & D. Gould (Eds.), *Sport for children and youth.* Champaign, IL: Human Kinetics.

Passer, M. W. (1982). Children in sport: Participation motives and psychological stress. *Quest, 33*(2), 231–244.

Piaget, J. (1951). *Play, dreams and imitation in childhood.* New York: W. W. Norton.
Pooley, J. C. (1984). A level above competition: An inclusive model for youth sport. In M. R. Weiss & D. Gould (Eds.), *Sport for children and youth.* Champaign, IL: Human Kinetics.
Purdy, D. A., & Richard, S. F. (1983). Sport and juvenile delinquency: An examination and assessment of four major theories. *Journal of Sport Behavior, 6*(4), 179–193.
Roberts, G. C., Kleiber, D. A., & Duda, J. L. (1981). An analysis of motivation in children's sport: The role of perceived competence in participation. *Journal of Sport Psychology, 3*(3), 206–216.
Sack, A. L. (1987). College sport and the student-athlete. *Journal of Sport and Social Issues, 11*(1,2), 31–48.
Sapp, M., & Haubenstricker, J. (1978). *Motivation for joining and reasons for not continuing in youth sport programs in Michigan.* Paper presented at the meeting of the American Alliance for Health, Physical Education, Recreation, and Dance, Kansas City, MO.
Scanlan, T. K. (1984). Competitive stress in children. In M. R. Weiss & D. Gould (Eds.), *Sport for children and youth.* Champaign, IL: Human Kinetics.
Seefeldt, V. (1987). *Handbook for youth sports coaches.* Reston, VA: American Alliance for Health, Physical Education, Recreation, and Dance.
Segrave, J. O. (1983). Sport and juvenile delinquency. In R. L. Terjung (Ed.), *Exercise and sport sciences reviews* (Vol. 11). Lexington, MA: D. C. Health.
Segrave, J. O., & Hastad, D. N. (1982). Delinquent behavior and interscholastic athletic participation. *Journal of Sport Behavior, 5*(2), 96–111.
Selman, R. L. (1971). Taking another's perspective: Role-taking development in early childhood. *Child Development, 42*(6), 1721–1734.
Selman, R. L. (1976). Social-cognitive understanding: A guide to educational and clinical practice. In T. Lickona (Ed.), *Moral development and behavior: theory, research, and social issues.* New York: Holt, Rinehart, & Winston.
Silva, J. M. (1984). Personality and sport performance: Controversy and challenge. In J. M. Silva & R. S. Weinberg (Eds.), *Psychological foundations of sport.* Champaign, IL: Human Kinetics.
Singer, R. N., & Gerson, R. G. (1980). Athletic competition for children: Motivational considerations. *International Journal of Sport Psychology, 11*(4), 249–262.
Smith, R. E., Smoll, F. L., & Curtis, B. (1979). Coaching effectiveness training: A cognitive-behavioral approach to enhancing relationship skills in youth sport coaches. *Journal of Sport Psychology, 1,* 59–75.
Smoll, F. L., & Smith, R. E. (1981). Preparation of youth sport coaches: An educational application of sport psychology. *Physical Educator, 38*(2), 85–94.
Smoll, F. L., & Smith, R. (1984). Leadership research in youth sports. In J. M. Silva & R. S. Weinberg (Eds.), *Psychological foundations of sport.* Champaign, IL: Human Kinetics.
Snyder, E. E. (1983). Identity, commitment, and type of sport roles. *Quest, 35*(2), 97–106.
Snyder, E. E, & Spreitzer, E. A. (1983). *Social aspects of sport* (2nd ed.). Englewood Cliffs, NJ: Prentice-Hall.
Stevenson, C. L. (1975). Socialization effects of participation in sport: A critical review of the research. *Research Quarterly for Exercise and Sport, 46*(4), 287–301.
Vallerand, R. J., Deci, E. L., & Ryan, R. M. (1987). Intrinsic motivation in sport. In K. B. Pandolf (Ed.), *Exercise and sport sciences review* (Vol. 15). New York: Macmillan.
Wankel, L. M., & Kreisel, P. S. J. (1985). Factors underlying enjoyment of youth sports: Sport and age group comparisons. *Journal of Sport Psychology, 7*(1), 51–64.
Weiss, M. R., & Bredemeier, B. J. (1983). Developmental sport psychology: A theoretical perspective for studying children in sport. *Journal of Sport Psychology, 5*(2), 216–230.
Wiggins, D. K. (1987). A history of organized play and highly competitive sport for American children. In D. Gould & M. R. Weiss (Eds.), *Advances in pediatric sport sciences.* Champaign, IL: Human Kinetics.

7

Moral Development and Sports Participation

Ignatius J. Toner
University of North Carolina at Charlotte

For when the One Great Scorer comes to write against your name,
He marks not that you won or lost, but how you played the game.

(Grantland Rice)

Winning isn't everything. It's the only thing.

(Vince Lombardi)

In the October 16, 1989 issue of *Sports Illustrated,* Bruce Newman described an event rare in professional competitive sport. Freeman McNeil, a running back for the New York Jets football team, in the course of making a legal block for another runner, accidentally inflicted a serious knee injury on linebacker O'Brien Alston of the Indianapolis Colts. What made the incident especially noteworthy were the subsequent reactions of McNeil and his coach. McNeil was overcome with remorse and unable to concentrate on the game after the incident. At the conclusion of the game, McNeil sought out the injured player and tearfully apologized. Jet coach Joe Walton was less sympathetic, remarking "I've never seen anything like it. I understand his feeling, but that's the way the game goes. Obviously, it [McNeil allowing his feelings to affect his play] was not a good thing . . . and he realizes that."

During and after the game, two men displayed distinctly different emotions, judgments, and actions in response to the moral dilemma. Clearly, to Freeman McNeil, he had determined that he had done something wrong when he hurt the other player. He judged the incident based on the consequences of his action and not on his innocent intentions. His emotional reaction was compassion and remorse. To his coach, the injury-producing action itself was not wrong. Instead, it was the effect of the remorse on McNeil's subsequent play that was wrong. Different men in different positions regarding competitive sport had distinctly different views of right and wrong.

In the January 15, 1990 issue of *Sports Illustrated,* Jay Greenberg described another moral conflict involving athletes. The new coach of the Tri-City Americans of the Western (junior) Hockey League used what were perceived by the players to be brutal tactics. The players called for a strike of team members. The dispute was settled soon after, but the players involved in the strike action were required to perform punitive community service to atone for their boycott. Goaltender Olaf Kolzig commented, "I don't think we should be punished for doing what we think was right."

On February 28, 1990, an unidentified teammate of Charles Shackleford claimed that members of the North Carolina State University basketball team had "shaved points" in games during the 1987–1988 season at the direction of gamblers. Shackleford had already admitted taking a considerable amount of money from boosters while still a student-athlete at North Carolina State University. The unidentified player justified such behavior by saying on ABC-TV that "it was basically just for the money . . . and it was justice to them in the sense that . . . they're bringing in thousands and thousands of dollars for them a year by playing on TV."

What determines how one judges right and wrong? What determines how one feels about transgressing? What determines how one acts in a moral conflict situation? In short, what determines an individual's personal morality and how does that morality develop?

To adequately understand the relationship between morality and sports participation requires a developmental perspective. The major theories of morality have consistently taken a developmental perspective because moral judgments, moral feelings, and moral behaviors appear to change substantially with age. Similarly, the dimensions of sports participation for the child may not be the same as those for the adolescent or adult. Does sports participation build character? Does the sports participant view the "rules of the game" in the same way throughout his or her life? What makes the participant more or less likely to follow the "rules of the game"? Clearly, there is likely no general statement about the relationship between morality and sports participation that will apply to all ages of participants.

In the present chapter, three psychological theories of moral development are presented in some detail. The application of these theories to contemporary sports participation will be made. However, it must be noted at the outset that such application is often speculative rather than demonstrated. Thus, it is often left to the reader to deduce the value of the theories to particular sports-related circumstances. An appreciation of the theories of moral development may guide sports researchers and practitioners in their efforts to understand how sports participants feel, think, and act in moral conflict situations. In this way, the present chapter, often unrestrained by data, may be viewed as promising rather than prescriptive.

PSYCHOLOGICAL THEORIES OF MORAL DEVELOPMENT: AN OVERVIEW

How one deals with issues and events involving right and wrong has been the concern of philosophers, theologians, and, more recently, psychologists. In fact, there has emerged, within this century, three distinct perspectives on the development of morality from childhood to adulthood, and each of these three theories has concentrated on distinctly different aspects of morality. Because they are oriented toward different domains of morality, rarely do the theories come into direct conflict with one other. The psychoanalytic perspective, notably that espoused by Sigmund Freud and Erik Erikson, has focused on the emotional or affective aspect of a developing morality. The cognitive-developmental perspective, especially that of Jean Piaget and Lawrence Kohlberg, has focused upon underlying judgmental and reasoning processes in moral thinking. Finally, the social learning perspective has focused upon the actual behavior of people when confronted with moral conflict situations. The three aspects of moral development—emotions, thinking, and behavior—have rarely been considered as a unitary phenomenon. Instead, the theorizing and research focusing on morality has typically taken a "three-track" approach. Each of the three aspects of morality will be dealt with separately in the present chapter because this approach has characterized the way psychology has found to be most useful in dealing with moral development.

THE PSYCHOANALYTIC PERSPECTIVE ON MORAL DEVELOPMENT

The psychoanalytic model of moral development focuses upon the manner in which children and adults deal with the emotional component of morality. For example, why did Freeman McNeil feel the way he did when he hurt the other player or Olaf Kolzig react to his punishment as he did in the incidents described earlier? What caused Canadian sprinter Ben Johnson to repent after the revelation of his steroid-enhanced performance at the Seoul Olympic Games? Why did baseball's Pete Rose and the basketball teammate of Charles Shackleford initially refrain from contrition following their scandals?

For the psychoanalytic theorist, moral standards are viewed as the outcome of an unconscious struggle between the pleasure principle (id), which is at once hedonistic and impulsive, and the developing "inner parent" provided by the superego. The id dominates the infant and the very young child because the superego has yet to be fully developed through socializing experiences. The id is part of the constitution of the individual and is influential from the beginning of life. As one gets older, impulsive gratification generally is on the wane, while more realistic, reflective means to achieve goals become more likely.

The focus of the psychoanalytic perspective on moral development is usually on how the individual deals with his or her own transgressions in moral conflict situations. Psychoanalytic theorists focus on such reactions as the development of the sense of remorse, compassion, guilt, confession, repression, reaction formation, and the other defense mechanisms. Dubbed the "original sin" orientation, the psychoanalytic perspective views the developing child as inherently selfish and immoral, and it is the task of a civilized society to socialize the developing individual so that he or she becomes a productive and nondestructive part of that society.

Freud (1935/1960) proposed that the superego develops most markedly during the preschool years. He maintained that children identify with the same-sex parent as an outcome of a conflict involving rivalry with that parent for the affection of the opposite-sex parent. Boys thus take on a wide range of characteristics of their fathers (including morals standards) and girls, in a similar manner, take on the characteristics of their mothers. The complete resolution of this intrafamilial conflict typically occurs by age 6 or 7, at which time the superego is a powerful inhibitor of immorality. However, Freud noted that girls do not develop as powerful a superego as boys because girls' fear of their mothers (fear being the instigator of identification) is not as intense as the fear boys feel toward their fathers.

Erikson (1963), from the psychoanalytic tradition, does not concur with many of Sigmund Freud's notions about the developing morality of the child. Erikson credits both parents (not just the same-sex parent) with a major role in developing a moral child. In his system, the id is never completely overwhelmed by the growing power of the superego. Erikson emphasized the role of the ego or reality principle in moral growth more so than Freud. For Erikson, moral growth is as much an intellectual as an emotional experience.

Research on the propositions advanced by psychoanalytic theorists has been inconclusive. Unlike other major theories of development, psychoanalytic models do not neatly fit the criteria of a scientific theory that can be directly tested and perhaps falsified. However, there are some data indicating that several of Freud's notions are perhaps less than accurate. For example, harsh, threatening parents, who should generate the most fear and therefore the strongest motivation for their children to identify with them, do not seem to produce children with the most clearly defined sense of morality (Hoffman, 1970), nor do boys appear to have a reliably higher level of morality than girls. Some researchers suggest, in fact, that girls may have a more clearly defined sense of morality than boys (e.g., Hoffman, 1975). Finally, morality does not seem to stop developing in early childhood. As we see in the discussion of the other major perspectives on moral development, morality appears to continue changing throughout childhood and perhaps even into adulthood for most individuals.

Research directly applying the psychoanalytic perspective on moral development to sports participation is nonexistent. The psychoanalytic perspective offers little to clarify the relationship between morality and sports other than to note that feelings resulting from transgressions are based on how a child deals with intrafamilial conflict, and that the resultant feelings should apply to all areas of life where one experiences moral conflict. Thus, the athlete who uses banned substances to enhance his or her performance, the amateur athlete who accepts payment, or the player who violates game rules may feel varying degrees of remorse, guilt, and soon. The extent of these feelings is determined for the most part by early childhood experiences. Such feelings should be consistently displayed in moral conflict situations whether the individual is engaged in sports participation or not. Unfortunately, how Freeman McNeil, Olaf Kolzig, Charles Shackleford, Ben Johnson, or Pete Rose reacted to transgressions cannot be predicted as precisely as it can be explained after the fact.

THE COGNITIVE-DEVELOPMENTAL PERSPECTIVE ON MORAL DEVELOPMENT

On what basis did McNeil, Kolzig, Shackleford, the unidentified North Carolina State teammate of Shackleford, Johnson, and Rose justify their actions? What determines how an individual thinks about and judges right and wrong? This is the essential question addressed by the cognitive-developmental theorists concerned with moral development.

In their 1983 review of research on developmental sport psychology, Maureen Weiss and Brenda Jo Bredemeier wrote: "Sporting contests may be viewed as moral situations in which many formal and informal agreements regulate interpersonal behavior. Because individuals at different levels of moral maturity reason differently about behaviors within the moral domain, sports psychologists need to consider morality within the cognitive-developmental framework" (p. 225).

The cognitive-developmental perspective has been presented most eloquently by Jean Piaget and Lawrence Kohlberg. Unlike the psychoanalytic approach, developing morality for the cognitive-developmental theorist is embodied in the development of moral reasoning. Moral development is a cognitive process, not merely or necessarily an emotional process. The cognitive-developmentalists view morality as essentially conscious judgments of the rightness or wrongness of decisions and actions in moral conflict situations. These theorists seek to determine developmental trends and underlying mental processes that form the basis of moral thinking. Further, unlike the psychoanalytic approach, this perspective is much more optimistic in its view of the developing sense of morality in individuals.

The development of moral thinking is proposed to be a stage-like phenomenon with the stages set in an invariant sequence. For the cognitive-developmentalist, each stage that the individual goes through in the development of moral reasoning is an integrated whole that leads to consistent ways of thinking about moral dilemmas. Each stage involves qualitatively different ways of reasoning about and judging right and wrong than the earlier and later stages. During development, each stage of moral reasoning is integrated into the next higher level of moral thinking and is thus replaced by it. Therefore, earlier, more primitive levels of moral thinking are necessary for the development of the later, more sophisticated levels of moral reasoning. No stages can be skipped, and once a new and higher level of moral reasoning is achieved, the individual will understand but will not be attracted to less sophisticated ways of thinking about moral issues. A final characteristic of the stages of moral thinking is that the movement through the stages is an active process. An individual develops new and higher levels of moral thinking only by dealing with moral issues that challenge him or her to think in newer, more sophisticated ways. Therefore, one can decide to arrest his or her own moral development at any point.

In the realm of moral thinking, athletes are sometimes expected to be more sophisticated than they actually are. The recent and continuing troubles of professional basketball player Chris Washburn provide an example of how athletes may not develop moral sophistication as readily as others. Washburn was very highly recruited young basketball player who enrolled at North Carolina State University. Although quite talented, his abbreviated college career was marked by a lack of personal discipline and by a conviction of theft. Washburn was drafted by the Golden State Warriors of the National Basketball Association. His use of banned substances then led him to be suspended for life from the league. Such difficulties were attributed by former teammate Doc Rivers of the Atlanta Hawks to a misperception by others of the sophistication of athletes who possess the physical stature of Washburn. Rivers remarked to Leonard Laye of the *Charlotte Observer* in January 1990: "I think what happens with a lot of guys like Washburn, people forget these big 6-10 men-look-alikes are kids. And people treat them like adults. They let them go on their own and get away with anything. How are we ever supposed to be responsible people?"

JEAN PIAGET'S APPROACH TO MORAL THINKING

The essence of morality for the famous Swiss psychologist Jean Piaget (1932/1965) was the individual's respect for rules of social order and his or her sense of justice. Piaget noted that his own children initially based their moral thinking on their respect and submission to authority figures, whereas, later in childhood, they based their moral thinking on self-generated ideals and self-determined distinctions between right and wrong. Piaget proposed two major stages of moral thinking. The first he called the stage of moral realism and the second he called the stage of moral autonomy. He also proposed that, when very young, the child is in a pre-moral period. Piaget was quite cautious about the use of the word *stage* as applied to moral thinking because individual differences in moral reasoning may be quite large at any age.

Piaget observed children playing the simple game of marbles. He asked children of different ages about the rules of the game. Then he watched the children play the game. The children were asked if they could make up new rules for the game and where the rules for marbles came from.

Piaget noticed that, before the age of 3 to 5 years, children were often uncon-cerned or unaware of the rules of the games and often did not play with the intention of winning the games. They seemed to be making up their own private rituals and, unconstrained by rules, seemed to display great joy in merely partici-pating in the activity. The game was almost free-play for such a young child. At most, there were only motor rules with the consideration of right and wrong ways of playing the game not entering into the thinking of the very young child. Thus, the preschool child was not immoral or moral but premoral. However, the sense of the need to adhere to rules comes soon thereafter. The young children observed older children following specific rules of game playing, and these younger chil-dren attempted to imitate their older playmates. Soon, the young child would enter the stage of moral realism, never to return to premoral reasoning.

In the stage of moral realism (also called the stage of moral heteronomy), the child feels the obligation to comply with rules at all times because these rules are sacred and unalterable. The rules are deemed sacred because they have been set by authority figures superior in knowledge and status to the child. The rules are deemed unalterable because such standards represent moral absolutes with no "shades of gray" between what is good and what is bad. Rules are viewed as eternal entities, and suggestions to alter rules are usually resisted. Behavior in compliance with specified rules is judged "right," and behavior not in compliance with these rules is judged "wrong." The morally realistic child further believes that everyone has the same view of the central importance of rules in determining the appropriateness of behavior. In the many situations in which specific rules of behavior are not clear, the moral realist will determine the rightness or wrongness of decisions and actions by noting the consequences the decisions or actions bring about. Beneficial outcomes confer rightness and detrimental outcomes confer wrongness. This is termed a belief in immanent justice. Because good acts and decisions will be rewarded, and bad acts and decisions will be punished in some way, life is fair and just for the morality realistic child.

It should be emphasized that Piaget focused upon how the individual judges right and wrong. At any age, one might behave in a "wrong" way, counter to his or her notions of good behavior. What an individual believes to be right and what he or she actually does in a moral conflict situation are two different aspects of morality. Piaget noted that, even though morally realistic children may believe in the sanctity of rules, they often play games without much reverence for the rules of the game. Yet children readily judge their own decisions and actions in moral conflict situations to be wrong if the rules are violated or punishing consequences result from their decisions or actions. This stage of moral realism generally dominates the thinking of children aged 6 to 10, although some adolescents and adults may display morally realistic thinking.

At around age 10 to 12, most children change their way of thinking about the basis for judging the rightness and wrongness of their own and others' decisions and actions in moral conflict situation. The enter the second stage: moral autonomy (or moral relativism). Rules are no longer perceived as rigid, unchangeable, eternal, divinely inspired prescriptions for behavior. The morally autonomous child or adult recognizes the importance of considering various aspects of the situation and the needs of others in judging good and bad. Thus, rules can be challenged and changed if necessary to serve human needs, provided that others agree to abide by them. In game playing, morally autonomous people can revise rules. Unlike the previous stage, moral autonomy reveals itself in the individual's willingness to accept that all moral dilemmas may not have a clearly right and a clearly wrong resolution. These people believe that there often exist "shades of gray," and that not everyone will always agree as to what decision or action is right and what is wrong. The morally autonomous person can and will put him or herself in the place of others and attempt to determine their intentions before judging their behavior. Likewise, when judging oneself, the actor takes his or her intentions into account. Rules are still important because they reflect the general needs of others and thus can be readily applied to many moral conflict situations. However, rules can be broken without the necessity of judging such rule breakage as inherently wrong.

As with the morally realistic child, the morally autonomous person often displays game-playing behavior at odds with this more sophisticated level of moral thinking. Morally autonomous children were observed by Piaget to display an even greater adherence toward the rules of games than did morally realistic children. Again, moral thinking and actual behavior are not necessarily reflected in each other. Furthermore, for the morally autonomous person, life is not always thought to be fair because good behavior may be punished while bad behavior may be rewarded. The belief in immanent justice is a thing of the past.

The transition from moral realism to moral autonomy is accomplished by a development of cognitive abilities and by specific social experiences. The reorganization of moral reasoning requires a more sophisticated level of thinking than the very young child may be capable of demonstrating. For example, very young children tend to think egocentrically. They view their own perspective as the only true perspective to consider and think that everyone shares their point of view. Only by outgrowing such egocentric thinking and developing role-taking skills can the child understand another person's intentions before judging them. The social experiences that assist the reorganization of moral thinking tend to be peer oriented rather than authority figure oriented. It is not uncommon for authority figures such as parents, teachers, or coaches to perhaps unwittingly hold the child at the level of moral realism. Certainly, telling a child what is right and what is wrong makes that child easier to handle for the person in authority. However, the peer group demonstrates to the child that rules are, to varying degrees, arbitrary. Rules depend on mutual consent. When there is conflict within the peer group, compromises may be struck to accomplish the group goal. The peer group may change rules to better suit their interaction and to take the individual child's needs into account. The child also may share in making decisions in the peer group.

Such experiences are necessary to give the child a new perspective on rules, authority, and right and wrong. Keasey (1971) found that children who engage more frequently in social activities, who are popular, and who take leadership roles are more mature in their moral thinking. Exposure to such new perspectives may leave the morally realistic child in a state of disequilibrium for a time from which he or she can emerge into a newer, higher level of moral thinking that is far more flexible and less dependent on total respect for the edicts of authority figures. Piaget did note that parents and authority figures need not impede the moral development of their children. He recommended that parents give up some of their power as the child matures so that a more mutual, egalitarian relationship develops. In this way, authority figures can facilitate rather than hinder the child's development of more sophisticated modes of moral thinking.

It has been noted (e.g., Turiel, 1978) that children may react differently to various types of rules. On the one hand, there are moral rules dealing with individual rights and privileges. On the other hand, there are social-conventional rules that are the result of group consensus and focus on actions and decisions within a prescribed, specific social setting such as sport and games. Children seem to distinguish between these two types of rules and react differently to them. Children as young as 3 have been found to consider deviations from moral rules far more serious than deviation from socioconventional rules. Thus, preschoolers may show great respect for moral rules while still allowing deviation from some sociocultural rules. Older children and adults may do the same.

LAWRENCE KOHLBERG'S APPROACH
TO MORAL THINKING

Lawrence Kohlberg (1969, 1981) may be considered the American counterpart to Jean Piaget. He extended the work of the Swiss psychologist into a theory of the development of moral thinking that divides such development into six distinct stages rather than two. Like Piaget, Kohlberg was more concerned with the underlying level of reasoning used in justifying moral decisions and moral actions than in what particular decision or action might be taken. Kohlberg found that very young children respect rules often out of a fear of being punished for violating them rather than out of profound respect for the rules themselves or for the authority figures who set these rules. In addition, the development of moral thinking seems to go beyond the ages of 10 to 12, which marked the entry into the final stage of Piaget's system. Moral thinking may continue to develop well into adolescence and early adulthood if not beyond. Kohlberg found much to support Piaget's notion of a stage-like pattern in the development of moral thinking, but Kohlberg's six stages may be thought of as a more precise approach to the description of the development of moral reasoning.

Each of Kohlberg's six stages deserves attention, especially for those dealing with athletes of various moral levels. Coaches, officials, and parents should be aware of the level of moral thinking of those in their charge. Although it may be tempting to ascribe ages at which each stage is most typical, it is more important and more accurate to note that (a) moral reasoning at any of the six stages may be found in older children, adolescents, and adults, and (b) young children are limited by their less sophisticated cognitive abilities to the earlier stages. Thus, although a young adult may typically function at any particular stage, a preschool child would be incapable of responding at the higher levels of moral thinking. For Kohlberg, as for Piaget, the stages have been found to develop in an invariant sequence, with each stage requiring more sophisticated reasoning abilities than the ones before it (e.g., Colby, Kohlberg, Gibbs, & Lieberman, 1983). When in a particular stage, the individual is fairly consistent in the level of reasoning used in making decisions in moral conflict situations and in judging one's self and others.

The first stage of Kohlberg's system is the stage of punishment and obedience orientation. Someone in this stage determines right and wrong based on the consequences of the moral decision or action. To avoid being punished, the Stage 1 moral thinker feels that they should defer to authority figures and obey them. However, if the person can escape unpunished, then it is considered appropriate for such rules and authority figures to be disobeyed. The greater the punishment, the more wrong is the decision or action. This stage is very similar to the premoral level and early phase of the stage of moral realism in Piaget's system.

The second stage is called the naive hedonism or instrumental orientation stage. Rules should be obeyed in order for the person to gain benefits and satisfy his or her own needs. If one does something for someone else, it is because the actor expects to gain in the long run. Intentions are thus to be considered in making moral judgments, but clearly the Stage 2 thinker thinks pragmatically in moral conflict situations. This stage is a combination of moral realism and some rudimentary parts of moral autonomy in Piaget's system.

Most adult Americans, including college students, are in stages 3 or 4 of Kohlberg's system where the overriding concern is being considered a good person and maintaining the social order. In fact, the third stage is called the "good boy" or "good girl" orientation. In this stage, judgment of moral decisions and actions is based upon what pleases others and will result in the person being considered as a nice person. Intentions are a prime consideration in judging one's self and others. In this stage and the ones that follow, the person may make moral judgments about right and wrong even when no authority figure is present.

The fourth stage is the authority and social order-maintaining morality. Social rules should be obeyed not because one fears punishment (Stage 1), seeks rewards (Stage 2), or wishes to be considered nice (Stage 3). Instead, obedience to rules is based on the conviction that rules uphold the social order, and the social order is worth maintaining. Good decisions and behavior are those that conform to the rules that preserve the social order.

The fifth stage of Kohlberg's system is called the morality of contract, individual rights, and democratically accepted law. Like the stage that follows it, Stage 5 thinkers are personally committed to a set of principles that go beyond the realm of authority figures in that morality is now internalized. The Stage 5 moral thinker displays a flexibility not seen in the earlier stages. Only those rules that are perceived to be for the good of the majority and that promote social welfare carry the moral imperative, whereas those rules perceived to compromise the rights of the majority do not require adherence and should be challenged.

The sixth and final stage is called the morality of individual principles of conscience, and few adults achieve it. Right and wrong is based on self-chosen ethical principles that take the form of abstract moral guidelines, which ensure that justice will reign in all situations. This stage of moral thinking is often accompanied by a desire to promote these principles in others.

Like Piaget, Kohlberg believed that moral development is an active process, and that an individual may indeed prematurely terminate his or her moral development if he or she is not exposed to new and higher levels of moral thinking or does not encounter the kinds of life experiences that might encourage a reevaluation of ways of thinking about right and wrong. For example, Kohlberg found that, although nearly 80% could be classified as Stage 1 or Stage 2 moral thinkers, more than 15% of 16 to 18-year-olds and one of 30 24 to 26-year-olds still expressed such reasoning.

Although it is appealing to believe that individuals are always firmly rooted in one or another of the six stages, there is reason to believe that people are not always consistent in the level of reasoning that they bring to moral conflict situations. Kohlberg proposed that individuals are predominantly in one stage, but may also show, on occasion, the level of reasoning of the prior stage (a remnant of earlier thinking) and, on occasion, the level of reasoning typical of the stage just beyond that typically used (promises of things to come). This accounts for the inconsistency we sometimes see in people's moral reasoning.

It is interesting to speculate about what happens in a confrontation between people of different moral judgment levels. If one is discussing a moral dilemma with someone using a less sophisticated moral framework, one is not drawn to emulate that more primitive reasoning even though it is readily understood. If one is discussing a moral dilemma with someone just beyond (i.e., one stage above) one's typical level of reasoning, there is a tendency to be attracted to this higher level of moral reasoning. In a similar way, morally realistic thinkers in Piaget's system may be attracted to morally autonomous reasoning but not vice versa. If, however, the level of moral thinking is two or more stages beyond one's own typical level, there is no impetus to emulate. One might say that the carrot is too far in front of the donkey.

It should be noted that Kohlberg's system initially was developed through his research on the moral thinking of male subjects. Do women develop their moral thinking in the same fashion as men? Gilligan (1977) claimed that there are similarities yet important differences between boys and girls in the development of their moral reasoning. Boys are usually raised to be independent, assertive, and achievement oriented, whereas girls are raised to be more nurturant and empathic. Thus, although Stage 4 may represent a modal male way of thinking, Stage 3 may represent a modal female orientation. Although most research has led to the conclusion that there are no clear sex differences in the development of moral thought, there is some evidence that women are more likely than men to be Stage 3 moral thinkers, and men are more likely to be in Stage 4 (Kohlberg, 1969). Rather than conclude that women are somehow less sophisticated than men, Gilligan proposed that this finding reflects culturally determined sex role standards.

Given the orientation of cognitive-developmental theorists like Piaget and Kohlberg to the development of moral thinking, what is the relationship, if any, of level of moral thinking to actual moral decisions and to actual behavior in moral conflict situations? Toner and Potts (1981) assessed children's level of moral reasoning, the type of decisions they made in hypothetical moral conflict situations, and their actual behavior in a moral conflict situation. The moral behavior measured was the children's ability or willingness to resist the temptation to break a rule in an authority figure's absence. These researchers found that the children's level of moral reasoning was not related in any consistent way to their moral decisions or to their moral behavior. Cognitive-developmental theorists do not claim that one's level of moral thinking can be used to predict which moral choices the individual might make or which actions the individual might demonstrate in moral conflict situations. Moral reasoning only predicts how such decisions and behavior are justified. Thus, moral reasoning is indeed an aspect of morality separate and distinct from specific moral decisions and specific moral behaviors.

THE COGNITIVE-DEVELOPMENTAL PERSPECTIVE ON MORAL DEVELOPMENT AND SPORTS PARTICIPATION

Unlike the psychoanalytic perspective, the cognitive-developmental perspective has led to direct investigation of the relationship between the development of morality (in this case, the development of moral thinking) and sports participation. For example, Piaget's stages have been found to be associated with game-related perceptions by children. In the sporting domain, Jantz (1975) found, for instance, that first- and second-grade children displayed less mature levels of moral reasoning than did children only a few years older than themselves when asked how they approached the rules of basketball.

Bredemeier produced a number of recent theoretical and empirical works focused upon the relationship between the development of moral thought and issues involved in sports participation. For example, she explored the relationship between the moral reasoning of male and female high school and college basketball players and their perceptions of the legitimacy of intentionally injurious sports acts (Bredemeier, 1985). She found that athletes exhibiting relatively high levels of moral reasoning were significantly less likely to endorse injurious acts as legitimate. Males were found to legitimize such acts at a higher level than were females. Also, college athletes were more likely to legitimize intentionally injurious sports acts than were high school athletes. In perhaps one of the most intriguing aspects of this investigation, Bredemeier found evidence that moral reasoning applied to sports contexts is often not predictive of moral reasoning applied to nonsports contexts, suggesting a situational morality by sports participants.

In a subsequent article, Bredemeier and Shields (1986a) noted that "sport may provide a temporary release from the constant demand to coordinate one's own sense of morality with the interests, needs, and perceptions of other moral beings" (p. 257). Sports-related morality was termed "bracketed" morality. It is bracketed within everyday morality rather than being completely separate from everyday morality. Sports participation is, after all, a part of life. The reason for such bracketing seems to stem mainly from the isolation of sport from everyday life in both time and space. Sports are basically short term and inconsequential in that participants, both winners and losers, regain their everyday life positions at the end of their participation in the sporting event. Bracketing also results from the concentration of authority surrounding the sporting events in coaches and officials and the consequent reduction in the accountability of the participant athletes themselves in what occurs. Finally, sporting events usually have very well-defined rules of action with little need to arbitrarily reset them.

Bredemeier and Shields found that, for high school and college athletes, the bracketed morality of sport was more egocentric than everyday morality; the divergence was greater for male athletes than for female athletes. Egocentrism, as we have seen, characterizes the less sophisticated levels of moral reasoning. It is as if sports participation provides the individual with the opportunity to center on his or her own interests while the everyday world is demanding less self-centered thinking.

In their comparative analysis of moral growth among athletes and nonathletes, Bredemeier and Shields (1986b) examined whether experiencing the bracketed morality of sports does indeed inhibit the overall development of sophisticated moral thinking in the participants. They found no direct relationship between athletic status and level of moral reasoning in college-age athletes involved in an individualized sport (swimming). However, the moral reasoning of college-age subjects who were team athletes (basketball players) was indeed lower than for nonathletes. This relationship did not emerge with high school-age basketball players. Male and Female swimmers did not differ in moral reasoning. For the basketball players, females demonstrated more sophisticated levels of moral reasoning than did males both at the high school level (in terms of everyday morality *and* sports-related morality) and at the college level (sports-related morality only).

It is clear that the cognitive-developmental perspective on the development of moral thinking can be directly and successfully applied to sports settings. The final theoretical perspective on moral development can be applied just as fruitfully, although little effort has been made to do so. This third perspective is that espoused by social learning theorists.

THE SOCIAL LEARNING PERSPECTIVE
ON MORAL DEVELOPMENT

What determines how one acts in a moral conflict situation? What kind of person breaks rules? What situations make rule breaking more or less likely?

Social learning theorists such as Albert Bandura (1977) and Ross Parke (1974) consider behavior in moral conflict situations as a form of behavior not unlike any other voluntary behavior. Behavior in situations where society labels one action right and another action wrong is considered to be a subset of freely emitted behavior in general. As such, moral behavior should be susceptible to the same environmental demands as other voluntary behaviors, namely, the influence of rewards, punishment, and observational learning. If, indeed, most voluntary behaviors, including moral behaviors, are learned, then how a person acts in a moral conflict situation is the outcome of an interaction between the demands of the particular setting with the learning history and personal characteristics of the individual. Social learning theorists have thus devoted their research energies to determine (a) what personal characteristics are most predictive of future "good" and "bad" behavior, and (b) what settings are most likely to encourage different types of moral behavior.

In their study of moral behavior, social learning theorists place an individual in a situation where behavioral choices between socially acceptable (good) and socially unacceptable (bad) alternatives are possible in a moral conflict situation. For example, a child might be left alone with attractive toys that an authority figure has prohibited him or her from touching. The child's adherence to or deviation from the prohibition is measured.

Social learning theorists believe that there are few if any individuals who are totally consistent in how they behave in moral conflict situations. An enduring example of this inconsistency was provided by the extensive research of Hartshorne and May (1928, 1929, 1930). The moral character of 10,000 children was studied in this massive project. It was found that children who cheated, lied, or stole in one situation may or may not cheat, lie, or steal in another. Virtually all of the children did in fact cheat, but the children varied greatly in how much effort and risk they would take to cheat. In fact, children who cheated in a particular situation were just as likely as those who did not cheat to state that cheating is wrong. Thus, there may not be completely good or truly bad people. Character, it seems, is somewhat situation specific. It is clear that, to understand one's moral behavior, one must take into account both the person and the situation.

All things being equal, what types of people are most likely to behave in morally acceptable ways and what types are most likely to behave in morally unacceptable ways? Good behavior is most likely demonstrated by individuals who tend to show greater ability to defer gratification, to be more intelligent, and to be less impulsive than their peers (Toner, Holstein, & Hetherington, 1977). These people are less likely to break rules as easily as their peers might.

Hartshorne and May reported that the greatest predictor of cheating in children was the degree to which their parents and peers cheated. Children raised in particular ways at home are also more or less likely than others to behave in morally correct ways. Hoffman (1970) suggested that children raised by parents who use inductive disciplinary tactics, which emphasize reasoning with the child and explaining to the child, are less likely to behave in socially unacceptable ways than those raised by parents who typically threaten withdrawal of approval or affection or who use physical punishment or threats of punishment.

Research by social learning theorists has tended in recent years to shift from a focus on these personal and historical characteristics to concentrate upon situational determinants of moral behavior.

In operant conditioning, when a consequence of a behavior strengthens that behavior, that behavior is said to be rewarded. Thus, it is not surprising that moral behavior has been found to be susceptible to the power of rewards. For example, Perry, Bussey, and Fisher (1980) increased resistance to temptation behavior in children confronted with a moral dilemma by simply offering them a present for such behavior. Previously, Perry and Parke (1975) found that children were less likely to violate a prohibition if they had been rewarded for alternative behaviors incompatible with the rule breaking. Thus, good behavior can be strengthened by rewards either directly or as a means to divert the behavior from bad activity. Of course, rewards can strengthen socially unacceptable behavior as well. For example, recent scandals involving the sale by college basketball players of complimentary tickets and athletic shoes, which resulted in monetary gain, can be viewed as rule breaking that was maintained and strengthened by rewards.

Much data have been gathered on the influence of punishment on morally unacceptable behavior. Punishment is the presentation of a consequence of a behavior, which weakens the behavior and lessens the likelihood that the behavior will be repeated. For example, if someone is reprimanded for violating some prohibition and thereafter refrains from violating that rule, punishment has operated to influence the rule-breaking behavior of the person. Like reward, punishment is defined in terms of its effect. In the case of the use of punishment, there are short-term and long-term outcomes possible. If the behavior is weakened even in the short term, it has been punished. However, punitive agents usually desire a longer lasting effect. Therefore, research on the influence of various punitive disciplinary techniques has assessed each technique with this long-range view of promoting self-control.

In a series of studies by Parke and his colleagues (e.g., 1972), it was found that punishment was generally more effective at suppressing rule-breaking behavior when (a) the punishment was administered immediately after the transgression rather than after a delay, (b) the punishment was administered consistently rather than erratically, and (c) the intensity of the punishment was neither too low (because it might be ignored) nor too intensely (because it might disrupt learning). In addition, a warm, caring punitive agent was far more effective than a cold, impersonal punitive agent. Clearly, the person's response to punishment is dependent on how the punishment is administered. However, Parke did warn disciplinary agents that the use of punishment as a primary disciplinary tool can cause increases in resentment, alienation, and aggression in one who is repeatedly punished.

Parke (1969) found that the provision of reasons or rationales for rule following may be the most important ingredient in administering any form of punishment. He found that the provision of even the simplest reason for compliance greatly increases the effectiveness of punishment. In subsequent work (1974), he noted that rationales that seem to match the prevailing moral reasoning level of the person are even more effective. For example, for very young children, rationales that are very concrete and focus on possible consequences of rule-breaking behavior may be ideal, whereas for older children more abstract reasons for compliance are most likely to promote rule following. In fact, when comparing the rule-following behavior of children who were punished without a rationale with those who were not punished but only provided with a rationale for compliance, Parke found the latter children to be somewhat more likely to obey the prohibition.

It should be noted that rule-following behavior may be weakened through an effective use of punishment and rationale provision as well. For example, the peer group or authority figure may prove very effective at weakening certain behaviors (e.g., sportsmanship) that the wider society deems more acceptable than they do.

Learning through observing the behavior of others (and then imitating their actions) is another way behavior, including moral behavior, might change. For example, Toner, Parke, and Yussen (1978) sought to determine whether children might be able to learn and imitate socially acceptable moral behavior by observing rule-following peer models on television. Previous research had clearly demonstrated that rule-breaking models can lead to greater rule violation in those who watch them (Stein, 1967). It was found that children as young as 3 years can indeed use the rule-following behavior of models to guide their own behavior, and that, in some cases, the observing child's moral behavior was influenced by the model's behavior for some time. In a follow-up investigation. Toner and Potts (1981) noted that the kind of justification a model might express to support his or her moral actions has a significant impact on whether observers will use the model's behavior as a guide to their own behavior. Rule-following models who expressed moral justifications at the level typically used by the observers were most likely to be imitated. In the case of rule-breaking models, however, the level of justification expressed by the models did not affect the likelihood of imitation by the observers. It should be noted that, in many studies, it appears far easier to show that giving into a temptation to break rules is more likely to be imitated than is resisting temptation (e.g., Stein, 1967). As is the case with reward and punishment, both good and bad behavior can be imitated.

Moral behavior has been shown to be influenced by other mechanisms beyond reward, punishment, and observational learning. For example, Bosserman and Parke (1973) showed that the moral behavior can be altered by allowing individuals to serve as enforcers of particular rules. The researchers found that children are more likely to follow moral rules that they have been asked to help enforce in others. Likewise, Toner, Moore, and Ashley (1978) found that having individuals serve as models of socially acceptable moral behavior for others greatly increases the likelihood of similar behavior in the models themselves.

Two other mechanisms have proved quite successful in influencing one's behavior in moral conflict situations. Casey and Burton (1982) demonstrated that people can become better rule followers if they are taught to periodically self-instruct, that is, to regularly remind themselves to follow the rules. The Pygmalion effect has also been clearly demonstrated by these researchers. When someone can be convinced that he or she is a good person, an honest person, a moral person, then he or she often fulfills the prophecy of this label.

Again, as with all other situational determinants of rule-following behavior in moral conflict situations, enforcement, serving as a model, self-instruction, and labeling can be used to promote undesirable behavior as well.

SOCIAL LEARNING PERSPECTIVE AND SPORTS PARTICIPATION

Sports is a rule-governed behavior. Participants are expected to adhere to these rules even when deviation from the rules may go undetected. What determines, in Grantland Rice's terms, "how one plays the game"? When does one follow the rules of sport? When does one cheat in sports? The answer depends on the person and on the situation.

As we have seen, some people violate rules more than others because of the way they are raised, whereas others adhere to rules for the same reason. However, the situation itself is a major determinant of breaking or following rules in moral conflict situations because people are not always consistent in the way they apply rules to themselves. If the individual believes that the cheating will go undetected and be rewarded (by winning the contest, for example), the likelihood of cheating increases, probably in proportion to the value of the reward. Olympic athletes, for instance, may be far more likely to give into the temptation to cheat than the intramural athlete. If punishment is considered probable, swift, and of at least moderate intensity, cheating is less likely. The threat of being banned from a sport for life makes cheating considerably less likely than being banned from the next contest only.

Rule breaking is also less likely if the individual understands the reasons why compliance to the rules is important. Understanding the need for all participants to play in accordance with mutually agreed-upon rules so that outcomes will be meaningful and valuable may lead to more rule following than would simply threatening some form of punishment if one is caught violating the rules. The level of reasoning that maximizes rule following changes with age and with level of intellectual functioning. The systems of Piaget and Kohlberg provide guidance in the selection of such rationales.

Cheating is more likely when the individual sees others cheat. Rule breaking is less likely when the individual sees others refrain from cheating. It is no accident that certain college football and basketball programs are beset by rule violations on a grand scale or that certain sports, such as weight lifting, seem to have a disproportionate number of rule breakers. Other college programs and other sports (e.g., golf) seem immune from the specter of rampant rule breaking. Imitation is indeed a potent determinant of moral behavior.

Rule breaking is less likely when the individual's own behavior serves as model behavior for others or when the individual is in a position to enforce rules for others. Athletes are often considered to be remarkable people by children and adolescents (e.g., Watkins & Montgomery, 1989). Individuals in sport thus serve as models for others and are under considerable pressure to remain purer in behavior than most others in society.

The expectancy effect (or self-fulfilling prophecy) may have a profound impact on sports participants within and beyond the moral sphere. Many aspects of athletic training are susceptible to the Pygmalion effect. For example, expectations about athletes by coaches have been found to influence the way these adult coaches reinforce children on their basketball teams (Rejeski, Darracott, & Hutslar, 1979). Children who were expected to perform well received more rewards from their coaches, whereas children expected to perform less well simply received more technical instruction.

Finally, cheating is less likely in individuals who consider themselves noncheaters and more likely in individuals who consider themselves cheaters. For example, problem athletes in college may well be problem athletes in the professional ranks. It is not unusual for professional sports teams to consider the past patterns of moral behavior of athletes as well as their athletic prowess when deciding whether to employ these individuals or not. Again, the Chris Washburn case demonstrates the pragmatism of this cautious approach.

In sum, the social learning perspective on rule following and rule breaking has direct implications for understanding the behavior of sports participants in moral conflict situations. Unfortunately, the link between this theoretical perspective and the demands of sports participation remains more speculative than empirical at present.

CONCLUSION

The present chapter represents a framework that delineates the relationship between moral development and sports participation. Morality encompasses the feelings, judgments, and actions that occur in situations where good and bad must be considered. Three distinct theories have emerged from psychology to focus on the three aspects of moral development. Psychoanalytic theory is oriented toward an understanding of the development of emotions in moral dilemmas. Cognitive-developmental theory is oriented toward an understanding of the changes in the basis of moral judgments of right and wrong. Social learning theory is oriented toward an understanding of behavior in moral conflict situations. Although the first of these three theories has provided little guidance in the domain of sports participation, the second has generated significant research, and the third holds considerable promise for future application. All moral dilemmas have emotional, cognitive, and behavioral components. Only by understanding the development of each aspect of moral development can sports participants and those who wish to understand sports participants begin to comprehend the various moral dimensions of such participation. For, after all, how you play the game isn't everything. It may be the only thing.

REFERENCES

Bandura, A. (1977). *Social learning theory,* Englewood Cliffs, NJ: Prentice-Hall.

Bosserman, R., & Parke, R. D. (1973, April). *The effects of assuming the role of rule enforcer on self-control in children.* Paper presented at the Biennial Meetings of the Society for Research in Child Development, Philadelphia, PA.

Bredemeier, B. J. (1985). Moral reasoning and the perceived legitimacy of intentionally injuries sports acts. *Journal of Sport Psychology, 7,* 110–124.

Bredemeier, B. J., & Shields, D. L. (1986a). Game reasoning and interactional morality. *Journal of Genetic Psychology, 147,* 257–275.

Bredemeier, B. J., & Shields, D. L. (1986b). Moral growth among athletes and nonathletes: A comparative analysis. *Journal of Genetic Psychology, 147,* 7–18.

Casey, W. M., & Burton, R. V. (1982). Training children to be consistently honest through verbal self-instructions. *Child Development, 53,* 911–919.

Colby, A., Kohlberg, L., Gibbs, J., & Lieberman, M. (1983). A longitudinal study of moral judgment. *Monographs of the Society for Research in Child Development, 48* (Nos. 1–2, Serial No. 200).

Erikson, E. (1963). *Childhood and society* (2nd ed.). New York: Norton.

Freud, S. (1960). *A general introduction to psychoanalysis.* New York: Washington Square Press. (Original work published 1935).

Gilligan, C. (1977). In a different voice: Women's conceptions of self and morality. *Harvard Educational Review, 47,* 481–517.

Hartshorne, H., & May, M. S. (1928). *Studies in the nature of character. Vol. 1: Studies in deceit.* New York: Macmillan.

Hartshorne, H., & May, M. S. (1929). *Studies in the nature of character. Vol. 2: Studies in self-control.* New York: Macmillan.

Hartshorne, H., & May, M. S. (1930). *Studies in the nature of character. Vol. 3: Studies in the organization of character.* New York: Macmillan.

Hoffman, M. L. (1970). Moral development. In P. H. Mussen (Ed.). *Carmichael's manual of child psychology* (Vol. 2). New York: Wiley.

Hoffman, M. L. (1975). Sex differences in moral internalization and values. *Journal of Personality and Social Psychology, 32,* 720–729.

Jantz, R. K. (1975). Moral thinking in male elementary pupils as reflected by perception of basketball rules. *Research Quarterly, 46,* 414–421.

Keasey, C. B. (1971). Social participation as a factor in the moral development of preadolescents. *Development Psychology, 5,* 216–220.

Kohlberg, L. (1969). Stage and sequence: The cognitive-developmental approach to socialization. In D. A. Goslin (Ed.), *Handbook of socialization theory and research.* Chicago: Rand McNally.

Kohlberg, L. (1981). *Essays on moral development* (Vol. 1). New York: Harper & Row.

Parke, R. D. (1969). Effectiveness of punishment as an interaction of intensity, timing, agent nurturance and cognitive-structuring. *Child Development, 40,* 213–235.

Parke, R. D. (1972). Some effects of punishment on children's behavior. In W. W. Hartup (Ed.), *The young child* (Vol. 2). Washington, DC: National Association for the Education of Young Children.

Parke, R. D. (1974). Rules, roles, and resistance to deviation: Explorations in punishment, discipline, and self-control. In A. Pick (Ed.), *Minnesota symposium on child psychology* (Vol. 8). Minneapolis: University of Minnesota Press.

Perry, D. G., Bussey, K., & Fisher, J. (1980). Effects of rewarding children for resisting temptation on attitude change in the forbidden toy paradigm. *Australian Journal of Psychology, 32,* 225–234.

Perry, D. G., & Parke, R. D. (1975). Punishment and alternative response training as determinants of response inhibition in children. *Genetic Psychology Monographs, 91,* 257–279.

Piaget, J. (1965). *The moral judgment of the child*. New York: Free Press. (Original work published 1932).

Rejeski, W., Darracott, C., & Hutslar, S. (1979). Pygmalion in youth sport: A field study. *Journal of Sport Psychology, 1,* 311–319.

Stein, A. H. (1967). Imitation of resistance to temptation. *Child Development, 38,* 157–169.

Toner, I. J., Holstein, R. B., & Hetherington, E. M. (1977). Reflection-impulsivity and self-control in preschool children. *Child Development, 48,* 239–245.

Toner, I. J., Moore, L. P., & Ashley, P. K. (1978). The effect of serving as a model of self-control on subsequent resistance to deviation in children. *Journal of Experimental Child Psychology, 26,* 85–91.

Toner, I. J., Parke, R. D., & Yussen, S. R. (1978). The effect of observation of model behavior on the establishment and stability of resistance to deviation in children. *Journal of Genetic Psychology, 132,* 283–290.

Toner, I. J., & Potts, C. R. (1981). Effect of modeled rationales on moral behavior, moral choice and level of moral judgment in children. *Journal of Psychology, 107,* 153–162.

Turiel, E. (1978). The development of concepts of social structure: Social convention. In J. Glick & A. Clarke-Stewart (Eds.), *The development of social understanding*. New York: Gardner Press.

Watkins, B., & Montgomery, A. B. (1989). Conceptions of athletic excellence among children and adolescence. *Child Development, 60,* 1362–1372.

Weiss, M. R., & Bredemeier, B. J. (1983). Developmental sport psychology: A theoretical perspective for studying children in sport. *Journal of Sport Psychology, 5,* 216–230.

8

Exercise, Fitness, and Aging: Psychological Perspectives

Bettie J. Glenn and J. Thomas Puglisi
University of North Carolina at Charlotte

More people are living into "old age" than ever before. At the turn of the last century, average life expectancy at birth in the United States was roughly 47 years (Special Committee on Aging, United States Senate, 1987–1988). At that time, only 10% of the American population was over the age of 55, and fewer than 4% were over age 65. By the mid-1980s, however, life expectancy at birth was almost 75 years, and 20% of all Americans were over age 55. Today, more than 12% of Americans are age 65 or older, and those who reach this age have an additional life expectancy of nearly 17 years.

Clearly we are now living, and aging, in a world that is very different from the one experienced by our forebears. As more and more of us live into later adulthood, it becomes increasingly important to understand the physical, social, and psychological factors underlying the aging process. In this chapter, we briefly review some basic issues related to "normal" and "successful" aging, and then examine the importance of exercise and fitness in later life.

NORMAL AND SUCCESSFUL AGING

What does it mean to be "old"? The period of later adulthood (in other words, "old age") is too often conceptualized in terms of stereotypical characteristics (Bennett & Eckman, 1973; Kermis, 1986). Early research investigating attitudes about "old age" and "old people" indicated that these stereotypes were predominately negative and devaluing. "Typical" older persons were thought to be sick and senile, depressed, and depressing to be around. Although more recent investigations indicate that society's beliefs about older people may be more complex and less globally negative than early research suggested (Gatz & Pearson, 1988; Samuelson, 1988), few would argue that widespread misconceptions about later life abound.

What is aging really like? What constitutes "normal" old age? The truth is that older persons display a wide range of variability in almost every area. Although average levels of functioning on certain physical and psychological dimensions clearly decline in later life, the range of functioning among older people is very great. Although some persons display deterioration, others maintain high levels of function that are quite comparable to those of younger persons (Rowe & Kahn,

1987). Older persons are as much different from each other as younger persons are. As a result, the tendency to describe old age in terms of generalized stereotypes results in a particularly inaccurate picture of older persons and their life experiences.

PSYCHOSOCIAL ADJUSTMENT

In terms of social and psychological functioning, most theorists now agree that successful aging and good mental health seem to be related to maintaining an active and meaningful involvement in one's world (Butler & Lewis, 1982). It stands to reason, for example, that older persons who maintain meaningful social relationships with friends and family members are much less likely to experience the social isolation and loneliness that are stereotypically identified with the later years. Moreover, psychological investment in family and friendship roles enhances the older person's feelings of self-worth and provides confirmation of self-identity, just as investment in such roles does in earlier life.

Maintaining involvement in meaningful activities is also an important component of good adjustment for most older persons. As is the case with social relationships, the activities that occupy an older person's time contribute to the individual's self-definition and feelings of worth, just as such activities contribute to the self-definitions of younger persons. To the extent that these activities are embraced psychologically and are perceived as meaningful by the individual, they lend feelings of worth and purpose to the elderly person's life, thereby fostering good adjustment and a happy, satisfying life-style.

It is important to remember, however, that "active," "involved," and "meaningful" are all, to some extent, subjective terms that must be applied differently to different people. Some older persons desire a great many relationships and engage in an incredible number of activities. Others prefer investment in just a few meaningful relationships or activities that provide a sense of fulfillment and satisfaction for them. Some older persons like to be "on the go" constantly and leave themselves little time for "rest and relaxation." Others prefer a more slowly paced life-style.

As Hayslip and Panek (1989) pointed out, the most important consideration involves an emotional or psychological investment in life rather than formal involvement in specific activities. Thus, individual differences in personality, health status, and social setting all mediate every older person's optimal formula for a "successful" old age. The important thing is achieving a successful mixture of relationships and activities that meets the individual needs of each person, and that allows each to maintain a meaningful and satisfying investment in life.

We turn now to an examination of specific issues related to exercise and fitness for the elderly. In the discussion that follows, we first consider how cultural expectations about old age interact with cultural attitudes about exercise to produce an elderly population that largely fails to act upon the well-documented importance of regular exercise for a healthful old age. We then examine the physical and psychological benefits of exercise and fitness for the elderly. In conclusion, we offer some observations regarding the development and maintenance of practical and livable exercise routines for elderly persons.

OLD AGE AND EXERCISE: CULTURAL INFLUENCES

One common notion about aging in our culture is that later adulthood is a time to relax, take it easy, and enjoy a rest from the rigors and responsibilities of a life well lived (Gray, Bassey, & Young, 1985; Hickey, 1980; Shephard, 1978). With family responsibilities satisfied and career obligations complete, the older person is viewed as free to enjoy a more restful, sedentary life-style. The idea that old age should be a time of restful relaxation is so ingrained in our culture that many persons accept it as simple common sense.

Benign as this attitude may seem, its implications for a healthful old age are particularly insidious. The older person comes to expect that physical activity will, and indeed should, be limited in later life, and that even moderate amounts of physical exertion are unnecessary, if not harmful. Nothing could be further from the truth. Yet well-meaning family members encourage their healthy elderly relatives to "take it easy," and caretakers often underestimate the exercise needs and capacity of frail individuals. Physicians rarely remind their older patients about the benefits of regular exercise or prescribe exercise routines as a means of preserving good health and preventing illness (Pardini, 1984; Sidney & Shephard, 1976).

Given these cultural expectations, it is not surprising that older persons display a variety of inaccurate and sometimes negative beliefs regarding exercise (Buell, 1984). In attempting to understand why "so many elders shun exercise," Ferrini and Ferrini (1989, p. 276) listed over a dozen contributing factors, including the misperception that exercise needs decrease with age, misinformation about the benefits of exercise, and a tendency to underrate one's own capabilities. Elderly men and women may also tend to misperceive their own levels of activity, believing that they are more active than they really are (Sidney & Shephard, 1977). Some older persons report embarrassment at the thought of being seen in T-shirts and gym shorts "at their age" (Sidney & Shephard, 1976, p. 250).

Elderly persons also face practical obstacles that may make participation in both formal and informal exercise programs less than appealing (Buskirk, 1985). Formal exercise programs designed specifically for the elderly are relatively few in number, and a lack of transportation makes participation in these programs impossible for many people. Older persons living in rural areas and in areas with a great deal of inclement weather find participation in formal programs especially difficult. Elderly persons interested in developing their own exercise program may lack the information needed to design an optimal regimen, or find it difficult to find companions with whom to share exercise activities.

All this does not mean that older people view exercise in an entirely negative light. In fact, older persons have been reported to hold many positive attitudes about exercise, recognizing its value for facilitating good health and enhancing one's vigor as well as for sheer enjoyment (Sidney & Shephard, 1976). Macheath (1984) reported that elderly persons in her studies "clearly see exercise as a beneficial and important contribution to health, independence, and a reasonable life-style" (p. 128). Nevertheless, these positive beliefs about exercise are too easily overshadowed by the cultural expectations about aging, the inaccurate information about exercise, and the practical obstacles to exercise that we have just outlined. The result, by and large, is an elderly population that fails to exercise sufficiently, and thereby reduces its opportunity for an optimal and successful old age.

PHYSICAL BENEFITS OF EXERCISE
FOR THE ELDERLY

Substantial data have been reported in the literature regarding the benefits of exercise in facilitating health and well-being. Regular exercise helps maintain muscle tone, decreases joint stiffness, and reduces fatigue by increasing endurance. Considerable research has been conducted demonstrating the need to remain physically active and fit throughout the life span.

According to Ashton and Davies (1986), evidence over the past 30 years clearly suggests that exercise has a major role in the prevention of disease. In their estimation, the entire population needs to become more physically active. As people age, the blood vessels become narrow, the blood pressure increases, and the ability to deliver oxygen to body tissues decreases to 50% of the young adult peak by age 75 (Brody, 1988). One of the effects of sustained exercise is to bring about a reduction in the oxygen requirements of the heart, allowing more efficient use of available oxygen to support the body's needs. Dynamic or aerobic exercise (i.e., regular and rhythmic exercise using large muscle groups) causes a substantial increase in heart rate and respiration, which appears to improve myocardial blood flow, thereby increasing the oxygen supply to the heart (Ashton & Davies, 1986). Such exercise includes jogging, cycling, swimming, and brisk walking, to name a few.

Excess weight gain, which is associated with the older years, is often the result of too little physical activity (i.e., too little energy expenditure) rather than excess intake. The proportion of body fat increases with age, so people must weigh less if they wish to maintain the same relative lean weight as they age (Brody, 1988). Intake of calories must be balanced by output. If calorie intake exceeds caloric expenditure, then the excess energy is stored as adipose tissue (body fat). Exercise, of course, increases energy expenditure and prevents its conversion to body fat. Moreover, metabolic rate increases during physical activity, and this higher rate of calorie burn off continues for a time after the exercise period. This facilitates the expenditure of excess calories, which helps maintain lean muscle mass (Ashton & Davies, 1986).

The elderly are just as susceptible to physical deterioration as children or young adults who lead a sedentary existence. In the past, it was assumed that the physiological declines associated with aging were inevitable. Recent evidence, however, substantiates the position that some of these "inevitable declines" are due in part to disuse. Disease and inactivity appear to be the real culprits in at least some forms of age-related decline. Several studies over the past decade have indicated that physical capacity declines with age rather than because of age. This hypothesis is theoretically defined as "deconditioning" (Bortz, 1982).

Bortz's investigations (1982) suggest that changes occurring in the cardiac, respiratory, and musculoskeletal systems normally attributed to aging are actually the result of long, sustained periods of inactivity. Even when exercise therapy has been initiated in older adulthood, research substantiates improved physical capacity (Posner, Gorman, Klein, & Woldow, 1986). Thus, regular exercise may retard or even reverse loss of functional capacity (Regensteiner, 1987). In fact, deVries (1970) reported that even people who had always been sedentary derived benefit from beginning an exercise or physical activity program. Given this data base, it is important that regular or even increased activity should be a high priority for all humans across the life span.

PSYCHOLOGICAL BENEFITS OF EXERCISE
FOR THE ELDERLY: COGNITIVE FUNCTIONING

The benefits of physical activity for elderly persons also extend to cognitive functioning. Birren, Woods, and Williams (1980) and Spirduso (1980) reviewed a number of studies that associate high levels of exercise and physical fitness with better performance on cognitive tasks, especially tasks involving psychomotor speed. Although these studies are not universal in their findings (e.g., Barry, Steinmetz, Page, & Rodahl, 1966; Botwinick & Storandt, 1974), Birren et al. concluded that "some of what now appears as a pattern of aging could in fact reflect diminished physical activity" (p. 305).

Two studies conducted by Spirduso (Spirduso, 1975; Spirduso & Clifford, 1978) are illustrative of the apparent relationship between exercise and psychomotor speed. These investigations compared reaction and movement times of physically active older men with those of nonactive older men as well as active and nonactive young men. In both studies, the performance of older active men was significantly faster and more consistent than that of nonactive older men. In fact, active older men reacted and moved "at least as quickly as sedentary men 40 years younger," responding overall in a manner "more similar to the young active groups than to either the young or old nonactive groups" (Spirduso & Clifford, 1978, p. 29). Rikli and Busch (1986) observed a similar pattern of motor performance on the part of active older women.

Stones and Kozma (1989) considered the evidence convincing that "exercise can compensate for age decrements in neuropsychological performance" (p. 190). Although the precise causal mechanism for the connection between cognitive functioning and physical fitness remains to be determined, Clarkson-Smith and Hartley (1989) suggested that "cardiovascular benefits derived from exercise may help to forestall degenerative changes in the brain associated with normal aging" (p. 183). They pointed out that this observation is entirely consistent with current theories of cognitive aging that link age-related deficits to physiological changes in the nervous system, either through a generalized, age-related slowing of nervous system processing (Salthouse, 1985) or through an age-related reduction in processing resources or capacity (Craik & Byrd, 1982).

Current research investigating the relationship between cognitive functioning and physical fitness has focused on determining precisely what sorts of cognitive functions and which components of particular cognitive tasks are affected by exercise activity. Elsayed, Ismail, and Young (1980), for example, found that physically fit groups of older and younger men displayed higher fluid intelligence scores than less fit groups, although there were no differences in crystallized intelligence scores. More recently, Clarkson-Smith and Hartley (1989) reported that older men and women who engaged in strenuous activity on a regular basis performed significantly better on measures of reasoning, working memory, and reaction time than did sedentary older persons, even when age, education, and vocabulary differences between the groups were statistically controlled.

Relative to specific task components, Baylor and Spirduso (1988) demonstrated that regular aerobic exercise affects both the central processing component and the peripheral contractile component of reaction time. Blumenthal and Madden's (1989) memory search data indicate that fitness may be "more closely associated with the encoding/response components" of the task, whereas age may be more associated with the comparison component. Stones and Kozma (1989) presented a model of coding performance that relates spatial localization processes both to age decrements and to the compensation effects of chronic exercise.

A related issue involves determining the conditions under which exercise programs might actually reverse decrements that have already occurred. Unfortunately, studies that have attempted to investigate the effects of specific exercise programs by measuring cognitive performance before and after participation have produced somewhat mixed results. In the Elsayed et al. (1980) study, performance on the series and matrices subtests of fluid intelligence increased after a 4-month exercise program, but scores on the conditions subtest decreased, and the exercise program had no effect on the classification subtest or on crystallized intelligence. Similarly, Blumenthal and Madden (1988) failed to obtain increased memory-search performance after 12 weeks of supervised aerobic exercise. Dustman et al. (1984) also reported mixed results of exercise training on cognitive functioning.

Negative findings notwithstanding, most researchers agree that there are important relationships among exercise, fitness, and cognitive functioning for older persons, and that these relationships warrant continued examination. In addition to determining the specific cognitive functions and task components that are affected by exercise, it will be important to determine the conditions under which exercise programs can reverse cognitive decrements. Even though the exact parameters of the relationship between fitness and cognition remain to be defined, it is clear that a life-style emphasizing regular aerobic exercise can be beneficial to the maintenance of optimal cognitive functioning in later adulthood.

PSYCHOLOGICAL BENEFITS OF EXERCISE
FOR THE ELDERLY: LIFE SATISFACTION
AND WELL-BEING

Not surprisingly, self-perceived good health tends to be associated with high levels of life satisfaction and good adjustment among older persons (Ferrini & Ferrini, 1989; Levkoff, Cleary, & Wetle, 1987; Willits & Crider, 1988). To the extent that good health is a necessary precondition for maintaining the activities, interests, and life-styles that give meaning to a person's existence, it is easy to understand why the relationship between perceived health and life satisfaction is particularly strong in the later years. Conversely, failing health would constitute a direct threat to these meaningful life experiences and would threaten good adjustment.

The ability to adapt successfully to one's environment and the resultant sense of mastery and competence that such successful adaption entails are essential components of a positive adult self-image. Indeed, successful adaptation to change is essential for adjustment throughout the life span (Schoenbach, 1985). Recognizing the psychological importance of adaptation and mastery, Whitbourne (1985) provided a detailed analysis of the relationship between the various physical changes that may accompany aging and the psychological consequences these changes may inspire.

Trivial but obvious signs of aging such as gray hair and wrinkles are likely to affect body image and may threaten the sense of continuity that characterizes self-concepts developed over the span of adult life. More dramatic changes such as a loss in strength or endurance, restricted flexibility of joints, or shortness of breath may be perceived as direct threats to the aging person's sense of mastery and to overall feelings of self-worth. To the extent that exercise and fitness programs can successfully ameliorate such age-associated physical changes, master, competence, and self-worth should be enhanced.

As we have indicated, exercise, even when begun late in life, is beneficial to the older person and "can enhance all five major components of fitness including cardiovascular endurance, muscle endurance, muscle strength, flexibility and balance—each of which helps promote independence and vitality" (Pardini, 1984, p. 20). It stands to reason, then, that older people who exercise regularly should be healthier, more independent, and more satisfied with life than those who do not exercise, and it is not surprising that exercise seems to improve "well-being, emotional stability, positive mood, and motivation" (Regensteiner, 1987, p. 52). Buccola and Stone (1975), for example, found increased self-sufficiency and de-creased surgency (as measured by the Cattell 16 Personality Factor scale) among participants in a 14-week program of walk-jogging. Similarly, Sidney and Shephard (1976) reported that older persons demonstrated increased well-being and decreased manifest anxiety after 14 weeks in a conditioning program.

Unfortunately, such positive effects of exercise on psychological functioning have not been demonstrated universally, especially in experimental studies that introduce exercise programs for short periods of time or in studies that examine underlying personality structures rather than attitudes (Folkins & Sime, 1981). Although Buccola and Stone (1975) did, indeed, obtain evidence of personality change among their walk-joggers, a comparable 14-week program of cycling ap-parently had no effect on personality. Likewise, Sidney and Shephard (1976) used a variety of measures in addition to well-being and manifest anxiety, including the behavior, mood, and feeling scales of the Cornell Medical Index, Neugarten's Life Satisfaction Index, Kenyon's Body Image scales, and McPherson's Real Me scale. No changes were observed as a result of conditioning on any of these measures.

Moreover, methodological limitations often make it difficult to determine the exact cause of psychological benefits that have been observed, and the precise physiological substrate for these psychological benefits remains uninvestigated (Is-mail, 1987). Nevertheless, Thomas and Rutledge (1986) are certainly not alone in concluding that exercise is "of marked psychological benefit" for older persons (p. 170). Indeed, few would argue with the belief that a healthy life-style that includes regular exercise can contribute significantly to overall psychological well-being. As Spirduso pointed out, "*mens sana in corpore sano* may, in fact, be more plausible than was thought—at least in the later decades of life" (p. 850).

DEVELOPING A LIVABLE PROGRAM
OF EXERCISE ACTIVITY

What precisely constitutes a healthful exercise or physical activity program for elderly persons? Simply stated, such a program must include active involvement in some form of physical exertion at regularly occurring intervals. However, the most desirable type of program and the optimal level of exertion depend, to some degree, on the individual. As a result, an accurate and sensitive recognition of the individual's health limitations, usual activity patterns, and overall level of interest in establishing or maintaining healthy practices is essential for defining the parameters of an appropriate physical activity program for any elderly person.

Assessment of the health status of an older adult is a necessary and basic prerequisite for the initiation of a regular exercise program (deVries, 1983). The health (or illness) status of all older adults should be determined before involvement in an exercise program. A routine physical examination by a qualified health professional is imperative, and it is this data base upon which an exercise program should be constructed. The strengths and limitations of the older adult must be determined to ensure safety and to enhance physical and psychological well-being.

Thus, older adults should be encouraged to seek a thorough health assessment before engaging in exercise therapy and to ask specific questions to secure sufficient information about exercise potential. Such questions often include concerns about the effects of exercise on one's heart or respiratory functioning, information regarding danger signs to be aware of when exercising, and questions about the safety of particular exercises or levels of exertion. Most older persons harbor a variety of these health and exercise questions, and obtaining satisfactory answers to them is important not only for protecting the individual's physical well-being but also for enhancing psychological security and self-confidence. No exercise program can be maintained successfully if the older person is preoccupied with concerns about the safety of exercise in general or the rigors of a particular exercise routine. Moreover, encouragement and reassurance from health care professionals regarding the benefits of exercise can be an important factor in motivating an older person to develop an appropriate exercise program and to maintain that program over time.

In general, any exercises that are performed consistently are preferable to none at all. The first consideration in beginning an exercise program is to start slowly and build toward maximal potential. It is important for elderly persons to begin with a level of activity that is comfortable and to use this initial level as a criterion for beginning regular activity. Once a regular pattern of activity is established, it can be increased gradually for optimal benefit.

WALKING: A HEALTHY EXERCISE ROUTINE

According to Adelman (1983), walking is probably the best overall exercise because it does not require special equipment, and it is efficacious and safe. Indeed, walking is a healthy form of exercise that can be initiated easily by the average older adult. It is a good activity with which to begin, develop, and end an effective and satisfying exercise regimen.

A good rule of thumb for older persons is to start with a comfortable walking distance, and to walk this initial distance at least twice per week for 1 or 2 weeks. The goal in the beginning should be comfort in all aspects of the exercise activity, including wearing comfortable clothing and supportive shoes, selecting a convenient easily maintained time schedule for exercise, and identifying a comfortable level of physical exertion. Once a comfortable pattern of exercise has been established on a regular basis, an additional "walk day" can be added each week. Speed and distance should also be gradually increased until an optimal level is reached.

Evidence suggests that three or four sessions of high-quality exercise per week (each lasting 30 to 45 minutes) will maintain an acceptable level of cardiac conditioning (Ashton & Davies, 1986). Ideally, men over 50 whose physical condition is fair should be able to walk between 1.0 and 1.25 miles in 12 minutes or 1.5 miles in 14 1/2 to 17 minutes. Women over 50 in fair physical condition should be able to walk 1.0 mile in 12 minutes or 1.5 miles in 16 1/2 to 18 1/2 minutes.

Overall, it is advisable for older adults to walk 2 to 5 miles at least three times each week using the time parameters just indicated. Continued involvement in such a program will ensure muscle and joint tone and general fitness. This level of walking as a dynamic physical activity will be brisk enough to challenge the cardiac system without being overtaxing (Ashton & Davies, 1986).

We must emphasize in the strongest possible terms, however, that all persons, and particularly older persons, differ in their overall physical activity levels, capability, and endurance. The times and distances that we have suggested are only general guidelines to assist in setting goals. What works best for any individual should be guided by personal health status, body cues, and periodic reevaluation of physical status after commencing regular conditioning. Ultimately any degree of regular, rhythmic physical activity/exercise is always superior to none.

PSYCHOSOCIAL FACTORS IN ENCOURAGING EXERCISE

Unfortunately, an exercise program like the one proposed in the preceding section is foreign, perhaps even unthinkable, for many older adults. Frequently the comment is made that "I am already old; why should I exercise?" Statements of this kind are reflective of the negative societal attitudes and social stereotypes we discussed previously, attitudes that fail to recognize the need to maintain maximal functioning capacity within the limitations of health status.

Until very recently, our society seemed oblivious to the need to maintain healthy life-style practices. Many people believed that good health was virtually automatic throughout young adulthood regardless of life-style, and that middle adulthood and older adulthood were inevitably associated with deterioration and decline. As we have seen, this attitude tends to encourage a gradual decrease in activity and exercise with an almost welcomed retreat into "old age."

What can be done to change this negative, self-destructive thinking? Over the past 30 years, researchers in the field of gerontology have begun to examine the behaviors of those persons who maintain youthful appearance and behavior in later adulthood. The trend toward exploration of the positive factors associated with later life has revealed not merely the need to talk about maintaining functional integrity, but to do something to facilitate it. With a more positive perspective on aging beginning to take hold in society, the future promises attitudinal changes that will ultimately result in a healthier, fitter, older population.

So it is that both health professionals and consumers are becoming increasingly cognizant of the need to develop and maintain healthy habits throughout the life-span. Walking, swimming, low-impact aerobics, and even wheelchair exercises are now enjoyed on a regular basis by adults of all ages. Living longer and healthier has become a popular theme for magazine articles, radio and television talk shows, and serious news reporting.

Nevertheless, people need to see models of successful and healthy aging. They need to be shown constantly through example that later adulthood does not necessarily mean that life must go "down hill." Fortunately, there are now around us many role models who personify active, healthy aging. These older adults are not simply "growing old gracefully." Graceful though they may be, these persons are able to maintain taut, firm, flexible bodies and positive self-images that provide dynamic living examples not only for their peers but for people of all ages. Indeed, the perpetuation of their positive approach to aging is clearly the wave of the future.

SOCIAL RELATIONSHIPS AND EXERCISE

Changing social attitudes and the availability of role models are important factors in encouraging increased exercise among older persons, but they are not enough. Many older adults need direct and consistent encouragement for exercise that is both positive and realistic. This encouragement can and should be provided through each older individual's personal social environment.

Health and social services personnel need to recognize their own importance as social contacts for older persons in addition to their traditional functions as providers of services. Elders tend to demonstrate particular confidence in health professionals, especially physicians and nurses. For this reason, health professionals must be mindful of the great influence they can wield in shaping the attitudes and behaviors of older adults relative to exercise.

One vehicle, then, for generating interest in exercise among older persons is the use of personal health care professionals in prescribing and encouraging active involvement. When elders seek medical or health assistance, primary care practitioners should be reminded to discuss a fitness maintenance regime. Moreover, praise and attention to increased muscle tone, decreased joint stiffness, and enhanced endurance should be included in follow-up visits with the older adult. Personal social reinforcement from health care professionals can be a major influence encouraging older persons to maintain an appropriate exercise routine and a generally healthy life-style.

Friends and family members are also important potential sources of encouragement. Family members should be advised to become actively involved in the exercise therapy of their significant elders. When exercise and fitness are incorporated into the daily conversation and routine of persons in frequent contact with each other, support is engendered within the group and exercise behavior is reinforced. When exercise can be viewed as a normal component of socialization rather than a chore, a burden, or a special program, it is more likely to become a positive aspect of health maintenance.

Younger adults, adolescents, and children who participate with elders in exercise therapy benefit as much as the older persons themselves. Together, family members can promote healthy habits for today's generation as well as for future generations of older adults. Reinforcement of positive thinking and active involvement are the key to successful, healthful practices and habits.

Indeed, the importance of social relationships and social reinforcement must be recognized as critical to the maintenance of an exercise program on the part of many older persons. Although exercising on a regular basis is intrinsically rewarding for some people, many elderly persons need an additional source of motivation if they are to persist in an exercise regime over an extended period of time. A program of regularly scheduled activity in which two or more persons exercise together can provide a valuable social outlet that is itself rewarding because it enhances the older person's social support network and fosters psychosocial adjustment in addition to promoting physical well-being. Moreover, the social rewards of sharing exercise experiences encourage continuation of the exercise program when and if the intrinsic rewards of exercise begin to wane.

THE IMPORTANCE OF BODY SELF-AWARENESS

A final psychosocial factor that we consider important for this discussion of exercise and aging involves body self-awareness. We have already pointed out that body image contributes to the older person's sense of self-identity just as it contributes to the self-identity of younger persons. Maintaining a healthy body reinforces feelings of mastery, competence, and self-worth.

Thus, both physical and psychological well-being can be enhanced by an overall body self-awareness that includes an accurate recognition of one's present physical status and a realistic appraisal of the potential for altering and improving that status. Certainly, the expertise and advice of health professionals are critical elements in achieving this type of recognition and conducting this type of appraisal. However, body self-awareness also depends on a sensitive attention to the internal cues and feedback that the body itself provides.

We consider body self-awareness to be a critical component in the development of a livable exercise program. Even when older persons do not see health care professionals on a regular basis, they can still engage in regular physical activity in a prescriptive manner. The body will provide cues regarding excessive activity, and listening to what the body has to say is one of the most effective means of monitoring capacity and endurance.

We emphasized in a previous section that the first consideration in beginning an exercise program is to start slowly with a level of activity that is comfortable. Obviously, body self-awareness is necessary for determining the initial activity level and, if optimal benefit is to be achieved, for increasing activity levels appropriately as the exercise program continues. For example, older persons who have initiated an exercise program that involves walking should assess how they feel before and after each walk. They should listen to their bodies as they walk and ask questions of themselves to monitor their physical state.

"Am I comfortable? Do I feel pain? If so, where, how severe, and is it relieved when I sit and rest? Is my body ready to increase speed? Can I walk more briskly?" Questions like these assist in focusing awareness on body cues and feedback, and they encourage a sensitive self-evaluation of progress in the exercise activity. This type of attention to and evaluation of body messages, together with periodic examinations by a qualified health professional, fosters a realistic body self-awareness that should become the primary control mechanism in developing and maintaining the older person's exercise program. In the end, we are all responsible for our own bodies, and we alone have access to the internal cues that the body provides.

CONCLUSION

Our goal in this chapter has been to review basic issues in physical and psychosocial aging, and to suggest how these two aspects of the aging process interact.

We have seen that there are myriad physical and psychological benefits of exercise for elderly persons, but that cultural expectations and practical obstacles tend to discourage them from getting the exercise they need to maintain an optimally healthy life-style. We have suggested that walking is a very desirable form of exercise for older persons and have provided suggestions for developing a livable program of exercise activity.

Finally, we have emphasized the importance of psychosocial factors in encouraging and maintaining exercise activity. In addition to changing social attitudes about the desirability of exercise for older persons, we have highlighted the importance of role models, social reinforcement from friends, family members, and health professionals, and the social rewards of exercising with others. We have concluded with the observation that a sensitive and realistic body self-awareness can enhance both psychological and physical well-being, and have illustrated its importance for maintaining an healthy exercise program.

REFERENCES

Adelman, R. D. (1983). Preventive medicine for the elderly. In S. Gambert (Ed.), *Contemporary geriatric medicine*. New York: Plenum.

Ashton, D., & Davies, B. (1986). *Why exercise? Expert medical advice to help you enjoy a healthier life*. New York: Basil Blackwell.

Barry, A. J., Steinmetz, J. R., Page, H. F., & Rodahl, K. (1966). The effects of physical conditioning on older individuals. II. Motor performance and cognitive function. *Journal of Gerontology, 21*, 192–199.

Baylor, A. M., & Spirduso, W. W. (1988). Systematic aerobic exercise and components of reaction time in older women. *Journal of Gerontology, 43*, P121–P126.

Bennett, R., & Eckman, J. (1973). Attitudes toward aging: A critical examination of recent literature and implications for future research. In C. Eisdorfer & M. P. Lawton (Eds.), *Psychology of adult development and aging* (pp. 575–597). Washington, DC: American Psychological Association.

Birren, J. E., Woods, A. M., & Williams, M. V. (1980). Behavioral slowing with age: Causes, organization, and consequences. In L. W. Poon (Ed.), *Aging in the 1980's: Psychological issues* (pp. 293–308). Washington, DC: American Psychological Association.

Blumenthal, J. H., & Madden, D. J. (1988). Effects of aerobic exercise training, age, and physical fitness on memory-search performance. *Psychology and Aging, 3*, 280–285.

Bortz, W. (1982). Disuse and aging. *Journal of the American Medical Association, 248*, 1203–1208.

Botwinick, J., & Storandt, M. (1974). Cardiovascular status, depressive affect, and other factors in reaction time. *Journal of Gerontology, 29*, 543–548..

Brody, J. E. (1988, Oct/Nov). Healthy words to live by. *Modern Maturity*, pp. 48–53.

Buccola, V. A., & Stone, W. J. (1975). Effects of jogging and cycling programs on physiological and personality variables in aged men. *The Research Quarterly, 46*, 134–139.

Buell, M. N. (1984). Psychosocial advantages of fitness programs for older people. In L. Biegel (Ed.), *Physical fitness and the older person: A guide to exercise for health care professionals* (pp. 27–40). Rockville, MD: Aspen.

Buskirk, E. R. (1985). Health maintenance and longevity: Exercise. In C. E. Finch & E. L. Schneider (Eds.), *Handbook of the biology of aging* (pp. 894–931). New York: Van Nostrand Reinhold.

Butler, R. N., & Lewis, M. I. (1982). *Aging and mental health: Positive psychosocial and biomedical approaches*. St. Louis: Mosby.

Clarkson-Smith, L., & Hartley, A. A. (1989). Relationships between physical exercise and cognitive abilities in older adults. *Psychology and Aging, 4*, 183–189.

Craik, F. I. M., & Byrd, M. (1982). Aging and cognitive deficits: The role of attentional resources. In F. I. M. Craik & S. Trehub (Eds.), *Aging and cognitive processes* (pp. 191–211). New York: Plenum.

deVries, H. A. (1970). Physiological effects of an exercise training regimen upon men aged 52–82. *Journal of Gerontology, 25*, 325–336.

deVries, H. A. (1983). Physiology of exercise and aging. In D. S. Woodruff & J. E. Birren (Eds.), *Aging: Scientific perspectives and social issues* (pp. 285–304). Monterey, CA: Brooks/Cole.

Dustman, R. E., Ruhling, R. O., Russell, E. M., Shearer, D. E., Bonekat, H. W., Shigeoka, J. W., Wood, J. S., & Bradford, D. C. (1984). Aerobic exercise training and improved neuropsychological function of older individuals. *Neurobiology of Aging, 5,* 35–42.

Elsayed, M., Ismail, A. H., & Young, J. R. (1980). Intellectual differences of adult men related to age and physical fitness before and after an exercise program. *Journal of Gerontology, 35,* 383–387.

Ferrini, A. F., & Ferrini, R. L. (1989). *Health in the later years.* Dubuque, IA: William C. Brown.

Folkins, C. H., & Sime, W. E. (1981). Physical fitness training and mental health. *American Psychologist, 36,* 373–389.

Gatz, M., & Pearson, C. G. (1988). Ageism revised and the provision of psychological services. *American Psychologist, 43,* 184–188.

Gray, J. A. M., Bassey, E. J., & Young, A. (1985). The risks of inactivity. In J. A. M. Gray (Ed.), *Prevention of disease in the elderly* (pp. 78–94). New York: Churchill Livingstone.

Hayslip, B., & Panek, P. E. (1989). *Adult development and aging.* New York: Harper & Row.

Hickey, T. (1980). *Health and aging.* Monterey, CA: Brooks/Cole.

Ismail, A. H. (1987). Psychological effects of exercise in the middle years. In W. P. Morgan & S. E. Goldston (Eds.), *Exercise and mental health* (pp. 111–115). Washington, DC: Hemisphere.

Levkoff, S. E., Cleary, P. D., & Wetle, T. (1987). Differences in the appraisal of health between aged and middle aged adults. *Journal of Gerontology, 42,* 114–120.

Kermis, M. D. (1986). *Mental health in late life: The adaptive process.* Boston: Jones and Bartlett.

Macheath, J. A. (1984). *Activity, health, and fitness in old age.* New York: St. Martin's.

Pardini, A. (1984, April/May). Exercise, vitality, and aging. *Aging,* pp. 19–29.

Posner, J., Gorman, K., Klein, H., Woldow, A. (1986). Exercise capacity in the elderly. *American Journal of Cardiology, 57,* 52C–58C.

Regensteiner, J. G. (1987). The benefits of exercise: Conditioning for elders. *Generations, XII*(1), 50–53.

Rikli, R., & Busch, S. (1986). Motor performance of women as a function of age and physical activity level. *Journal of Gerontology, 41,* 645–649.

Rowe, J. W., & Kahn, R. L. (1987). Human aging: Usual and successful. *Science, 237,* 143–149.

Salthouse, T. A. (1985). Speed of behavior and its implications for cognition. In J. E. Birren & K. W. Schaie (Eds.), *Handbook of the psychology of aging* (2nd ed., pp. 400–426). New York: Van Nostrand Reinhold.

Samuelson, R. J. (1988, March 21). The elderly aren't needy. *Newsweek,* p. 68.

Schoenbach, V. J. (1985). Behavior and life style as determinants of health and well-being in the elderly. In H. T. Phillips & S. A. Gaylord (Eds.), *Aging and public health* (pp. 183–216). New York: Spring.

Shephard, R. J. (1978). *Physical activity and aging.* Chicago: Year Book Medical.

Sidney, K. H., & Shephard, R. J. (1976). Attitudes towards health and physical activity in the elderly: Effects of a physical training program. *Medicine and Science in Sports, 8,* 246–252.

Sidney, K. H., & Shephard, R. J. (1977). Activity patterns of elderly men and women. *Journal of Gerontology, 32,* 25–32.

Special Committee on Aging, United States Senate. (1987–1988). *Aging America: Trends and projections.* Washington, DC: U.S. Department of Health and Human Services.

Spirduso, W. W. (1975). Reaction and movement time as a function of age and physical activity level. *Journal of Gerontology, 30,* 435–440.

Spirduso, W. W. (1980). Physical fitness, aging, and psychomotor speed: A review. *Journal of Gerontology, 35,* 850–865.

Spirduso, W. W., & Clifford, P. (1978). Replication of age and physical activity effects on reaction and movement time. *Journal of Gerontology, 33,* 26–30.

Stones, M. J., & Kozma, A. (1989). Age, exercise, and coding performance. *Psychology and Aging, 4,* 190–194.

Thomas, G. S., & Rutledge, J. H. (1986). Fitness and exercise for the elderly. In K. Dychtwald (Ed.), *Wellness and health promotion for the elderly* (pp. 165–177). Rockville, MD: Aspen Systems.

Whitbourne, S. K. (1985). *The aging body: Physiological changes and psychological consequences.* New York: Sprinter-Verlag.

Willits, F. K., & Crider, D. M. (1988). Health and life satisfaction in the later middle years. *Journal of Gerontology: Social Sciences, 43,* S172–S176.

III

THEORETICAL
CONTRIBUTIONS

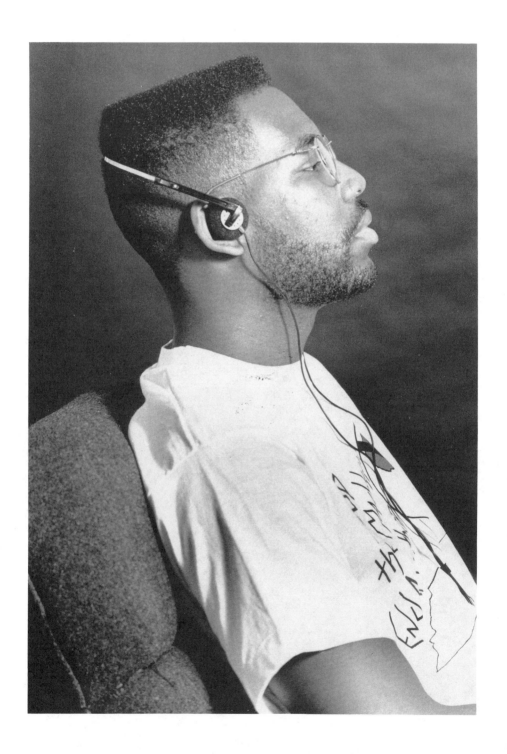

9

Sports, Athletes, and Games
In a Psychoanalytic Perspective

Dan Dervin

would you chant the glory of games,
look never beyond the sun
by day for any star shining brighter through the deserted air

(Pindar, ''Olympia 1'')

BALL GAMES

We may acquire a fundamental psychoanalytic insight into sports if we proceed exactly as if we were at an athletic event, ideally a football game or a tennis match, and fix our gaze carefully on that all-important object, the ball. After reading Tim Gallwey's *The Inner Game of Tennis* (1974), anyone would agree that the ball *is*, but *is* what? That is our question.

If we watch that ball, any ball, for a while, we are struck by how little it can do for itself. It seems poles apart from Aristotle's prime mover, Thomas Aquinas's unmoved mover, or Abraham Maslow's self-actualizing ego. The ball is completely at the mercy of the rules, the assault of the players, and the whistle of the official. To all these external forces, the ball can only react; yet it is all important to the game. The player who has it is transformed. Without it, the greatest star in the world cannot win. Yet the ball itself is powerless to act for itself.

The ball is helpless. It is carried, stroked, nudged, shot, kicked, flung, paddled, batted, bounced, and hugged throughout the various contests, as if every effort were being made to overcome this obvious fact. The ball soars, flies, sails—it can do anything so it seems—until at last it comes to a stop.

The ball informs us that athletic events, at some level, involve helplessness. Not true, we may object: They are everything but. They are about power, the triumph of effort over adversity, the celebration of pure skill, and so forth. However, if we can assume for a moment that opposites often presume each other, we might also consider that this theoretical center of helplessness displaced onto the ball is at least on a continuum with denials of helplessness and grandiose wishes for conquest, as well as with realistic efforts toward mastery. In so considering, we are also adopting a psychoanalytic viewpoint.

Now our attention has shifted from the ball to the ball carriers, the players, as if the ball were just another object and could not interest us until it is placed on a field and set in motion. Yet this acknowledgment of player privilege should also make us, as spectators, aware that we too share relatively in the ball's helplessness, and that even athletes may not participate until they have been properly uniformed and enfranchised as players in a given contest. So let us keep our eye on

163

this *sine qua non* object a while longer and summon the psychoanalytic spirit not to nail in hard facts but to probe, to suggest analogies, to tease out latent dimensions.

Take football for example. There an indifferent, oblong object lies inert until it has been handed between the legs of one player to another. It is a signal for literal action that our present context implies may be overdetermined. Does activating the ball, which in turn animates teams, evoke if only remotely the act of giving birth? At least the excitement generated by an effective play, especially if it yields valuable yardage, tends to validate the transformation from inert to living and helps account for such otherwise inconsequential sporting events' becoming so overladen with significance. Consider further how in such games as soccer, basketball, and hockey the object must always be controlled, never abandoned for even an instant, for then nothing is as exciting to a crowd or as dangerous to a team as a loose ball or puck out of control. A loose ball is called a "live" ball. As the players activate the ball, so the ball assumes magical powers, decides points, and focuses our most intense attention on the ball handler. However, it remains to be seen how the biological power to generate life, with which nature has seen fit to bypass men, leaving them on this fundamental level virtually helpless, has been transformed by male-dominated games into the power to score, to generate statistics, victories, vast public acclaim, and, for a few, to achieve the semblance of immortality. A potential bias in this area should be explicitly addressed. Apart from women's footraces, athletics in the ancient world were dominated by men, and most games that women participate in today are male-originated. For these reasons it is logical if not altogether fair to slip into a scenario of male development; yet the question of gender remains intriguing. Certainly the issue of surmounting helplessness is shared by both sexes, but the implication of male mimicry of female procreative powers, with its compelling analogues in primitive societies, suggests a separate line of male development in the service of disidentifying with things maternal and overcoming envy of women's life-bearing faculties. This would appear to play a lesser role in motivating female athletes, and a separate scenario may be needed. Consequently, for the most part the term athlete has reference to men and is not intended to subsume women.

Be that as it is, although ball games may function on one level as a denial of helplessness by generating life, they also encompass a range of psychosexual levels for both sexes from the most primitive to the relatively mature, and affect not only the composition of the games but the levels of performance within them. Deutsch (1926) and Fenichel (1939) were the earliest psychoanalysts to explore, albeit within a clinical setting, the counterphobic aspects of sports, which imply prior states of helplessness out of which grow the need for mastery. Deutsch's patient had been injured as a child by a flying ball and later took to baseball where he could ward off the dangerous object by catching it first. Ego capacities come visibly to the fore.

The necessity for subordinating and adapting the purely infantile—what Freud (1905) distinguished as the pregenital, component drives—to the larger aims of the game underscores the values attendant on postponing instant gratification. Exhibitionism serves skillful achievement and becomes maladaptive when the wish to be seen overtakes the need to observe the ball or the play: The ritual end-zone dance is permitted only after the touchdown. Spectators with their collective eye on the game both complement the players' need to be seen and provide a regulating role, but what can be called the Wimbledon response (impartial applause) is rare, and more typically crowds behave as the classic Freudian superego, inconsistently, often belligerently, chauvinistically, or perversely (Suarez-Orozco, 1982), often blinded and bribed into reliving a real or imaginary grandiose past, owing largely to the proximity of the superego to the dangerously seductive id. However, in major athletic events, sheer exhibitionism, like the exhibition game, is rarely seen and never counts.

Although the ball (as fetish) also confers a judicious degree of exhibitionism on those in its aura, it more seriously represents the means for overcoming the displaced helplessness of the athletic self within a whirling ambience of motion. Thus temporarily released from this debilitating self-representation, the player moves into action, and the ball in turn sheds its helplessness as it becomes a "subjective object" (following Winnicott, 1953) or a "self-object" (following Heinz Kohut, 1971). Either way, the ball not only becomes part of the self but is self-empowering as it passes hands or until the whistle stops play. The ball (likewise discus, javelin, and so on) functions to make sure the player's overcoming of helplessness is witnessed.

However, if the ball is to a degree personalized as part of the self, the self also meets it halfway by being impersonalized into part of the world of objects. In a wider range of athletic events, the hand is extended into a glove, paddle, stick, bat, or racquet; the foot into cleats, ski, or skate; the head into a helmet. In some games, such a helmeted and heavily padded player with the ball may be attacked like an inhuman monster or an insensate object, oblivious to pain. In football, one player may turn himself into a missile diving over the goal line, while a second may launch himself to intercept the first. Other bodies become walls, blocking the goal.

In other athletic events, downhill skiers and high divers come perilously close to insensate free-falling objects. The athletes' tolerance of the physical world's intrusion that gives sports so much of its excitement of risk has subtle analogies with tribal rituals in which the dancers are possessed by the gods and handle snakes or walk on fiery coals with impunity. The analogy is irresistible as well as apposite because it introduces questions of drive displacement and sublimation. Allowing for differences in function, the similarity of a painted visage behind a face mask and helmet to a tribal dancer concealed inside a spirit mask is striking in their empowerment. The one is dominated by the gods of nature, the other by laws and forces within the natural world, often personified in rituals by costumed opponents. However, costumes, masks, and ritual painting continue the process of overcoming the original helpless condition. In this respect, athletic events as secular rituals of enormous cultural power form a cogent connection.

These analogies need not be too surprising because sports in its important prehistory is intimately associated with the emergence of society from hunting ceremonies, fertility rituals, and other magical rites as it advances toward a gradual secularization and separatism favoring spectatorship and outstanding personal or team feats. It is well established that in Greece, for example, the Olympic games no less than the rise of the classic theater owe a great deal to preexisting rituals and seasonal celebration (Raschke, 1988). Nor is it surprising that Freud's (1927) contribution to the origins of religious beliefs was to connect them with the same unbearable condition of helplessness out of which is generated omnipotent father deities (LaBarre, 1978). The need for certainty, which religion provides, Freud added, is a remnant of childhood that later life cannot provide. Perhaps athletic events should have been exempted, for they never frustrate our persisting needs for certainty. Not only are we guaranteed clearly delineated winners and losers, but we are comforted by reams of records down to the last hundredth of a second. Today, cults still spring up around teams as the bearers of good fortune; fans often behave as fanatics, and their devotion to their cherished stars is just shy of idolatry. Thus, in many ways an anthropology of games underlies a psychoanalysis of sports.

GAMES AND THEIR PROTOTYPES

but Herakles founded the Olympiad
out of the spoils of his warfare

(Pindar, "Olympia 2")

Pindar's premise sounds intriguing until we reflect that Herakles was one of the Titans, a figure of fantasy, although the name had also been assigned to one of the runners in the mythical races. His name simply means the "Glory of Hera," son of the year goddess. In his mythical past, the athlete may be thought of as enjoying, along with the dancer and the actor, a second or cultural history, which, like an unconscious structure, forms part of his total (and unavoidably male) reconstruction.

The original Olympic games, which were played in view of the conical Mount Cronos, date formally from 776 B.C.; but long before the Olympian gods had assumed the mountaintops and renamed them, other religions and cults thrived in the same places. It is among these older races that events that came to resemble the athletic contests of today first began. Before athletic fields, there were sacred groves; and before the celebration of sky gods, there was the observance of earth deities and vegetation cults. Even within the reverent spirit for earth goddesses, according to Drees (1968), there were stages and progressions. Gaia, who lived in caves and clefts, was the earth, the source of life, and possibly the original goddess of Olympia; tellus mater, with her divine child, was the mother of vegetation; magna mater, who consummates a marriage with her divine son, is associated with sowing seed, crops, and harvest. When later marauding tribes occupied these lands, they retained the same sacred terrain even as they substituted their own patriarchal deities. Perhaps because these stages are so basic to individual as well as cultural evolution, these stages persist in the sports arena. There the playing field is still a sacred space removed from the spheres of labor and home; and earth's boundaries, while retaining their importance, are regulated and enforced by a male-dominated regime of rules and arbiters. However, the establishment of boundaries suggests the very earliest operations of a self emerging from the maternal environment. Rules and guidelines of later developmental stages may facilitate this project, but they never supersede or supplant it. In fact, sports generally affirm this duality, which coincides with the earliest female and the later male components of the superego. The analogy of a so-called territorial instinct observable in other species may shed some additional light on these processes, but it disregards the more obvious explanations found in individual development, and it would be as misleading to read courtship rituals or aggressive drives into athletics as it would be to deduce a survival of chivalry in sports simply because some players resemble knights in armor (although chivalry itself was a highly coded social game with its own sporting or jousting contests).

In athletic events, then, it may well be that the continuum of gender-derived boundaries and rules, with their intricate gender-free overlap and interplay, harmonizes early female and male introjects or positions within the psychic structure, and in so doing provides one of the greatest pleasures, along with a key to the motive force of athletic mastery as the emphasis shifts from the magical procreation of life to the harmonious recreation of lively and enlivening events. Cultural events are then replays of developmental periods in those special spaces created by sublimation (for lack of any clearer word). We can now appreciate how the non-specific condition of helplessness with which we began is an internalized condition in which the domination of powerful authorities (impersonalized into boundaries and rules) can be mastered by skillful and appropriate performance. In addition, a collateral fear of abandonment is mitigated and forestalled by team support and fan clubs, or when it comes is compensated for by trophies, plaques, and admission to various halls of fame.

Although operating within a matriarchal/patriarchal milieu, early athletic events also included libidinal and aggressive components for similar purposes of mastery, often symbolized by the nature of prizes. Footraces, which signified—or had actually intended to induce—the emergence of the new year from the womb of mother earth, were run by either sex, and the fertility role was emphasized by bestowing the wreath woven from the sacred olive tree or by apples and pomegranates. The victory of the new year was also a conquest over the old, a destruction of winter, which may be personified and may require an actual contest or duel to bring about his demise. This aspect of the ritual could eventuate in wrestling matches or other hand-to-hand contests presumably replacing blood sacrifice while still shedding blood. The overthrow of a rival, often a superior enemy, clearly points to positive oedipal conflicts embedded in the athlete's prehistory. The negative oedipal side may be mastered by the athlete's shift from a narcissistic body cathexis to the embrace of an ideal within his sport and his acquisition of the stamina to withstand pain. The annual event in early Greece, which probably derived from rites of sacrifice or initiation, was the voluntary scourging of young men until the blood flowed over a god's grave. Flogging, usually a penalty reserved for slaves, as Finley (1976) noted, was invoked by judges during the later Olympic festivals. Sansone (1988) interpreted the athlete as conducting a "ritual sacrifice of physical energy" on himself as the true meaning of sports, a view that transcends losers and winners.

The ball games of Meso-American Indians were also ceremonial and as often as not sacrificial (Stern, 1966). Sometimes the losing team would be honored by losing their heads; sometimes the winning team would be so honored (even then, winning was not everything). It may be that the ball itself originally represented the helpless victim to be sacrificed and became a sort of substitution. Indian balls differed greatly as to size and weight, from our handball to our medicine ball, the latter heavy enough to crush ribs; taboos against touching also determined the way games were played. Some of our modern balls may retain primitive animal or human associations: the feathery shuttlecock, the pigskin nickname for the football, the furry tennis ball, golf or ping-pong balls as testicles, and so on. In addition, if for no more than the interest of speculation, various ball sizes approximate head sizes, animal or human, shrunken or normal, which may have first rolled free from the blade of sacrifice and were kicked about but could not be otherwise touched fear of pollution.

The wild olive wreath that crowned the winner's locks in ancient Greece, or the vase of oils with which he was bathed, has clear libidinal overtones and may suggest something about the symbolism of modern cups and New Year's Bowl games. According to Drees, the grain mother Demeter slept with her lover, whose name resembled that of one of the mythical Olympic footracers, on a nuptial couch that was a litter of wild olive branches. Thus, the winner's olive wreath suggests an oedipal victory of a sort, a favored son/lover of the goddess as magna mater. On another level, it also represents the child's interest in the parent's nuptial relations, the primal scene, and many of the coital-like acts of games may represent reenactment of fertility forces inherent in the primal scene. The vulgarization of "scoring" to signify male prowess obviously makes similar connections.

Whatever one should finally conclude about the libidinal-aggressive components of the athlete's prehistory, we shall come to see that the athlete *qua* athlete has assimilated his or her early drives and object relations; the location of the cheerleaders on the sidelines, along with the emergency medical attendants, may remotely symbolize the promise of orgy or the threat of sacrifice but also, and more importantly, the subordination of the more primitive drives or threats. Although his behavior may often seem to replicate many phase-specific conflicts, an athlete is also emerging from them, for he displays in his poise, his powers of concentration on present tasks, his relative even temper, an unmistakable degree of autonomy.

This view may appear to undermine our point of departure. Undeniably, the popular idealization of athletes into superheroes distracts from our noticing the ways in which they share in the ball's helplessness, mediating that of the spectator, and enabling them to compromise by meeting the ball halfway. This is manifested most ingeniously in the touchability of the ball: In racquet or paddle games the ball cannot be touched by the hand at all once it is set in motion; in volleyball it can be touched but not held; in soccer it can be touched by portions of the body exclusive of the hands; in basketball it can be held only while one is motionless and then only briefly; in football it can be passed forward only from behind the line of scrimmage and only to eligible receivers; and the rules go on. As ancient as the games themselves, these various handicaps comprise the rubrics of play, but also restrict a player's freedom and in certain respects render him helpless. In effect, they acknowledge the hypothetically prior condition of the athlete, suggesting the already noted sympathetic rapport with the ball's condition. More important, these handicaps function to force the player to develop and emphasize special skills, such as the soccer player's educated foot or a basketball player's finesse at dribbling. Such skills so effectively overcome imposed handicaps that the latter are repressed by being countercathected (i.e., originally defensive restrictions become sources for distinctive pleasures of their own), and we no longer view handicaps as such, our attention being directed to the adroitness of the performance.

Although these rules are highly arbitrary, as anyone who has compared rugby with football knows, they are treated at any given moment as fixed and absolute. Moreover, those sports that do not include a ball do manage to impose handicaps on the player's freedom to act, which only contributes to what we think of as the contest. Thus, divers perform delicate acrobatics during their descent; runners face hurdles; skiers must negotiate treacherous obstacle courses; and generally athletes must endure the hardships of training, a phenomenon of interest in itself.

SYMBOLIC MEANINGS

so I, bringing poured nectar of victory,
gift of the muses, the mind's sweet yield

(Pindar, "Olympia 7")

Insofar as the idea of helplessness is most thoroughly repressed in sports, the symbolism of the ball seems to emanate from the unconscious. However, all the elaborate restrictions over proper handling of the ball place us squarely in the line of ego development where effort, skill, and self-discipline come to the fore. We also enter the larger sphere of play proper: the unique area so well defined by Huizanga (1955), as well as in the transitional sphere delineated by Winnicott (1953), in which illusion and reality, inner and outer, and self and other are in continual fluctuating interaction.

The question of boundaries, for example, is a literal issue in almost all sports where stepping outside will cost one possession of the ball or touching the net will cost one the point. End zones, baskets, goals, and nets are, like the ball, invested with great affect and may be touched or entered only indirectly or in special circumstances. Boundaries, as we have seen, are of great importance and are protected in both directions: If players cannot step out, spectators cannot step in. Thus, the playing area, like the primitive community's dancing ground and the classic stage, is special for *homo ludens* and must be respected. This inviolability of boundaries further points to associations with the most archaic level of ego formation, when the self is first beginning to separate from the mother. From Gaia, the mother of boundaries, the athlete passes onward to issues of growth, coordination, and training associated with tellus mater, and ultimately on to the libidinal mother who rewards for scoring achievements.

Taboos against touching may be seen within this larger context. Certain taboos apply to players on the other team, who may not be improperly touched (e.g., no elbowing in basketball, no holding or clipping in football), whereas a greater range of touching, embracing, back-slapping, cuffing, and the like is permitted among members of the same team and usually signifies the achievement of an ideal. As in carnivals, theater festivals, and other communal celebrations, certain social rules are suspended and license prevails to a degree.

However, the ball remains the focal point of touching. In one situation, it manifests prohibitions against the body. Yet in view of the peak excitement concentrated on the quasisexual performance of the ball as it swishes into the hoop and through the lace, sails between the uprights, penetrates the soccer or hockey nets, the ball may be either made into a phallus or into the incestuous object itself, depending on whether one desires more to launch or possess it. Here Freud's (1912) analysis of the duality or ambivalence of incest taboos—a (conscious) attraction for an (unconscious) forbidden object—is also played out in terms of the touching/no touching dialectic. The incestuous play within the play, as it were, is legitimized along the same lines: The tendency of football teams, for example, to be named after animals or idealized authority figures endows them with the totemic power of the (oedipal) father. On the most primitive dyadic level, they are two tribes competing to regain the lost territory of the mother's bountiful organism, while on a more advanced dyadic level mastery, strength, coordination, and other allied skills come to the fore. On a simple triadic level, scoring ability may symbolize oedipal victories, while on more advanced levels teams may compete for only a token of esteem, the wreath, or the cup of her favor.

Fans respond to the excitement over touching and boundaries by running off with balls, goalposts, and the like, reaching out for a player who may have passed out of bounds, and rushing onto the field to make contact with the players after the final whistle. In these instances the suspension of repression and the life-giving powers of touching become evident.

Thus, while drawing clearcut restrictions on the impulse to touch, sports also allow for limited gratification and sustain an overdetermined excitement over every aspect of the game. When the ball becomes a part of the self affected by the taboo, the opposing players symbolize the object world, which is threatening and must be warded off by a ritualization of contact and avoidance. The ball as the untouchable part of the self may obviously stand for any part of the bodily surface or zone, and particularly may be an acted-out defense against masturbation and later against incest, or castration—both the fear of it and the wish to inflict it. Here too the immediate and underlying response to the imposition of these barriers may be one of helplessness, which the game then helps an individual to master. Although the fear of helplessness emanating from boundary barriers is more primitive and pervasive than the fear of helplessness from castration, sports are sufficiently overdetermined to accommodate both levels simultaneously or in turn.

The ball as fetish may also symbolize part of the object world that elicits the same ambivalent excitement—maternal breast, paternal phallus—and in which forbidden impulses become legitimized by stealing the ball in soccer, football, and basketball. At times the ball may in addition represent the younger sibling who may be touched in certain ways but not in others, and whom one may wish to paddle, boot, or hurl away. Down distant corridors away from the playing field, one hears the dire admonitions of the nursery: Hands off! Don't touch! We recall that it is okay for a runner to steal bases, but if he gets tagged by the ball (taboo object), he's out (ostracized). Go to your room! (The dugout). Here the ball's contact in a dangerous act is equivalent to being seen by the parent in a forbidden act. The ball as penetrating eye emanates from the object world in contrast to its more usual function as vehicle of players' desire. Its power is based on the highly mobile energy of the id.

By now we may summon a context of early family relationships and conflicts that various games restructure and permit to be played out and mastered, if need be, in a special area of safety where the original objects of one's early environment cannot enter and hence cannot be harmed, while the early conflicts and emotions can enter symbolically. As a matter of fact, those same family members who play so crucial a role in one's development are reduced by the conventions of games to mere inactive spectators, who can only watch, occasionally shout or cheer from a distance, and provide what is nicely called "moral support." This is indeed because they are in certain respects superfluous to the athletic contest, for the players have incorporated the demands of authority transmitted to them by the early, predominantly parental environment in two apparent ways: (a) They have submitted themselves unquestioningly to the rules of the particular game, and (b) rules, in turn, support and reinforce boundaries as the paternally derived superego implements the archaic maternal identifications and prohibitions.

However, the spectators do have vital functions. Their cheers and boos are analogous to the chorus in Greek tragedy and to the chant of the earlier tribal community gathered around the dancing ground; their principal function today is to legitimize the event and, by their presence, to incorporate it into the seasonal calendar. They may not directly intrude on the event, and, if need be, a referee, server, or quarterback will hush them, thus reversing the tables on reality. For now the children (athletes) tell the parents (spectators) that they may be seen but not heard. Too much rowdiness in the stands will not be tolerated.

The fact that rules are never questioned within a game conveys how thoroughly they have been internalized. How difficult this process has been is dramatized by the players' relationship with the consciously visible embodiments of superego in the games, namely the referees, umpires, and linesmen, whose calls on particular rules are indeed often hotly disputed. This is permitted; in some sports, like baseball, it has become part of the game. Even a degree of aggression may be unleashed at these sturdy surrogates, who often reveal primitive features of sadism and masochism in their overt behavior and embody a taboo against touching. Balancing them and serving to regulate the excesses of the players are the more approachable and hence benevolent superego figures known as coaches and trainers. In some sports, coaches will even take on the role of haranguing officials so that players' attention need not be diverted from the pressing matters at hand. What seems to protect these various officials from becoming scapegoats for the players and spectators, apart from their own skills, is the unquestioned authority of rules and boundaries backing them up. This adherence to rules underscores the validity of players' having internalized early object relations.

Sports as developed and competitive play partake of various stages of boundary establishment, ego development, and superego formation. All of these processes are continuous on the playing field and apparently reverberate through the stands as well. Although some sports foster extensive body contact, as in wrestling or the football pileup, and others a mere handshake over the net, it is so difficult as to be virtually impossible to structure a hierarchy of athletics along a psychosexual plane. However, the nature of spectator responses provides clues to the relatively primitive or more developed events on the field. Spectators display a sense of energy unbinding itself in fluid anticipatory phases as it is becoming reattached to a given event. Consequently, they are often in a volatile, highly suggestible state: The appearance of primitive aggressive behavior on the field often reverberates through the stands. Spectators tend to get overexcited by brutal body contact as has been the case in hockey games, and they also tend to confuse opportunities for unlimited emotional response with dangerous impulsive behavior when, for example, they feel taken advantage of or when teams personify ideals associated with group superiority or survival—hence some of the violence attendant with boxing and soccer matches. However, boundaries and rules must also be observed by fans. Their overinvolvement is usually handled by crude forms of mimicry, such as hurling objects or engaging in fist fights. Other primitive drives and wishes may be allayed or neutralized by indulging in food and drink, although often to excess because of the degree of excitement and the extension of license to encompass the total arena.

On the other hand, a more gentle sport like tennis, with a discreet net always separating opponents, is usually reflected by the more courteous, genteel variety of spectators, who impartially applaud points as well as players. However, this varies from culture to culture. Italy and South America, for example, are notoriously chauvinistic about their athletes. Oddly enough, these variants seem to have little to do with the players themselves. Football players often can be quite mild and decent fellows, even on the field, for example, when helping an opponent to his feet, and boxers often embrace after a match. Tennis players on the other hand may behave like hideous brutes in a match, although the crowd may come to its senses and exercise a restraining influence in certain cases, at least in countries with a developed sense of fair play.

If we now survey the whole field of sports with the analyst's even-hovering attentiveness, we can tune in on how well all three psychic agencies are engaged: The superego is manifested through boundaries, rules, rigorously assigned roles, spectators, traditions, heroic ideals; the ego is operating in the transitional sphere of play, of skillful competition in the service of mastery, of loyalties, and of the regulated pleasures mediated by compromise formations; the id charges the action with overdetermined motives and meanings in which, for example, the ball as fetish-phallus is necessary for denying helplessness and for "scoring." (As fetish, the winning object—ball, bat, stick, and so on—is coveted by fans, autographed by player, locked in trophy cases, and generally assigned great value, or mana, i.e., magic.).

THE QUESTION OF AGGRESSION

success for the striver washes away the effort of striving

(Pindar, "Olympia 2")

Many varieties of sports are often interpreted through some cultivation or refinement of the aggressive instinct. One readily recalls Veblen's (1899) high barbarism theory or Tiger's (1969) analogy with the male-bonding pattern in the hunt. Certainly, aggression toward rivals is manifest in many games, and combat sports among the ancient Greeks were brutal grueling affairs (Poliakoff, 1987). Moreover, the more primitive aggression toward prey in contests from the Spanish bullfight to the English foxhunt (their so-called blood sports) and the American rodeo may represent an extremity of overt aggression, while in subtle ways it may be powerfully latent in so static a contest as chess were we to tune in on the players' florid paranoid fantasies. Interestingly, however, none of the participants in predatory contests are called athletes, and I think some kind of distinction implying deflected aggression is intended. However, even in the most widely endorsed games of the Western world—football, soccer, hockey—injuries not only abound but are considered part of the game. Violence appears to be implicitly sanctioned. There is arguably some blood-lust carryover from origins outside of play from warfare or hunting parties or sacrificial rites (i.e., a continuous line rather than the double parallel ones of analogy), but scholars disagree (Poliakoff, no; Sansone, yes).

Although focusing narrowly on aggression, as many studies have done, can be misleading, the specter of the ruthless gladiator looming above the playing fields is difficult to vanquish. Certainly there are aggressive components in sports just as there are also libidinal ones, yet it would be mistaken to conclude that sports are exclusively about destructive drives as to say they are about homosexual feelings, although obviously both may play some sort of affirming/negating role. The proponents of the aggressive motive, however, have two strong claims to our attention. First, some athletic contests resemble in microcosm the military campaign; and by way of extending the analogy, both occur on fields where certain martial virtues are summoned to the fore for the same ultimate purpose of victory. Thus, as one may be preparatory for the other, each may readily blend into the other, as Napoleon was supposedly defeated on the playing fields of Eton.

The other case for aggression moves in the opposite direction. Sports are not a preparation for warfare at all, but a form of socialization because they deflect the destructive drive into harmless spheres and drain off the dangerous energy in merely physical feats. This engages Aristotle's catharsis theory of tragedy as the purging of dangerous emotions, although it is interesting that his mentor, Plato, felt the state was more threatened by poets than by athletes. In any case, the Aristotelian javelin thrower will not return at the end of the day to transfix his wife; the suburban homemaker who bats the tennis ball around will not subsequently do the same to her children, and so forth. Undoubtedly, there is something to the athletic catharsis theory if one does not examine it too closely or ask too much from it. Just as athletic skills may be more readily adapted to martial aims than to any other, so one could reason that sports are preadaptations for battle.

I remain persuaded that if we study athletic phenomena as they develop and reach some state of excellence in professional competition, we are likely to find things of a rather different order. Let us study, with the aggressive instinct still in mind, what serious athletes actually do. For example, if they have Olympic ambitions, they may literally spend years practicing until their respective skills are near perfect, the margin for error being near zero; when the moment of truth at last arrives they are pitted as much against time clocks and record books as against any flesh-and-blood foe whom they are determined to vanquish. If we want to bring forward a prehistory of ritual sacrifice, we would have to conclude that the athlete has to a marked degree directed inward the lust for sacrifice.

This tendency to neutralize the athletic contest applies as well to games, in which every professional football viewer is drenched with statistics about all-time passing records or field attempts in the course of a game. (So abstract and impersonal can the media make events that occasional injuries on the field seem necessary just to remind one about what is happening.) More than a revulsion toward bloodshed or a defensive evasion, this shift in focus has something in its own right to tell us, and we shall return to it.

Let us quickly get back to the typical situation of athleticism as training, as practice, as drill, drill, drill, as continuously working out. This is how athletes spend their time. To succeed, athletes must be determined, of course, but they must also be capable, as it is often said, of taking much punishment: all those push-ups in the morning, the sit-ups, and the chin-ups. Whether they can endure it is the question: lifting weights, smashing into the tackling dummy, running until they want to heave, and sometimes do. This self-testing by ordeal never ends.

In training, which is by far the greatest part of competitive athletics, an enormous amount of aggression may be summoned, but it is initially directed onto the self, turned inward, made part of the athletic self, measurable as muscles, coordination, speed, stamina, and the rest of the equipment. Athletes become tough on themselves in training so that they can more readily withstand whatever the game, opponent, or environment may dish out. Then some aggression may be directed outward on to the event or toward the opponent, but this is after it has gone inward into the building up of a self, and so by then it may be in an altered, that is, more civilized position. When a fight occasionally breaks out, we immediately become aware that the game has broken down. Raw aggression is not only rare but anomalous. The biological instinct, which is to kill, inflict injury, or harm in the interest of self-preservation, has no place in games; but the general psychological drive, which may be defined as the aim to "annihilate that which causes displeasure," is far more problematic.

Eissler (1975), whom I am quoting, pointed to a path out of this thicket. In two far-reaching articles, he injected the terms *ambivalence* and *narcissism* into the human aggression equation. The effect of the former term is to soften the aggressive drives, whereas the latter raises the possibility of assigning a subsidiary role to the aggressive drive in sports. As spectators may be struck by the kindness of a player extending a hand to help up the ball carrier he has just moments ago crushed, we may remind ourselves that athletes never really forget that their opponents are fellow athletes whom they may admire or envy, and with whom in another season they may be cooperating rather than competing. However, the ambivalence displayed among prizefighters is even more visible. The press (Whittemore, 1979) has noted that the slurs and insinuations exchanged between two contestants show esteem for the box office rather than hatred for each other. One of the first comments made by Larry Holmes following his 1979 heavyweight title bout against Ernie Shavers, whom he pounded mercilessly for 15 rounds, was "I love ya, Ernie!" Ernie may have been entitled to skepticism at that moment, but Holmes was being sincere. However modulated, ambivalence clearly modifies any simple theory of athletic aggressiveness. This is not to say that paranoid rage cannot be artificially whipped up, although the relative ease in turning on or off such affects at the sound of a whistle or bell signals ego mastery.

Even more intriguing is Eissler's suggestion that "man is prone to be aggressive in order to regain the narcissistic level optimal to him." Eissler suggested that the enjoyment of talent or wealth often functions as a "negative enjoyment," based on its relative rarity, and is therefore a source of "narcissistic differentiation," paraphrasing Freud's (1921) "the narcissism of minor differences." Although he did not include athletes in his cultural analysis, they seem an ideal example of aggression in the service of narcissistic goals.

In other words, there are very sound reasons for one's not encountering predominantly raw aggression in athletes; rather what one looks for is what one expects to find in other polished performances: poise, composure, adroitness, beauty of movement, and transcendence of the coarse and vulgar. Along with these may be an affective state resembling free-floating anger, which may at certain bad moments be vented on the environment or on the self, but which normally is maintained as determination. Jimmy Conners described himself as ferocious as a tiger or a prizefighter in a match, and so he impresses the public. After a slump in 1979, however, he asserted that his infant son had rekindled his enthusiasm. Not only does he now claim to see himself as the breadwinner (who must return with valuable trophies like the hunter of old), but also as the object of his son's future admiration: "He's going to grow up and watch me, he's going to think I'm the best. If I'm not the best player, he won't be proud of me." He wants to perform well for his latest idealized spectator.

In addition, it is fair to conclude that the exponential increase of spectators thanks to the televising of all major sporting events, which arouses the imaginations of countless young athletes, has tilted the emphasis away from crude aggressive display to pleasing attentive play. In living color, athletes want to look their best. Their fantasy is not of a gloating victor with his foot on a slain foe, but of a beaming attractively shaped youth tilting his or her head for an Olympic gold medal, the ultimate emblem of narcissistic differentiation. Not only do medals, trophies, certified checks, and advertising accounts hail the uniqueness of the winner, they also assure him or her that he or she is virtuous and strong, not helpless.

THE QUESTION OF MOTIVE: NARCISSISM

Great is his fame forever whom your bright victory befalls

(Pindar, "Olympia 8")

The more we are prepared to view athletic events as performances, the better we are able to recognize how they occur in the area of self and transitional phenomena (Winnicott, 1953). Indeed, in athletics, the perfected self is on exhibition as in no other comparable performance, except dance. Like other performers, the athlete's goal of winning comprises a narcissistic triumph, accompanied by restored self-esteem and elation, not an aggressive triumph accompanied by fatuous gloating or sullen guilt.

Before proceeding further, we need a clearer notion of what it means to perform, a curiously modern word, heard in unusual, often ambiguous contexts. Certain cars are said to perform well in adverse conditions; certain men are preoccupied with how they perform in bed where one might hope the conditions are not so adverse. Actors who perform may be slightly different from those who play parts. The dictionary is a slight help here, telling us that to perform is to carry out or fulfill a task while leaning heavily on a public component in the performance. The real point of reference is the arts, and even literature is seen as presenting in the Norman Mailer-type of writing "the performing self" (Poirier, 1971).

If we reconsider acting for a moment, is it fair to say that we would go to the theater to see Lawrence Oliver perform, while we might otherwise go to see an unknown actor play Othello? If we went to the New York experimental theater in recent years, we would either seek out a new work somewhere or we would go the Richard Schechner's Performance Group less to see a play than to see the company perform. The inference to be drawn seems to be that the performers or group per se have not so completely buried themselves in the role as the traditional actors, and that some kernel of the self is kept and affirmed either by the performer or by the public. That the sense of illusion is not as pervasive may be another way of putting it. The performer does not disappear in the performance as the actor in the role; the original self is still a felt presence. Some observing part of the performer is watching the performance.

The actual mode of performing is as elusive as it is ubiquitous. It is neither creating nor relating personally, but remains similar to both. To be truly creative, one must let go at some point and let chaos sweep in because only in this way can a new reordering of experience take place; the performer hangs onto him- or herself, does not let go, performs with great skill and imagination, but does not create (although he or she may recreate). That both athletics and the arts exist in a highly symbolic world suggests that developmentally we have entered a stage of separation—individuation, noted by Melanie Klein et al. as the depressive position in which early attachment to objects are being relinquished and being recreated internally. This is also the stage of concern that Winnicott described as the acquiring of ruth, and before which one was ruthless, that is, primitively aggressive in ways that would clearly be as inappropriate for the artist as for the athlete. However, the artist, one might say, is born under Saturn and enters more deeply into the depressive phase than the athlete. The artist gains approval and immortality indirectly through the work into which he or she has "died" and been reborn through the creative process, and only when this fails does he or she become another performer. The athlete as performer retains his or her own selfhood and attains favor more directly. Like the performing artist, however, the athlete must play in others' games and never invent his or her own, never become an original. Unlike artists who produce a self-subsisting legacy, performers like the athlete remain their own work.

Does the performer relate personally (i.e., to the audience or to someone)? It seems more precise to say that he or she relates primarily more impersonally to something. Gymnasts perform on the bars, acrobats on the high wire, divers on the board, musicians with their instruments, actors with their scripts, entertainers with their scenarios, and so forth. It is the primacy of the self that performers always affirm, a paradoxical triumph through the medium or over the medium, and while objects may serve or assist them, persons, individually or collectively, insofar as performers would have to relate to them, get in their way. The performers are finally themselves, and the rest of us know it as well as they.

We may return now to the proposition that athletes perform, and that their performance, whatever other components it may bring along, takes place preeminently in the area of the self. Team play does not negate this position, because it may allow for outstanding individual performances or may temporarily induce the sense of a collective self. It is worth noting, however, that contests in ancient Greece were highly competitive as well as individualistic: Team sports arose later or elsewhere.

Players primarily relate to their game and to the skills enlisted for it; they may also relate to their opponent's game; but for them to relate to the opponent as a person rather than as another performer would be distracting and defeating. This is precisely what unscrupled players like John McEnroe often achieve, however, in their court antics. If John McEnroe can turn himself into a target, as he does for the fans, the other player's ball will more likely miss the baselines. Some aggression in the impersonal sphere of skillful performance is both evident and appropriate. However, if this energy is transformed into an affective state like anger or rage, the performing athlete focuses on the opponent as a person, and in losing the vital balance of concentrating on the game, usually draws a penalty, although in the hunt or in the battle, anger or rage may indeed be adaptive.

In terms of psychic economy, the disposal of aggressive energy into skilled performance is cut off or diminished by rage or anger, and the effort needed for the perfected performance suffers accordingly. Thus, we return to the maxim that the athlete's first victory is over himself: Without this mastery he cannot overcome an opponent. Indeed, there is a Zen of athletics as Tim Gallwey suggested, and between the ascetic and the athlete there may be subtle affinities.

One can reason further that, far from vanquishing a foe as in a military or hunting operation, the athlete must protect his opponent at all costs, for the two are in a reciprocal, yin/yang relationship. The issue in light of aggression is not why so many quarterbacks are sacked on a Sunday afternoon, but given the destructive potential of the game, why so many survive for so long.

It is interesting to examine how in this state of affairs the ball plays a mediating role to such an extent that what may look like aggression can become in more than a punning sense, both object-inhibited and aim-inhibited. Thus, in tennis and cognate sports, the name of the game is to strike the ball, never the opponent, even though these strokes are often called "shots" and reinstated into a lethal context by announcers. However, if aggressive wishes have been thwarted at the outset, a second frustration is soon to follow. For the shot to be successful, it must miss the opponent by as great a margin as possible while still being in bounds. Thus, one practices overheads, lobs, passing shots, cross-courts, or whatever it takes to hit away from the other player. The real joy—not to mention the more tangible reward—of winning arises from this very skill. One exception that may prove the rule was given dramatic emphasis when Arthur Ashe rather casually mentioned that a nice way to win points at the net in mixed doubles was to aim for the other net player's chest. This brought a cry of protest from those who were misled into thinking that Ashe was speaking as a man and not as an athlete discussing legitimate and time-honored court strategy. However, if the ball serves to deflect aggression, and thereby contributes to its transformation into disciplined control and precision, then these new values create their own priorities. This study is not primarily a study of motives, but suffice it to say that the aggressive personality in our society can find many more directly gratifying outlets than those provided by sports.

The risk of harming oneself is generally greater than the likelihood of injuring others; this is the secret dread, along with failure, lodged in every athlete's heart that threatens to cripple his performance. As noted, the phenomenon of grudge fights is much more the product of sales promotion and media warfare than of individual or team animosity. Various economic and social forces contribute to a brotherhood of athletics regardless of team identity, which indeed may fluctuate.

The relative impersonality of athletic performances and the preeminence of the performing self can also be demonstrated from many contests in which the opponent is the track, the stopwatch, the elements, the laws of gravity, a panel of judges, and so forth. Along with the worthy-opponent concept, the vaporization of flesh-and-blood foes in certain contests emphasizes the role of aspiration and the primacy of victory over self that reign in many more contests. If we recall that sports especially draw on the need to deny or master the sense of helplessness, we will have no difficulty in recognizing why many youngsters adjust to confinement following injuries, accidents, and illnesses chiefly by planning and then implementing plans for excelling in a difficult athletic area. The inspirational literature on this theme is legion.

These factors may issue from an interface of the ball as self-representation and the player's physical self as part of the object world. This partial merging allows him to decathect his body as target of attacks and source of injury, while projecting affects onto the ball or its equivalent. The performing self fears failure, shame, and damage to self-esteem; the athlete fears these too and, in addition, injury to the actual body, behind which lurks the specter of helplessness, a terrifying merging with the inert object, the still environment. Victory over self mitigates these dangers and provides the athlete with an internal goal when an external challenge appears too overwhelming. Along with the analogies between performing athletes and performing artists (or entertainers), some important differences arise. Not only does the athlete expose himself to real dangers through competition, he is also more bound to a rigidly enforced codification of behavior. Entertainers' boundaries and rules are much looser and so they often find themselves at the mercy of the audience where narcissistic mortification and enthusiastic acclaim are balanced on the perilous rope of taste and whim. The values affirmed in winning by the rules and its corollary in how you played the game mean that a player who has not lived up to his ideals of victory need not be humiliated as long as he has succeeded in playing by the book and thereby has preserved his self-esteem. His conscience is clear. There does seem to be something in the familiar adages about character building in sports, for social values are upheld through an adequate superego, which can rescue narcissism from the double defeat of losing and of cheating. Thus, there are good psychological reasons for the apparent overvaluation of rules in sporting events. On the other hand, the formation of moral character on the field is often a poor guarantee of ethical behavior off the field, especially without cultural reinforcement.

As the rigors and rituals of these contests produce unique stresses, a certain splitting often occurs within the athlete with which most followers of sporting events are quite familiar: He begins talking to himself, and the voice he uses may resemble that of the coach or some benevolent and helping figure, although he may also administer himself a vigorous tongue lashing. This splitting both of self and of task returns us to that symbol of the split-off, helpless self: the ball. Ideally, the athlete must reintegrate this component into the total performance so that in his performing the newly perfected self will be freed from the dread of helplessness, including its allied forms of injury and failure, and hence will become worthy of the crowd's applause, the judge's trophies, and his nation's medals. These awards dramatize the triumph of self, the self performing as athlete, and they may be passed on to other winners over the years, as in Yeats' poem the dancer becomes indistinguishable from the dance, the year god from the year.

The Olympic games began in prehistory as a footrace to achieve honor and win prizes, but also to embody the god. The hero becomes the "daimon" or spirit, and for a few moments shares in the god's immortality. For the Greeks, who made the invading Persians wait until they had finished their games, the apotheosis of the self was worth more than the glories of battle. The modern athlete is heir to this ideal; the public still basks in the aura of his immortality. His triumph occurs in a highly articulated microcosm governed by space and time, systems of law, rubrics of behavior, taboos, and prohibitions, an environment endowed with values and goals and rich in symbols and representative figures, wherein he so regulates his behavior to avoid dangerous aggression or overt libidinal impulses. Unless he can master all of these elements, he will never win any game. Winning or losing, he can still triumph by the quality of his performance, for the arena of sports thrives in the area of the self. It is a strange place this world of sports, and it is properly our own.

What makes sports properly and supremely still our own today is clearly other than mock combat or vestigial territorial instincts or survivals from hunting parties; it is something more naturally allied with the aesthetic pleasures and self-regenerative energies, produced by the body-mind integrations of skilled performers. Its everlasting secrets are nicely hinted at by a remark of veteran quarterback Billy Kilmer, who until this last game had been relegated to the sidelines and compelled to watch a younger teammate and rising star perform. When the old-timer got back in and hit receivers twice for winning scores, what he had to say later was about something other than simple triumph: "It felt good to get hit again. I hadn't been hit in eight games." It must have taken some kind of jarring after those numbing weeks on the bench for him to feel alive again; but that was what the game did for him. As his coach had already said, every defeat is a death, but to win is to be born again. Whether we take the anthropological route and place sports on a continuum with renewal rituals marking the arrival of the new year god and birth of the new season, or whether we see it as mimicking reproductive processes by variously scoring, athletic events spell a bringing-to-life process, be it of an event, of players and teams by their performance, or of spectators animated through their participation.

Sports' true and lasting victory is over the numbness that comes from fear or boredom or over the deadness that comes from being helpless or inert; for it is fundamentally a continuous regeneration of the self that sports can induce. The need to stimulate the sense of inner aliveness is specific to the human species. Perhaps we have after all now struck the nerve of motive.

This motive may remind us of the example used earlier of the football's passing through a player's legs as both a mimicry of birth and the birth of a play. By way of closing, I would like to speculate whether every play does not individually recapitulate the hallmarks of the athlete's early development from the state of poise to that of performing and on to scoring. Plays open with the players stationary but in a mobilized state of alertness, readiness, and composure. It is the moment before the pitch, the face-off, the jump ball, the serve, the kick-off, or pass from center; the players are poised. The state of poise has been carefully studied by Leo Rangell (1954) as being related to the earliest skills the infant displays of oral stage mastery; it coincides with our previous discussions of early separation and boundary establishment. The activating of the ball (or puck) also animates the players into the game proper; now they must perform, and this implies mastery at the second stage of drive and ego development: the anal period, where the child first performs or carries through a task demanded by the parent. Players also enter a field of limits and demands, of right and wrong steps, where others are observing and judging, and where shame or failure is a real possibility. If they can maintain their performance by learning to aim well and by developing skills among all the bodily parts, without losing control, breaking rules, inflicting or suffering injuries, or being overcome by crippling guilt, they may achieve the phallic-genital stage: the success of scoring and winning. Performance has then become allied with generative power.

The virtues of poise, performance, precision, and their allied skills may be considered ego capacities that, whatever the origins in drive development or early object relations, now culminate in the realm of self and flexibly serve the needs of the individual athlete.

REFERENCES

Deutsch, H. (1926). Contributions to the psychology of sport. *International Journal of Psycho-Analysis, 7,* 223–227.

Drees, L. (1968). *Olympia: Gods, artists, and athletes*. New York: Praeger.

Eissler, K. R. (1971). Death drive, ambivalence, and narcissism. *Psychoanalytic Study of the Child, 26*, 25–78.

Eissler, K. R. (1975). The fall of man. *Psychoanalytic Study of the Child, 30*, 589–646.

Fenichel, O. (1939). The counterphobic attitude. *International Journal of Psycho-Analysis, 20*, 263–274.

Finley, M. (1976). *The Olympic games: The first thousand years*. London.

Freud, S. (1905). *Three essays on the theory of sexuality* (Standard Edition 7). London: Hogarth Press.

Freud, S. (1912). *Totem and taboo* (Standard Edition 13). London: Hogarth Press.

Freud, S. (1921). *Group psychology and the analysis of the ego* (Standard Edition 18). London: Hogarth Press.

Freud, S. (1927). *The future of an illusion* (Standard Edition 21). London: Hogarth Press.

Gallwey, T. (1974). *The inner game of tennis*. New York: Random.

Huizinga, J. (1954). *Homo ludens*. Boston: Beacon.

Kohut, H. (1971). *The analysis of the self*. New York: International Universities Press.

LaBarre, W. (1978). *The ghost dance*. New York: Dell.

Pindar. (1947). *The odes* (Richard Lattimore, Trans.). Chicago: University of Chicago Press.

Poirier, R. (1971). *The performing self*. New York: Oxford.

Poliakoff, M. (1987). *Combat sports in the ancient world*. New Haven, CT: Yale.

Rangell, L. (1954). The psychology of poise. *International Journal of Psycho-Analysis, 35*, 313–332.

Raschke, W. (Ed.). (1988). *The archaeology of the Olympics*. Madison: University of Wisconsin Press.

Sansone, D. (1988). *Greek athletes and the genesis of sports*. Berkeley: University of California Press.

Stern, T. (1966). *The rubber-ball games of the Americas*. Seattle: University of Washington Press.

Suarez-Orozco, M. (1982). A study of Argentine soccer: The dynamics of its fans and their folklore. *Journal of Psychoanalytical Anthropology, 5*, 1:7–28.

Tiger, L. (1969). *Men in groups*. New York: Random.

Veblen, T. (1899). *The theory of the leisure class*. New York: Viking.

Whittemore, H. (1979, March 4). Ali vs. Frazier: outside the ring they didn't mean it—usually. *Parade*.

Winnicott, D. (1953). Transitional objects and transitional phenomena. *Collected papers*. New York: Basic Books.

Winnicott, D. (1958). The manic defense. In Name of Editor (Ed.), *Collected papers*. New York: Basic Books.

10

A Behavioral Approach to Health Psychology

P. A. Lamal
University of North Carolina at Charlotte

THE COMPLEXITY AND CONTEXT OF BEHAVIOR

Our focus is on behavior, that is, whatever people say or do. Our definition of behavior also includes the products of behavior, what people produce as a result of their behavior. Thus, the score on an achievement test, which is a product of behavior, may well be the focus of our attention, even though the score itself is not a behavior. Likewise, the amount of weight than an individual has lost over some period of time may also be of interest to us, although the change in weight is not itself a behavior but the result of behaviors that have changed.

Our approach emphasizes the idea of contextualism, which means taking into account the fact that our behaviors do not occur in a vacuum. It also alerts us to the fact that most, if not all, of the things we do and say have more than one isolated cause. Put another way, we acknowledge that there are myriad influences or sources of control over our behaviors. To make matters even more complex, we must realize that most, if not all, of our behaviors have multiple results. So just as there are multiple factors determining the rate and extent of an individual's weight loss, there is typically more than one result of an individual's losing a significant amount of weight. The complexity of behavior and behavior change has been emphasized at the outset for two reasons. One is that behaviorism has long been erroneously depicted by some as being a simple-minded, cookbook approach to behavior that fails to grasp the complexity of human life. This characterization of the field is, however, erroneous. Those in the field who work to bring about significant behavior change in everyday settings are well aware of the complexity of human behavior. The second reason for emphasizing the complexity of behavior and behavior change is to try to forestall the view that therapeutic behavior change requires only an acquaintance with a few basic principles of behavior, such as positive reinforcement and extinction. Anyone who is no better equipped and experienced than that and who attempts to function as a practitioner may well do more harm than good.

RELEVANT PRINCIPLES OF BEHAVIOR

The paradigm for a behavioral approach to health is the same for a behavioral approach to virtually all topics. This paradigm is the three-term contingency which consists of antecedents, behaviors, and consequences. Antecedents are those stimuli and events that come to exercise control over certain of a person's behaviors.

That is, certain behaviors are much more likely to occur in the presence of certain stimuli than in the absence of those stimuli. Many smokers, for example, are much more likely to light up in the presence of others who are smoking than when other smokers are not present. Obese people are more likely to eat as a result of seeing food—regardless of how long it has been since they last ate—than are people who do not have a weight problem. The converse is also true. That is, some antecedents may result in certain behaviors being less likely to occur. For an obese person, the sight of food will make it less likely that the person will walk away from it.

We have already defined the second component of the three-term contingency. We have stipulated that behaviors are everything that we do and say, and that for our purposes we include the products of behaviors in this component.

The third component of the three-term contingency consists of the consequences of behaviors. We are concerned here with two classes of consequences. One class of behavioral consequences has the effect of strengthening or maintaining certain behaviors that it follows. By strengthening or maintaining, we mean that this class of consequences results in the kind of behavior that it follows being more likely to occur again in the future (strengthened) or to continue to have a high likelihood of occurring (maintained). The class of consequences that strengthen or maintain the behaviors they follow are reinforcers.

The second class of consequences has the effect of weakening certain behaviors that it follows. By weakening we mean that this class of consequences results in the kind of behavior that it follows being less likely to occur again in the future. The class of consequences that weakens the behaviors they follow are punishers. It is important to note that this is a technical, behavioral definition of the word *punisher*; it should not be confused with our everyday use of the word.

Note also the important difference between antecedents and consequences. Antecedents occur before the relevant behavior occurs; consequences occur after the relevant behavior occurs.

There are two basic behavioral principles concerning the consequences of behavior, both reinforcers and punishers, that are critical in our consideration of health psychology. One principle concerns the immediacy of consequences. The notion is that the more immediately reinforcers or punishers follow certain behaviors, the more effect they will have on those behaviors, other things being equal. The principle of immediacy helps us to understand many health-threatening behaviors. Smoking, for example, is often reinforced within seconds by the effect of nicotine. Overeating is usually immediately reinforced by the taste of food. In the case of both behaviors, however, the deleterious effects are often far in the future. A major problem in health psychology is that the immediate reinforcement of many unhealthy behaviors overrides the delayed negative consequences of those behaviors.

The principle of immediacy can also operate in a converse manner. That is, some health-promoting behaviors may not occur or continue because the immediate consequence of the behavior is punishing, although the long-term consequence might well be reinforcing. Many people start exercising but stop after one or two sessions. This may be because, in many cases, the immediate consequences of exercising are aversive (punishing). For example, the person may experience soreness and may have his or her customary work schedule disrupted as a result of exercising. At the same time, the positive consequences of exercising may not be at all clear; the positive consequences remain far in the future. Given these circumstances, it is not surprising that many people start to exercise but then stop. The same analysis applies to overeating and other behaviors that result in morbidity and mortality.

The principle of frequency of consequences is also critical in attempts to understand and change health-related behaviors. According to this principle, the more frequently a class of behaviors is followed by reinforcers, the more the behavior class will be strengthened, up to some (usually unspecified) limit. Also, the more frequently a class of behaviors is followed by punishers, the more the behavior class will be weakened, again to some limit, the limit often being no occurrence at all of the behavior. We said that the principle of immediacy of consequences was to be understood in the context of other things being equal; the same is true for the principle of frequency of consequences.

To understand and change health-related behaviors, we must avoid the simplistic notion of discrete instances of behaviors occurring in discrete situations. It may often be advantageous to study discrete instances of behavior in our roles as behavioral scientists, but in our attempts to understand and change the everyday health-related behavior of people, we must consider that these behaviors are often chains of behavior. If we concern ourselves only with the last link in the behavior chain, we may fail in our change attempt. If, however, we realize that many health-related behaviors are the last links in a behavior chain, and we then concern ourselves with breaking or strengthening earlier links in the chain, we may be successful in changing the relevant behaviors occurring later in the chain.

For example, smoking may be considered to involve a number of behavioral links that terminate in a smoker puffing on a cigarette. The first link in the chain might be the purchasing of cigarettes, the second link opening the pack, the third link raising it to the lips, the fourth link lighting it, and the last link might (for our purposes) consist of taking the first puff. It may well be that intervention early in behavior chains will result in a more significant outcome than dealing only with the last one or two links. Indeed, there is evidence that behaviors are more likely to be eliminated or significantly reduced if the behaviors leading up the terminal behavior are consistently and immediately punished. The converse is also true; that is, if we want to increase healthful behaviors, we may need to reinforce precursor behaviors. If we want to increase the likelihood, for example, that someone will start a walking program, one of the behaviors to be reinforced might be the purchase of a pair of appropriate walking shoes.

BASIC FOCUS AND GOALS

Behaviorists have typically been concerned in both their research and practice with individuals rather than groups. There are at least two reasons for behaviorists' emphasis on the individual. One may be thought of as more germane to research than practice, although it may also occasionally be relevant to practice. In their research, behaviorists typically eschew the group designs that are favored by psychologists. Instead, behaviorists study one or a few individuals at a time. The rationale for not using group designs is that the results of such designs can be seriously misleading. In a typical two-group design, one group is treated in a particular manner (the experimental group) and the other group is not so treated (the control group). After the experimental treatment, the two groups are compared to determine if there is a statistically significant difference between the two groups. If such a difference is found, it is assumed that the experimental treatment was responsible.

From a behavioral point of view, this concern with groups is ill-advised. This is because the results from group designs, by their nature, mask the performance of the individuals in the groups. Thus, it could well be the case that no individual in the experimental group actually performs at the average performance of the group. The same situation may be true of the control group, but this is not the only problem. It may also be the case that some members of the experimental group perform at significantly higher or significantly lower levels than some members of the control group. The reverse may also be true. However, with the typical group design, these important individual results are rarely considered.

The concern with statistically significant differences that is a hallmark of group designs entails another problem. This is the failure, typically, to ask whether there is a clinically significant difference (as opposed to a statistically significant difference) between the groups being studied (cf. Sohn & Lamal, 1982). Many studies that report statistically significant differences between groups do not report clinically significant differences, and it is clinically significant differences that will often be of most value with respect to health promotion programs. What do we mean by clinical significance? Sohn and Lamal (1982) used the following definition: "(a) magnitude of behavior change effected during the treatment period, and (b) persistence of the treatment effect beyond the termination of treatment . . ." (p. 196).

The second reason for behaviorists' emphasis on individuals rather than groups is that when all is said and done it is (or should be) the individual, rather than a group, whose behavior we are trying to change. In clinical settings the level of success or failure of our treatments must be evaluated in terms of the changes brought about with individuals who present themselves for help. It is of little or no consolation for a member of a group undergoing treatment to know that other group members are changing in the desired direction when that individual is not.

A corollary of the emphasis on the individual is the necessity of tailoring treatments to the individual. At the outset, we affirmed the complexity of human behavior and its causes. It follows from this that the same treatment unthinkingly used with every person will vary in its effectiveness. There well may be certain techniques that work effectively with almost everyone. However, there are some individuals with whom those techniques will not work. Because individuals differ in important ways, the ways in which we treat them must also differ in important ways. A cookbook approach to helping individuals will invariably result in a large percentage of failures. The points we have just made are corroborated by Anderson and Gross (1988) in their consideration of behavioral treatments of obesity. They pointed out that "evidence suggests that the use of group studies may hinder efforts to develop effective treatment programs as well as obscure evidence of effective treatment when it occurs" (p. 144). A common problem with obesity studies has been their failure to individualize treatment.

Our success in dealing with behaviors that have a high likelihood of resulting in illness or death depends upon the extent to which we are able to achieve four goals: (a) having clear definitions of the relevant behaviors, methods, goals, and measures; (b) effecting increases in certain behaviors; (c) effecting decreases in certain behaviors; and (d) establishing stimulus control. Each of these goals is now discussed.

Our first goal, having clear definitions, may seem to be noncontroversial. Almost all of us might agree that it surely is a good idea to be clear about what we are trying to do. This goal, nevertheless, is often not met. "Having a healthy lifestyle," for example, is not a clear definition of any behavior; "jogging 4 miles every Monday, Wednesday, and Friday" is a clearer definition, and would be even more clear if the time were taken into account. The methods by which health-promoting behaviors are to be established and maintained must also be amenable to specification. "Providing reinforcement for participation in an exercise program" is not a specification of a method because it leaves unanswered such questions as how much exercise of what kind will be required for how much reinforcement of what kind. It also leaves unspecified who is to deliver the reinforcement and when and where it is to occur. There is an old saying that if you don't know where you are going, you don't know if you have gotten there. This notion is relevant to the specification of goals. "Exercising more" is not a sufficiently specific goals, nor is "cutting down on my smoking." The obvious question in the first case is, just what does "more" mean; and in the second case, just what does "cutting down" mean? In both cases, the person would either explicitly or implicitly still have to decide whether or not the goal was achieved, and this decision would have to be based on some evidence.

There are different kinds of evidence, or measures, of behavior change, each of which has advantages and disadvantages. A widely used measure of behavior change, self-reports, has the advantage that it is relatively easy to obtain. We can simply ask someone, for example, how many cigarettes he or she smoked yesterday. The serious disadvantage with self-report measures is that they may be inaccurate to varying degrees, compounded by the fact that in the absence of other measures, we cannot know to what extent, if any, the self-reports are inaccurate. Thus, if we ask someone how many cigarettes they smoked yesterday, and they tell us "none", we do not know if the statement is true unless we have other sources of information, that is, other measures.

Another measure of behavior change—direct observation of behavior—has the advantage of increased accuracy. That is, when we can directly observe someone we can avoid the problem of having to accept self-reports. Leaving aside issues of the reliability and accuracy of behavioral observation (which have been addressed by behaviorists), direct observation of behavior is one of the best measures we can have of health-promoting behaviors. You will doubtless, however, not be surprised to learn that there are disadvantages to the direct observation of behavior, and you may have already thought of one obvious disadvantage: feasibility or logistics. That is, it is often very difficult if not impossible to obtain systematic direct observations of the behaviors of other people. Consider, for example, trying to systematically observe the eating or smoking behavior of another person over a number of months. We may be able to obtain samples of such behaviors, but the samples may be too infrequent, for durations that are too short, and in an insufficient number of locations.

Physiological measures are obviously important when we are concerned with health behaviors. Most physiological measures, with such exceptions as blood pressure and heart rate, are usually not readily obtainable, however. It may be important to have various physiological measures, but often they will be obtained only after relatively long periods of time during which the person is engaging in health-related behaviors.

In many cases, an important measure may be the product or result of behavior change. We said, for example, at the outset that change in weight is not a behavior, but the result of behaviors that have changed. Weight gains or losses obviously, however, are important measures. Furthermore, they have the advantage of being unambiguous (assuming our scales are reliable).

Because virtually all of our measures have shortcomings, the best practice, when possible, is to obtain two or more measures. Thus, we may supplement our limited direct observations of eating behaviors with measures of weight loss (or gain). In general, we would attach less weight (no pun originally intended) to self-report measures than to any other of our measures.

The second of our four goals is the effecting of increases in relevant behaviors. Recall that one of the terms of the three-term contingency was consequences of behaviors. We labeled as reinforcers those consequences that strengthen (increase) or maintain the behaviors they follow. A fundamental procedure in almost any health-promotion program is to follow health-promoting behaviors with reinforcers. Examples of the reinforcement of health-promoting behaviors are presented in the next section.

Our third goal is the effecting of decreases in relevant behaviors. Again, recall that we labeled as punishers the type of consequence that weakens (decreases) the behaviors it follows. Note again that this is not the same use of the word "punisher" that is used by the person on the street. A fundamental procedure in some health-promotion programs is to follow health-threatening behaviors with punishers.

Our fourth goal is the establishment of stimulus control. Stimulus control involves the first two terms of the three-term contingency. You may recall that these terms were antecedents and behaviors. We said that antecedents are those stimuli and events that come to exercise control over certain behaviors. When stimulus control is in effect, certain behaviors are much more likely to occur in the presence of certain stimuli then in the absence of those stimuli. Much of our everyday behavior, starting with our arising in the morning when the alarm clocks sounds, is under stimulus control.

Stimulus control can be planned or unplanned. When trying to establish and maintain health-promoting behaviors and eliminate health-threatening behaviors, we must take stimulus control into account. For example, to eliminate health-threatening behaviors, we may have to eliminate the antecedent stimuli that control the appearance of those behaviors. A friend of the author's smokes cigarettes (unfiltered at that) only in a certain kind of locale, when he has a few beers with friends at a local bar. That is the only time he smokes. Clearly, the combination of friends, beer, and bar exercises stimulus control over his smoking.

INTERVENTIONS

There are two principles that should be adhered to as closely as possible when we consider interventions whose purpose is the establishment and maintenance of health-promoting behaviors. One principle is that prevention is preferable to remediation; the notion is that it is usually easier to prevent problems than to solve them after they appear. Thus, it may be easier and less costly to prevent individuals from overeating than to deal with obesity. The second principle is that simpler interventions should be tried first. Behavioral interventions vary greatly in terms of their complexity, cost, and intrusiveness. It seems unarguable that less complex, less costly, and less intrusive interventions should be tried before we try ones that are more complex, costly, and intrusive in individuals' lives. This principle holds unless we have good reason to believe that a simpler intervention will be ineffective. If, for example, we are dealing with someone with a 20-year history of smoking three packs of cigarettes a day, we can reasonably assume that an intervention consisting solely of admonishing them twice a day will be a failure.

Interventions can vary with respect to the degree to which they are controlled by the subjects of the interventions or controlled by others (e.g., a clinician, parent, spouse, or friend). We do not place much faith in self-control. Indeed, the notion of self-control may be a myth (Sohn & Lamal, 1982). Many interventions may require that control be initially exercised primarily by others. This could well be the case in the treatment of obesity and excessive drinking. The goal would be to decrease the degree of such control by others, so that the client is able to maintain health-promoting behaviors in the absence of others.

To maximize the likelihood of success, any intervention must have certain characteristics. We have already discussed the importance of having clear specifications of the relevant behaviors, methods, goals, and measures to be used. Another important characteristic is the importance assigned to the consequences of the relevant behaviors. Many health-promotion interventions fail because an erroneous assumption is made that certain things and events will function as reinforcers to strengthen health-promoting behaviors. The assumption is erroneous because people vary greatly with respect to what is reinforcing for them. Although one person's participation in a walking program may be reinforced upon receipt of a T-shirt, the shirt might not be at all reinforcing for someone else in the program. For the second person, the camaraderie of program participants may be what reinforces staying in the program. Recall that we said that treatments must be individualized (Anderson & Gross, 1988). Later the feeling of better tone may reinforce the continuing participation of both.

Mention of a T-shirt and tone leads naturally to a consideration of another important characteristic of interventions. This concerns the difference between contrived versus naturally occurring consequences of behavior. Health-promoting programs may initially rely on the use of such contrived reinforcers as T-shirts, ribbons, and the prompted approval of other participants to reinforce the relevant behaviors of participants. Within varying degrees of time after initial changes in health-relevant behaviors, however, naturally occurring consequences may come to sufficiently reinforce the new health-promoting behaviors to ensure their continuation after contrived reinforcers are no longer provided. One important naturally occurring consequence of many health-promoting behaviors is simply that the person feels better.

Another characteristic of successful interventions is that they usually include the ongoing monitoring of results. This is also a hallmark of behavioral research and practice. In the realm of practice, the rationale of monitoring results throughout the course of a program is to ensure that the program is working. If information about program results were only obtained long after the intervention began, time and resources would have been wasted if the results indicated that the program was not working.

Related to the ongoing monitoring of results is the collection of follow-up data. Many programs that seem to successfully strengthen healthful behaviors fail to report whether these behaviors are maintained over significantly long time periods, after the programs have ended. There is evidence that there often is no further improvement. In their review of self-reinforcement programs for weight loss, for example, Sohn and Lamal (1982) concluded that "in not one instance was there significant continued weight loss beyond the formal treatment period" (p. 200). A behavioral approach takes seriously the importance of programming maintenance of healthful behavior over long periods of time with minimal or if possible no formal program support.

From a behavioral point of view, interventions intended to strengthen health-promoting behaviors will "emphasize the positive." This means that such programs will focus on the development of new health-promoting behaviors to replace health-threatening behaviors. The emphasis is thus on reinforcing behaviors that can take the place of undesired behaviors. There may be occasions when health-threatening behaviors may be eliminated by punishing them rather than by replacing them. This procedure is, however, the exception. Behaviorists tend to be wary about the use of punishment because its use often has undesirable side effects that work against program success. For example, people tend to avoid or escape from sources of punishment. Thus, if a weight-loss program were to emphasize punishment of its participants when they failed to follow the program, the program might soon have no participants. Another problem with punishment is that, although it may indeed eliminate health-threatening behaviors, there is no guarantee that health-promoting behaviors will somehow magically occur in their place. Rather, to be sure that health-promoting behaviors occur and are maintained, we must systematically (at least at first) reinforce them.

EXAMPLES OF BEHAVIORAL INTERVENTIONS

Eating

Behavioral procedures for the treatment of overeating typically include the following components: monitoring food intake, eating in the same places and at the same times every day (stimulus control of eating), eating small portions, eating slowly, rewarding oneself for maintaining proper eating behaviors, and not focusing on weight-scale readings.

It should be realized that in spite of the great attention paid by researchers to the problems of eating, this area is one in which there definitely is no such thing as a "quick fix." Over 10 years ago Wooley, Wooley, and Dyrenforth (1979) described obesity as "one of the most perplexing and refractory of all disorders" (p. 3). That characterization remains true today.

Of course what is eaten is just as important as how it is eaten. The diet of most Americans is too high in fat and too low in complex carbohydrates. In this context, Winett, Kramer, Walker, Malone, and Lane (1988) evaluated procedures designed to change people's food purchases. Two of their goals were to reduce the fat content and increase the complex carbohydrate content of households' food purchases. The two procedures found to be most effective were modeling with feedback and participant modeling. The first procedure involved having all adults in a household view a 30-minute video. The video presented a couple in various scenes and began with a rationale for nutritious food purchases and gave relevant information about food (e.g., that complex carbohydrates are low in calories). The video showed the couple reaching a decision to change their diets, finding relevant information, and trying out new procedures and new meals, as well as overcoming obstacles. Besides viewing this video, participants in the modeling-with-feedback procedure received written feedback on their weekly food purchases. The feedback showed a percentage breakdown for the baseline period of, among other things, complex carbohydrates, simple carbohydrates, total fat, and saturated fat. The same breakdown was shown for the food items last purchased. Standardized written statements indicated how far the participants were from specified goals, and additional evaluate statements were given for positive or negative change relative to the goals. Every second week, participants received a second similar form that provided a cumulative analysis and summary of their food purchases to date.

The participant-modeling procedure also involved showing the video to participants. In addition, however, one of the program's directors also met with participants to assist them in developing complete shopping lists and performing nutritional reviews. The program director also took each participant on a prearranged shopping trip at the participant's usual supermarket. During this trip the director walked about the store with the participant and answered any questions. Weekly feedback included the written form used in the other procedures as well as feedback provided by the director in a telephone call. The call reviewed all feedback items and goals on the written form, and participants were able to ask and receive answers to any relevant questions.

Of the various procedures, the modeling-with-feedback procedure resulted in the largest increase in complex carbohydrates (5.4%) and the largest reduction in total fat (6.7%). The participant-modeling procedure resulted in the largest increase in simple carbohydrates (5.1%) and the largest reduction in saturated fat (2.2%).

Exercise

Reinforcement programs and behavioral contracting have been used successfully to increase levels of exercise (e.g., Libb & Clements, 1969; Wysocki, Hall, Iwata, & Riordan, 1979). Elementary school children who scored low on tests of health fitness participated in a behavioral program reported by Taggart, Taggart, and Siedentop (1986). The children accumulated points each week for engaging in such activities as running, bicycling, and practicing soccer, and their parents collected the data about their activities.

Contracts between the parents and children were established according to which the children agreed to increase daily/weekly activity levels progressively to meet preset criteria. In return, the parents agreed to provide various rewards when the children's activity levels increased. The specifics of each contract varied for each participant. Thus, the rewards varied, and included money, tangibles (headbands, toys), social outings, favored foods, praise, and watching favorite television programs.

When the contracts were in effect, all participants increased the number of activity points they earned. The increases ranged from 52% to 500%. Also the amount of time spent in the various activities increased by 49%. In addition, all but one of the participants scored better on the health fitness tests; many of them scored significantly better.

Maintenance data collected on 3 of the participants showed lasting effects of the program 12 weeks after the study's conclusion.

Wysocki et al. (1979) used behavioral contracting to increase college students' exercise. The students deposited items of personal value with the experimenters, which they could earn back in part by meeting weekly aerobic exercise goals. This contingency was effective with 7 of the 8 students. Also, in a follow-up questionnaire completed 12 months after the end of the study, 7 of the 8 students reported that they were earning more aerobic points per week than they had during the first (baseline) phase of the study.

Smoking

Money as a consequence, which was provided when the participants reduced their smoking (more precisely their breath carbon monoxide [CO]), was used in a study by Stitzer, Rand, Bigelow, and Mead (1986). The participants had been smokers for an average of 17.2 years and smoked an average of 19.6 cigarettes per day. This program included a cut-down test in which the participants could earn money on a sliding scale for reducing their weekday CO reading from baseline levels. The payments ranged from $1 for a 30% reduction from the baseline level to $6 for reductions of 80% or more. On the final day of the cut-down tests, the participants were informed that during the last 2 weeks of the study they could earn $12 per day if they quit smoking and their CO readings were consistent with abstinence. Participation in this phase of the study was voluntary.

The participants were divided into two groups based on their CO readings during the first day of the abstinence test. Those whose CO readings were ≤ 11 ppm were classified as abstainers and those with higher readings were classified as nonabstainers. During the contingent payment cut-down week, the average CO had decreased for both groups, dropping to 15 ppm for abstainers and to 24 ppm for nonabstainers from baseline levels of 30 to 35 ppm. During the 2-week abstinence test, average CO readings for abstainers were 5 to 7 ppm, and those for nonabstainers were about 25 ppm.

A 3-week follow-up assessment of the 22 abstainers found a variable pattern of relapse to smoking following withdrawal of the contingent money payments.

The measure used in this study, breath CO, has the advantage of being an objective measure of smoking. One disadvantage is that CO has a short half-life (1 to 4 hr) in the body, thus requiring frequent monitoring.

CONCLUSION

In physical education and sports, behavior analysis strategies and tactics appeared only rarely until the 1970s. Even today there are few examples of the application of behavior analysis in these domains. Siedentop and Taggart (1984) outlined impediments to the widespread application of behavior analysis in these domains. First, the direct and frequent measurement of behavior seems to be a problem for physical educators and, to a lesser extent, coaches. Second, the spaces where sports and physical education take place are relatively large, and the participants move around in them a good deal. The pace is often rapid and there may be frequent changes of activity. These factors work against the accurate observation of participant's behaviors. Third, in many areas, there is lack of agreement about what constitutes important outcome measures. "There are no standardized measures, except for fitness outcomes. There are few content valid tests for skill performance, especially in those activities where performance is interactive, such as all of the team games and many of the dual activities . . ." (Siedentop & Taggart, 1984).

A behavioral approach to health-related behaviors, on the other hand, emphasizes the clear specification and careful observation of the behaviors, ongoing monitoring of results, and decision-making based on obtained data. Such an approach also concerns itself with the antecedents and consequences of behavior that may be changed in systematic ways to bring about systematic behavior change. Emphasis is placed on the individual rather than groups. In addition, although not addressed in this chapter, a behavioral approach also encourages programs that are designed in such a way that significant behavioral changes can be attributed to the program, and not to other possible causes. Such programs are designed as experiments or at least quasiexperiments, and the long experience of behaviorists with experiments involving small numbers of subjects makes them uniquely qualified to contribute significantly to the analysis and promotion of health-related behaviors.

REFERENCES

Anderson, J. E., & Gross, A. M. (1988). Behavioral obesity research: Where have all the single subjects gone? *The Behavior Analyst, 11,* 141–148.

Libb, J. W., & Clements, C. B. (1969). Token reinforcement in an exercise program for hospitalized geriatric patients. *Perceptual and Motor Skills, 28,* 957–958.

Siedentop, D., & Taggart, A. (1984). Behavior analysis in physical education and sport. In W. L. Heward, T. E. Heron, D. S. Hill, & J. Trap-Porter (Eds.), *Focus on behavior analysis in education.* Columbus, OH: Charles E. Merrill.

Sohn, D., & Lamal, P. A. (1982). Self-reinforcement: Its reinforcing capability and its clinical utility. *The Pyshcological Record, 32,* 179–203.

Stitzer, M. L., Rand, C. S., Bigelow, G. E., & Mead, A. M. (1986). Contingent payment procedures for smoking reduction and cessation. *Journal of Applied Behavior Analysis, 19,* 197–202.

Taggart, A. C., Taggart, J., Siedentop, D. (1986). Effects of a home-based activity program. *Behavior Modification, 10*(4), 487–507.

Winett, R. A., Kramer, K. D., Walker, W. B., Malone, S. W., & Lane, M. K. (1988). Modifying food purchases in supermarkets with modeling, feedback, and goal-setting procedures. *Journal of Applied Behavior Analysis, 21,* 73–80.

Wooley, S. C., Wooley, O. W., & Dyrenforth, S. R. (1979). Theoretical, practical, and social issues in behavioral treatments of obesity. *Journal of Applied Behavior Analysis, 12,* 3–25.

Wysocki, T., Hall, G., Iwata, B., & Riordan, M. (1979). Behavioral management of exercise: Contracting for aerobic points. *Journal of Applied Behavior Analysis, 12,* 55–64.

11

Sport Involvement and Identity Formation

Douglas A. Kleiber
University of Georgia

Carol E. Kirshnit
University of Illinois at Chicago

Recent work in the study of human development has emphasized the intentionality of the individual in being a producer of his or her own development, especially from adolescence onward (e.g., Lerner & Busch-Rossnagel, 1981). The selection of action options is frequently a matter of managing developmental imperatives and stretching toward maturity (Silbereisen, Eyferth, & Rudinger, 1986). Sport involvement is one such option, and despite the fact that it is largely intrinsically motivated in its beginning phases, it often becomes part of the acting out of an individual's developmental agenda.

In middle childhood there is, arguably, very little sense of future. Interest in sport typically emerges out of play values and the desire to be with one's peers. Yet even during this period, there are predictable psychosocial issues that children address in relation to an emerging awareness of self. As children approach adolescence, the choice to stay involved in organized sport reflects a sense of one's abilities and potentials as well as one's interests and an awareness of the expectations of others.

The essence of our thesis here is that it is often difficult to manage these often conflicting viewpoints, making development through adolescence a precarious, if sometimes rewarding, business for one who is committed to one or more sports. In addition, contrary to popular assumption, it may be more difficult for boys than for girls, a question that is also addressed throughout this analysis.

Our general contention is that organized sport is an important context within which developmental issues may be addressed, and that sport involvement may itself be regarded as a form of developmental action. Nevertheless, despite considerable debate in the popular press and among the public at large as to the value of sport, psychology has devoted little attention to the impact of sport on the development of those who take it seriously, a fact that may be attributed less to a lack of interest than to a need to define the problems more clearly. Given the complexity of the subject and the diversity of influences and effects, any evaluation or analysis of sport must be circumscribed even to raise appropriate questions. The choice here is to focus on the subject of identity formation and the manner in which it may be affected by the action of sport participation. More specifically, preliminary

The authors acknowledge the contributions of Reed Larson and Thomas Greening, who have regularly offered information and insight into this material.

193

answers are sought for the following questions: How does a child's emerging sense of self change as a result of an ongoing encounter with one or more sports? What are the liabilities, if any, of committing heavily to this domain? At what age are such problems likely to be particularly troublesome? Finally, how do these dynamics differ for males and females?

To address these questions, the meaning of identity formation is considered first. The contributions of sport to identity formation are then addressed by examining variations in the meaning of sport and by clarifying its relationship to play and work in each of several developmental periods. Variations in experience and patterns of influence for males and females are examined with respect to alternative outcomes. Finally, the matter of gender differences is addressed from a broader sociohistorical perspective, and implications are drawn for optimizing the developmental potential of sport.

THE FORMATION OF A SENSE OF IDENTITY

What exactly is identity and how is it formed? Definitions of this concept have often been excessively vague. Erik Erikson, perhaps the foremost theorist examining identity, readily admitted his own frustration in trying to make a definitive statement about this concept:

> So far I have tried out the term identity almost deliberately—I like to think—in many different connotations. At one time it seemed to refer to a conscious sense of individual uniqueness, at another to an unconscious striving for continuity of experience, and at a third, as a solidarity with a group's ideals. (1968, p. 208)

Relying on the theories of Erikson, Waterman (1985) noted that identity is discussed as a mechanism, a framework, a sense of continuity, and a sense of direction. He regarded it as "self-definition comprised of those goals, values and beliefs which a person finds personally expressive and to which he or she is unequivocally committed" (p. 6). He noted that identity formation occurs differently with respect to different domains (vocational, ideological, and so on), and that it varies considerably from individual to individual.

One important source of difference that has gained a great deal of attention in recent years is that attributable to gender. The original views on identity put forth by Erikson were based on a male model of development. Realizing the significant influence of biology, culture, and social norms on the developing individual, however, Erikson acknowledged the potential for gender differences in identity formation (1968). What he came to recognize was the relational focus in the lives of women, such that women derived their identities more through their relationships with others and less through the individuation process typical of male identity development. Although Erikson believed that a man needed to establish a firm sense of identity as an individual before being able to enter into an intimate relationship with another person, the establishment of intimacy was considered the foundation upon which a woman's identity was built.

The implications of Erikson's ideas regarding gender differences in identity development are far reaching with regard to the discussion at hand. His theory could be interpreted to mean essentially that individuation occurs earlier than reference group identification in the process of male identity development, whereas the temporal sequence of these two aspects is reversed in female identity formation. Extending this line of reasoning further, it may be that the element that occurs first in the course of identity development—individuation for males and reference group identification for females—is perhaps that which is more basic and fundamental, hence more significant, to the resultant identity. Therefore, men would be more likely to define themselves in terms of what they do, whereas women would tend to define themselves by the people with whom they do things.

It is important to note, however, that the differences are a matter of emphasis and primacy; both aspects are critical to identity formation in men and women alike. Most of those who write about identity formation recognize an internal individuation imperative that separates one from others and establishes autonomy and also a relational imperative that locates the person effectively within his or her social world. A dialectic is necessitated in the course of individuation, however different a person may become, because validation is sought through association with others and from their recognition. As Erikson put it,

> *The young individual must learn to be most himself where he means most to others—those others, to be sure, who have come to mean the most to him. The term identity expresses such a mutual relation in that it connotes both consistent sameness within oneself (selfsameness) and a persistent sharing of some kind of essential character with others. (1959, p. 102)*

Conversely, the communality that is established in association with others must be interpreted in individual ways to contribute anything much to a sense of identity. Total investment in the perspective of the group runs the risk of deindividuation (cf. Diener, 1977).

In examining the course of identity formation in human development, psychologists typically focus on work, religion, sex roles, and ideology as the substantive matters around which adolescents, anyway, shape an identity. Values and beliefs that can be articulated in some manner generally have to do with such matters. Yet the process of identity formation is a dynamic one requiring opportunities for self-expression and social feedback and ample room for revision. The perspective to be advanced here is that although social, institutional, and cultural commitments may reflect the stabilization of identity, it is in the liberating context of leisure that identity alternatives are often addressed initially through the expression of personal interests. In addition, as Erikson pointed out, when these childhood interests are connected to what is expected in adulthood, the necessary continuity is created for what he called an "inner identity."

The importance of physical action in the process of identity formation is addressed by Chickering (1969). In relating identity to education, Chickering interpreted identity as being at home in one's body, and noted that although physical activity is generally neglected in the study of identity, it provides an action basis for developing a sense of competence. "The development of physical and manual skills can foster development in other areas by permitting objects and events to be tied to symbols through action" (p. 31). Learning to ride a bicycle extends one's range of enterprise and makes other bike riders part of an accessible reference group. Furthermore, the overt demonstration of abilities, with opportunities for failure as well as success, provides direct experience in the management of emotions, which Chickering also regarded as critical in the course of identity formation.

The context of leisure thus affords opportunities for action and self-development that may be more self-affirming than those afforded in more socially constrained circumstances (cf. Kelly, 1983). In particular, the opportunity to play is seen here as especially important because play is the active, creative interpretation of values and abilities, and thus is an essential aspect of individuation.

The formation of identities requires commitment, however, and only those forms of play that capture one's serious attention are likely to transform the self in any meaningful way. Only those that move experimentation and playfulness into alignment with the values of others are likely to be of any substantive value to an enduring identity. Although sport involvement is generally initiated in response to play impulses, the earnestness with which many young people commit themselves to sport activities and the significance it holds socially tends to push it out of the realm of the experimental and playful, but at the same time brings it in closer alignment with the work and achievement meaning systems of the wider world. The question here is what is the relevance of that transformation in the course of identity formation? Does that make sport more or less compelling or useful in the development of a sense of self?

On one hand, borrowing from Piaget's (1962) assimilation model of play, we can return to the point that the relative triviality of leisure activities makes them merely a buffer for assuaging the conflicts of socialization (see also Roberts & Sutton-Smith, 1962). Even as identity can be a mixture of things, it might be argued that only those matters that society regards as serious and important will have any relevance to values central to identity. So whether a person is "serious" about his or her fun or not will ultimately be just a blip on the developmental trajectory, a temporary and perhaps therapeutic departure, but not ultimately sustaining to an emerging sense of self.

On the other hand, in taking a leisure activity seriously, the individuating power of play is turned into something more responsive to the developmental tasks of establishing one's integrity as an individual in society. Serious leisure is that which has both a following and an audience that supports an individual's commitment, offering a behavioral structure with established performance standards and providing feedback about one's competence (Stebbins, 1982). Activities such as sport that are physically expressive and therefore recognizable by others, with explicit rules and standards of performance, contribute experiential data for the formation of identity. Embodied experience that is expressive, challenging, and socially integrating may contribute more to identity formation than has been previously acknowledged.

Erikson (1959) pointed out that "favored capacities" are among the important elements integrated into the evolving configuration of identity formation (p. 116), and certainly many of those capacities are physical. Of course, patterns of physical expressiveness are not confined to sport. Music and the other arts are often embraced initially as play, shaped into competencies through instruction and self-discipline, and sometimes emerge as clearly defined vocational alternatives. Even as avocations within the context of leisure, such activities are both personally and socially significant. For example, participation in juvenile jazz bands in Scotland was shown in a recent study by Grieves (1989) to be both self-defining and socially integrative for the girls involved. It provided a sense of friendship and identification and an opportunity to practice discipline and develop a sense of pride and commitment.

It may still be argued that avocational interests contribute little to identity formation; vocational and ideological issues come to dominate the attention of most maturing adolescents. However, the freely chosen expressive activities of leisure are especially self-affirming, because behavior in that context is more a matter of personal discretion than in other contexts (Haggard & Williams, 1990). Certainly choices can be digressive or regressive, but to the extent that they reflect on the continuity of self from one time to the next, or alternatively, to the extent that they proffer new alternative values for examination in more constrained contexts, they can be identity defining (cf. Hendry, 1983).

Voluntary activity involvement may be very emblematic for a young person. Being a skater, an artist, a tennis player, or a computer "jock" offers a personal statement through which varying degrees of commitment are expressed. Such self-statements can be trivial, temporary, and merely assimilative, or they can be taken very seriously and developed in conjunction with the standards and norms of an activity association, however loosely organized. When activities are serious and accommodative in that way, we may call them "transitional" (Csikszentmihalyi & Larson, 1984; Kleiber, Larson, & Csikszentmihalyi, 1987; Larson & Kleiber, 1990). Transitional activities are those that connect childhood with adulthood by blending the enjoyment of childhood play with the seriousness and investment of adult work. In transitional activities, a child's intrinsic interests are engaged with meaning systems that are valued by adults. A girl who collects antique toy farm implements, first for amusement and later as an ongoing endeavor that she shares with other enthusiasts of all ages, is engaged in a transitional activity. Membership in a sports team or club would very likely have the same effect.

In sports, discipline, endurance, persistence, and achievement are characteristics and behaviors that adults espouse and youth accept as important. However, unlike school, where such indoctrination tends to be imposed, there is at least the premise of choice in sport and recreational activities. As Porter (1967) pointed out:

> Sport may offer a fresh opportunity to find instruction a desired rather than an imposed experience, especially where coaching is received as part of team membership, generally welcomed by the peer group, and offered by an older boy or man who may be much admired for his skills and willingness to share them. (p. 81)

It is identification with others as much or more than establishing one's distinctiveness that is important in this view of identity formation. Not surprisingly sociologists make more of the inclusive character of identity formation (cf. Stryker, 1987) than do psychologists, who tend to emphasize the independence-seeking character of adolescence. However, even in developmental psychology, the idea of individuation is not inherently individualistic. As noted previously, the consensual validation of peers, parents, and society more generally allows and confirms one's uniqueness, and interrelatedness serves in varying degrees as a foundation for identity formation.

VARIATIONS IN MEANING OF SPORT ACTIVITIES

A given sport activity can have different meanings for different people, and this is especially true with respect to gender. Because boys are typically encouraged to excel in instrumental achievement situations, whereas girls are socialized to define themselves and their success through their relationships with others, it is not surprising that sport is associated with different meanings and correspondingly different experiences for males and females.

Joan Duda (1988) found that female athletes were much less oriented toward mastery and social comparison in their sports than were male athletes. In a study of high school varsity soccer players, Borman and Kurdek (1987) observed that girls' motivation to play soccer was associated with the desire to have many friends, whereas boys' motivation to play soccer was related to an instrumental achievement orientation (i.e., a desire to get ahead and wanting to participate in varsity athletics). Croxton and Klonsky (1981) noted that males often emphasize winning and personal achievement as the primary goals in their athletic participation, whereas females typically rate opportunities for socializing and intrinsic satisfaction as most important.

In a study of sports involvement during early adolescence (Kirshnit, 1989), boys were observed to approach sports as a context for achievement and an opportunity for developing skills and competing with others. Parents expected and encouraged this behavior in their sons, and boys produced accordingly. Girls, on the other hand, tended to approach sport as leisure and as activities to be pursued primarily for fun, and they received little parental encouragement for sports participation. Perhaps the most interesting finding was the fact that girls derived much more enjoyment from their athletic involvement than did the boys in this study.

Professionalism is a term that has often been used in discussions of children's involvement in organized sports to refer to an adult orientation toward games, in which success and skill become the primary goals of participation and fairness is deemphasized (Theberge, Curtis, & Brown, 1982; Webb, 1969). Gender differences have emerged in studies of professionalism among athletes; male athletes are far more likely to have a professional orientation toward sports than are female athletes. Interestingly enough, these gender differences in professionalism have not been observed to be nearly as pronounced among nonathletes (Snyder & Spreitzer, 1976). Clearly, males and females are being socialized into different models of athletic involvement with different sets of values and correspondingly different goals and expectations.

Of course, times have changed, and these gender differences are lessening to some degree. We are in the middle of a historical transition with regard to the role of women in sport. We have come a long way from the first Olympic games in ancient Greece, when the only contact women had with competition was through their role as potential "prizes" for the successful male participants (Twin, 1985). Title IX of the Educational Amendment Act of 1972 has been a major landmark in the history of women's athletics in the United States, guaranteeing both sexes equal opportunity for participation in programs in all schools receiving federal funds. This legislation has resulted in a tremendous increase in funding and involvement for women in sports at both the high school and collegiate levels (Rivers, Barnett, & Baruch, 1979). The scholarships and other extrinsic rewards now available for female athletes are indications that the gap in sport socialization is beginning to narrow. Elite male and female athletes are, in many respects, more similar to one another than they are different. Because sport has for so long been defined as a traditionally masculine domain of experience (e.g., Birns, 1976; Eitzen & Sage, 1978; Griffin, 1973; Malumphy, 1971), female athletes at the highest levels of competition have generally accepted the prevailing male model of sport and have risen to the demands and performed well within this structure.

Moreover, what have often been called gender differences are perhaps more precisely sex role differences. For example, Kirshnit's (1989) findings indicated that young adolescent girls with nontraditional sex role attitudes approached and experienced sport in a manner similar to that of their male peers and differed from that of the more traditional girls in the study. Certainly the issues are both subtle and complex, but it does appear that as sports are taken more seriously by females, as they become athletes and commit to the prevailing model, a more masculine identity formation pattern may be the result. Is this inevitable? What are the consequences, and what are the alternatives?

Sex role differentiation has important implications for the study of athletic involvement. The qualities that we typically associate with being athletic are many of the same agentic and instrumental characteristics that are subsumed under traditional definitions of masculinity (Bardwick, 1971; Harris, 1981). That is, successful athletes are thought to be aggressive, competitive, tough minded, determined, and driven (Marsh & Jackson, 1986). Clearly, these traits are antithetical to what are considered to be socially desirable feminine qualities. On the other hand, the qualities associated with athleticism and masculinity are virtually interchangeable. Consequently, the male athlete is seen as behaving in a manner consistent with gender role stereotypes, whereas the female athlete has traditionally been viewed as more of an anomaly because of her "unladylike" behavior (Allison & Butler, 1984).

Much of the literature on female athletes has focused on sex role stereotypes and the notion of the "role conflict" in being both a woman and an athlete. The assumption implicit in this body of research is that being feminine and being athletic are somehow mutually exclusive, such that opting to capitalize on one role necessitates sacrificing the other (Anthrop & Allison, 1983; Harris, 1979; Sage & Loudermilk, 1979; Snyder & Kivlin, 1975; Snyder, Kivlin, & Spreitzer, 1979). Griffin's (1973) finding that the most unflattering roles for women were that of the female athlete and the female professor highlights this point clearly.

Among adolescents and adults, the idea that female athletes will feel a greater degree of role conflict than their nonathletic female peers has received only modest empirical support. Sage and Loudermilk (1979) studied 268 collegiate female athletes from a variety of different sports and found that 56% of their sample experienced little or no role conflict with being female and being athletic. Anthrop and Allison (1983) conducted a similar study with 1,343 female high school athletes in various sports and found that 50% of these athletes had experienced little or no conflict.

Research on female athletes in different types of sports has generally been based on the assumption that women participating in more traditionally feminine sports will be more comfortable and experience less conflict around the athlete role than their female counterparts who choose to engage in less traditionally feminine sports. Del Rey (1978) coined the term *apologetic* to explain her empirical observations of female athletes involved in more masculine sports espousing more traditional sex role attitudes than those involved in more appropriately feminine sports. Del Rey (1978) asserted that women who are committed to masculine athletic pursuits apologize for being unfeminine in this area by being ultrafeminine in other aspects of their lives. Empirical support for Del Rey's notion of the apologetic has been inconsistent, and although there is research demonstrating a higher degree of role conflict among female athletes participating in sex-inappropriate sports (Felshin, 1974; Harris, 1975), there is also a body of literature suggesting that female athletes, regardless of sport type, feel better about themselves and are less traditional with regard to sex roles than their nonathletic female peers (Anthrop & Allison, 1983; Hall, Durborow, & Progen, 1986).

The meaning of participation in sport for males and females can, of course, be characterized by similarities as well as differences. For anyone, being an athlete implies some degree of physical prowess as well as an affinity for competition. Moreover, the athlete is one who has established some enduring commitment to at least one sport and is recognized by others as having that commitment. Persistence and endurance in the course of physical training, as with any other area of competence, is culturally valued as an important socialization experience. However, commitment may also be reflected in loyalty to the collective; and all the celebration of "male bonding" notwithstanding, it may be the team aspect of sport experience that females find particularly satisfying, as well as being that which may offer sport its most humanizing interpretation. We address this point further in the final section of the chapter. Let us now turn to a developmental analysis of sport and identity formation.

SPORT AND SELF-AWARENESS IN CHILDHOOD

"Young athletes" (among 10- to 12-year-olds) may be so labeled because of the aspiration of coaches and program leaders, and this may be a misnomer with respect to commitment. When sport involvement does not reflect a child's personal preference, when he or she is forced to "play" by parents, or when a gifted adolescent betrays his or her recalcitrance in half-hearted efforts, the label of athlete is inappropriate. It is at this point in the life course, however, that physical skill and sport contests are first taken seriously, and a child may begin to see him or herself as an athlete. Projections of continued sport involvement for years to come allow the athlete role to feature prominently in what Markus and Nurius (1986) referred to as one's possible self.

According to Erikson (1963), a sense of competence is a prerequisite for adolescent identity formation. This issue of relative competence is very much on the minds of prepubertal children. Yet despite the fact that the child's principal way of comparing his or her skill level with others is through observable action, developmental psychologists have devoted relatively little attention to the significance of physical competence during this period. On the other hand, sociologists and sport scientists have clearly established the importance of physical and athletic skill to social status and self-esteem in elementary school, especially among boys (Coleman, 1961; Eitzen, 1976; Kleiber & Roberts, 1987; Roberts, Kleiber & Duda, 1982). In a study of adolescents' self-perceived competencies, Gilmore (1979) found that 80% of those mentioned were athletic in nature.

At this point, we may begin to recognize a cost to identity formation from sport involvement that begins as athletic prowess gains some degree of social currency.

Although the social significance of sport involvement may contribute to the identi-fication aspect of identity formation, its individuating power may begin to be compromised. For young children, the association of sport with play is still strong enough to sustain their interest and involvement. Sports are more likely to have a light-hearted quality, being pursued as games for fun and enjoyment, with little emphasis on performance or outcome (Kirshnit, 1989). Doing what coaches and teammates want may be felt as confining by a child and the notoriety from success an unnecessary, if exciting, reward. However, to the extent that satisfaction be-comes contingent upon the reactions of others to one's performance, failure is likely to lead to early abandonment of the activity, whereas success sets one into a progressive achievement pattern predesigned by others. Whether a selection effect or an age-related change, as a child approaches adolescence, satisfaction derived from various sports comes to be contingent upon the reactions of others to his or her performance. As the adolescent's world becomes more serious and adult-like, competence, as measured by success or failure in the eyes of others, becomes increasingly more relevant to the decision about whether or not to continue in the role of "athlete." It is no longer simply a matter of enjoying an activity; one must also be good at it.

ADOLESCENT SPORT INVOLVEMENT AND IDENTITY FORMATION

Part of the identity-formation process in adolescence involves abandoning the role of child. A person who voluntarily commits to a pattern of activity in which gratification is predictably delayed and preceded by discomfort is saying that he or she is no longer a child. Beyond simply playing competently, an adolescent athlete is able to think of him or herself as one who persists and endures in the face of obstacles, perhaps one who is courageous and can embrace adversity with poise and composure. The possibility that such self-statements then transcend the context of sport becomes a basis for a more substantial contribution to identity achieve-ment and also the premise whereby society can assert that sport builds character.

There is, however, very little empirical evidence for such assertions (Ogilvie & Tutko, 1985; Stevenson, 1975). Nomothetic studies have suggested that such char-acteristics, to the extent that they are more common among athletes, are more likely to be there at the start as prerequisites in an often ruthless selection process. There are likely those who mature substantially or develop further as a result of their sport experience, but they have not been adequately identified in the correla-tional studies typically performed. Furthermore, the context of sport competition, where the outcome often has importance to players and spectators that extends far beyond the contest itself, is just as likely to promote unethical and antisocial behaviors (e.g., cheating to win or hurting an opponent) that might not be as easily incorporated into one's emerging identity (cf. Bredemeier & Shields, 1987).

Of course, suffering alone is not likely to be perceived as particularly virtuous if it does not produce some positive effect. Competence would appear to be neces-sary for a person to take pride in and identify with an ability to struggle and persist. In an ethnographic investigation of climbers and rugby players, Donnelly and Young (1988) established a process of identity construction associated with proficiency and experience in the activity and the acquisition of an appropriate style as well as the skills for participation. In a study of the consequences of involvement in extracurricular activity (Kleiber & Roberts, 1990), a measure of identity (Rosenthal, Gurney & Moore, 1981) failed to show any relationship with sport involvement per se. However, when level of involvement and perceived ability were taken into account, a modest relationship was revealed. Additionally, competent athletes were significantly more likely to endorse the statement, "You would get a better understanding of me through my extracurricular activity than through my schoolwork," and less likely to agree that "My personal identity is reflected more in the work that I would like to do than in my current extracurricular activities" than less talented athletes, students in other performance-oriented extracurricular activities, or other high school students more generally.

In spite of these indications of a relationship, the amount of variance accounted for was small, suggesting many other influences or identity as well as many variations among athletes. The narrowing of attention on sport may, in fact, undermine the formation of a more elaborate configuration of identity. David Elkind (1981) suggested that talented youth in sports and other areas who are nurtured aggressively in the development and display of those talents are subject to a kind of "premature structuring" that deprives them of other important experiences. In *The Hurried Child,* he noted that those who fit this pattern are likely to have personalities that are underdeveloped in other respects (p. 179). If being successfully involved in sports affords a greater degree of self-acceptance and a sense of identification with significant others, it may also attenuate consideration of other aspects of oneself. Former professional basketball player and now United States Senator Bill Bradley referred to his adolescent awareness of "having entered the tunnel of narrowing perspective at age 14" (Lipsyte, 1976; see also Bradley, 1976). This realization may not come until years later, if at all, for some athletes (cf. Kleiber, 1983).

One theoretical advance in the study of identity formation that may be relevant to this discussion is Marcia's (1980) description of identity statuses. Marcia conceptualized identity development as a two-fold process involving crisis/exploration of the various roles and life-styles available to the individual and the subsequent commitment to a relatively enduring definition of self. On the basis of presence or absence of exploration and commitment in various areas (e.g., occupation, religion, sex roles), Marcia postulated the existence of four distinct styles of resolution of the identity crisis of adolescence, which he referred to as identity statuses. A person who has explored a variety of possible options within a specific area and is successfully committed to one of these options is said to be in the status of identity achievement within that area. Conversely, one who has neither explored alternatives nor made any sort of commitment falls within the identity diffusion status. Individuals who are in the process of considering their options but have not yet made any firm commitment are considered to be in a state of moratorium. People who have not actively reviewed their choices and have instead relied upon their childhood identifications with authority figures to arrive at premature commitment are considered to be in the status of foreclosure.

It seems reasonable to suspect that many athletes would find themselves in the diffusion or foreclosure statuses in most areas if they become singularly committed to sport and are reinforced and insulated in that commitment. An athlete identity may become crystallized if other interests are disregarded, if commitments lead to financial and temporal investments, and if future activities (educational and vocational) are contingent upon athletic involvement. To that extent, the premature structuring associated with an athlete identity may be quite limiting. This would be especially true where the approval of significant others makes sport other-directed and accommodative rather than playfully expressive or assimilative. This is perhaps the explanation for the frequently observed association between athletic involvement, conservatism, and conventionality (King & Chi, 1974; Malmisur, 1976; Sage, 1985; Snyder & Spreitzer, 1983).

In a study by Malmisur (1976), college athletes were found to be less advanced than nonathletes in terms of ego development, predominantly fixated at a conventional level, far short of more autonomous and principled thinking. There is also evidence, albeit modest, that college athletes are more foreclosed than nonathletes (Petipas, 1981). Using the Objective Measure of Ego Identity Status (Adams, Shea, & Fitch, 1979) with 278 college students, Petipas found that athletes scored significantly higher on the foreclosure scale than nonathletes. This, and the fact that they were also higher on a measure of authoritarianism, led the author to conclude that "the results allow the hypothesis to remain tenable that participation in college athletics stunts psychosocial maturation."

Both of these studies involved only male athletes; the impact of sport involvement on the ego development of female athletes remains to be determined. It may be that in keeping with other gender differences in meanings associated with sport, the effects would not be as great or would at least be different. Perhaps for females, the lack of general social reinforcement, the more limited focus on instrumental achievement objectives, the lack of professional vocational alternatives, and a more communal orientation would make foreclosure a less likely outcome.

THE INEVITABLE METATHESIS OF RETIRING ATHLETES

Although there is considerable debate about the process of identity formation using the identity status model (e.g., Côté & Levine, 1988), Waterman (1985) argued that one may move between statuses in a variety of ways (Figure 1). With regard to foreclosure, he suggested several possible patterns that can be applied to our understanding of the retiring athlete.

Challenged by the aging process, the athlete role endures well only after considerable revision, if at all. The social salience of athleticism depends on peak performance. With aging—25 is considered old in some sports—declines are predictable. If there is enduring intrinsic interest in playing at the sport or opportunities to compete more informally, some semblance of an athlete identity may endure well into middle age and beyond. At these later stages, however, being an athlete must become only a peripheral aspect of the self, giving way to alternative role identities and self-definitions consistent with taking one's place in adult society.

In this regard, females must again be considered separately from males, however much the culture of sport for women is changing. It seems reasonable to expect that women would be likely to find the transition out of sport easier than men, because they have traditionally been discouraged from defining themselves solely in terms of instrumental achievement. Consequently, women are more likely than men to have cultivated alternative roles over the course of an athletic career, thereby making more possibilities available to themselves at the point of retire-

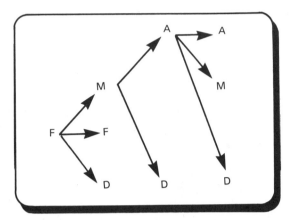

Figure 1 Model of the sequential patterns of ego identity
development. (D = identity diffusion; F =
foreclosure; M = moratorium; A = identity
achievements) (Adapted from *Identity in
Adolescence: Processes and Contents* (p. 15) by
A. S. Waterman, 1985, San Francisco:
Jossey-Bass. Copyright 1985 by Jossey-Bass.
Adapted by permission.)

ment. There has been little empirical research on the subject, but a study of female
former college athletes indicated little evidence of transition difficulties (Greendorfer & Blinde, 1986). Ironically, the obstacles that make it difficult for women to
wholeheartedly pursue the athlete role provide the impetus for the development of
coping strategies that facilitate a graceful departure from that role (cf. Kleiber &
Kane, 1984).

The abandonment of the foreclosed identity may leave an athlete "diffused"
(see Figure 1). Such might be expected in cases where ex-athletes seem to degen-
erate, abusing drugs and alcohol and engaging in other self-destructive patterns. In
some cases, economic success may simply delay this process. This is the pattern
that gains the most attention in the popular press and for which there is at least
some evidence (McPherson, 1980). In fact, such patterns may be established even
before retirement as evidenced, for example, by reports of drug use among professional athletes. It is possible that the committed athlete at leisure experiences a
sense of emptiness based on a lack or underdevelopment of challenging role alternatives, and turns to maladaptive coping strategies to fill the void and recapture the
"highs" associated with the excitement of sports.

In other cases, the foreclosed identity may be just slightly recast subsequent to a
decline in relative ability and competitive success. A kind of prolonged athlete
identity is thus maintained, for example, or by living vicariously through the
sports achievements of one's children.

For those who are more fortunate, the abandonment of the identity precipitates
a search for alternatives in a period of moratorium. An identity must in some ways
be reconstructed through the discovery of fundamental values that transcend the
physical achievement context. New commitments come slowly, but there is a clear
crisis, an "inevitable metathesis" (Hill & Lowe, 1974), that revolves around the

relinquishing of identity-defining attachments to a sport and the examination of alternatives.

The extant research on retirement from sport has not given adequate attention to the psychological process associated with leaving that role. The available literature on professional and collegiate athletes has not substantiated the downward spiral often suggested in the popular press (Coakley, 1983). Nevertheless, to assert that this adjustment is therefore painless is to ignore the normal stress associated with identity formation, which is simply delayed in this case. The outward signs of diffusion discussed earlier (i.e., drug use, alienation) are likely to give way to some identity reconstruction over time and sooner for some than for others. Research is needed to determine whether delays in the process of identity formation in sports have any significant impact on other developmental processes.

A question worthy of consideration in that regard involves how the establishment of intimate relationships is affected by foreclosure of an identity around a sport. Establishing intimate relationships is the normative crisis that Erikson (1963) and others associate with young adulthood, and which, at least with males (cf. Gilligan, 1982), requires some identity resolution. If an athlete is foreclosed around that identity or is only beginning to divest him or herself of it, intimacy is likely to be elusive. Furthermore, the combative, aggressive style reinforced in athletics is likely to further undermine a process that requires a degree of surrender to another.

The problem becomes even more complex when gender differences and sex role expectations are taken into account. Given that intimacy and identity formation are thought to be more closely associated for women, the female athlete may be faced with a particularly difficult dilemma. In some cases, she has to decide between differentiating herself as an athlete and defining herself in relationships with others. The more traditional woman is likely to be uncomfortable in sacrificing intimate relationships in the interest of athletic achievement, perhaps apologizing for being an athlete by behaving in ultrafeminine ways when she is not playing her sport (Del Rey, 1978). Although this woman is unlikely to have overlooked other identity-relevant areas outside of sport, the cost in terms of her commitment to the athlete role, and perhaps her athletic success may be painfully apparent.

In contrast, nontraditional women probably experience less conflict between the demands of the athlete role and the desire for an intimate relationship (Matteo, 1986). It may be easier for such women to define themselves in terms of their athletic involvement as well as to find intimacy with another who is capable of accepting the significance of sport to their overall sense of themselves. These women, however, may also experience some of the negative effects of athletic involvement on identity formation described for men. If sport participation comes at the cost to intimacy for such women, the effect of this trade-off on their resultant identity development becomes a matter of some concern.

SPORT, GENDER, AND PERSONAL LIBERATION

From a feminist perspective, it is easy to become discouraged by the manner in which women have been largely excluded from the traditionally male-dominated sport subculture. Until very recently, society has neither expected nor encouraged female sports participation, and the slow progress that has been made in the institutionalization of sports for women since Title IX was enacted speaks to our culture's ambivalence in fully accepting the female athlete. This may be a blessing in disguise. Although no doubt unintentional, women may actually have been spared the agonies and pressures of the male athlete role. With fewer social expectations, role models, and performance standards, the female athlete has more freedom than the male athlete to define the athlete role in a more personally meaningful way and thereby have more ownership over her identity in this regard. The athlete role is not something imposed on her by society, but rather an identity of her own making.

There is inconsistent evidence of psychological turmoil among female athletes, which is thought to arise primarily from status inconsistency in the public domain (i.e., the lack of encouragement and recognition from significant others, the athletic establishment, and the media community) rather than from any uncertainty or discomfort regarding their perceived femininity (Allison & Butler, 1984; Anthrop & Allison, 1983). Considering the possibilities of premature structuring and over-identification referred to earlier, some amount of conflict could serve as an effective deterrent to identity foreclosure. Although the assertions of role conflict among female athletes are often overstated, any reluctance to commit wholeheartedly to the athlete role must be regarded as advantageous in terms of the ultimate course of identity formation. Foreclosure is less likely where the value of sport to one's developmental trajectory continues to be examined rather than simply assumed.

On the other hand, although women may be in less danger of finding themselves foreclosed around the athlete role, the mechanisms that prevent such an eventuality are the same ones that increase the likelihood of a perpetual state of moratorium for the majority of female athletes. If females are encouraged to explore within the realm of athletics but not provided with significant support for commitment, the path to identity achievement as an athlete is virtually closed off. Faced with such a situation, one is likely to begin looking elsewhere for potential commitments.

There is certain irony in the fact that a women's interest in the world of sport was increased during a time when researchers and theorists have come to question the value of athletics. Critics of organized, competitive sport have challenged the conventional wisdom that sport builds character and assert instead that the playing field may not be a healthy place for anyone (Lasch, 1979, Ogilvie & Tutko, 1985). Yet in spite of the growing realization that sport may not be as positive an experience as was once assumed, there may be solace in the fact that females tend to approach sports differently than males. Criticism of sport has been, more precisely, criticism about the traditionally masculine model of athleticism and its inherently exploitive and professionalized character. The feminization of sports may ultimately provide us with the answers about how best to humanize the experience of sport. This is not to say that sports cannot and should not be a context for achievement, but rather that we need to broaden our perspective considerably to allow space for other possible goals and outcomes of the athletic experience.

There are certainly limitations and drawbacks in the traditionally feminine model of sport. Whereas the lack of social pressure and expectations to achieve in sport may allow young female athletes greater freedom to pursue sports as physically expressive leisure activities, the motivation to sustain a serious self-defining commitment to athletics is insufficient in the absence of concrete future goals toward which to strive. Because the masculine sport as work model has been criticized for its failure to incorporate expressive and play-like qualities of sport, the feminine sport-as-leisure model is equally limited in its exclusion of the instrumental and achievement-oriented aspects of sport.

Because our current structure for socialization into sport has a tendency to produce uninspired female and oppressed male athletes, it would seem advantageous to reconsider the prevailing views about sport and attempt to construct a more comprehensive model of sport socialization that would be applicable to both males and females. Such a model of sport would very likely incorporate both the enjoyable aspects of leisure and the productive qualities of work. In support of this view is recent research demonstrating that liking of a sport is greatest among players who describe their participation as a combination of both work and leisure compared with those who view their sport solely as either work or leisure (Wagner, Lounsbury, & Fitzgerald, 1989).

Mary Duquin (1978) described an androgynous model of sport that would integrate the expressive "process-oriented" qualities of feminine sport with the instrumental "product-oriented" aspects of masculine sport, thus creating a sort of gender-free form of athletic experience. Like the more general concept of psychological androgyny, Duquin suggested that this would represent the healthiest approach to sport. Although the main thrust of the model revolves around making sport more accessible and enriching to females, the implications of her argument are much broader. To extend her line of reasoning further, male sport participants would be encouraged to appreciate and focus on their expressive qualities as athletes. Hence, both males and females would learn to balance both the expressive and instrumental (play and work) aspects of the athlete role, making sports more available to all participants.

Perhaps equally as important, this orientation to experience sport in new ways would break the hold of sex role prescriptions and contribute to the circumspection necessary to become a more responsible producer of one's own development. Opening the context of sport to alternative interpretations should reinforce its potential to provide action alternatives that are self-enhancing and growth producing.

CONCLUSION

Marxist and Neomarxist critiques of sport (e.g., Rigauer, 1981) emphasized the tendencies of sport to dehumanize and exploit disenfranchised human beings in the course of accepting the mechanistic, specialized, rationalized, and bureaucratic character of capitalist society (a point that was apparently lost in the factory-like sport training institutions in Eastern Europe in the not-so-distant past). Rather than finding it a realm of liberating and playful self-expression, these critics regard sport as both repressive and distracting. However, Guttman (1981) noted that it is the relatively advantaged rather than the powerless in society who covet the experience of sport and that "exhilaration and joy and self-realization" are so common and significant in sport that it cannot be written off as false consciousness. Guttman referred to Bouet's (1969) assertion that "sport is a form of play, an assertion of their human freedom to do what they choose, an experience of self actualization quite unlike the routine experience of work."

However, for whom would we favor the association of sport to play rather than work and for whom the contrary? Both play and work seem to be evident in sport expression to varying degrees. In addition, what difference does it make to identity formation? Perhaps in view of the gender differences previously discussed, it might be argued that the pattern of identity development for women—giving primacy to the interpersonal—would allow them to better tolerate and perhaps even benefit from the professionalization of play into achievement-oriented work values (cf. Lever, 1976). For males, on the other hand, given the evidence that identity formation may be more readily retarded, derailed, and foreclosed as a result of premature structuring around achievement-oriented sport involvement, maintaining a large dose of play would perhaps serve as an antidote to some extent. However, given the changes taking place in women's sport, it is probably best to suggest that all forces that would divorce sport from play should be confronted, as it is the mixture of play and work that gives sport its power as a transitional experience.

It is partly because play precedes work ontogenetically that sport is associated first and foremost with play. The enduring insistence on preserving a play quality in sport may reflect a combination of ambivalence about work and freedom and a recognition, at some level, that it is the play quality that ultimately makes sport most enriching to life. However, for those committed to being athletes, there is also the matter of success and achievement. Sport has certainly become recognized as an achievement domain, and that is precisely where the compromising specter of commodified labor appears. In what sense is the young child who is inspired by the virtuosity of a professional athlete, his or her own joy at improvement in skillful execution, or the desire simply to "play" with others physically drawn into an inexorable dialogue with the social conventions and regulations of sport in a way that is distorting to a more personally controlled pattern of growth? Certainly we should give this question further attention.

REFERENCES

Adams, G. R., Shea, J., & Fitch, S. A. (1979). Toward the development of an objective assessment of ego-identity status. *Journal of Youth and Adolescence, 9,* 223–237.

Allison, M. T., & Butler, B. (1984). Role conflict and the elite female athlete: Empirical findings and conceptual dilemmas. *International Review of Sport Sociology, 19,* 157–168.

Anthrop, J., & Allison, M. T. (1983). Role conflict and the high school female athlete. *Research Quarterly, 54,* 104–111.

Bardwick, J. (1971). *Psychology of women: A study of biocultural conflicts.* New York: Harper & Row.

Birns, B. (1976). The emergence and socialization of sex differences in the earliest years. *Merrill-Palmer Quarterly, 22,* 229–254.

Borman, K. M., & Kurdek, L. A. (1987). Gender differences associated with playing high school varsity soccer. *Journal of Youth and Adolescence, 16,* 379–400.

Bouet, M. (1969). *Les motivations des sportifs.* Paris: Edition-Universitaires.

Bradley, W. (1976). *Life on the run.* New York: New York Times Books.

Bredemeier, B. J., & Shields, D. L. (1987). Moral growth through physical activity: A structural/developmental approach. In D. Gould & M. R. Weiss (Eds.), *Advances in pediatric sport sciences* (Vol. 2). Champaign, IL: Human Kinetics.

Chalip, L., Csikszentmihalyi, M., Kleiber, D., & Larson, R. (1984). Variations of experience in formal and informal sport. *Research Quarterly for Exercise and Sport, 55,* 109–116.

Chickering, A. W. (1969). *Education and identity.* San Francisco: Jossey-Bass.

Coakley, J. (1983). Leaving competitive sport: Retirement or rebirth? *Quest, 35,* 1–11.

Coleman, J. S. (1961). *The adolescent society.* Chicago: Free Press.

Côté, J. E., & Levine, C. (1988). A critical examination of the ego identity status paradigm. *Developmental Review, 8,* 147–184.

Croxton, J. S., & Klonsky, B. G. (1981). Causal attributions of college athletes as a function of performance outcome and sex of participant. In S. L. Greendorfer & A. Yiannakis (Eds.), *Sociology of sport: Diverse perspectives.* West Point, NY: Leisure Press.

Csikszentmihalyi, M., & Larson, R. (1984). *Being adolescent.* New York: Basic Books.

Del Rey, P. (1978). The apologetic and women in sport. In C. Ogelsby (Ed.), *Women and sport: From myth to reality.* (pp. 107-111). Philadelphia: Lea and Febiger.

Diener, E. (1977). Deindividuation: Causes and consequences. *Social Behavior and Personality, 5,* 143-155.

Donnelly, P., & Young, K. (1988). The construction and confirmation of identity in sport subcultures. *Sociology of Sport, 5,* 223-240.

Duda, J. L. (1988). The relationship between goal perspectives, persistence, and behavioral intensity among male and female recreational sport participants. *Leisure Sciences, 10,* 95-106.

Duquin, M. (1978). The androgynous advantage. In C. Ogelsby (Ed.), *Women and sport: From myth to reality* (pp. 89-106). Philadelphia: Lea and Febiger.

Eitzen, D. S. (1976). Sport and social status in American public secondary education. *Review of Sport and Leisure, 1,* 139-155.

Eitzen, D. S., & Sage, G. (1978). *Sociology of American sport.* Dubuque, IA: Wm. C. Brown.

Elkind, D. (1981). *The hurried child.* Reading, MA: Addison-Wesley.

Erikson, E. (1959). Identity and the life cycle: Selected papers. *Psychological Issues, 1*(1), 5-165.

Erikson, E. (1963). *Childhood and society.* New York: Wiley.

Erikson, E. (1968). *Identity: Youth and crisis.* New York: W. W. Norton.

Felshin, J. (1974). The triple option . . . for women in sport. *Quest, 21,* 36-40.

Gilligan, C. (1982). *In a different voice.* Cambridge, MA: Harvard University Press.

Gilmore, G. E. (1979). Exploration, identity development and the sense of competency. In J. G. Kelly (Ed.), *Adolescent boys in high school.* Hillsdale, NJ: Erlbaum.

Greendorfer, S., & Blinde, E. (1986). Female sport retirement: Descriptive patterns and research implications. In L. Vander Velden & J. Humphrey (Eds.), *Psychology and sociology of sport: Current selected research* (Vol. 1). New York: AMS Press.

Grieves, J. (1989). Acquiring a leisure identity: Juvenile jazz bands and the moral universe of 'healthy' leisure time. *Leisure Studies, 8,* 1-9.

Griffin, P. S. (1973). What's a nice girl like you doing in a profession like this? *Quest, 45,* 96-101.

Guttman, A. (1981). Introduction. In B. Rigauer (Ed.), *Sport and work.* New York: Columbia University Press.

Haggard, L., & Williams, D. (1990). Self-identity benefits of leisure activities. In B. Driver, P. Brown, & G. Peterson (Eds.), *The benefits of leisure.* State College, PA: Venture Press.

Hall, E. G., Durborow, B., & Progen, J. (1986). Self-esteem of female athletes and nonathletes relative to sex role type and sport type. *Sex Roles, 15,* 379-390.

Harris, D. V. (1975). Psychosocial consideration. *Journal of Physical Education Research, 46,* 32.

Harris, D. V. (1979). Female sport today: Psychological considerations. *International Journal of Sport Psychology, 10,* 168-172.

Harris, D. V. (1981). Feminity and athleticism. In G. R. F. Luschen & G. H. Sage (Eds.), *Handbook of social science of sport.* Champaign, IL: Stipes.

Hendry, L. (1983). *Growing up and going out: Adolescents and leisure.* Aberdeen, Scotland: University of Aberdeen Press.

Hill, P., & Lowe, B. (1974). The inevitable metathesis of the retiring athlete. *International Review of Sport Sociology, 9*(4), 5-32.

Kelly, J. (1983). *Leisure identities and interactions.* London: Allen & Unwin.

King, J. P., & Chi, P. S. K. (1974). Personality and the athletic social structure: A case study. *Human Relations, 27,* 179-193.

Kirshnit, C. E. (1989). *Athletic involvement during early adolescence: Factors affecting sport participation and the effects of athleticism on perceptions of self.* Unpublished doctoral dissertation, Loyola University of Chicago.

Kirshnit, C. E., Ham, M., & Richards, M. H. (1989). The sporting life: Athletic activities during early adolescence. *Journal of Youth and Adolescence, 18,* 601-616.

Kleiber, D. (1983). Sport and human development: A dialectical interpretation. *Journal of Humanistic Psychology, 23*(4), 76-95.

Kleiber, D., & Kane, M. J. (1984). Sex differences and the use of leisure as adaptive potentiation. *Leisure and Society, 7,* 165-173.

Kleiber, D., Larson, R., & Csikszentmihalyi, M. (1987). The experience of leisure in adolescence. *Journal of Leisure Research, 18,* 165–176.

Kleiber, D., & Roberts, G. (1987). High school play: Turning it to work in organized sport. In J. Block & N. King (Eds.), *School play.* New York: Garland.

Kleiber, D., & Roberts, G. (1990). *Extracurricular activity and identity formation in high school students.* Unpublished manuscript, University of Georgia, Athens.

Larson, R., & Kleiber, D. (1990). Free time activities as factors in adolescent adjustment. In P. Tolan & B. Cohler (Eds.), *Handbook of clinical research and practice with adolescents.* New York: Wiley.

Lasch, C. (1979). *The culture of narcissism.* New York: Norton.

Lerner, R., & Busch-Rossnagel, N. (Eds.). (1981). *Individuals as producers of their own development.* New York: Academic.

Lever, J. (1976). Sex differences in games children play. *Social Problems, 23,* 478–487.

Malmisur, M. (1976). Ego development of a sample of college football players, *Research Quarterly, 47,* 14–153.

Malumphy, T. (1971). Athletics and competition for girls and women. In D. V. Harris (Ed.), *DGWS research reports: Women in sports.* Washington, DC: American Association for Health, Physical Education, and Recreation.

Marcia, J. E. (1980). Identity in adolescence. In J. Adelson (Ed.), *Handbook of adolescent psychology.* New York: Wiley.

Markus, H., & Nurius, P. (1986). Possible selves. *American Psychologist, 41,* 954–969.

Marsh, H. W. & Jackson, S. A. (1986). Multidimensional self-concepts, masculinity and femininity as a function of women's involvement in athletics. *Sex Roles, 15,* 391–415.

Matteo, S. (1986). The effect sex and gender-schematic processing on sport participation. *Sex Roles, 15,* 417–432.

McPherson, B. (1980). Retirement from professional sport: The process and problems of occupational and psychological adjustment. *Sociological Symposium, 30,* 126–143.

Ogilvie, B., & Tutko, T. (1985). Sport: If you want to build character, try something else. In D. Chu, J. Seagrave, & B. Becker (Eds.), *Sport and higher education.* Champaign, IL: Human Kinetics.

Petipas, A. (1981). *The identity development of the male intercollegiate athlete.* Unpublished doctoral dissertation, Boston University.

Piaget, J. (1962). *Play, dreams and imitation in childhood.* New York: W. W. Norton.

Porter, R. (1967). Sports and adolescence. In R. Slovenko & J. Knight (Eds.), *Motivation in play, games, and sport.* Springfield, IL: Charles C. Thomas.

Rigauer, B. (1981). *Sport and work.* New York: Columbia University Press.

Rivers, C., Barnett, R., & Baruch, G. (1979). *Beyond sugar and spice: How women grow, learn, and thrive.* New York: Ballantine Books.

Roberts, G., Kleiber, D., & Duda, J. (1981). An analysis of motivation in children's sport: The role of perceived competence in participation. *Journal or Sport Psychology, 3,* 206–216.

Roberts, J., & Sutton-Smith, B. (1962). Child training and game involvement. *Ethnology, 1,* 166–185.

Rosenthal, P., Gurney, R., & Moore, S. (1981). From trust to intimacy: A new inventory for examining Erikson's stages of psychosocial development. *Journal of Youth and Adolescence, 10,* 525–537.

Sage, G. H. (1985). American values and sport: The formation of a bureaucratic personality. In D. Chu, J. Seagrave, & B. Becker (Eds.), *Sports and higher education* (pp. 267–273). Champaign, IL: Human Kinetics.

Sage, G. H., & Loudermilk, S. (1979). The female athlete and role conflict. *Research Quarterly, 50,* 88–96.

Silbereisen, R., Eyferth, K., & Rudinger, G. (1986). *Development as action in context: Problem behavior and normal youth development.* Berlin, West Germany: Springer-Verlag.

Snyder, E. E., & Kivlin, J. E. (1975). Women athletes and aspects of psychological well-being and body image. *Research Quarterly, 46,* 191–199.

Snyder, E. E., Kivlin, J. E., & Spreitzer, E. (1979). The female athlete: An analysis of objective and subjective role conflict. In A. Yiannakis, T. D. McIntyre, M. J. Melnick, & D. P. Hart (Eds.), *Sport sociology: Contemporary themes.* Dubuque, IA: Kendall/Hunt.

Snyder, E. E., & Spreitzer, E. (1976). Correlates of sport participation among adolescent girls. *Research Quarterly, 47,* 804–809.

Snyder, E. E., & Spreitzer, E. (1983). *The social aspects of sport.* Englewood Cliffs, NJ: Prentice Hall.

Stebbins, R. A. (1982). Serious leisure: A conceptual statement. *Pacific Sociological Review, 25*(2), 251–272.

Stevenson, C. L. (1975). Socialization effects of participation in sport: A critical review of the literature. *Research Quarterly, 46,* 287–301.

Stryker, S. (1987). Identity theory: Developments and extensions. In K. Yardley & T. Honiss (Eds.), *Self and identity: Psychosocial perspectives* (pp. 89–103). Chichester, England: Wiley.

Theberge, N., Curtis, J., & Brown, B. (1982). Sex differences in orientations toward games: Tests of the sport involvement hypothesis. In A. O. Dunleavy, A. W. Miracle, & C. R. Rees (Eds.), *Studies in the sociology of sport.* Fort Worth, TX: Texas Christian University Press.

Twin, S. L. (1985). Women and sport. In D. Spivey (Ed.), *Sport in America: New historical perspectives.* Westport, CT: Greenwood Press.

Wagner, S. L., Lounsbury, J. W., & Fitzgerald, L. G. (1989). Attribute factors associated with work/leisure perceptions. *Journal of Leisure Research, 21,* 155–166.

Waterman, A. S. (1985). *Identity in adolescence: Processes and contents.* San Francisco: Jossey-Bass.

Webb, H. (1969). Professionalization of attitudes toward play among adolescents. In G. Kenyon (Ed.), *Aspects of contemporary sport sociology.* Chicago, IL: Athletic Institute.

12

Psychological Motivation in Sport, Exercise, and Fitness

Dorcas Susan Butt
The University of British Columbia

Applications of psychology to sport and fitness have advanced enormously over the past 20 years. It was 1969 when I published my first brief article on psychology and sport. At that time, it seemed interest was just beginning, although some pioneers had made or were about to make major contributions (e.g., Beisser, 1967; Morgan, 1972; Ogilvie & Tutko, 1966; Singer, 1972; Whiting, 1969). Today the application of psychology to sport and fitness is a two-way street, and the interchange is booming. Books, journals, clinical practices, sections in the major psychological associations as well as the media, athletes, and many coaches have made the applications of psychology to sport and fitness a specialized field of inquiry and investigation. Not only have many in sport benefited from learning from psychologists and psychology; but psychology has benefited by entering into the field of sport practice and sport studies to test and to expand some key theories and hypotheses.

However, all is not well in the field of application or investigation. There is a malaise afoot, which I intend to address in this chapter. The malaise arises from too earnest a search for general laws of behavior centered on performance enhancement and too little emphasis on individual and group understanding and development. This results in a superficial application of psychology and psychological principles and people who expect too much too soon from both psychology and from their own pursuit of sport or fitness. The malaise is caused not only by false expectations but also by people failing to take into account dynamic conceptions of human motivation and emotions.

I am calling for the restoration of equanimity to our field, and a broadening of perspective with which to prepare for the year 2000 and beyond. In applying psychology to sport in an achievement-oriented zeitgeist, we are leaning too heavily toward principles of human behavior and the search for laws of human behavior without taking into account the less examined world of individual adjustments, emotions and motivations. Not only are the latter the source of great heights reached by the mind and body; but they are also a source of great peril if ignored. Thus, I am calling for more comprehensive and dynamic exploration of the human psyche in relationship to sport and fitness activity.

I intend to present a vignette that introduces the common and everyday problems we are faced with in applying psychology to sport. I follow with a description of the motivational framework from which I have worked and which offers one attempt to capture the complexities of human motivation. Third, I comment on the studies that shed light upon the model. Fourth, I address the question; "Where do we go from here?", and suggest that the field of individual differences and health psychology is where future energies need to be concentrated.

A VIGNETTE: CONFUSION AMONG CONSUMERS

At a recent training camp for figure skaters, I was confronted by a 14-year-old skater who proceeded to tell me what an eager customer of psychology she was. "Sport psychology has helped me a lot," she said, "although it has been very expensive for my mother. I have been hypnotized. I know how to think positively, I don't think any negative thoughts, I use biorhythmics and sophrology. I think like a champion and I know I will be a champion. I have seen five sport psychologists. I like hypnosis best."

This statement from an adolescent may sound positive to some, but it sounded very troublesome to me. Although the skater was precocious enough to have the psychological lingo down pat, I already knew she had difficulty relating to other skaters and coaches, had extreme mood swings, seemed to get little enjoyment from her sport, and was limited in talent. In essence, this case raises questions about what people in sport expect from psychology and whether those expectations are realistic.

Athletes and the general public are barraged with claims in the media and by some practitioners that athletic performance is enhanced through the application of special psychological techniques. In fact, there is little evidence that many of these techniques in the short run are a major source of performance improvement. I have said many times, and I will say it again that I do not know of any quick and easy method from psychology that will increase performance. Where such results are claimed, one should first question placebo effects.

Then why do national and Olympic teams frequently hire psychologists for precompetition training camps? Schilling (1980) of Switzerland attributed it to the bandwagon effect. He reasoned that national Olympic bodies whose athletes had failed in the previous Olympics had a tendency to rationalize the losses as being due to the absence of psychologists. The winning nations had hired psychologists. Thus, the inevitable groundswell of interest in psychological techniques before any Olympics allows sport organizations to justify to themselves and to others that they have left no stone unturned in preparing their teams. However, hiring a psychologist on a short-term basis before the Olympics is not likely to win anybody medals.

It is understandable that athletes are always looking for ways to jump higher, run faster, score more goals, or become fit with the least amount of effort. They wonder if they should rely entirely upon their own powers of self-discipline and determination or whether they should count on a coach or another source of help. They wonder if the team pep talk given before a game really does unite and motivate them. They wonder whether hypnosis can help maximize performance or if taking steroids and amphetamines will pay off. Frequently, in spite of training and investment in equipment and lessons, the athlete may not improve. Although there is strong desire, backed by enthusiasm for the sport, something is still missing. Both the amateur and professional athlete have this feeling and they sometimes attempt to overcome it in a typical way: They look for a shortcut or an easy way to improve.

Beware: Athletes looking for shortcuts to excellence are ripe for exploitation by merchants, unscrupulous teachers, and those who use psychological gimmicks to affect what is often thought to be the last frontier in sport—the human mind.

What psychology does have to offer takes time to learn, practice, and develop just as any other skill or part of sport and fitness. Some examples follow. The importance of mental practice in acquiring skills has been demonstrated in studies across the years in psychology (Feltz & Landers, 1983). Other studies show how team morale and cohesion can improve performance (Deutsch, 1960, 1982). Yet another line of research has come from the study of the positive relationship of fitness training to mental and physical health and to mood elevation (Folkins & Sime, 1981). Studies of the benefits of special psychological techniques and their long-term effects on performance are now emerging as a fourth major research area (e.g., Suinn, in press).

I have long argued that the best coaches in sport stress developing the total athlete rather than just training them to beat people. Within the North American system, it is unfortunate that misguided coaches and psychological practitioners pop up in response to the prevailing social value of winning at all costs. This value dictates that winning is more important than the athlete's internal feelings of well-being and competence when performing in sport.

Athletes and their mentors are increasingly turning to professional psychologists and others in the quest for a competitive edge. This is a beneficial trend to the extent that qualified psychologists have gone through long training in which respect for individual welfare is a basic ethic. A danger lies in the degree to which practitioners are caught up in the drive for success at the expense of athlete welfare.

Besides, people need to know that most of today's trendy techniques have been around for centuries. For example, cognitive-behavioral techniques (usually a system of relaxation followed by mental practice, reward, and sometimes punishment) is now in vogue. Variations on such themes have been present through much of human history in various forms, for example, in religious training and Eastern philosophies.

The reader may well ask why psychologists use new names for variations on old techniques. The answer is that technology, fragmentation of specialties, and changing styles lead to cycles of popularity. Each generation takes the responsibility for casting psychological beliefs in the language most appropriate to the spirit of the times.

The use of psychological training can be an important component of an athlete's overall development. However, it should be a long-term process worked into the athlete's developmental program along with sport skill and fitness training. None of these training programs is short, easy, or magical. Psychologists are valuable because they can describe techniques in specific language and make the progressive steps more precise and understandable. The psychologist also often acts as a trainer or tutor for the athlete in practicing the techniques. However, the decision to use any psychologist or any technique is always up to the athlete and his or her coach.

In spite of the many ideas the sports person can gain from psychology today, the enjoyment and improvement of sport performance remain exactly where they have always been—in the body mind, and soul of the athlete.

MOTIVATIONAL THEORY: A STARTING POINT

How, then, do we grasp or understand the body, mind, and soul of another? Further still, how do we apply that understanding or knowledge to facilitate growth and adjustment? A theory or position is needed to understand and apply knowledge. Recent writers in the performance field are calling for such theory. For example, Tomporowski and Ellis (1986) argued that a theory-based parametric approach is needed to test the effects of exercise on cognitive processes. Neiss (1988) called for more research attention to both affect and cognition in the study of performance physiology. Most experts, when asked to criticize the field of sport and fitness psychology, will also note that comprehensive theories are lacking. The studies and the literature tend to be molecular and esoteric. Not only is the person lost in personality psychology, and the social lost in social psychology (Carlson, 1984), but we can make a good case for the athlete being absent in much work on sport and fitness. Present are molecular studies, statistical records, steroids, experts, equipment manufacturers, image makers, governments, and corporations, but what about the athlete (whether a fitness buff or an elite performer)?

I have found the following model of motivation most helpful in my work and I have described it in several publications (Butt, 1987). Because the theory provides the type of framework that many are calling for, I review it briefly here. The theoretical model is presented in Figure 1.

Involvement in sport provides times of elation, progress, and mastery as well as times of frustration, boredom, and self-doubt. As people persevere in sport, they may even find themselves increasingly on the negative side of the sports experience, to the extent that they consider dropping out, or do drop out, of their program or activity. To enable a discussion of such sports experiences, one may apply the following theory, which proposes four levels of motivation. Each level is already richly supported by research and theory. For a full set of references, the reader is again referred to Butt (1987, pp. 1–92). Only some major examples from the literature are cited in the following summary.

Sport motivation evolves from the interaction of biological and environmental processes. Both have important effects on the psychological and social motivations that intervene. Five psychological and social motivations are used to account for variations in sport behaviors and sport experiences.

The biological level is the source of motivation and provides the energy or life force common to all living things. Most psychological theories include the assumption of a life force or energy, although some do not state it explicitly. Learning theorists (Hilgard, 1981), while accepting the notion of biological drives, then have constructed their analyses by focusing on acquired behaviors. Freud (1961), Erikson (1950), Maslow (1970), and others assumed an evolution of motivation over the life span and used terms such as instinct, need, or drive to describe the biological forces behind evolution.

The psychological level yields three styles of energy expression. The three styles arise when biology and environment interact, producing individual differences. The classic names associated with the concepts are Lorenz (1966) on aggression, Freud (1961) on conflict, and White (1959, 1963) on competence. Each of these theories provides an approach to the study of psychological motivation and features a basic energy model. More recent research and thinking on the concepts offer expansion and adjustment. For example, consider the updates of

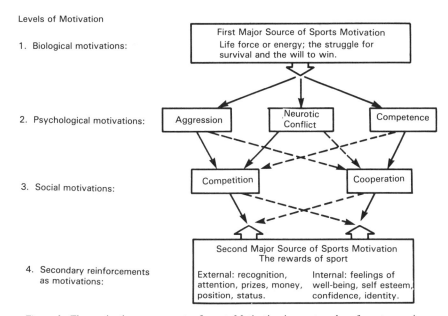

Figure 1   The motivation components of sport. Motivation in sport evolves from two major
sources or influences: biological motivation and the reinforcements conferred
through the sports enterprise. Psychological motivation is represented in the three
basic energy models of aggression, neurotic conflict, and competence. The solid and
dotted arrows indicate the greater and lesser degree of a connection thereafter.
Aggressive motivation and neurotic conflict are most likely to lead to competitive
social motivation and, to a lesser extent, to cooperation. Competence motivation is
most likely to lead to cooperative social motivation. Both the competitively and
cooperatively motivated will be affected by the reinforcements of sport. The external
rewards will usually be most important to the competitor, however, and the internal
rewards to the cooperator.

Wilson (1975–1980) on sociobiology, Lazarus and Folkman (1984) on stress, and
Bandura (1977, 1982; Bandura & Cervone, 1983) on self-efficacy. In turn, each of
these theories in the modern form are not without critics. However, their purpose
here is to assist in the understanding of both individual differences in sport motivation and extremes in sport behaviors. It is important that one considers these
categories to be fluid and not static states; therefore, it should be possible to assess
athletes in terms of the degree to which they feel aggressive, conflict, or competence motivations across time and in various situations. Aggressive athletes are full
of energy and power, but are frequently lacking in control. They are as likely to
direct energy against people and things as into skill at sport. Aggressive individuals react quickly to frustration and blame things other than themselves for failure.
Quick to temper and subject to physical and mental outbursts, aggressive athletes
are sought after in some sports. However, even in boxing, football, and ice
hockey—sports that require aggressiveness—the athletes' energy must be directed
in the service of skill at sport if they are to mature and to develop. Conflict-
oriented athletes tend to be troubled, unhappy, and a burden to self and to others.
Unrealistic expectations, excuses, and physical and mental symptoms may plague

them as will nervousness, moodiness, and unpredictable reactions to coaches and other athletes. Often talented and promising, these athletes have difficulty fulfilling that potential. When on occasion they do succeed, they tend to make life miserable for those around them and for themselves because of their worries and self-absorption. The competence-oriented athletes are easily recognized as eager to pursue new challenges in sport. They are able to do this because their major motivation stems from the reward of developing skill and mastering the environment. This in turn leads to the growth of self-confidence, self-esteem, and feelings of well-being. For the competence-oriented athletes, sport is an expression of and an exploration of self. This style is largely free of the difficulties and bitterness that can characterize the aggressive and conflict orientations. Such individuals are predictable, reliable, and realistic. In summary, these three orientations describe the internal psychological states of the athletes and theoretically all athletes possess varying and measurable amounts of each motivation.

The social level of motivation describes ways in which athletes relate to the sports environment and to the people in it including coaches, officials, and other athletes. Two styles are important here: competitive social motivation and cooperative social motivation. A pioneer researcher of cooperation and competition has been Deutsch (1960, 1982), but many others have followed (see e.g., Axelrod, 1984; Johnson, Maruyama, Johnson, Nelson, & Skon, 1981). These terms as used here refer to how individuals perceive their social environment. Thus, individuals may be basically cooperative psychologically and yet engage in contests in which they compete against others. Similarly, individuals could be competitive by nature and yet cooperatively conform to the rules of the contest or behave cooperatively toward team members. Focusing on how the athletes think and feel about others, those falling on the competitive side of the model see sport as a struggle in which they must defeat others, sometimes at all costs. They see others as antagonistic to their goals and wish to dominate them or demean them. This is the type of athlete who must hate opponents, who is jealous of the successes of others, and who is happy only when he or she is outdoing others. In contrast, the cooperatively oriented sees other athletes as partners in the sports event and can be found in good-natured interchange with them after a contest, win or lose. The cooperatively oriented is willing to help others, is joyful for the successes of others, and offers support to group and coach. It is hypothesized that these individuals can perform as well in contests as the competitive type providing they are motivated by competence on the psychological level.

Finally on the reinforcement level are two categories of reward: external and internal. External rewards are outside of the self as in gaining money or recognition and status from others. Internal rewards are ingrained in self such as in feelings of well-being, self-confidence, and elation at having reaped new skills or experiences through sport. The objective fact of the reinforcement as well as the expectancy of external or internal control of reinforcement have been shown to be important in a long line of studies (for review, see Strickland, 1989).

The implications of the model are as follows. Because of the reward system in organized sport, a negative socialization is too often encouraged in participants. That is, aggressive and conflict-ridden athletes are caught up in a competitive social environment where emphasis is placed primarily on winning, prizes and money, recognition and status. Thus, youngsters are encouraged to participate and compete for external reward while sacrificing the pleasures they might once have found in sport. Competence and cooperation are often not sufficiently encouraged because the internal rewards of skill development, mastery, and maturity are often not emphasized. Yet the person most needed in sport is the one who does their best, loves the sport, and assists others. This is also the person who will grow in personal and performance stature through sport because of the self-confidence resulting from each subsequent achievement.

If this theory is applicable, then the greater relationships should occur between aggression and competition, conflict and competition, and competence and cooperation. Athletes developing down the right-hand side of the chart will show largely positive psychological and social adjustments, whereas athletes developing toward the left-hand side will show more problematic adjustment. Furthermore, great team and individual potential and performance will be associated with the right-hand side of the model.

The advantages of this model are:

1. It is comprehensive, allowing for the integration of many theories of human motivation.
2. It allows for both biological predispositions and acquired styles of motivation and for the interaction between the two.
3. It allows for individual variation as well as for the study of situational and other determinants of motivational style (e.g., type of sport, coach, time, position played, culture, sex).
4. The constructs are measurable, and scales have been developed that are available in five languages (other than English).
5. A number of predictions and hypotheses result from the theories and the research results that preceded the proposed model.
6. The model lends itself readily to clinical and consulting work with individuals, teams, or clubs that present with varying problems and questions for the psychologist.

STUDIES: MEASURES AND RESULTS

We have developed scales to measure the three psychological motivations of aggression, conflict, and competence and the two social motivations of competition and cooperation. These are the crucial variables upon which individual differences are predicted. Scales have been psychometrically tested, validated, and used in numerous studies. One of the attractions of performing studies in sport is the variety of validation indexes available such as rankings, standings in competitions, time in timed sports, position played, coach and peer ratings, changes over time, and several more. The scales we use are self-report and very simple. The Sport Motivation Scales read as follows: "During the last month while participating (training or competing) in _____ (fill in activity) did you ever feel. . . .?" The respondent then answers a series of questions. Two examples follow for each construct.

Aggression: Full of energy?
Impulsive?
Conflict: Listless or tired?
Moody for no real reason?

Competence:	*Thrilled?*
	Happier than you have ever been?
Competition:	*Determined to come in first?*
	Like winning is very important to you?
Cooperation:	*Like helping someone else to improve?*
	Like part of, or very friendly toward the group (partner, team or club)?

We first developed a 25-item version of these scales (Butt, 1979b). This was combined with other scales and questions in the research and counseling instrument called The Sports Protocol (Butt, 1987, pp. 83–92, 213–223). Recently, we developed a 50-item version of the scales to increase the reliability of the scales. The profile sheet we use for counseling clients is presented in Figure 2. so that readers may easily survey the content of the constructs.

All questions are answered "yes" or "no" and the participant therefore obtains a score for each scale out of 10. Reliabilities for groups range between .56 and .97 (varying with the group responding). Item-test correlations are checked as are the proportions of variance attributable to person, item, and error before proceeding with analyses for any group. Means and standard deviations vary, of course, with the group studied. For 55 university men and 90 women, the means varied from 1.8 for women on competition to a high of 6.7 for both men and women on competence. These scores reflect the fact that a university group is choosing a leisure or sport activity that for the most part they engage in for fun. The group results are quite different when elite groups of athletes are tested under the pressures of competition (e.g., see Butt, 1985). However, there are also extreme individual variations. Standard deviations for these university groups were lowest for women on aggression and highest for both groups on cooperation (1.8 in the case of women on aggression and 3.0 and 3.3 for men and women, respectively, on cooperation). When the predicted relations between the constructs are tested, the results are consistent with other studies. Aggression and conflict relate more highly to competition than cooperation whereas, competence relates more highly to cooperation than to competition. For the two groups previously mentioned, the results are reported in Figure 3.

These trends have been replicated many times (see Butt, 1987, p. 89) with the 25-item scales and clearly support the theoretical predictions.

Further, the pattern of correlations with other variables supports the tendency of those individuals higher on aggression, conflict, and competition to report more problematic sport adjustments. As a group they score higher on negative affect (unhappiness), whereas those athletes who score higher on competence and cooperation also score higher on positive affect (happiness) (e.g., see Butt, 1979a, 1979b, 1980).

Because these results are based on self-report, we have also used peer and coach ratings of the team member's contribution to morale and performance of the group, and find validation across different sources of data (Butt, 1985).

Let me review three illustrative sets of results from past studies to demonstrate the importance of and the emergence of competence as the key variable in several studies. These same illustrations were used in a recent review by the author (Butt, in press).

The first results are from one of our earlier studies (Butt, 1979b) and show the

Profile sheet with five vertical scales, each numbered 10, 9, 8, 7, 6, 5, 4, 3, 2, 1, 0.

AGGRESSION

— 5 full of energy
— 9 impulsive
— 13 powerful
— 18 telling someone off
— 22 let someone have it if in your way
— 26 angry
— 31 excited
— 36 impatient
— 41 enraged
— 46 vicious

CONFLICT

— 1 listless or tired
— 6 moody for no reason
— 12 guilty for not doing better
— 14 very nervous
— 17 like crying
— 27 wanted to give up
— 32 defensive
— 37 no one understands
— 42 a failure
— 47 lost and confused

COMPETENCE

— 3 thrilled
— 11 happier than ever
— 16 performed at best yet
— 19 more interest than in anything else
— 23 accomplished something new
— 28 trustworthy
— 33 improving
— 38 confident
— 43 like to know more about your sport
— 48 pleased with abilities

COMPETITION

— 2 determined to come in first
— 7 winning is very important
— 10 irritated by some one did better
— 20 annoyed you didn't win
— 24 others get more than deserve
— 30 bitter at other's success
— 35 out perform other's key to success
— 40 others use you
— 45 you should be in charge
— 50 better than anyone else

COOPERATION

— 4 helping others to improve
— 8 like part of group, pair team
— 15 pleased someone else did well
— 21 doing something to help team or group
— 25 congratulated someone else who did well
— 29 staying late to help
— 34 sharing responsibility for failure
— 39 you and people you work/play with pull together
— 44 everyone seems to help
— 49 team has common goals

ID #:
SPORT:
AGE:
SEX:
COMMENTS:

Figure 2 Profile sheet for 10-item Sport Motivation Scales. Copyright Butt . . . (see Figure 1).

221

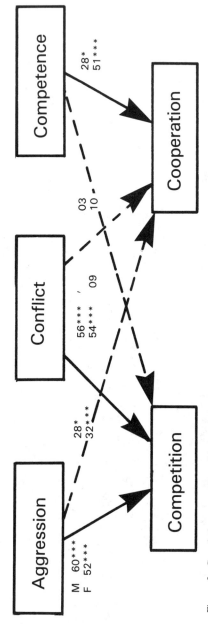

Figure 3 Correlations are reported between the three psychological motivations of aggression, conflict, and competence and the two social motivations of competition and cooperation. The solid lines predict the greater relationship, and the dotted lines the weaker relationship. All predictions hold, for example, aggression has a greater relationship to competition than it does to cooperation for both boys and girls, respectively. Correlations are based on results from 10-item scales for each construct. Samples are 55 university men and 90 university women. *p < .05; **p < .01; ***p < .001.

Table 1 Coach ratings of athlete potential correlated with sport motivation scores of 73 swimmers

Potential	Aggression	Conflict	Competence	Competition	Cooperation
Coach 1	− 04	.06	.23*	.07	.18
Coach 2	− 10	.02	.022**	.20**	.06

*p < .05. **p < .10.

correlations between the sport motivations of 73 members of a competitive swimming club and their male and female coaches' ratings of the swimmers' potentials. Note that although the correlations are low (reliability having an inverse relationship to the number of items in a scale), the association of competence with potential emerges most strongly. Note the trend for the second coach to pick up also the swimmer's self-rating of competition (.20). This coach was a former national champion swimmer and stressed the value of competitiveness. A frequent finding is that the preexpressed philosophy of the coach links his or her ratings of potential to the individually reported styles of the athletes, an important theme for follow-up study.

The second set of results (Butt, 1979a) represents the correlations between the ratings of figure skaters' potential by two nationally prominent figure skating coaches and the skaters' motivation scores. The skaters rated were training with the respective coaches. Note again the emergence of competence as the motivation picked up in the ratings of potential as well as its opposition to competition in the ratings of the second coach.

The third set of results (Butt, 1985) is from the study of 15 national field hockey teams competing in a world championship. The correlations of the Japanese team's peer ratings of performance and morale contribution to their sport motivation scores stood out markedly. They were of special interest because of the validity provided: (a) by the reputation of the Japanese team and (b) by predominant Japanese social values. Note the almost-perfect congruence of the results with the motivational theory.

Not all teams reflect the theory. For example, for a team in which the coach stresses and demands aggressive play, coach ratings of potential have correlated most highly with the self-report of aggression in the athletes. It is clear that sport, atmosphere, situation, and individual consistencies all affect scale responses. We are currently working on sorting out the proportions of numerical variance attributable to each of these sources.

Table 2 Figure skating coach ratings of potential correlated with sport motivation scores

Coach ratings	Aggression	Conflict	Competence	Competition	Cooperation
Potential coach X[a]	− 12	− .04	.44 (p < .03)	.00	.15
Potential coach Y[b]	− 33	.27	.46 (p < .11)	− .39 (p < .15)	.00

[a]N = 18.
[b]N = 9. This coach's ratings of potential correlate positively with competence and negatively with competition. (Significance of difference between correlation < .01.)

Table 3   Japanese team results: The correlations of the average peer performance and morale ratings with the Sport Motivation Scales for the Japanese National women's field hockey team

Peer ratings	Aggression	Conflict	Competence	Competition	Cooperation
Performance		−55 (p < .02)	.39 (p < .08)	−65 (p < .06)	
Morale	−40 (p < .08)	−52 (p < .03)	.48 (p < .04)	−55 (p < .02)	.51 (p < .03)

Note: N = 14 women.

THE FUTURE: THROUGH THE LOOKING GLASS

To return to the case of the 14-year-old figure skater who was described in the vignette, I suggest that all of the techniques and psychological fees being paid and directed toward increased performance would be better directed toward personal development and psychological maturity—the maturity that comes with competence development (not attainable by external means). That is, the appropriate starting point is the internal world and adjustment of the athlete and not an externally defined quest for increased performance. A very good example of an externally defined quest is provided in the case of Ben Johnson, the Canadian sprinter stripped of his 1988 Olympic gold medal and world record as the world's fastest man because of steroid use. A steroid regimen controlled by others is perhaps as clear as any an external method of improving performance but with absolutely no guarantee of personal maturity or competence feedback for the athlete.

In this chapter, I have presented the approach to motivation upon which I have been working. There are many other approaches, also addressed in this book. However, my conclusion is that in the field of sport, exercise, and fitness, we must inevitably focus upon the pursuit of health and well-being as basic pillars of psychology. Performance enhancement techniques may be valuable, and people need to know about them and practice them if they find them useful. However, I think the application of blanket techniques is limited and the pendulum has swung too far in psychology for many years toward the search for basic laws of human cognition and behavior. Along with this we have observed increased dependence upon experts for advice and techniques to be applied to all manners of human experience whether it be sport excellence, mood problems, marital or relationship problems, childbirth, child rearing, smoking cessation, and so on. The problem is that all of these human experiences and their evolutions and resolutions are most constructively cast as adventures in self or quests for competence or control. The emergence of the health psychology movement is in my mind the most important event of the century for psychology. The central theme of health psychology is the transfer of power and knowledge back to the individual so that he or she may chose wisely and experience a sense of well-being. Such individuals through their wisdom and experience will perhaps influence others, thus contributing to the future and to the general good. The psychologist can assist in this process not only by searching for general laws, but more importantly by applying dynamic, individual approaches that lead directly to the growth of the individual.

REFERENCES

Axelrod, R. M. (1984). *The evolution of cooperation.* New York: Basic Books.

Bandura, A. (1977). Self-efficacy: Toward a unifying theory of behavioral change. *Psychological Review, 84,* 191–215.

Bandura, A. (1982). Self-efficacy mechanism in human agency. *American Psychologist, 37*(2), 122–147.

Bandura, A., & Cervone, D. (1983). Self-evaluative and self-efficacy mechanisms governing the motivational effects of goal systems. *American Psychologist, 45*(5), 1017–1028.

Beisser, A. R. (1967). *The madness in sports.* New York: Appleton-Century-Crofts.

Butt, D. S. (1979a). *Psychological motivation in figure skating: Some considerations for coaches.* Paper presented at the meetings of the Figure Skating Coaches of Canada, Victoria, British Columbia.

Butt, D. S. (1979b). Short scales for the measurement of sport motivation. *International Journal of Sport Psychology, 10,* 103–216.

Butt, D. S. (1980). Perspectives from women on sport and leisure. In C. S. Adamec (Ed.), *Sex roles: Origins, influences and implications for women* (pp. 70–88). Montreal: Eden.

Butt, D. S. (1985). Psychological motivation and sports performance in world class women field hockey players. *International Journal of Women's Studies, 8*(4), 328–337.

Butt, D. S. (1987). *Psychology of sport: The behavior, motivation, personality and performance of athletes* (2nd ed.). New York: Van Nostrand Reinhold.

Butt, D. S. (in press). *Critical issues in promoting competence in health and sport.* In D. N. Cox & K. D. Craig (Eds.), *Psychology, sport and health promotion.* Proceedings of the XXI Banff International Conference on Behavioral Science; Banff, Alberta, March 19–23, 1989.

Carlson, R. (1984). What's social about social psychology? Where is the person in personality research? *Journal of Personality and Social Psychology, 35,* 1055–1074.

Deutsch, M. (1960). A theory of cooperation and competition. In D. Cartwright & A. Zander (Eds.), *Group dynamics: Research and theory.* New York: Harper & Row. (Original work published in 1949).

Deutsch, M. (1982). Interdependence and psychological orientation. In V. J. Derlega & J. Grzelak (Eds.), *Cooperation and helping behavior.* New York: Academic.

Erikson, E. (1950). *Childhood and society.* New York: W. W. Norton.

Feltz, D. L., & Landers, D. M. (1983). The effects of mental practice on motor skill learning and performance: A meta analysis. *Journal of Sport Psychology, 5,* 25–57.

Folkins, C. H., & Sime, W. E. (1981). Physical fitness training and mental health. *American Psychologist, 4,* 373–389.

Freud, S. (1961). *The ego and the id.* In J. Strachey (Ed.), *The standard edition of the complete works of Sigmund Freud* (Vol. 19). London: Hogarth. (Original work published in 1923).

Hilgard, E. R. (1981). *Theories of learning* (5th Ed.). Englewood Cliffs, NJ: Prentice-Hall.

Johnson, D. W., Maruyama, G., Johnson, R., Nelson, D., & Skon, L. (1981). Effects of cooperative, competitive, and individualistic goal structures on achievement: A meta-analysis. *Psychological Bulletin, 89,* 47–62.

Lazarus, R. S., & Folkman, S. (1984). *Stress, appraisal, and coping.* New York: Springer.

Lorenz, K. (1966). *On aggression.* New York: Harcourt, Brace & World. (Original work published in 1963).

Maslow, A. (1970). *Motivation and personality.* New York: Harper & Row. (Original work published in 1954).

Morgan, W. P. (Ed.). (1972). *Ergogenic aids and muscular performance.* New York: Academic.

Neiss, R. (1988). Reconceptualizing arousal: Psychobiological states in motor performance. *Psychological Bulletin, 103*(3), 345–366.

Ogilvie, B. C., & Tutko, T. A. (1966). *Problem athletes and how to handle them.* London: Pelham.

Schilling, G. (1980). Psycho-regulative procedure in Swiss sport: More as an alibi or fire-brigade? *International Journal of Sports Psychology, 11*(3), 189–201.

Singer, R. N. (1972). *Coaching, athletics, and psychology.* New York: McGraw-Hill.

Strickland, B. R. (1989). Internal-external control expectancies: From contingency to creativity. *American Psychologist, 44,* 1–12.

Suinn, R. M. (in press). Visualization for Olympic athlete performance enhancement. In D. N. Cox & K. D. Craig (Eds.), *Psychology, sport and health promotion.* Proceedings of the XXI Banff International Conference on Behavioral Science; Banff, Alberta, March 19–23, 1989.

Tomporowski, P. D., & Ellis, N. R. (1986). Effects of exercise on cognitive processes: A review. *Psychological Bulletin, 99*(3), 338–346.

White, R. W. (1959). Motivation reconsidered: The concept of competence. *Psychological Review, 66,* 297–333.

White, R. W. (1963). Ego and reality in psychoanalytic theory: A proposal regarding independent ego energies. *Psychological Issues, 3*(3, No. 11).

Whiting, H. T. A. (1969). *Acquiring ball skill: A psychological interpretation.* London: Bell.

Wilson, E. O. (1975–1980). *Sociobiology: The new synthesis.* Cambridge, MA: Harvard University Press.

13

Personality Traits and Athletic Performance

Louis Diamant
University of North Carolina at Charlotte

John H. Byrd
University of North Carolina at Charlotte

Melissa J. Himelein
University of North Carolina at Charlotte

Understanding human behavior is the raison d'etre of the professional psychologist, and we have developed concepts and theories to that end. Even though research may sometimes seem tirelessly dedicated to running rats or talking to apes, the meat of it all is understanding and predicting the how and why of people's thoughts, moods, and actions.

One of the most fascinating areas studied in psychology is personality. Every student in a personality course has some idea of what personality is, and many such notions are not bad, although quite informal. Schultz (1990) recognized the similarity between these informal, personal theories and the formal theories of science. "We all have some idea of the concept of personality and we all make suppositions about the personality of those with whom we interact" (p. 29). Schultz called these supposition theories frameworks within which we put the data of our commonplace observations. What sharply distinguishes the formal theories of psychology from supposition theories is our ability to objectively test the data.

Psychologists have generated a number of recognized formal theories of personality. Some are more relevant and useful in research with athletes than others. Elsewhere in this book are presented personality theories built around basic drives and the unconscious mind (psychoanalytic theory), holistic and epigenetic principles of a natural and determined unfolding and development of personality (humanistic theory), and an almost nonpersonality theory that describes the shaping of a human persona through reinforcers and punishments (behaviorism) and its neo-structure (cognitive behaviorism).

However, most personality research with athletes is grounded in trait theory. This view—that more or less enduring traits comprise the basic personality structure—is based in large part on the work of Raymond B. Cattell. Although Gordon Allport (1961) previously developed a personality theory based around a concept of traits, the theory's detail and analysis owes much to the work of Cattell. Cattell saw traits as hypothetical constructs inferred from the objective observation of behavior. These traits produce the basic elements of behavior. Understanding traits is vital to any prediction about people.

Cattell described 16 basic traits and developed a standardized test to quantify them: the 16 Personality Factor Questionnaire (16 PF) (Cattell, Eber, & Tatsuoka, 1970). Cattell's instrument, which assigns a value of 1 to 10 to each of these factors, has been useful in sport-specific personality research.

Other formalized instruments that have been used with varying degrees of success include the Minnesota Multiphasic Personality Inventory (MMPI) (Hathaway & McKinley, 1967), Eysenck's Personality Inventory (EPI) (Eysenck & Eysenck, 1962), and the Profile of Mood States (POMS) (McNair, Lorr, & Droppleman, 1971). With the exception of the POMS, each of these instruments is designed to assess enduring personality characteristics with the goal of enhancing investigators' ability to make predictions about behavior. In the past 15 years, the POMS has been used by a number of investigators in sports-related personality research who have built a strong case for its value as a predictive tool (Bell & Howe, 1987; Fuchs & Zaichowsky, 1983; LeUnes & Nation, 1982; Morgan, 1980a, 1980b; Morgan & Johnson, 1978; Morgan & Pollock, 1977; Morgan, O'Connor, Ellickson, & Bradley, 1988; Morgan, O'Connor, Sparling, & Pate, 1987; Silva, Shultz, Haslam, Martin, & Murray, 1985). Indeed, Iso-Ahola and Hatfield (1986) argued that a specific pattern of responses on the POMS, which Morgan (1980a) christened "the Iceberg Profile," can be viewed as evidence of a specific, enduring personality trait seen in successful athletes.

WINNERS AND LOSERS

Since the beginning of life and according to Darwinian principles, there have been winners and losers. On first look, the reason seems obviously simple: Some organisms, be they protozoa or professional basketball players, are simply better than others, stronger, smarter, or just more suited to their environments.

Yet our near-universal fascination with sports and competition suggests that the quality of better is anything but simple. Is better a sum of traits whose components can be isolated, measured, or changed? If so, which traits add up to a superior athlete, and what are their relative weights? Is there an interaction among traits?

Singer, after reviewing much of the literature in the mid-1970s, questioned the broader significance of much of the research. "The attempt to associate personality traits with athletic interests and accomplishments is certainly fascinating. Attempting to verify through science that which has been popularly conceived is quite understandable. But what exactly has been proven?" (Singer, 1975, p. 99).

Researchers continue to study the personality aspects of sports, but a consensus regarding the appropriate direction for research has been slow to evolve. Efforts focusing on traits and mood states have been subject to criticism (e.g., Dwyer & Carron, 1985; Geron, Furst, & Rotstein, 1986; Iso-Ahola & Hatfield, 1986; Kumar, Pathak, & Tahkur, 1985; Nieman & George, 1987; Singer, 1988; and others). The most troublesome problem has been the frequent failure to differentiate elite athletes from recreational sportspeople or even from the general population. A related difficulty is the weak evidence of trends in the personality traits of athletes. In addition, when a study does report evidence of a differentiating characteristic, it raises the question of whether investigators have uncovered only an artifact.

From the practical standpoint of applying sport psychology research to traits and success, other questions emerge. Do more confident, less confused athletes excel because of their positive mental states? Alternatively, does their upbeat mental state reflect the fact that they have been performing well at their respective sports?

For clues to these complex interactions, investigators must continue to depend on the observation of behavior, the assessment of self-reports of mental states, and the evaluation of responses to probing questions. Sport research has some particular difficulties: although such psychological and mental factors as motivation, confidence, and concentration undoubtedly influence athletic performance, it is sometimes difficult to separate their effects from such important physical variables as strength, speed, or training.

WHY STUDY PERSONALITY VARIABLES?

So why study the psychological makeup of athletes? What answers to what questions can be gained through research into this aspect of sport?

Since antiquity, participation in sports has been associated with psychological well-being—the healthy-mind-in-a-healthy-body notion. In the 1980s, this notion persists in certain biochemical theories that associate vigorous aerobic exercise with enhanced production of endorphins in the brain (Steinberg & Sykes, 1985).

Another reason for interest in personality psychology related to sports has been interest in sports generally. The 1970s and 1980s witnessed a virtual explosion in athletic participation by the general population. It is not unusual today to see several thousand recreational athletes compete in 26.2-mile marathons in dozens of cities around the United States. Twenty years ago, it would have been impossible to even imagine such large numbers of "ordinary" people undertaking the arduous task of training for a marathon, but today it is common.

There are also very practical possibilities for the application of personality psychology to sports. Much has been written in the past two decades about Eastern European sports programs and the inordinate success enjoyed on the international level by such small nations as East Germany. What role has psychological testing and candidate selection played in this success? What of counseling and motivational techniques? Can personality studies improve sports performance in the West?

Some researchers have suggested that psychological testing has a role in the selection of team athletes. Knowledge of personality type may also be helpful in matching an athlete or recreational sportsperson to a specific sport. If regular athletic participation does indeed promote healthier psychological states, then perhaps sports therapy has a role in the treatment of emotional disturbances.

Perhaps the most compelling reason for sport-oriented personality research is related to the reason we are interested in sports in the first place. Few other human activities offer such well-defined challenges to the personality as sports competition. In sport, it is easy to define winners and losers, success and failure. From a scientific standpoint, isolating or manipulating those factors responsible for winning or losing a contest might be as relevant as the game itself.

PREDICTING SUCCESS

The ability to make predictions about human behavior is particularly useful in the field of sports. Coaches who can accurately assess an individual's attributes are well prepared in making team selections and assignments. Moreover, knowledge and understanding of a particular athlete's traits and motivations could prove invaluable in prescribing more training and drills versus a period of rest.

A review of the literature has to start with attempts to isolate those psychological factors that can predict success in an athletic contest. In any game matching highly skilled and trained athletes, the outcome may well depend as much on the contestants' psychic condition as on their physical abilities. Coaches call it the right "attitude," but exactly what constitutes "attitude" and how to induce it have so far escaped precise definition.

Considerable disagreement exists in the literature as to whether athletes differ from population norms in key personality measures, whether athletes exhibit less or more neurotic attributes than the general population, and whether psychological variables are a factor important enough to predict success or failure in competition. In fact, some studies that set out to isolate personality factors in a success formula conclude that no psychological factor even approaches more easily measured physical factors in predictive value.

For instance, one study of marathon runners (McKelvie, Valliant, & Asu, 1985) had little difficulty in documenting a runner's training pace and previous race times as highly significant predictors of finishing time in a given race. The authors had considerably more trouble establishing whether or not the runners' locus of control contributed to marathon performance.

In fact, using Rotter's Social Reaction Inventory (SRI), the authors noted that they were surprised to find runners no more internally controlled than the general population. The SRI is a 29-question instrument designed to measure whether respondents are influenced more by external, environmental factors or internal, personal factors (Rotter, 1966).

Two interesting findings of this study were that faster marathon runners tended to be more sensitized to bodily signals, as measured by the 127-item Revised Repression-Sensitization Scale (Byrne, Barry, & Nelson, 1963), and that there seemed to be no correlation between prerace anxiety—as measured by a modified version of the 15-question Illinois Competition Questionnaire Form A—and marathon times. These two latter findings shed some light on the cognitive strategies used by elite athletes facing pain and fatigue.

The relatively faint evidence of the predictive value of psychological factors when compared with physical factors shows up starkly in several studies. For instance, a study of competitors in the 1,100-mile Iditarod Trial Internal Sled Dog Race (Stillner, Pierce, Popkin, & Callies, 1983) found metabolic changes in blood chemistry, indicating greater aerobic fitness to be the best selector of top-half finishers. Higher L-Scale scores (indicating less truthful responses) on the EPI were associated with poorer performances, but the association only approached significance ($p = .061$). Other personality factors showed no correlation to performance.

Similarly, a study of professional women golfers (Crews, Shirreffs, Thomas, Krahenbuhl, & Helfrich, 1986) found that percentage of body fat was the best single predictor of both the golfers' ranking on the Ladies' Professional Golf Association Tour and money winnings.

Implicit in many of the studies attempting to find personality traits that predict athletic success is a hypothesis that successful athletes possess more "positive" traits such as dominance or confidence and fewer "negative" traits such as anxiety.

However, this is not always the direction of the hypothesis. One interesting series of studies concerned controversies regarding the possible pathology of compulsive running. Yates et al. posed a negative mental health model of "obligatory" runners in reports that first appeared in the *New England Journal of Medicine* (Yates, 1987; Yates, Leehey, & Shisslak, 1983).

The authors suggested that male obligatory runners resembled anorectic women in that they tended to inhibit anger, held unusually high self-expectations, and could tolerate physical discomfort while denying potential serious disability. Moreover, Yates asserted, the compulsive running masked or compensated for an underlying depression. "The compulsive or obligatory athlete is typically a depressed male who has learned to treat his depression through running" (Yates, 1987, p. 201).

It would be difficult to replicate Yates' research, which is more in the way of a report on the comparisons of case studies. Three other studies responded with attempts to quantify the incidence of eating disorders among runners or to compare runners' and anorectics' responses on standardized questionnaires. All studies tended to discount Yates' hypothesis.

Runners tended to score within normal ranges on the MMPI, whereas anorectics did not. Moreover, more anorectics scored elevations on more MMPI scales than did runners, with depression and psychopathology being noteworthy (Blumenthal, O'Toole, & Chang, 1984). A measure of perfectionism and satisfaction, the SCANS questionnaire (Slade & Dewey, 1986), was administered to female runners, who scored high on perfectionism and, unlike anorectics, also scored high on satisfaction (Owens & Slade, 1987). Owens and Slade concluded that only superficial similarities exist between runners and anorectics.

Finally, Weight and Noakes (1987) administered two questionnaires specifically designed to elicit abnormal concern with eating and weight to a group of female marathoners. They concluded that "the incidence of anorexia nervosa is no more common among competitive female runners than it is among the general population" (p. 216). They further noted that although some regular runners exhibit abnormal concerns about eating and weight, they "may be at less risk for anorexia nervosa than non-running individuals with similar vulnerabilities" (Weight & Noakes, 1987, p. 216).

This is a frequent corollary of the mental health model as a predictor of success: Regular exercise of athletic competition is seen as a contributor to mental health or a reinforcement of positive personality traits. Although many studies have reported an association between the two, investigators still debate whether one causes or results from the other.

TRAITS AND SUCCESS: A POSITIVE LINK

Cattell's trait theory and his standardized questionnaire to quantify 16 core traits of the personality have helped to highlight certain factors associated with success in sports. Some studies suggest that complementary traits such as reserve, detachment, and tough-mindedness may be associated with success.

Magni, Rupolo, Simini, DeLeo, & Rampozzo (1985) administered the 16 PF to high-altitude mountain climbers who were preparing to attack K-2 in the Tibetan Himalayas. Comparing the climbers with a matched control group, the authors characterized the climbers as "cooler" or more emotionally detached (Magni et al., 1985). The climbers differed significantly from controls on three factors: They reported lower anxiety, had weaker superegos, and exhibited greater gregariousness. The investigators cautioned that the finding of weaker superegos may be specific to high-altitude mountain climbers, many of whom leave family and jobs to pursue their sport, and cannot be applied generally to other sports.

Evans and Quarterman (1983) used the 16 PF with black female college basketball players. They reported significantly higher scores among successful players when compared with population norms on tough-mindedness and suspiciousness.

Nieman and George (1987) reported that competitive runners differ significantly from 30-year-old norms on 9 of the 16 PFs scales, with higher scores for reserve, intelligence, dominance, social reticence, suspiciousness, shrewdness, experimentation, self-sufficiency, and unconventionality. Likewise, Jackson et al. (1978) found that 16 PF scores indicating tough-mindedness, detachment, and reserve were associated with fewer injuries among high school football players.

It is worth remarking on at least one other area indicative of personality differences between successful and less successful athletes. As previously noted, McKelvie found evidence of a greater sensitivity to bodily signals by elite runners.

Morgan, whose work is usually associated with a specific pattern of scores on the POMS, supported this finding through interviews with runners. In one early study, Morgan reported that he was surprised to find an "associative cognitive strategy" adopted by runners in coping with physical discomfort during competition. In other words, the runners concentrated on bodily signals during their races rather than try to distract themselves with other thoughts (Morgan & Pollock, 1977). Previous interviews with nonelite marathon runners had caused the authors to expect to find the reverse: a dissociative cognitive strategy.

Indeed, the ability to concentrate on bodily signals may be indicative of a trait that distinguishes the superior athlete from those in the middle of the pack. Morgan et al. (1987) found further evidence of this pattern in a study of female distance runners. Many runners did not rely on just one cognitive strategy: These runners associated at some times and dissociated at others. A significant finding was that during competition the more successful runners tended to associate, whereas the less successful runners tended to distract themselves with other thoughts. This difference was present only during competition: during training runs, no runners reported associative strategies.

The studies mentioned so far suggest a link between low trait anxiety and a cool detachment and athletic success. They do not, however, answer the question of whether athletes succeed because of personality variables, or whether athletic participation and success contribute to changes in personality traits over time. This would be a fruitful area for longitudinal studies of personality traits and athletic success.

THE TIP OF THE ICEBERG

Although Cattell's 16 PF has been used with some success to highlight the traits of low anxiety, detachment, and tough-mindedness as possible contributors to athletic success, it has not been used to predict successful competitors on the basis of test scores. The studies most frequently cited to support the prediction of success are those reported by Morgan, who began using the POMS in the mid-1970s to assess runners and other athletes.

More so than the MMPI or the 16 PF, the POMS is easy to administer and purports to measure fairly specifically a small number of variables that Morgan reported to have high predictive value. Numerous studies have produced a distinctive pattern when plotted on a graph that Morgan called the "Iceberg Profile." This pattern is characterized by POMS scores below the mean for the general population on measures of tension, depression, fatigue, and confusion (the "underwater" part of the iceberg) and a score above the population mean on vigor (the "tip" of the iceberg).

An early study demonstrating the Iceberg Profile included the POMS in a battery of tests administered to male marathon runners of varying levels (Morgan & Pollock, 1977). This study attempted to identify personality variables that enabled certain marathoners to tolerate high levels of discomfort in their sport. It used a variety of measures, including the State-Trait Anxiety Inventory (STAI), Somatic Perception Questionnaire, Depression Adjective Checklist, the EPI, Physical Estimation and Attraction Scale, and the Hidden Shapes Test. Morgan and Pollock reported only one significant trait difference between runners and published population norms: The runners scored significantly lower on trait anxiety as measured by the STAI than the general population. Contrary to the authors' expectations, the runners did not score outside norms on measures of introversion-extroversion or neuroticism.

The Iceberg Profile has been replicated in numerous studies with a wide variety of athletes, including female runners (Morgan et al., 1987), triathletes (Bell & Howe, 1987), football players (LeUnes & Nation, 1982), body builders (Fuchs & Zaichowsky, 1983), and wrestlers (Silva et al., 1985).

Morgan's ability to link the Iceberg Profile to successful sports performance so frequently has led him to pose a mental health model for sports success. In short, the less pathology evident in athletes' psyches, the more likely they are to succeed. In fact, Morgan reported 70% and 80% accuracy in identifying rowers and wrestlers who qualified for national teams and as high as 90% for other sports (Morgan, 1980a; Morgan & Johnson, 1978). Moreover, using a global POMS score, or a composite of all the tests' six subscales, plus results of the STAI (Spielberger, Gorsuch, & Lushene, 1971), Morgan reported an unusually high success rate in predicting the performances of distance runners in 10,000-meter races over a 2-year period ending in 1988.

According to Morgan and colleagues, a combination of the global POMS score and the STAI's measure of trait anxiety accounted for nearly half (45%) of the performance variance among 14 elite distance runners. They suggested that physical and biomechanical differences explain the remaining 55% (Morgan et al., 1988). To a lesser extent, the EPI neuroticism measure was negatively correlated with running performance. Eysenck's extroversion and conformity scales had no significant correlation.

Morgan presented modern evidence of the ancient maxim of "a healthy mind in a healthy body" but, to repeat Singer's question, what has been proved? For instance, can we assume that adolescents who exhibit the Iceberg Profile before beginning their athletic careers are destined to be tomorrow's Olympic champions? Alternatively does vigorous sports activity in some way influence mood as measured by the POMS?

Morgan's Iceberg Profile has turned up so consistently in studies of athletic success that Iso-Ahola and Hatfield suggested that it could be indicative of a stable personality trait or traits. The existence of specific athlete traits predictive of success would allow for the development of an assessment tool for athletes. "An ultimate extension of this testing would be the development of an instrument to measure what might be called athletic intelligence. This construct refers to a person's overall psychological capacity or aptitude to perform in highly stressful competitive situations. Morgan's Iceberg Profile might measure only a small portion of such a broader construct" (Iso-Ahola & Hatfield, 1986, p. 157).

One practical benefit for coaches of being able to isolate personality variables that contribute to success would be improved selection of athletes. Given equivalent physical abilities between two athletes, the better candidate for a team or competition would be the one exhibiting those personality variables associated with success. American coaches have shown little inclination, however, to rely on standardized personality tests in selecting team candidates.

Singer (1988) suggested that studies so far have not shown convincingly that performance can be predicted on the basis of personality variables alone. "[M]uch more confirming evidence in a variety of sports and with a more comprehensive battery of tests is necessary before we can be *reasonably* certain of the generality of Morgan's findings. . . . [T]he ability to determine the athlete who will make an elite team by overcoming intense competition probably requires the use of a battery of composite tests. These might measure skill level, tactical knowledge, morphology, body composition, physical condition and attributes, and psychological attributes—all of which should be directly related to potential success in the sport" (Singer, 1988, p. 101).

Frazier (1988) suggested that, rather than measuring stable traits that can accurately predict athletic success, the POMS scores actually show the effect of athletic success on the mood and personality of the athlete. He noted that well-trained runners would be expected to respond positively to the POMS descriptors for vigor (e.g., "energetic," "full of pep," "cheerful") and negatively to the descriptors for fatigue (e.g., "listless," "weary," "sluggish"). "[T]he mental health model may not be an accurate predictor of athletic performance. . . . Since previous research has indicated that exercise may influence transitory states such as those measured by the POMS (Dienstbier, 1984), the real value of the instrument may be to discern between fitness levels rather than ability levels" (Frazier, 1988, p. 69).

Although he has found a measure of success in predicting athletic success with the POMS and other measures, Morgan (1980a) did not endorse it as a test of ability. Morgan noted that the variables measured by the POMS and other scores account for only half of observed variances in performances, and he suggested that predicting success may not be the best application of psychological testing of athletes. Although those athletes that do exhibit the Iceberg Profile are more likely to succeed, many athletes who do not show the distinctive profile also excel at their sports. The POMS' best practical application may be in monitoring an athlete's mood changes during training, Morgan speculated. Such monitoring might enable a coach to spot "staleness" and to adjust training levels or provide additional psychological support.

Personality research using sports subjects has concentrated on identifying those personality factors associated with success in competition. One goal in the 1970s and 1980s was to develop enough understanding of psychometric variables to be able to make accurate predictions of success or failure. A result has been the emergence of an image of the cool, detached athlete as the most likely candidate for success. However, as Morgan noted, personality tests can quantify variables that at best account for only about half the variance in performance between athletes. Physical attributes, the degree of skill, and training levels are at least equally important in determining winners and losers.

REFERENCES

Allport, G. (1961). *Patterns and growth in personality.* New York: Holt.

Bell, G. J., & Howe, B. L. (1988). Mood state profiles and motivations of triathletes. *Journal of Sport Behavior, 11,* 66–77.

Blumenthal, J. A., O'Toole, L. C., & Chang, J. L. (1984). Is running an analogue of anorexia nervosa? An empirical study of obligatory running and anorexia nervosa. *Journal of the American Medical Association, 252,* 520–523.

Byrne, D., Barry, J., & Nelson, D. (1963). Relation of the revised repression-sensitization scale to measures of self description. *Psychological Reports, 13,* 323–334.

Cattell, R. B., Eber, H. W., & Tatsuoka, M. M. (1970). *Handbook for the sixteen personality factor questionnaire (16PF).* Champaign, IL: Institute for Personality and Ability Testing.

Crews, D. J., Shirreffs, J. H., Thomas, G., Krahenbuhl, G. S., & Helfrich, H. M. (1986). Psychological and physiological attributes associated with performance of selected players of the Ladies Professional Golf Association Tour. *Perceptual and Motor Skills, 63,* 235–238.

Dienstbier, R. A. (1984). The impact of exercise on personality. In Sachs, M. L., & Buffone, G. W. (Eds.), *Running as therapy: An integrated approach* (pp. 439–446). Lincoln: University of Nebraska Press.

Dwyer, J. J., & Carron, A. V. (1985). Personality status of wrestlers of varying abilities as measured by a sport specific version of a personality inventory. *Canadian Journal of Applied Sport Sciences, 10,* 19–29.

Evans, V., & Quarterman, J. (1983). Personality characteristics of successful and unsuccessful black female basketball players. *International Journal of Sport Psychology, 14,* 105–115.

Eysenck, H. J., & Eysenck, S. B. G. (1962). A factorial study of an interview questionnaire. *Journal of Clinical Psychology, 18,* 286–290.

Frazier, S. E. (1988). Mood state profiles of chronic exercisers with differing abilities. *International Journal of Sport Psychology, 19,* 65–71.

Fuchs, C. Z., & Zaichowsky, L. D. (1983) Psychological characteristics of male and female bodybuilders: The iceberg profile. *Journal of Sport Behavior, 6,* 136–145.

Geron, E., Furst, D., Rotstein, P. (1986). Personality of athletes participating in various sports. *International Journal of Sport Psychology, 17,* 120–135.

Hathaway, S. R., & McKinley, J. C. (1967). *Minnesota Multiphasic Personality Inventory: Manual for administration and scoring.* New York: Psychological Corp.

Jackson, D. W., Jarrett, H., Bailey, D., Kausek, J., Swanson, J., & Powell, J. W. (1978). Injury prediction in the young athlete: A preliminary study. *American Journal of Sports Medicine, 6,* 6–14.

Kumar, A., Pathak, N., & Tahkur, G. (1985). Death anxiety and locus of control in individual, team and nonathletes. *International Journal of Sport Psychology, 16,* 280–288.

LeUnes, A. D., & Nation, J. R. (1982). Saturday's heroes: A psychological portrait of college football players. *Journal of Sport Behavior, 5,* 139–149.

Magni, G., Rupolu, G., Simini, G., De Leo, D., & Rampazzo, M. (1985). Aspects of the psychology and personality of high altitude mountain climbers. *International Journal of Sports Psychology, 16,* 12–19.

McKelvie, S. J., Valliant, P. M., & Asu, M. E. (1985). Physical training and personality factors as predictors of marathon time and training injury. *Perceptual and Motor Skills, 60,* 567–574.

McNair, D. M., Lorr, M., & Droppleman, L. F. (1971). *Profile of mood states manual.* San Diego, CA: Educational and Industrial Testing Service.

Morgan, W. P. (1980a). Test of champions: The iceberg profile. *Psychology Today.* pp. 92.

Morgan, W. P. (1980b). The trait psychology controversy. *Research Quarterly for Exercise and Sport, 51,* 50–76.

Morgan, W. P., & Johnson, R. W. (1978). Personality characteristics of successful and unsuccessful oarsmen. *International Journal of Sport Psychology, 9,* 119–133.

Morgan, W. P., O'Connor, P. J., Ellickson, K. A., & Bradley, P. W. (1988). Personality structure, mood states, and performance in elite male distance runners. *International Journal of Sports Psychology, 19,* 247–263.

Morgan, W. P., O'Connor, P. J., Sparling, P. B., & Pate, R. R. (1987). Psychological characterization of the elite female distance runner. *International Journal of Sports Medicine, 8,* 124–131.

Morgan, W. P., & Pollock, M. L. (1977). Psychological characterization of the elite distance runner. *Annals of the New York Academy of Science, 301,* 382–402.

Nation, J. R., & LeUnes, A. D. (1983). Personality characteristics of intercollegiate football players as determined by position, classification and redshirt status. *Journal of Sport Behavior, 6,* 92–102.

Nieman, D. C., & George, D. M. (1987). Personality traits that correlate with success in distance running. *Journal of Sports Medicine, 27,* 345–356.

Owens, R. G., Slade, P. D. (1987). Running and anorexia nervosa: An empirical study. *International Journal of Eating Disorders, 6,* 771–775.

Rotter, J. B. (1966). Generalized expectancies for internal versus external control of reinforcement. *Psychological Monographs,* 80(No. 1).

Schultz, D. (1990). *Theories of personality.* Pacific Grove, CA: Brooks/Cole.

Silva, J. M. III, Shultz, B. B., Haslam, R. W., Martin, T. P., Murray, D. F. (1985). Discriminating characteristics of contestants at the United States Olympic Wrestling Trials. *International Journal of Sports Psychology, 16,* 79–102.

Singer, R. N. (1975). *Myths and truths in sport psychology.* New York: Harper & Row.

Singer, R. N. (1988). Psychological testing: What value to coaches and athletes? *International Journal of Sport Psychology, 19,* 87–106.

Slade, P. D., & Dewey, M. E. (1986). Development and preliminary validation of SCANS: A screening test for identifying individuals at risk of developing anorexia nervosa and bulimia nervosa. *International Journal of Eating Disorders, 5,* 517–538.

Spielberger, C. D., Gorsuch, R. L., & Lushene, R. E. (1971). *Manual for the state-trait anxiety inventory.* Palo Alto, CA: Consulting Psychologists Press.

Steinberg, H., & Sykes, E. A. (1985). Introduction to symposium on behavioral processes: Review of literature on endorphins and exercise. *Pharmocology, Biochemists and Behavior, 23,* 857–862.

Stillner, V., Pierce, C. M., Popkin, M. K., & Callies, A. L. (1983). Predicting successful behavior indicators in an athletic contest. *Military Medicine, 148,* 668–672.

Weight, L. M., & Noakes, T. D. (1987). Is running an analog of anorexia?: A survey of the incidence of eating disorders in females distance runners. *Medicine and Science in Sports and Exercise, 3,* 213–217.

Yates, A. (1987). Eating disorders and long-distance running: The ascetic condition. *Integrative Psychiatry, 5,* 201–211.

Yates, A., Leehey, K., & Shisslak, C. M. (1983). Running—an analogue of anorexia? *New England Journal of Medicine, 308,* 251–255.

14

Exercise, Mood States, and Neuroendocrinology

Robert G. McMurray
University of North Carolina at Chapel Hill

A runner prepares for a 10-mile race. He quietly stretches, does some easy running, and calmly talks to other competitors. The gun goes off and without any fanfare he starts his run. As he continues to run he begins to feel better. In fact, as the run continues, he does not even realize the time! He is "into" the run. After he finishes he still feels good, refreshed and rejuvenated.

On the same day a football team runs out onto the playing field before the game starts. They are running hard, jumping, throwing their fists into the air, and yelling. They run to the coach on the sideline and gather into a huddle, still yelling and screaming. As the huddle grows, the players are jumping on top of each other to be a part of the team. In the middle of the huddle, the coach is starting a chant. The players join in. Some are crashing shoulder pads into each other, while others are beating their helmets. Finally, the huddle breaks and the players run onto the field to start the game. They are "psyched up" to play.

Both the runner and the football players experience changes in their mood; however, the stimulus for the induced mood is quite different. In the case of the football players, they are inducing a psychological state that will result in a ballistic, all-out effort and simultaneously reduce the pain of physical contact. The chant in the huddle is designed to emotionally arouse each football player, inducing a mental stress to physically prepare the athlete. Conversely, the runner is letting the event induce the psychological state. The runner may also be attempting to reduce any pain from the run, but he is letting the body make the adjustment as needed. The runner is using the physical effort of the exercise to induce the mood alteration. The point of these two different scenarios is that there is an interaction between the psychological and physiological states such that either one can and does affect the other; both are stressors.

Stress is a general concept that is extremely complex and difficult to fully appreciate. However, if stress is viewed as any external or internal situation that tends to grossly disturb homeostasis (Grossman, 1989), the concept can be simplified. Furthermore, examining stress from a neuroendocrinology basis limits the definition even more to situations that cause significant changes in the endocrine system. The neurohormones of particular concern to the stress response include the catecholamines (epinephrine and norepinephrine), the opioids (endorphins and enkephalins), and serotonin.

Previous research on stress by Selye (1936) seemed to indicate the existance of a nonspecific stress response. All stress, regardless of the origin, caused increases in the stress hormones, cortisol, and the catecholamines norepinephrine and epinephrine. More recent evidence suggests that a specific stress causes a specific response. Obrist et al. (1978) suggested that active coping, such as shock avoidance, results in a beta-adrenergic (catecholamines) response, whereas passive coping such as inescapable shock does not. Williams, Bittker, Buchsbaum, and Wynne (1975) showed that attempting to complete a jigsaw puzzle with noise distraction resulted in elevations of norepinephrine but not epinephrine. Conversely, playing "Pong" (a computer game) with harassment increased epinephrine but not norepinephrine. Forsman and Lundberg (1982) noted lower levels of catecholamines in women than in men during achievement situations but not in vigilance tasks. Thus, there is reason to believe that differences in stress response exist. The evidence seems most conclusive for mental stress, but concomitantly there is evidence suggesting that differences in the stress response for exercise exist as well. For example, Winder, Hickson, Hagberg, Eshani, and McLane (1979) aptly demonstrated that training induces a change in the catecholamine response to a given level of exercise. Carr, Bullen, and Skrinar (1981) showed that physical conditioning may facilitate the beta-endorphin release in women. McMurray, Hardy, Roberts, Forsythe, and Mar (1989) showed that coronary-prone behavior types (Type A) may have a different neuroendocrine profile during high-intensity exercise than Type B personalities.

This chapter is an attempt to encapsulate the material on exercise-induced neuroendocrine responses and to relate these neuroendocrine responses as possible mechanisms to changes in mood. The importance of other factors that affect mood are not to be disregarded. However, they are not included in this discussion. Specifically, three neurohormones are discussed: the catecholamines, opioids, and serotonin. There is ample evidence to link the catecholamines to changes in psychological state. However, the present knowledge of the endogenous opioids and serotonin is not consistent and has led to a great deal of speculation. The chapter attempts to separate speculation from fact. The chapter also examines exercise in terms of an acute response, which may occur during or immediately following exercise, and includes chronic exercise exposure as well.

AFFECTIVE BENEFITS OF EXERCISE

Exercise has been shown to induce a positive affective state. Several recent publications have reviewed this information in detail (Hatfield & Landers, 1985; Morgan, 1985). There seems to be general agreement that an acute bout of exercise can reduce depression, anxiety, and tension, and the effect can last for up to 5 hours. Several long-term studies have indicated that depression can be reduced and self-concept improved. Folkins, Lynch, and Gardner (1972) examined the Multiple Affect Adjective Checklist depression scale responses after a semester of jogging and found significant improvements on the scores, especially in those individuals who were worse psychologically. On the basis of these results, the authors applauded the benefits of exercise. Several other authors (Folkins & Sime, 1981; Murphy, Bennett, Hagen, & Russell, 1972; Sachs, 1981) have also recommended exercise to improve emotional health, and similar results have been noted in postmyocardial infarction patients (Kavanaugh, Shephard, Tuck, & Quaveshi, 1977). However, the absence of a mood change with exercise has also been reported

(Bahrke & Morgan, 1978; Grossman et al., 1984; McGowan, Robertson, & Epstein, 1985; Morgan, 1985).

Several authors have proposed that exercise can result in feelings of euphoria, or a runners high (Appenzeller, 1981; Pargman & Baker, 1980; Sachs, 1984). This theory is based on the premise that exercise releases beta-endorphin and enkephalins (the body's endogenous opioids), which induces a feeling of euphoria. Although this theory is popular in the lay press, there exists little scientific evidence to substantiate the claim (McMurray, in press).

CATECHOLAMINES

Dopamine, epinephrine, and norepinephrine are collectively classified as the catecholamines. All three amines are derived from phenylalanine and tyrosine; dopamine is the most basis structured from which the other two are synthesized. The body's response to the release of the catecholamines is dependent upon the receptor. Norepinephrine stimulates the alpha-adrenergic receptor, whereas epinephrine stimulates the beta-adrenergic receptor. The difference in receptors accounts for the differences in response, because the catecholamines seem to have a "mass discharge" into the blood and affect many organ systems.

There are no distinct pools from which the catecholamines can be released; the adrenal gland and the sympathetic nervous system (SNS). The SNS postganglionic neurotransmitter is mostly norepinephrine, with only a small portion of epinephrine. The discharge from the SNS seems to have its greatest effect by causing arteriolar vasoconstriction: splanchnic, renal, and cutaneous. This generalized vasoconstriction results in an elevation of blood pressure. Norepinephrine is also a major neurotransmitter in the central nervous system (CNS); it is involved with the hypothalamus and limbic systems, both of which are essential to emotional responses and stress. The second source of the catecholamines is the adrenal glands, and the majority of their discharge seems to be epinephrine. The effects of epinephrine are concerned with increasing metabolism by increasing plasma sources of energy and by increasing the rate of glycolysis within the muscle cell. Epinephrine also has a strong cardiogenic effect, increasing both rate and contractility of the heart. Dopamine originates from a variety of tissues including the SNS and adrenal glands. It responds to stress, exercise, standing, and hypovolemia, but its actual importance is still poorly defined (Van Loon & Sole, 1980). Antelman and Caggiula (1977) demonstrated that several behavioral disorders can be explained by an nonnormally functioning dopamine system within the brain. Because dopamine and norepinephrine seem to have emotional involvement, they will be of primary concern in the rest of the discussion.

As Morgan and O'Conner (1988) pointed out, the amine hypothesis was derived from animal studies on psychoactive drugs in which it was demonstrated that when the affective state was altered, brain amine levels correspondingly changed. Proponents of this hypothesis state that even inactivity can be viewed as a component of an affective disorder and exercise improves affect. Also, it has been demonstrated that low levels of brain norepinephrine have been associated with depression (Hatfield & Landers, 1987). In addition, Stern and McDonald (1965) took an interesting approach to determining the importance of a biochemical factor in psychomotor control. They taught dogs to run a maze and then injected the blood from manic-depressed patients during their depressed phase. They found that the injection reduced maze run times significantly, thus suggesting that a biochemical factor, probably a catecholamine inhibitor, has considerable control of depression. However, their research does not indicate which factors are important.

The response of the catecholamines during acute exercise is dependent upon the intensity, duration, and psychological perception of the exercise. Several authors have shown that a direct relationship exists between circulating plasma catecholamines and exercise intensity (Kotchen et al., 1971; McMurray, Forsythe, Mar, & Hardy, 1987; Seals, Victor, & Mark, 1988; Weicker, 1986). However, there still may be some question as to whether very low levels of exertion increase catecholamines (Seals et al., 1988). During low-level exercise, the anticipation of the laboratory experience may be contributing to the response (Donald, Ferguson, & Milburn, 1968; Peronnet et al., 1986; Rushmer & Smith, 1959), as could Type A behavior personality traits (McMurray et al., 1989). The duration of exercise is another factor that increases plasma catecholamines (Weicker, 1986). Maron, Horvath, and Wilkerson (1977) showed that marathon running results in elevated catecholamines, which can remain elevated for up to 3 days. Galbo (1983) showed that exercise at 60% to 75% VO$_2$max results in a significant increase in norepinephrine and epinephrine after 40 minutes of exercise, with a continuous rise until peaking at exhaustion. Kindermann et al. (1982), in their study of acute supramaximal exercise and prolonged aerobic exercise, indicated that the intensity seems to be a stronger stimulus than duration in eliciting a catecholamine response.

Training alters the catecholamine response. Winder et al. (1979) found that, with as little as 3 weeks of training, the catecholamine response to a given submaximal exercise bout is reduced. Hull, Young, and Ziegler (1984) and Bloom, Johnson, Park, Rennie, and Sulaiman (1976) also noted that fit, or trained, subjects have a lower catecholamine response to a given stressor than untrained normals. However, at maximal exertion, the catecholamine responses may be greater than normal (Hull et al. 1984; Kjaer & Galbo, 1988) as the capacity to secrete catecholamines may become increased. It is interesting to note that Hull et al. (1984) not only examined the response of aerobic fitness on the amine response during exercise but also during other forms of stress: industrial accidents film, cold pressor task, and word-color tasks. Their measurements of depression and anger taken before and immediately after the accident film revealed a significant inverse relationship with fitness. A study by Sinyor, Schwartz, Peronnet, Brisson, and Seraganian (1983) also showed that fitness is inversely related to anxiety at the end of a psychosocial stress session. Southmann, Ismail, and Chodepko-Zajiko (1984) used a factorial analysis to examine the relationship between fitness, catecholamines, anxiety, depression, hysteria, hypochondriasis, psychasthenia, and hypomania. They found a consistent relationship between psychological status, fitness, and catecholamines. Generally, few differences existed at rest, but following exercise the more fit individuals had lower concentrations of catecholamines as well as less depression and anxiety. Hypochondriasis, hysteria, and psychasthenia were positively associated with fitness, whereas hypomania was negatively associated. Thus, there is information indicating that aerobic fitness, or training, reduces the catecholamine response and improves the psychological status to a given physiological or psychological stressor. However, a direct cause and effect relationship has not been demonstrated.

The elevation of the plasma catecholamines during exercise can be mostly attributed to the adrenal gland and the metabolic needs (Christensen & Galbo, 1983;

Winder, Beattie, & Holman, 1982). However, we know little about the role of the CNS amines during exercise. This is because there is a blood-brain barrier, which does not allow for free diffusion of brain and peripheral pools. Elevated catecholamines during exercise do not allow for the determination as to whether the release was from the SNS or the adrenals. Early researchers believed that is the predominant catecholamine response was norepinephrine, the SNS and brain were the origin. Conversely, if the predominant amine was epinephrine, then the adrenals were the source.

Morgan and O'Conner (1988) pointed out that many investigators have examined urinary levels of 3-methyl-4-hydroxphenylglycol (MHPG) in an attempt to estimate brain and SNS reactivity. The theory was that because most norepinephrine is SNS or brain in origin, the amount of metabolite in the urine should approximate the SNS activity. Also, it seems that MHPG, a metabolite of norepinephrine, is low in depressed patients, and the administration of dopamine precursor can assist in reducing the depression (Ransford, 1982). Therefore, a link is found between the catecholamines and psychological state. Schildkraut, Orsulak, Schatzberg, and Rosenbaum (1983) noted that between 20% to 60% of the MPHG is derived from the CNS. Thus, peripheral sources of MHPG are significant. However, Maas and Leckman (1983) found a direct relationship between brain and peripheral adrenergic systems. Hence, regardless of the amount of MHPG, peripheral change can be used as an indicator of central responses. One must also keep in mind that Young, Rosan, and Laudsberg (1984) showed that, under certain conditions when the SNS is suppressed, the adrenals can release considerable norepinephrine. Thus, interpretation of plasma catecholamines is difficult.

Brain levels of norepinephrine during exercise has been previously measured in animals. Barachas and Freedman (1962) studied rats swimming and found significant elevations of brain norepinephrine. Similarly, Brown and Van Huss (1973) also reported that running exercise increases brain amines. Thus, although we have little direct evidence that exercise enhances brain norepinephrine activity in humans, we have collaborative animal studies. However, no studies have explored the purpose of the increased amines.

The research on the psychological effects of catecholamines during exercise seems circumstantial. The relationship between arousal and catecholamines is obvious. The research on depression supports this role. However, other psychological changes known to occur with exercise, such as reduced anxiety, a calmness, a reduction in neuroticism, and self-confidence, cannot be accounted for by a catecholamine effect. Thus, the catecholamines may contribute to the changes in affect, but they are not the only mechanism. Studies in normal humans in which psychological status is measured before and after the injection of catecholamines are needed to clarify the psychological role of catecholamines.

SEROTONIN

Serotonin (5-hydroxytryptamine, or 5-HT) is an aromatic monoamine derived from the amino acid tryptophan. Most of the 5-HT is found within the brain; the majority is bound and considered inactive, whereas a smaller pool of the active form is in the free form. Plasma and platelet pools are also evident (McMurray et al. 1989; Artigas, & Gelpi, Ortiz, 1988); most of the plasma serotonin is bound and therefore may be inactive. The exact role of 5-HT is not clear; it has been implicated with blood clotting

(Palermo et al., 1986), blood pressure (deLeeuw & Birkenhager, 1985), and obesity (Hoebel, 1975). The effects of serotonin on blood pressure have been questioned, because most of the serotonin in the blood is bound and thus inactive (Brodie & Shore, 1957). Also serotonin's role in obesity has also been recently questioned. Serotonin is involved with nervous transmission and processing. Animal studies indicate that 5-HT may be involved with nociceptive functioning by decreasing the animal's response to pain or reducing the effects of arousal stimuli (Brown et al., 1979; Harvey, Schlosberg, & Younger, 1975). Other studies (Bogdanski, Bonomi, & Brodie, 1963; Brodie & Shore, 1957) suggest that 5-HT may function as a parasympathetic modulator inhibiting the "fight or flight" mechanism.

The effect of exercise on serotonin has been minimally investigated. A perusal of the literature revealed only three studies examining the effect of exercise on 5-HT. Barachas and Freedman (1962) reported that in rats swimming to exhaustion brain serotonin levels were significantly elevated. Palermo et al. (1986) found that a graded exercise test increased platelet serotonin but not in all subjects. Palermo et al. suggested that the elevated 5-HT may potentiate platelet reactivity to subthreshold stimuli and increase prostacyclin or induce a vasodilator response, thus modulating sympathetic tone. McMurray et al. (1989) examined plasma serotonin and found that maximal exercise elevates serotonin, but the response varied. The variability in response seemed to be related to behavior type. McMurray noted that Type B personalities had higher circulating concentrations of serotonin than the Type A personalities. Also, Type B personalities exhibited a direct relationship between exercise intensity and plasma serotonin, whereas Type A personalities had no systematic response. None of the literature has related plasma and brain pools of 5-HT, and this relationship is important because any known nociceptive effect occurs in the brain.

Brown et al. (1979) examined the effects of endurance training on rat brain serotonin concentrations. When comparing exercise-trained and sedentary rats, they found that training resulted in significantly higher concentrations of 5-HT in most areas of the brain except for the cerebral cortex where it was lower. They suggested that the elevated midbrain serotonin could decrease appetite and improve weight control, thus indirectly controlling obesity (at least in rats).

Because most individuals report "feeling good" or "feeling better" after exercise, the previously mentioned studies seem to indicate that serotonin (5-HT) could be involved with the reduction of tension and anxiety after exercise. If serotonin contributes to a reduction of arousal and nociception, and serotonin is elevated in the brain, the hypothesis is feasible. Also, the elevation of serotonin with training may contribute to a reduced stress response that is reported to occur with physical training (Morgan, 1985). However, this is purely speculation because no studies have been completed to directly link serotonin to postexercise mood. The fact that not all exercise seems to elevate serotonin (McMurray et al., 1989), and yet reports have indicated that changes in psychological state can occur during exercise, suggests that serotonin has no role or an extremely limited role. Concomitantly, serotonin may be a significant factor in the development of coronary prone behavior.

ENDOGENOUS OPIOIDS

The endogenous opioids are a class of peptides that mainly includes beta-endorphin, dynorphin, leuenkephalin, and metenkephalin. They are chemical produced within the body that have many of the same characteristics of opiates or morphine. Each endorphin and the enkephalins are derived from a precursor molecule and are distributed extensively in both central (brain) and peripheral tissues and fluids. Adams, Brase, Welch, and Dewey (1986) pointed out that not all endogenous opioids are peptides. Some of these substances have been isolated in the brains of other animals, but their present status is unknown in humans. To add to the complexity of endogenous opioids, it is recognized that multiple types of receptors exist. Adams et al. (1986) indicated that along with the original mu, kappa, and sigma receptors, delta and epsilon receptors have been postulated, each with a specific function.

The enkephalins appear to be involved with the stress response and minor pain analgesia, and do not seem to produce any euphoric effects (Allen, 1983). The endorphins are slower to be released than the enkephalins, but are longer lasting and have an effect on many organ systems. They also seem to be directly involved with the stress response and pain analgesia (Allen, 1983). The dynorphin is the least known of the opioids. At present, its detection in plasma has not been reliable. However, dynorphins seem to have an effect in the adrenal gland, vasopressin, and possibly the cardiovascular system (Grossman, 1989). Because of the available information, the present article focuses on beta-endorphin.

Beta-endorphin is produced in the brain, primarily in the pituitary gland, and is cleaved from the compound beta-lipotropin, which is also responsible for the production of adrenocorticotropin (ACTH) and metenkephalins. Although many parts of the brain produce beta-endorphin, it seems that only the pituitary contributes to the peripheral pool. Most research suggests that beta-endorphin has two distinct origins: (a) that which is produced in the brain and does not cross the blood-brain barrier and (b) a peripheral pool that may come from other organ systems or the pituitary (Akil et al., 1984; Bunny et al., 1979; Rossier et al., 1977). Some studies have indicated that the pools may respond differently to the same stimulus (Rossier et al., 1977). However, Carr, Jones, and Bergland (1985) demonstrated a direct relationship between the peripheral pool and central pool. This concept is important for human research because access to the brain for blood and fluid sampling is extremely hazardous.

The importance of beta-endorphin has been studied directly by measuring the endorphin response to a stimulus or injecting beta-endorphin and monitoring the response. Early studies directly measuring beta-endorphin have been confounded by the fact that the assays used had considerable cross-reactivity with the endorphin precursor or ACTH. Thus, care should be taken when interpreting the absolute data. Concomitantly, indirect methods of using the drug naloxone or naltrexone to block the opioid response are very prevalent.

There have been many proposed purposes of beta-endorphin. Early works have suggested that the primary purpose of endorphins was pain analgesia (reviews by Adams et al., 1986; Bunny et al., 1979; Foley et al., 1979; Krieger, 1982). Studies have shown that foot shock and other painful stimuli increase endorphins. Studies using naloxone to block the endorphins have also shown that pain tolerance is reduced in the presence of the drug (see review by Allen, 1983; Kreiger, 1982). Many studies have also linked acupuncture analgesia to pituitary endorphin release (Allen, 1983).

Beta-endorphin has been correlated to the functioning of other systems. Research using naloxone has indicated an effect of endorphins on the respiratory system such that the drug increases ventilation (Santiago & Edelman, 1985). Studies by Petty, deJong, and deWied (1982) and Moss and Scarpelli (1981) have also indicated that beta-endorphin lowers blood pressure and heart rate. Feldman, Kiser, Under, and Li (1983) suggested a link between high dosages of endorphins (40-fold increase) and glucose metabolism. However, physiologically 40-fold increases in beta-endorphin are not normally seen in humans. Also, El-Tayeb, Brubaker, Lickey, Cook, and Vramic (1986) and McMurray et al. (1988) failed to find an effect of naloxone on glucose kinetics; thus, the link is tentative. Beta-endorphin may also have a role in temperature regulation, particularly during heat exposure, but the role is presently obscure (deMeirleir, Arentz, Hollman, & Vanhaelst, 1985; Kelso, Herbert, Gwazdauskas, Goss, & Hess, 1984). Considerable research now suggests that beta-endorphin is an important intermediary in the release of gonadotropin hormones. Morris et al. (1987) showed that in rats beta-endorphin produced in the testis can reduce follicle-stimulating hormone functioning. Similarly, a review of the data on females by McArthur (1985) suggests a role of beta-endorphin in menstrual dysfunction.

The elevation of concentrations of plasma beta-endorphin with exercise was first reported in 1981. Colt, Wardlow, and Frantz (1981) examined the effect of easy and strenuous long-distance running and found that beta-endorphin was significantly elevated compared with levels measured during rest. Similarly, Carr, Bullen, and Skrinar (1981) found that 1 hour of high-intensity cycle ergometry resulted in elevations of beta-endorphin. Since then, many studies have shown that exercise induces an endorphin response (see review by Sforzio, 1988). However, these results have not been without contradiction. DeMeirleir et al. (1986) found that anaerobic cycle ergometry induced an endorphin response, whereas 1 hour of cycling below the anaerobic threshold did not. Conversely, Melchionda et al. (1984) found that isometric knee extension exercise did not cause elevated endorphins. McMurray et al. (1987) noted that 20 minutes of cycle ergometry at 40% and 60% of maximal capacity did not elicit an endorphin response. Langenfeld, Hart, and Kao (1987) found that 1 hour of cycling or running at 60% did not elevate beta-endorphin. Generally, all maximal capacity exercise tests or tests involving high-intensity exercise lasting longer than 10 minutes have resulted in an increased beta-endorphin. Also most long-distance runs or cycles have also caused an elevation of plasma beta-endorphin. It is also necessary to note that considerable variability exists within and between individuals. Results varying from 4.5 to over 85 pmol/1 have been reported for the same 10-mile run and individuals may vary as much as 20 pmol/1 for the same run under the same conditions (Sheps, Koch, Bragdon, Ballenger, & McMurray, 1988).

Several authors have examined the effect of exercise intensity on the endorphin response. Early research by Colt et al. (1981) suggested that an intensity-related response exists. The research of Farrell, Gates, Muksud, and Morgan (1982) does not support an intensity relationship, because their subjects responded to running at 60% of maximum with significant increases but no significant changes during the 89% trials. McMurray et al. (1987) attempted to clarify the relationship using standardized intensities and found a curvilinear or exponential relationship between exercise intensity and beta-endorphin. Low-intensity exercise resulted in no significant change, but moderate-intensity exercise resulted in a 65% increase over baseline, whereas high-intensity exercise caused an increase of 155%.

The effects of training on beta-endorphin have also been investigated. Early studies by Carr et al. (1981) suggest that 3 weeks of training augments the endorphin response to a standard exercise bout. Conversely, Appenzeller, Appenzeller, Standefer, Skipper, and Atkinson (1984) and Howlett et al. (1984) found that a longer interval of training actually depresses the endorphin response to a given exercise. Similarly, Mikines et al. (1985) found no differences between trained and untrained subjects' beta-endorphin response to insulin-induced hypoglycemia. Thus, the data are not clear concerning the effect of physical training on the beta-endorphin response to exercise.

The improvement in psychological status has been linked to the endogenous opiates (Appenzeller, 1981; Eichner, 1988; Speroff, 1981). This seems quite logical given the opiate characteristics of the endorphin/enkephalins. The earliest report of a relationship was by Pert and Bowie (1979) in which rats either swam in ice water for 5 minutes or ran for 5 minutes; an increased opiate receptor binding was found. They summarized that such binding would cause an alteration in the psychological state of the animal. Haier, Quaid, and Mills (1981) demonstrated that jogging altered the pain threshold. They found that it took more time to notice pain after running. Furthermore, when they administered naloxone, which blocked the endorphin response, the postexercise pain threshold was increased. They reasoned that this provided a basis for the reported mood alteration with exercise. Wildmann, Kruger, and Schmole (1986) found a degree of correlation between the elevation of endorphins after running and the amount of positive mood change.

Most of the studies attempting to determine a psychological role for endorphins during exercise used the opiate antagonist naloxone or naltrexone. Allen and Coen (1987) completed naloxone/placebo running trials on untrained runners. Their measurements of Profile of Mood States (POMS) and the Visual Analogue Scale indicated a significant trend toward calmness during the placebo trials that was not evident during the naloxone trials. Concomitantly, the subjects felt more negative after the naloxone trials than after the placebo trials, therefore suggesting that activity-generated endorphins produce a calming effect. Janal, Colt, Clark, and Glusman (1984) administered naloxone intravenously and found attenuated self-reports of euphoria after a 6-mile run. Similarly, Surbey, Andrews, Cervenko, and Hamilton (1984) found a trend toward an increased affective component of pain and reduced endurance times to exhaustion with the administration of moderate dosages of naloxone. Thus, there seems to be ample indirect evidence to support a role of endogenous opioids in altering psychological status during exercise.

However, there is still controversy because not all data support an endorphin/mood relationship. Farrell et al. (1982) had individuals run at 60% and 80% of VO$_2$max as well as at a preferred pace. They measured POMS and ratings of perceived exertion at the end of each run. The found no statistically significant improvement in the POMS after the 60% and 80% trials. Concomitantly, the endorphins were elevated only after the 60% trials. Farrell, Gates, Morgan, and Pert (1983) also evaluated 14 runners following a 10-mile race. POMS results indicated a decrease in anxiety; however, the leucine-enkephalin activity did not change from prerace levels. McMurray, Berry, Hardy, and Sheps (1988) and McMurray, Berry, Vann, Hardy, and Sheps (1988) measured the endorphin, rating of perceived exertion, and general affect scale responses to three separate 10-mile runs. They found no significant differences in the ratings of perceived exertion or general affect when comparing the trials, yet some individuals had as much as a four-fold difference in endorphin response. It is also interesting to note that the beta-endorphin had not significantly increased by the eighth mile of the run, yet positive affect changes had all ready occurred. If endorphins were the cause of the mood changes, the measures of mood should mirror the endorphin response. The data presented do not clearly show this association. Also Colt et al. (1981) pointed out that the reported increases in beta-endorphin during exercise are much smaller than those used to treat psychiatric patients; therefore, mood changes during running are unlikely to be attributed to the exercise-induced endorphin change. As an aside, we recently measured resting beta-endorphin concentrations in pregnant women and found them to be higher than the responses to exercise in nonpregnant subjects. Yet we found no feelings of calmness or euphoria. Our data (in preparation) also show that a circadian rhythm exists for beta-endorphin that does not seen to be related to mood state.

The data concerning the use of naloxone to reveal significant mood shifts are also equivocal. Many of the studies (Allen & Coen, 1987; Janal et al., 1984; Surbey et al., 1984) that have used naloxone are based on the assumption that endorphins have been elevated by the stressor and have not documented the endorphin response. As we have seen, not all exercise induces an increase in endorphin. Thus, we do not know if the naloxone is blocking an endorphin-mediated response. This is an important consideration because naloxone may have effects independent of endorphins and can even induce a mild dysphoric mood change in humans (Grossman et al., 1984; Sawynok, Pinsky, & LaBella, 1979). Also Steinberg and Sykes (1985) pointed out that in some cases even high dosages have not been found to intensify pain in humans. Another problem with the use of naloxone is the dosage. Several studies have used a low dosage based on clinical trials indicating that the dose is sufficient to reverse opiate-induced coma (Sawynok et al., 1979). These studies have found varying results. In contrast, studies using large dosages have found significant results. The last problem to mention is the timing of the dose of naloxone. Naloxone takes effect in 10 to 15 minutes and has a half-life of 30 to 81 minutes depending upon the individual. Thus, the timing of the dose is critical.

Several exercise studies using naloxone have found no significant differences in mood. Markoff, Ryan, and Young (1982) had subjects complete runs under placebo and naloxone conditions. They administered the POMS before and after exercise and again after the administration of the drug. Anxiety as well as total POMS scores were reduced with exercise; however, the naloxone did not significantly alter the psychological state. McMurray et al. (1983) administered naloxone during a maximal capacity test and found no differences in ratings of perceived exertion. Similarly when they administered naloxone during 10-mile runs, no significant changes in ratings of perceived exertion or general affect were evident. Ellestad and Kuan (1984) infused naloxone in coronary patients during a graded exercise test in an attempt to alter the onset of anginal pain. They also found no effect of naloxone. Thus, there seems to be substantial evidence against an endorphin effect on mood via the use of drugs.

It is interesting to note that many authors attempt to equate changes in pain threshold with mood change or euphoria. Logic suggests that there exist quite a difference between pain and euphoria. Just because the pain threshold is modified does not indicate a change in euphoric state. Many of the authors have also suggested that the exercise does not induce a "high" feeling, but rather a calmness. If this were truly the mood, then a stronger case could be presented for an effect of serotonin, which has been previously shown to reduce arousal.

If endogenous opioids are truly opiates, then repeated and prolonged elevation could lead to an addiction. This implies that the substance produces an emotional high, a tolerance can be developed, and there are withdrawal signs if the administration is continued (Steinberg & Sykes, 1985). Although exercise may meet these criteria (Christie & Chester, 1982; Yates, Leehey, & Shisslak, 1983), the present evidence is not conclusive (Blumenthal, O'Tode, & Chang, 1984). Many people exercise regularly to the extent that endorphins would elevate, but do not demonstrate withdrawal symptoms when the exercise is removed. As Steinberg and Sykes (1985) pointed out, the idea of an addictive personality based on opioids has received little support, but exercise researchers have continued to examine the personality characteristics of exercisers, especially runners.

The final question is if endorphins are not the cause of mood changes, what is the function of their exercise-induced increase? Our present state of knowledge does not allow an answer. It seems that the purposes of opioids are complex and diffuse, affecting not only pain but energy availability, hormonal systems, and food intake. It appears that all work together so that the body can withstand the stress of exercise.

BODY TEMPERATURE

The use of heat to induce therapeutic effects has been known for centuries. In fact, the major purpose of the sauna and hot tub is to induce a relaxed state (deVries, Wiswell, Bulbulian, & Movitani, 1981). Bennett, Cash, and Hoekstra (1941) showed that elevating body temperature could normalize electroencephalogram activity in persons with increased alpha-wave activity. DeVries et al. (1981) also showed that warming significantly reduces tonic muscle activity. Similarly, Raglin and Morgan (1985) showed that a 5-minute warm shower can reduce anxiety. Avery, Wildschiodtz, and Rafaelsen (1982) compared patients with affective disorders with normal patients, and concluded that the former group had higher nocturnal body temperatures and a suppressed diurnal variation in core temperature. It has also been hypothesized that the elevated body temperature at rest may influence the synthesis, release, and uptake of neurotransmitters.

There is a body of literature indicating that exercise results in an increase in body temperature. However, very short-term exercise may not elevate temperature. Thus, it seems that to obtain an elevated core temperature the exercise must last at least 10 to 20 minutes depending upon the intensity. Some studies have indicated changes in psychological status after less than 10 minutes of exercise. Thus, the temperature hypothesis awaits confirmation.

DISTRACTION

Some researchers have suggested that a physiological mechanism is not required; affective changes do not rely on the physiology (Morgan & O'Conner, 1988). The data for this hypothesis are tenuous at best. Bahrke and Morgan (1978) showed that vigorous exercise of moderate intensity reduced tension and anxiety to the same level as did 20 minutes of meditation or sitting in a sound-filtered room. They concluded that the exercise acts as a distraction from stressors. Csikszentmihalyi (1977) also demonstrated that rhythmic exercise may enhance affect by the participant being in with the flow. Considerable research is necessary to confirm or deny this hypothesis.

CONCLUSION

Initially, two scenarios for mood alteration in sport were described. The first was a football team getting ready for play. The attempt of their antics was to elevate catecholamines. The coach believed that the increased catecholamines would allow them to hit harder and endure more pain associated with physical contact. There is some evidence that vocalization is effective in power events. Competitive weight lifters are an example. However, there is no evidence that catecholamines have an analgesic effect. There is evidence that a positive relationship between catecholamines and endogenous opioids exists: An increase in catecholamines may be accompanied by a rise in endorphins (McMurray et al., 1987). Thus, although the coach might not be aware, his stressor may be elevating both catecholamines and endorphins to bring about his desired pregame psychological state.

On the other hand, the runner is using the act of running to fine-tune his psyche. The running will have a significant effect on elevating opioids, serotonin, and the catecholamines. The running will also cause a slow increase in body temperature and could also result in the distraction. Thus, as the run progressed, the combined effect would result in a positive mood shift, such that he finishes feeling good. Because of the thermogenic effect or continued elevation of serotonin after exercise, he may continue to feel good for quite some time.

There seems to be a number of plausible explanations for the mood shifts or changes in affect that can occur with exercise. Acute changes in brain catecholamine, serotonin, and endogenous opioids have all been shown to alter psychological status or have a possible analgesic effect. However, the present data infer a relationship, but do not show a cause and effect relationship. If one considers that exercise reduces tension and anxiety and causes a calmness, then our knowledge of catecholamines seems to negate their implications. Conversely, our knowledge of serotonin and endogenous opioids seems to support their involvement. The distraction and thermogenic theories are also attractive, but like the neuroendocrine theories they lack proof. It is possible that the affective response is a result of redundant or interactive mechanisms. For example, Brown et al. (1979) suggested that the change in affect is related to an interaction of norepinephrine and serotonin within the brain. Many systems within the human body have redundant controls (e.g., respiration, endocrine, cardiovascular, metabolism). Logically, the psyche may be organized in the same manner. Future research is necessary to elucidate the relationship between the physiology and psychology during exercise.

REFERENCES

Adams, M. L., Brase, D. A., Welch, S. P., & Dewey, W. L. (1986). The role of endogenous peptides in the action of opioid analgesics. *Annals of Emergency Medicine, 15*, 1030–1035.

Akil, H., Watson, S. J., Young E., Lewis, M. E., Khachaturian, H., & Walker, J. M. (1984). Endogenous opioids: Biology and function. *Annual Review of Neuroscience, 7*, 223–255.

Allen, M. (1983). Activity generated endorphins: A review of their role in sports science. *Canadian Journal of Applied Sports Science, 8*, 115–133.

Allen, M. E., & Coen, D. (1987). Naloxone blocking of running-induced mood changes. *Annals of Sports Medicine, 3*, 190–195.

Antelman, S. M., & Caggiula, A. R. (1977). Norepinephrine-dopamine interactions and behaviors. *Science, 195,* 646–653.

Appenzeller, O. (1981). What makes us run? *New England Journal of Medicine, 305,* 578–580.

Appenzeller, O., Appenzeller, J., Standefer, J., Skipper, B., & Atkinson, R. (1984). Opioids and endurance training: A longitudinal study. *Annals of Sports Medicine, 2,* 22–25.

Avery, D. H., Wildschiodtz, G., & Rafaelsen, O. (1982). Nocturnal temperature in affective disorders. *Journal of Affective Disorders, 4,* 61–71.

Barachas, J., & Freedman, D. (1962). Brain amines: Response to physiological stress. *Biochemical Pharmacology, 12,* 1232–1235.

Bahrke, M., & Morgan, W. (1978). Anxiety reduction following exercise and meditation. *Cognitive Therapy and Research, 2,* 323–333.

Bennett, A. E., Cash, P. T., & Hoekstra, C. S. (1941). Artificial fever therapy in general paresis with eletroencephalographic studies. *Psychiatric Quarterly, 15,* 750–771.

Bloom, S. R., Johnson, R. H., Park, D. M., Rennie, M. J., & Sulaiman, W. R. (1976). Differences in the metabolic and hormonal response to exercise between racing cyclists and untrained individuals. *Journal of Physiology, 258,* 1–18.

Blumenthal, J. A., O'Toole, L. C., & Chang, J. L. (1984). Is running an analogue of anorexia nervosa? An empirical study of obligatory running and anorexia nervosa. *Journal of the American Medical Association, 252,* 520–523.

Bogdanski, D. F., Bonomi, L., Brodie, B. B. (1963). Occurrence of serotonin and catecholamines in brain and peripheral organs of various vertebrate classes. *Life Science, 2,* 80–84.

Brodie, B. B., & Shore, P. A. (1957). A concept for a role of serotonin and norepinephrine as chemical mediators in the brain. *Annals of the New York Academy of Sciences, 66,* 631–642.

Brown, B. S., Payne, T., Kim, C., Moore, G., Krebs, P., & Martin, W. (1979). Chronic response of rat brain norepinephrine and serotonin levels to endurance training. *Journal of Applied Physiology, 46,* 19–23.

Brown, B. S., & Van Huss, W. D. (1973). Exercise and rat brain catecholamines. *Journal of Applied Physiology, 34,* 664–669.

Bunny, W. E., Pert, C. B., Klee, W., Costa, E., Pert, A., & Davis, G. C. (1979). Basic and clinical studies of endorphins. *Annals of Internal Medicine, 91,* 239–250.

Carr, D. B., Bullen, B. A., & Skrinar, G. S. (1981). Physical conditioning facilitates the exercise-induced secretion of beta-endorphin and beta-lipotropin in women. *New England Journal of Medicine, 305,* 560–563.

Carr, C. B., Jones, K. J., Bergland, R. M. (1985). Causal links between plasma and CFS endorphin levels in stress: Vector ARMA analysis. *Peptides, 6*(1), 5–10.

Christensen, N. J., & Galbo, H. (1983). Sympathetic nervous activity during exercise. *Annual Review of Physiology, 45,* 139–153.

Christie, M. J., & Chester, G. B. (1982). Physical dependence on physiologically released endogenous opiates. *Life Science, 30,* 1173–1177.

Colt, E. W. D., Wardlow, S. L., & Frantz, A G. (1981). The effect of running on plasma B-endorphin. *Life Sciences, 28,* 1637–1640.

Csikszentmihalyi, M. (1977). Play and intrinsic reward. *Journal of Human Psychology, 15,* 41–64.

deLeeuw, P. W., Birkenhager, W. H. (1985). Chronic effects of serotonin inhibition in hypertensive patients: Hemodynamic and hormonal findings. *Journal of Cardiovascular Pharmacology, 7*(7), S137–S139.

deMeirleir, K., Arentz, T., Hollman, W., & Vanhaelst, L. (1985). The role of endogenous opiates in thermal regulation of the body during exercise. *British Medical Journal, 290,* 739–740.

deMeirleir, K., Naaktgeboren, N., Van Steirteghem, A., Gorus, F., Olbrecht, J., & Block, P. (1986). Beta-endorphin and ACTH levels in peripheral blood during and after aerobic and anaerobic exercise. *European Journal of Applied Physiology, 55,* 5–8.

deVries, H. A., Wiswell, R. A., Bulbulian, R., & Moritani, T. (1981). Tranquilizer effect of exercise. *American Journal of Physical Medicine, 60,* 57–66.

Donald, D. E., Ferguson, D. A., & Milburn, S. E. (1968). Effect of beta-adrenergic receptor blockade on racing performance of greyhounds, with normal and denervated hearts. *Circulation Research, 22,* 127–134.

Eichner, E. R. (1988). A profile of the mature athlete. In W. A. Grana, J. A. Lombardo, B. J. Sharkey, & J. A. Stone (Eds.), *Advances in sports medicine and fitness* (pp. 1–22). Chicago: Year Book.

Ellstad, M. H., & Kuan, P. (1984). Naloxone and asymptomatic ischemia: Failure to induce angina during exercise testing. *American Journal of Cardiology, 54,* 982–984.

El-Tayeb, K. M. A., Brubaker, P. L., Lickey, H. L. A., Cook, E., & Vranic, M. (1986). Effect of opiate-receptor blockage on normoglycemic and hypoglycemic glucoregulation. *American Journal of Physiology, 250,* E236–E242.

Farrell, P. A., Gates, W. K., Morgan, W. P., & Pert, C. B. (1983). Plasma leucine enkephalin-like radioreceptor activity and tension-anxiety before and after competitive running. In H. G. Knuttgen, J. A. Vogal, & J. Poortmans (Eds.), *Biochemistry of exercise* (pp. 637–644). Champaign: Human Kinetics.

Farrell, P. A., Gates, W. K., Muksud, M. G., & Morgan, W. P. (1982). Increases in plasma B-endorphin/B-lipotropin immunoreactivity after treadmill running in humans. *Journal of Applied Physiology, 52,* 1245–1249.

Feldman, M., Kiser, R. S., Under, R. H., & Li, C. H. (1983). Beta-endorphin and the endocrine pancrease. *New England Journal of Medicine, 308,* 349–353.

Foley, K. M., Kourides, I. A., Inturrisi, C. E., Kaiko, R. F., Zaroulis, C. G., Posner, J. B., Houde, R. W., & Li, C. H. (1979). B-endorphin: Analgesic and hormonal effects in humans. *Proceedings of the National Academy of Sciences, 76,* 5377–5388.

Folkins, C. H., Lynch, S., & Gardner, M. M. (1972). Psychological fitness as a function of physical fitness. *Archives of Physical Medicine and Rehabilitation, 53,* 503–508.

Folkins, C. H., & Sime, W. E. (1981). Physical fitness training and mental health. *American Psychology, 36,* 373–389.

Forsman, L., & Lundberg, U. (1982). Consistency in catecholamine and cortisol excretion in males and females. *Pharmacology Biochemistry & Behavior, 17,* 555–562.

Galbo, H. (1983). *Hormonal and metabolic adaptations to exercise.* Stuttgart, West Germany: Thieme.

Grossman, A. (1989). Opioids and stress: The role of ACTH and epinephrine. In Y. Tache, J. F. Morley, & M. R. Brown (Eds.), *Neuropeptides and stress* (pp. 313–324). New York: Springer-Verlag.

Grossman, A., Bouloux, P., Prince, P., Drury, P. L., Lam, S. L., Turner, T., Thomas, J., Besser, G. M., & Sutton, J. (1984). The role of opioid peptides in the hormonal responses to acute exercise in man. *Clinical Science, 67,* 483–491.

Haier, R. J., Quaid, K., & Mills, J. S. C. (1981). Naloxone alters pain perception after jogging. *Psychiatry Research, 5,* 231–232.

Harvey, J. A., Schlosberg, A. J., & Younger, L. M. (1975). Behavioral correlates of serotonin depletion. *Federation Proceedings, 34,* 1796–1801.

Hatfield, B. D., & Landers, D. M. (1987). Psychophysiology in exercise and sport research: An overview. *Exercise and Sport Sciences Reviews, 15,* 351–388.

Hoebel, B. G. (1975). Brain reward and adversion systems in the control of feeding and sexual behavior. In M. R. Jones (Ed.), *Nebraska symposium on motivation.* Lincoln: University of Nebraska Press.

Howlett, R. A., Tomlin, S., Hgahfoong, L., Rees, L. H., Bullen, B. A., Skrinar, G. S., & McArthur, J. W. (1984). Release of B-endorphin and met-enkephalin during exercise in normal women: Response to training. *British Medical Journal, 288,* 1950–1952.

Hull, E. M., Young, S. H., & Ziegler, M. G. (1984). Aerobic fitness affects cardiovascular and catecholamine responses to stressors. *Psychophysiology, 21,* 353–360.

Janal, M. N., Colt, W. D., Clark, C. W., & Glusman, M. (1984). Pain sensitivity, mood, and plasma endocrine levels in man following long distance running: Effects of naloxone. *Pain, 19,* 13–25.

Kavanaugh, T., Shephard, R. J., Tuck, J. A., & Quareshi, S. (1977). Depression following myocardial infarction: The effect of distance running. *Annals of the New York Academy of Science, 301,* 1029–1038.

Kelso, T. B., Herbert, W. G., Gwazdauskas, F. C., Goss, F. L., & Hess, J. L. (1984). Exercise-thermoregulatory stress and increased plasma B-endorphin/B-lipotropin in humans. *Journal of Applied Physiology, 57,* 444–449.

Kindermann, W., Schnabel, A., Schmitt, W. M., Biro, G., Cassens, J., & Weber, F. (1982). Catecholamines, growth hormone, cortisol, insulin, and sex hormones in anaerobic and aerobic exercise. *European Journal of Applied Physiology, 49,* 389–399.

Kjaer, M., & Galbo, H. (1988). Effect of physical training on the capacity to secrete epinephrine. *Journal of Applied Physiology, 64,* 11–16.

Kotchen, T. A., Hartley, L. H., Rice, T. W., Mougey, E. H., Jones, L. G., & Mason, J. W. (1971). Renin, norepinephrine and epinephrine responses to graded exercise. *Journal of Applied Physiology, 31,* 178–184.

Kreiger, D. T. (1982). Endorphins and enkephalins opioids. *Disease-a-Month, 28,* 1–53.

Kruger, A., Wildmann, J., Schenk, H., Schmole, M., Niemann, J., & Matthias, H. (1985). Inter- and intraindividual variations in plasma B-endorphin-like immunoreactivity: The effect of running 10 km. *Annals of Sports Medicine, 2,* 111–116.

Langenfeld, M. E., Hart, L. S., & Kao, P. C. (1987). Plasma B-endorphin responses to one-hour bicycling and running at 60% VO2max. *Medicine and Science in Sports and Exercise, 19,* 83–86.

Maas, J. W., & Leckman, J. F. (1983). Relationship between CNS noradrenergic function and urinary MHPG and other norepinephrine metabolites. In J. W. Mass (Ed.), *MHPG: Basic mechanisms and psychopathology* (pp. 33–42). New York: Academic.

Markoff, R. A., Ryan, P., & Young, T. (1982). Endorphins and mood changes in long-distance running. *Medicine and Science in Sports and Exercise, 14,* 11–15.

Maron, M. B., Horvath, S. M., & Wilkerson, J. E. (1977). Blood biochemical alterations during recovery from competitive marathon running. *European Journal of Applied Physiology, 36,* 231–238.

Mason, J. W. (1971). A re-evaluation of the concept of 'non-specificity' in stress theory. *Journal of Psychiatric Research, 8,* 323–333.

McArthur, J. W. (1985). Endorphins and exercise in females: Possible connection with reproductive dysfunction. *Medicine and Science in Sports and Exercise, 17,* 82–88.

McGowan, C. R., Robertson, R. J., & Epstein, L. H. (1985). The effect of bicycle ergometer exercise at varying intensities on the heart rate, EMG and mood state responses to a mental arithmatic stressor. *Research Quarterly, 56,* 131–137.

McMurray, R. G. (in press). Beta-endorphin and mood state during exercise: The controversy continues. *Annals of Sports Medicine.*

McMurray, R. G., Berry, M. J., Hardy, C. J., & Sheps, D. S. (1988). Physiologic and psychologic responses to a low dose of naloxone administered during prolonged running. *Annals of Sports Medicine, 4,* 21–25.

McMurray, R. G., Berry, M. J., Vann, R. T., Hardy, C. J., & Sheps, D. S. (1988). The effect of running in an outdoor environment on plasma beta endorphins. *Annals of Sports Medicine, 3,* 230–233.

McMurray, R. G., Forsythe, W. A., Mar, M. H., & Hardy, C. J. (1987). Exercise intensity-related responses of B-endorphin and catecholamines. *Medicine and Science in Sports and Exercise, 19,* 570–574.

McMurray, R. G., Hardy, C. J., Roberts, S., Forsythe, W. A., & Mar, M. H. (1989). Neuroendocrine responses of type A individuals to exercise. *Behavioral Medicine, 15,* 84–91.

McMurray, R. G., Sheps, D. S., & Guinan, D. M. (1984). Effects of naloxone on maximal stress testing in females. *Journal of Applied Physiology, 56,* 436–440.

Melchionda, A. M., Clarkson, P. M., Denko, C., Freedson, P., Graves, J., & Katch, F. (1984). The effect of local iosmetric exercise on serum levels of beta-endorphin/beta-lipotropin. *The Physician and Sportsmedicine, 12,* 102–109.

Mikines, K. J., Kjaer, M., Hagen, C., Sonne, B., Richter, E. A., & Galbo, H. (1985). The effect of training on responses of B-endorphin and other pituitary hormones to insulin-induced hypoglycemia. *European Journal of Applied Physiology, 54,* 476–479.

Morgan, W. P. (1985). Affective beneficence of vigorous physical activity. *Medicine and Science in Sports and Exercise, 17,* 94–100.

Morgan, W. P., & O'Conner, P. J. (1988). Exercise and mental health. In R. K. Dishman (Ed.), *Exercise adherence: Its impact on public health* (pp. 91–121). Champaign, IL: Human Kinetics.

Morris, P. L., Vale, W. W., & Bardin, C. W. (1987). B-endorphin regulation of FSH-stimulated inhibin production is a component of a short loop system in testis. *Biochemical and Biophysical Research Communications, 140,* 1513–1519.

Moss, I. R., & Scarpelli, E. M. (1981). B-endorphin central depression of respiration and circulation. *Journal of Applied Physiology, 50,* 1011–1016.

Murphy, J. B., Bennett, R. N., Hagen, J. M., & Russell, M. W. (1972). Some suggestive data regarding the relationship of physical fitness to emotional difficulties. *Newsletter of Research in Psychology, 14,* 15–17.

Obrist, P. A., Gaebelein, C. J., Teller, E. S., Langer, A. W., Grignolo, A., Light, K. C., & McCubbin, J. A. (1978). The relationship among heart rate, carotid dP/dt, and blood pressure in humans as a function of the type of stress. *Psychophysiology, 15,* 102–115.

Ortiz, J., Artigas, F., & Gelpi, E. (1988). Serotonergic status in human blood. *Life Science, 43,* 983–990.

Palermo, A., del Rosso, G., Costantini, C., Bertalero, P., Rizzi, S., & Libretti, A. (1986). Platelet content of serotonin and response to stress. *Journal of Hypertension, 4,*(1), S43–S45.

Pargman, D., & Baker, M. C. (1980). Running high: Enkephalin indicated. *Journal of Drug Issues,* *10,* 341–349.

Peronnet, F., Blier, P., Brisson, G., Diamond, P., Ledoux, M., & Volle, M. (1986). Reproducibility of plasma catecholamine concentrations at rest and during exercise in man. *European Journal of Applied Physiology, 53,* 555–558.

Pert, C. B., & Bowie, D. L. (1979). Behavioral manipulation of rats causes alterations in opiate receptor occupancy. In Usdin, E., Bunny, W. E., & Kline, N. S. (Eds.), *Endorphins and mental health* (pp. 93–104). New York: Oxford University Press.

Petty, M. A., deJong, W., & deWied, D. (1982). An inhibitory role of B-endorphin in central cardiovascular regulation. *Life Sciences, 30,* 1835–1840.

Raglin, J. S., & Morgan, W. P. (1985). Influence of vigorous exercise on mood state. *Behavior Therapist, 8,* 179–183.

Ransford, C. P. (1982). A role for amines in the antidepressent effect of exercise: A review. *Medicine and Science in Sports and Exercise, 14,* 1–10.

Rossier, J., French, E. D., Rivier, C., Ling, N., Guillemin, R., & Bloom, F. E. (1977). Foot shock-induced stress increases B-endorphin levels in blood but not in brain. *Nature* (London), *270,* 618–620.

Rushmer, R. F., & Smith, D. A. (1959). Cardiac control. *Physiological Reviews, 39,* 41–68.

Sachs, M. L. (1981). Running addiction. In M. H. Sachs and M. L. Sachs (Eds.), *The psychology of running* (pp. 116–126). Champaign, IL: Human Kinetics.

Sachs, M. L. (1984). The runner's high. In M. L. Sachs, & G. W. Buffone (Eds.), *Running as therapy: An integrated approach* (pp. 273–287). Lincoln: University of Nebraska Press.

Santiago, T. V., & Edelman, N. H. (1985). Opioids and breathing. *Journal of Applied Physiology, 59,* 1675–1685.

Sawynok, I., Pinsky, C., & LaBella, F. S. (1979). Minireview on the specificity of naloxone as an opiate antagonist. *Life Science, 25,* 1621–1630.

Schildkraut, J. J., Orsulak, P. J., Schatzberg, A. F., & Rosenbaum, A. H. (1983). Relationship between psychiatric diagnostic groups of depressive disorders and MHPG. In J. W. Maas (Ed.), *MHPG: Basic mechanisms and psychopathology* (pp. 67–83). New York: Academic.

Seals, D. R., Victor, R. G., & Mark, A. L. (1988). Plasma norepinephrine and muscle sympathetic discharge during rhythmic exercise in humans. *Journal of Applied Physiology, 65,* 940–944.

Selye, H. A. (1936). A syndrome produced by diverse nocuous agents. *Nature*(London), *138,* 32–34.

Sforzio, G. A. (1988). Opioids and exercise. *Sports Medicine, 7,* 109–124.

Sheps, D. S., Koch, G., Bragdon, E. E., Ballenger, M. N., & McMurray, R. G. (1988). The reproducibility of resting and post exercise plasma beta-endorphins. *Life Science, 43,* 787–791.

Sinyor, D., Schwartz, S. G., Peronnet, F., Brisson, G., & Seraganian, P. (1983). Aerobic fitness levels and reactivity to psychosocial stress: Physiological, biochemical and subjective measures. *Psychosomatic Medicine, 45,* 205–217.

Southmann, M. S., Ismail, A. H., & Chodepko-Zajiko, W. (1984). Influence of catecholamine activity on the hierarchical relationship among physical fitness condition and selected personality characteristics. *Journal of Clinical Psychology, 40,* 1308–1317.

Speroff, L. (1981). Getting high on running. *Fertility and Sterility, 36,* 149–151.

Steinberg, H., & Sykes, E. A. (1985). Introduction to symposium on endorphins and behavioural processes; review of literature on endorphins and exercise. *Pharmacology, Biochemistry & Behavior, 23,* 857–862..

Stern, J. A., & McDonald, D. G. (1965). Physiological correlates of mental disease. In P. R. Farnsworth (Ed.) *Annual Review of Psychology,* Palo Alto: Annual Reviews.

Surbey, G. D., Andrews, G. M., Cervenko, F. W., & Hamilton, P. P. (1984). Effects of naloxone on exercise performance. *Journal of Applied Physiology, 57,* 674–679.

Van Loon, G. R., & Sole, M. J. (1980). Plasma dopamine: Source, regulation and significance. *Metabolism, 29,* 1119–1123.

Weicker, H. (1986). Sympathoadrenergic regulation. *International Journal of Sports Medicine, 7,* 16–26.

Wildmann, J., Kruger, A., & Schmole, M. (1986). Increase of circulating beta-endorphin-like immunoreactivity correlates with the change in feeling of pleasantness after running. *Life Sciences, 38,* 977–1003.

Williams, R. B., Bittker, T. E., Buchsbaum, M. S., & Wynne, L. C. (1975). Cardiovascular and neurophysiologic correlates of sensory intake and rejection. I. Effect of cognitive task. *Psychophysiology, 12,* 427–433.

Winder, W. W., Beattie, M. A., & Holman, R. T. (1982). Endurance training attenuates stress hormone response to exercise in fasted rats. *American Journal of Physiology, 243,* R170–R184.

Winder, W. W., Hickson, R. C., Hagberg, J. M., Eshani, A. A., & McLane, J. A. (1979). Training-induced changes in hormonal and metabolic responses to submaximal exercise. *Journal of Applied Physiology, 46,* 766–771.

Yates, A., Leehey, K., & Shisslak, C. M. (1983). Running: An analog to anorexia? *New England Journal of Medicine, 308,* 251–255.

Young, J. B., Rosa, R. M., & Landsberg, L. (1984). Dissociation of sympathetic nervous system and adrenal medullary responses. *American Journal of Physiology, 247,* E35–E40.

15

Mental States and Physical Performance

Leif Robert Diamant and Richard M. Baker
Community Wholistic Health Center, Carrboro, NC

Athletes and other performers of physical skills often find a wide variation in the quality of their performance on a given day. Sometimes, a person is "on a roll" or "out of their mind," and it seems that their performance is superlative. There are other days when the same person performs below par and seems to have regressed to an inferior level of skill. Physiological factors can contribute to variations in performance; these include health, conditioning, sleep, and drug use. Other less tangible factors also influence performance such as stressors, stress-management skills, luck, biorhythms, self-esteem, ability to process mistakes, emotions, and various difficult-to-quantify factors.

For centuries, yogis of India, as well as members of certain religious and military orders, have practiced developing mental states that allowed them to control autonomic body functions such as heartbeat and blood pressure (Green & Green, 1977). Until recently, Western science did not believe this was possible. Aspects of these practices, along with development of sports psychology during the past several decades, definitively correlate physical performance of sports and other skills with mental states that can be influenced and controlled by the performer.

It is now widely agreed by athletes, coaches, and sports psychologists that much of how well a game is played is mental. Jack Nicklaus is reputed to have said that golf is 90% mental preparation and only 10% skill. A common adage of sports performance is "90% inspiration and 10% perspiration." Jimmy Connors estimated that winning at the top is 95% mental (Williams, 1988). Mental preparation, emotional response, inspiration, inner game, "psyching up," processing mistakes, and self-hypnosis are some of the mental behaviors that influence physical performance.

PREPARING FOR PERFORMANCE

Complex behaviors, like a tennis serve or shooting an arrow with a bow, are often called psychomotor skills to emphasize the vital integration of the psyche with the body. The implication is most important for teaching psychomotor skills: The learner must integrate the necessary intellectual and spiritual aspects of the skill (spiritual meaning the quintessential nature of the sport or skill; it is more than the sum or the parts; it is what gives meaning, beauty, joy, to the experience) in addition to mastering the movements to perform well. The need for this balance is often seen in figure skating, where the free-form exercises look wooden and joyless when the more artistic aspects of mind and spirit have not received enough emphasis. Good teaching of psychomotor skills requires the inclusion of: (a) efforts to motivate learning, (b) information about how and why the components of the skill are performed, (c) demonstration of the skill in a way that the learner can understand, (d) feedback from a source that the learner believes in, and (e) opportunity to practice, with remotivation, more information, and more feedback when necessary.

The tennis backhand can be an example. Ideally, the novice learner would desire to learn the sport of tennis and is old enough to be able to perform the movements with adequate strength and coordination. Specific motivation may be added for the backhand, as an essential, although difficult, part of the sport. The special movements can be described in words, with the reasons why they have the best chance of working well in actual play. Then the backhand is demonstrated slowly, dissected into its components, and then together, volleying with the best form possible. The learner tries the movements with the coach's feedback. At a certain point, all the correctly applied motions work; self-consciousness evaporates and it "feels right." When there is the oneness of mind and body, the spiritual aspect is experienced.

The method of teaching psychomotor skill is described in some detail to emphasize the importance of integrating mental states and physical performance in any complex behavior. Performing well in a sport or skill combines the knowledge, feelings, attitudes, and spirit with the movements. On one hand, sports like golf, swimming, or volleyball are incredibly complex and difficult to perform in the "ideal" way. On the other hand, these sports offer endless challenges to attain new heights within one's limitations, and people can be fascinated by trying to play with more skill, consistency, and joy.

RELAXATION AND PSYCHING UP

It could be generalized that coaches emphasize increasing their players' arousal before sports events, whereas sports psychologists tend to focus on teaching athletes relaxation and control of mind and body. Coaches who teach a wide variety of skills and techniques often have encouraged high levels of energy, aggression, and strong drive as the fuel for winning ("win one for the Gipper"). This particular psyching-up strategy is useful at some times in some events.

There are increasing data to show that different people have individualized ways to psych up, and this is usually accomplished through internal dialogue, imagery, verbalization, and vocalization. This is the "fight" of the "fight or flight" response.

For a number of reasons, this extreme arousal technique is antithetical to many types of performance. The fight or flight cues trigger a series of body responses that increase adrenaline and noradrenaline. Breathing, blood pressure, and heart rate increase, and muscles tense or tighten. As these physiological responses increase, often the individual will find him or herself worrying and increasing anxiety. This can lead to an even greater increase in heart rate, breathing, blood pressure, and more muscle tension. This is, obviously, contraindicated for optimal performance. The physical performance situation often requires strategizing, subtle awareness, refined motor skills, and complex decision making. The high-level strength response, which becomes available with "flight or fight", is often not readily usable in the complex tasks of performance, and the high level of mental arousal has a high probability of making the athlete edgy and prone to mistakes.

If psyching up is a means of creating optimal arousal of mind-body resources, relaxation is the most effective foundation of psyching up. Relaxation involves the releasing of any unnecessary tension, tightness, or concerns. Relaxation means the muscles do nothing and the mind, effortlessly, does as little as possible. Relaxation means heart rate, blood pressure, and respiration slow down. Relaxing (to make loose again) often is accomplished by slower brain wave activity and heightened endorphin production. Relaxing allows the athlete to develop awareness of his or her muscles and thought processes in subtle and beneficial ways.

The ability to be aware of individual muscles and muscle groups loosening increases a person's capacity to more finely isolate and control those muscles. Noticing the difference between relaxation and tension allows the physical performer to notice unnecessary tension while at rest or in action. This is a very useful skill because unnecessary tension uses extra body energy and tightens muscles, which often reduces agility. Body tension is often correlated with anxious or self-doubting thought processes. Relaxation provides a way to recharge during an athletic event or physical activity.

There are many different ways to relax. All involve a combination of loosening muscles and reducing involvement in mental activity. To relax is to feel safe and comfortable enough to let go of control. Active and passive body relaxation (as described in the self-hypnosis section of this chapter) are effective and easily learned methods of relaxation.

Breathing effectively is probably the most fundamental and usable relaxation technique. Deep, slow breathing relaxes the mind and the body. This type of breathing involves drawing the breath deeply into the lungs. The diaphragm expands and the stomach extends outward as the lungs fill with air. Most people were taught the kind of "good" posture that involves having a flat tucked-in stomach. To breathe deeply, the abdomen must expand. This is a much more physiologically satisfying way to breathe than shallow breaths into the upper chest.

An easy way to become more relaxed is to take a slow, deep breath through the nose, inhaling comfortably and fully into the lungs so that the stomach pushes out during inhalation. Now one slowly exhales through the nose or mouth, comfortably expelling most of the air from the lungs. One can imagine "breathing in comfort, breathing out relief." Another breathing technique is, after the deep inhalation, to hold the breath for a count of 5 or 10 and then let out the breath for a count of 5 or 10.

The particular breathing technique that one uses depends on what is comfortable and what works. Some people visualize their breath filled with white light. Some people count as they breathe, taking a longer time to exhale than to inhale. As with many things in life, it is important to customize breathing for relaxation in a way that best suits the individual.

Relaxation through breathing is a complete tool in itself. It is also an effective foundation for other psyching behaviors and strategies. These include self-hypnosis, rehearsal, visual imagery, self-affirmation, and self-confidence building.

SELF-HYPNOSIS, IMAGERY, AND REHEARSAL

Self-hypnosis is a mental method through which individuals maximize their ability to perform physically. Many competitive athletes use self-hypnosis skills to prepare for competition as well as during the actual sport events. Individuals also use self-hypnosis to improve their own levels of performance in noncompetitive situations (Alman & Lambram, 1983; Hadley & Staudacher, 1985).

Preparing for performance is not the same as just physically practicing the same skills repetitively. Studies (Feltz & Landers, 1983) showed that basketball players who practiced free throws on the court performed less well than those who only used mental rehearsal to practice free throws. Mary Lou Retton (at the age of 16) mentally rehearsed every routine and every move in each routine before winning her 1984 Olympic gold medal in gymnastics (*Time* magazine).

Self-hypnosis techniques involve a multi-fold strategy that includes: relaxation, concentration, physical and psychological rehearsal, and posthypnotic cues and suggestions.

The theory behind the experience that mental rehearsing creates improved physical performance is based on an ideomotor model of learning. It has been scientifically observed for over 50 years that ideas in the mind create muscular changes (Jacobson, 1938). When a physical skill is mentally practiced, the muscles involved in the skill are stimulated as if the skill were being physically practiced. The body learns to incorporate and repeat the skill outside of conscious thought or direction. This means a skill can be repeated and refined in a person's mind and their body can repeat the skill automatically.

Self-hypnosis involves three basic components. They are: (a) induction (the process of going into trance); (b) trance (altered state of consciousness that usually involves relaxation, inner awareness, and concentration; and (c) posthypnotic suggestions and cues (desired responses that are arranged in the trance state to take place during the physical performance) (Diamant, 1986).

Relaxation is usually the induction process. There are many ways to relax. Cardiologist Herbert Benson (1975) coined the phrase "relaxation response" to describe the body's response to deep, slow, rhythmic breathing. The heartbeat slows, blood flows better as blood pressure decreases, and muscles relax. Brain waves slow down and, it seems likely, endorphins are released. Step-by-step body relaxation and breathing exercises are frequently used methods of relaxation or induction. Breathing (discussed earlier) can include techniques such as inhaling energy and exhaling tension or inhaling comfort and exhaling relief. A slow, deep breathing technique is usually the most beneficial. Step-by-step progressive body relaxation can be active (such as by tightening and loosening each body part) or passive (by imagining each body part relaxing).

Either can be done sitting or lying in a comfortable position. As always, whenever one performs self-hypnosis, it is helpful to be in a place where one feels safe and relaxed.

During active progressive body relaxation, subjects systematically tense muscles in their body and then release the tension. Although some prefer to begin at the feet and progress to the head, any order of progression can be chosen. To begin, bring awareness to the right foot, curling the toes and tightening the foot, bending at the ankle. Hold this tension for a moment and then slowly release and relax. It is okay to make a sound or a sigh as tension is released. Then tighten the calf and thigh and again hold and then slowly release and relax. Repeat for the left foot and leg and then progress to other areas of the body, tensing different body parts (these body parts are tensed in different ways, e.g., the stomach tightened, the lungs filled, the jaw stretched, the face wrinkled), holding for a moment and then slowly releasing and relaxing.

It is important to relax all body parts during active or passive progressive body relaxation. These body parts and muscle groups are: feet and legs; genital and pelvic area; buttocks; abdomen, stomach, and chest; back, spine, and shoulders; hands and arms; neck, head, and face. In passive progressive body relaxation, each body part is relaxed without tensing. One might imagine that each part is actually relaxing. Perhaps some other imagery will work better, such as imagining the muscles "unwinding" like a spring, softening, or the tension melting away like it does during a hot bath. Like active relaxation, passive progressive body relaxation is done systematically, one part at a time, until the entire body is relaxed and comfortable.

The breathing exercises and the progressive body relaxation are methods of going into a self-hypnotic trance. These techniques relax the body and when one's body is relaxed, the mind also relaxes. Relaxation and inner focused awareness are key aspects of being in a self-hypnosis trance.

Other often-used methods for relaxation include: going to a special, safe place; countdown (e.g., 20 to 1); meditative techniques (such as focusing on a phrase or the breath as it comes in and out); or remembering the last trance experience and using that as a cue to go into that relaxed state of consciousness.

Once a person has entered into that deeply relaxed state and is in trance (the "trance state of consciousness" become more easily recognizable and accessible with practice), the exquisitely detailed rehearsal takes place. A dancer, for instance, might rehearse in his or her mind every detail from predance warm-up through all aspects of a routine to postdance finish. Details seem essential, because this is an ideomotor rehearsal and the rehearsal is a replication of the performance. This is often broken into tiny details with focus not only on body movement, but also on other sensory and mental aspects. These could include auditory and visual awareness, mental attitude, emotional state, temperature sensations, and even olfaction and taste if appropriate.

Posthypnotic suggestions and cues are an essential part of the self-hypnosis process. Suggestions might include some behavioral responses: "I can concentrate fully on what I'm doing"; "I can be relaxed and alert"; "I have a winning attitude"; "I will play or do my best today." Cues are responses that take place in reaction to a stimulus. For instance, distracting thoughts can be a cue to take several deep and relaxing breaths, or the sight of an opponent stimulates the feeling of extra alertness, or the last 5 minutes on the clock is a cue to release the remaining reserves of energy.

In the initial stages of learning self-hypnosis, 20 minutes to more than an hour are appropriate learning times. As an individual becomes competent in the process, often a much shorter period of induction is needed. Even a few breaths are enough to go into a trance. In many sports, the athlete relaxes, rehearses, and then performs. For instance, a tennis player tosses the ball in the air a few times, pauses, imagines where the serve will land in the opponent's court, and then serves. The same type of relaxation, internalization of desired actions, and then externalized behavior fits many different types of physical activity from bowling to ballet, free throws to headstands. These could be appropriately called "mini-trances."

X The person who uses self-hypnosis for athletic and physical performance usually finds the process highly reinforcing. Sometimes the results come quickly, other times more gradually. Often the benefits and efficiency of the process are increased by learning self-hypnosis from a professional who not only teaches the techniques but also reinforces (through suggestion and practice) the individual's ability to enter into this state on his or her own.

MECHANISMS FOR ENHANCING BODY-MIND PERFORMANCE

Around 1970, an opiate- or morphine-like chemical was found in the brain and blood (Pert & Snyder, 1973; Snyder, 1977). There were receptor sites for this chemical, called endorphins, in the brain and elsewhere in the body. Now, several similar systems of neurotransmitters have been discovered as connections between positive moods and exercise. Although researchers initially linked endorphins to euphoric states in exercisers, such as "runner's high" (Pargman & Baker, 1980), the real effect may be more like calmness. In addition, endorphins and related compounds may be linked to pain tolerance, appetite, and satiety. Finally, immune system activity and reproductive hormone cycles seem to be influenced.

Beta-endorphin has been shown to increase by at least five times its resting level in the brain. This group of chemicals is now called endogenous opioids, and more research is in progress to identify specific effects and regulation mechanisms (McArdle, Katch, & Katch, 1986). Many states have been postulated to increase the level of endogenous opioids (Sherman & Liebeskind, 1980), but the only known mechanism currently is aerobic exercise. Massage, affection, sexual stimulation, heat, and some medications may also prove to be effective mechanisms. The pleasurable feelings associated with endorphin production have been theorized as a motivator for exercise. Positive addiction to various physical activities are reinforced by "endorphin highs" (for a complementary review of the endogenous opioids literature see MacMurray's chapter in this book).

Amphetamines mimic the effects of the sympathetic nervous system by increasing alertness and other aspects of arousal, such as blood pressure, pulse, blood glucose, and metabolic rate. The improvement of performance has not been demonstrated in studies of actual effects during exercise or sporting events. Some athletes still use these "pep pills" for the psychological effect of psyching up for the game or event. The physiological effects and the potential for addiction make the use of these drugs very undesirable, and the deleterious health affects have caused them to be banned from most sports competition.

Caffeine, on the other hand, has been shown to improve performance while helping exercise feel easier (McArdle et al., 1986). The metabolism of fat during exercise seems to be increased, and muscles may be made more efficient at lower levels of exercise. The subjective affects of arousal and the physiological effects on the cardiovascular system are similar to the amphetamines, although milder. Preparation for endurance events, such as marathons, is often recommended to include two cups of coffee before the event. We should note, however, that caffeine and other drugs or vitamins are seldom compared with placebo's effect on performance. These "stimulants" may possibly have their beneficial effects through the release of endogenous opioids.

THE INNER GAME

During performance, "the inner game" has a crucial role in the outcome. By outcome, we mean the performer's satisfaction or dissatisfaction rather than winning or losing, which may be incidental. Outcome is highly correlated, however, with doing what is perceived as one's best. Peak performance requires integration of a good mental state with proper preparation and physical ability. Aspects of a good mental state are: emotional readiness, positive thinking, self-esteem, toughness, presentness, and relaxation.

The emotional states of the athlete directly affect the ability to perform. Anxiety, frustration, worry, jealousy, anger, boredom, and tension are all emotions that reduce maximum performance and, at times, can be debilitating. The successful physical performer usually learns to manage, reduce, or transform these feeling states to have optimal physical and mental energy available. Although all of these emotional experiences are a normal part of human experience and competitive situations often stimulate and exacerbate these feelings, the usually hinder performance.

Anxiety is usually connected to the anticipation of performance or competition when the outcome of an even it important to the individual. Certain characteristics of this anxiety state can be interpreted as negative indicators. Thoughts of self-doubt and inadequacy inhibit ability by focusing awareness from the experience to the individual's ability to perform competently. Physical tension, nervousness, self-criticism, focus on external factors (those that are out of control such as weather, officiating luck), and exaggerating outcome value often accompany anxiety. Because many types of physical performance require some combination of accessible power, endurance, or physical control, it is easy to understand how excessive anxiety would reduce the ability to perform. Anxiety is energy draining. Anxiety reduces the ability to focus energy as it tenses muscles, increases blood pressure and heartbeat, and reduces calmness and control. Anxiety shifts thinking awareness from the experience back to the individual. All of these aspects reduce performance competence.

Generally, emotions have an impact on the body's functioning through the endocrine (glandular) system, the sympathetic nervous system, and the voluntary nervous system. Each individual responds to his or her stresses (sport competition, for example) with a unique set of hormonal responses. The most important known for performance are adrenaline, noradrenaline, cortisol, insulin, sex hormones, and thyroid hormones. Over 20 other hormones are known to change in stressful conditions. Those mentioned here have immediate and direct effects on the body in ways that influence performance: altering metabolic rate, kidney function, heart rate or output, blood pressure, or behavior, such as aggressiveness. There is also evidence that individuals have some degree of control over their hormonal responses. For instance, communicating stressful feeling with others can change hormonal responses. Good preparation for the event is also known to affect adrenaline levels.

The autonomic, or involuntary, nervous system prepares the body quickly for fight or flight responses. Pulse, blood pressure, glucose in the blood, and muscle tension rise to some extent. This varies depending upon past experience, degree of stress, and individual characteristics. Often the "jitters" get in the way of smooth, coordinated muscle action, and they are a frequent rationalization for poor performance, especially early in "big games" or pressure situations. Here, again the individual has a good deal of control over the quantity of autonomic activity through good preparation and coaching.

The voluntary nervous system also has a direct role in performance when anger or anxiety are present. Tense skeletal muscles result partly from hormonal stimulation and from the sympathetic nervous system. In addition, individuals tend to tense particular muscle groups during anxiety or anger. Shoulder and neck muscles, jaw muscles, chest muscles, and low back muscles are favorites. Relaxation techniques can modify this tension.

On the other hand, optimal performance needs a level of arousal that may be difficult to create in some athletes or in some circumstances. Good coaching and self-preparation seek to balance the tension, avoiding overstress and understress. This level of stress is called "eustress." It is a zone of arousal state that contributes to good performance without overtaxing the body's physiological mechanisms. Eustress levels will vary according to the particular sport (e.g., golf vs. rugby), the importance of performing well (e.g., a practice dive vs. the Olympic finals), and the individual's makeup (e.g., the lackadaisical young football player vs. the high-strung gymnast).

"Positive thinking" is a discipline of the mind in better performers that allows them to use their experience and current sensory input in the most constructive ways. There is considerable overlap with self-esteem, discussed next, but the discipline of positive thinking can be more easily operationalized and changed.

Positive thinking can be shaped by increasing the praise one expresses to oneself for good performance and the optimism and appreciation one expresses for good skills or attitudes that improve performance. At the same time, self-criticism, pessimism, and other expressions of negativity are reduced.

Relaxation skills must be used intermittently throughout the performance when appropriate. Some sports have times of critical need, such as the tennis serve or the foul shot in basketball, when relaxation techniques will let the mind and body function well together. The player often will focus on eliminating any areas of muscle tightness while taking several deep breaths and going through a set routine of preparation. In other sports, such as running or swimming, relaxation can be called up at intervals or when tightness is perceived as a developing problem.

"Mental toughness" is a more elusive concept that encompasses aspects of positive attitude and self-esteem, but adds important elements of concentration and disciplined competitiveness. Ivan Lendl is an example of a tough tennis player. He is well known for his consistent pressure on opponents, using high-percentage shots with measured aggressiveness, and he seldom "lets down." For marathoners, toughness keeps the long training runs in inclement weather steadfast. Tough performers are better able to control negative emotions, maintain motivation, and preserve a positive attitude. He or she may gain the "challenge response," sport psychologists' name for the peak self-confidence of the superior athlete who can summon maximal effort in the "clutch" situation. An example is the college tailback who demands the football on fourth down and five when his team is 5 points behind near the end of the game. Even weekend athletes have the occasional opportunity to summon extra energy and self-confidence to put out a special performance for their team or for their own gratification in the challenging situation.

Self-esteem is the basic self-perception that one is okay. Basically, the individual with good self-esteem accepts his or her behavior as a part of being an "okay" person even if improvement is needed in the behavior. The best athletes seem to be self-confident people who think well of themselves, although they may criticize parts of their performance. For optimal performance, one often needs the mind-set of positive self-regard to gain strength from the situation rather than losing ground in a vicious circle of playing worse as one judges oneself to be a bad person or a bad athlete.

These mistake-spurred communications of blame can probably be best understood through the transactional analysis model (Harris, 1969). The parent ego state processes information either in a critical or nurturing style. In its critical style, it blames the self in a negative punitive way (e.g., "What the hell is wrong with me that I missed that easy shot?") or blames others ("You're cheating," "The officiating is terrible"). This style assigns blame for any mistake or unsuccessful outcome in an angry critical way.

Guilt, shame, and condemnation are some of the styles in which this critical response manifests. It is, consciously or unconsciously, based on the belief or experience that the best way to learn is through anger and punishment. Because optimal performance states involve the ability to focus, a relaxed state of alertness, and internal energy resources (psychic and physical) being available, these negative responses to mistakes reduce performance ability, morale, and enjoyment. Instead, these feeling states create tension, distraction, unpleasant associations and feelings, and often self-fulfilling prophecies.

Sometimes these negative reactions can change because of a recognition of the inefficiency of these responses. Sometimes an awareness of pain and loss of pleasure motivate learning a new way to deal with mistakes. Sometimes a more intense or complex learning process is involved, for example, psychotherapy, behavior modification, hypnosis, or some more intensive or introspective approach.

A more effective and enjoyable method for processing mistakes is based on a model of affirmation of the worth of oneself, reviewing data from the framework of self-support and objective analysis in a direction toward the denied outcome. (This is contrasted to negation and devaluation of self, exaggerated description of the mistake and its consequences, and focus on the undesired outcome). In the transactional analysis model, this healthier way to process mistakes would mean having a nurturing parent and adult (data processing) ego state engaged in the review and focus on improvement.

This response to mistakes could be a three-fold process. The first part would be to maintain a loving and accepting attitude to the mistake maker (i.e., oneself; e.g., "I am a lovable and good person even when I make mistakes"). This keeps self-esteem intact. Second would be to learn from the mistake, that is, what was the mistake and how did it happen (e.g., "I held the racquet wrong because I was distracted by thinking of the fight I had yesterday with my friend or I thought my opponent was going to move to the left because of the way her feet were pointed and instead she moved right and "faked me out"). The third component would be what can I learn from this mistake to reduce the chances of it recurring or to prevent it from recurring or to improve myself. This might include developing specific strategies for dealing with distractions or making a mental note of "fake right move left" or remembering to look for more details the next time I compete with that person.

A person can learn and benefit from mistakes. Any champion has become a champion through a process of success and loss, mistake and mastery. Errors and mistakes are essential in the development and mastery of skills. The negatively critical person curses him or herself for mistakes and erodes self-esteem. The person with self-love processes the information of mistakes with less agony, intact self-esteem, and a more rapid learning curve.

REFERENCES

Alman, B., & Lambram, P. (1983). *Self-hypnosis: A complete manual for health and self-change.* San Diego, CA: International Health Publications.

Benson, H. (1975). *The relaxation response.* New York: Morrow.

Diamant, Leif R. (1987). How to introduce self-hypnosis to clients. *North Carolina Society of Clinical Hypnosis Newsletter,* 6–9.

Feltz, D. L., & Landers, D. M. (1983). The effects of mental practice on motor skill learning and performance: A meta-analysis. *Journal of Sport Psychology, 5,* 25–57.

Green, E., & Green, A. (1977). *Beyond biofeedback.* New York: Dell.

Hadley, J., & Staudacher, C. (1985). *Hypnosis for change.* Oakland, CA: New Harbinger.

Harris, T. A. (1969). *I'm OK, you're OK.* New York: Avon.

Jacobson, E. (1938). *Progressive relaxation: A physiological and clinical investigation of muscle states and their significance in psychology and medical practice* (2nd ed). Chicago: University of Chicago Press.

McArdle, W. D., Katch, F. I., & Katch, V. L. (1986). *Exercise physiology* (2nd ed.). Philadelphia, PA: Lea and Febiger.

Pargman, D., & Baker, M. (1980). Running high: Enkephalin indicated. *Journal of Drug Issues, 10,* 341–349.

Pert, C. B., & Snyder, S. H. (1973). Opiate receptor: Demonstration in nervous tissue. *Science, 179,* 1011–1014.

Sherman, J. E., & Liebeskind, J. C. (1980). An endorhinergic, centrifugal substrate of pain modulation: Recent findings, current concepts, and complexities. In J. J. Bonica (Ed.), *Pain.* New York: Raven.

Snyder, S. H. (1977). Opiate receptors and internal opiates. *Scientific American, 3,* 44–56.

Index